THE SEED OF ABRAHAM

Aḥmad al-Kinānī and Raphael Patai in Hebron (1933)
At the Entrance to the Traditional Tomb of
Their Common Ancestor, Abraham

The Seed of Abraham

JEWS AND ARABS IN CONTACT AND CONFLICT

Raphael Patai

CHARLES SCRIBNER'S SONS
New York

Library of Congress Cataloging-in-Publication Data

Patai, Raphael, 1910–
The seed of Abraham.
Bibliography: p.
Includes index.
1. Jews—Arab countries. 2. Arab countries—Ethnic relations.
3. Jews—Arab countries—Folklore. 4. Folklore—Arab countries.
5. Judaism—Relations—Islam. 6. Islam—Relations—Judaism.
7. Jewish-Arab relations—1917– .
I. Title. DS135.A68P37 1986b 305.8′924′0174924 86-26276
ISBN 0-684-18752-3 (pbk.)

Originally published as *The Children of Abraham* by the University of Utah Press

Published simultaneously in Canada by Collier Macmillan Canada, Inc.
Manufactured by Fairfield Graphics, Fairfield, Pennsylvania
First Paperback Edition 1987

Contents

To the Memory of My Friend
SHAYKH AḤMAD FAKHR AL-DĪN ALKINĀNĪ
Who Introduced me to Arab Jerusalem
And My Lifelong Contact with Whom
Never Took the Form of Conflict

Preface

This book grew out of a series of lectures I gave at the University of Utah in the fall of 1983 under the auspices of its Middle East Center, at the initiative of Professor Harris M. Lenowitz. Arab-Jewish relations had been for decades one of the main areas of my scholarly interest, as witnessed by my early monograph, *On Culture Contact and Its Working in Modern Palestine*,[1] my books *Golden River to Golden Road: Society, Culture and Change in the Middle East*,[2] *The Arab Mind*,[3] and *The Jewish Mind*,[4] and a number of articles. However, the present book goes far beyond my previous writings on the subject in that it is devoted in its entirety to the presentation of what I consider the most significant aspects of the historical and psychological relationship between the Muslim Arabs and the Jews, and to an analysis within that context of the varied influences which radiated in both directions between the two communities.

In the course of the last 150 years the subject of Jewish-Arab relations has attracted the attention of several of the greatest Jewish Arabists, from Abraham Geiger and Ignaz Goldziher to S. D. Goitein and B. Lewis, and of several dozens of others in between. Each of them has made important contributions to the elucidation of the subject, and the present book could not have been written without utilizing some of their insights and research results. If, despite the existence of hundreds of studies on Jewish-Arab relations, I nevertheless decided to write *The Seed of Abraham*, my motivation in doing so was twofold: first, I felt that there were a number of chapters in the overall great story of Arab-Jewish symbiosis that had been tackled by none of my predecessors and that needed telling; and second, I wanted to connect the historical relations between the two peoples with the present situation in which, for the first time since the days of Muhammad, there is, in the midst of the many large and small Arab countries, a Jewish state with a sizable Arab minority in its population. As far as I know, no other scholar has sought a connection between the traditional Arab attitude to the downtrodden Jewish *dhimmīs*, who were a fixture in their midst for some thirteen centuries, and the present Arab attitude to the new State of Israel.

I wish to express my thanks to Professor Harris M. Lenowitz and Professor Laurence D. Loeb of the University of Utah, and to Professor Victor D. Sanua of St. John's University, New York, with whom I discussed certain points in my lectures that ultimately found their way into the book; and to Professor Howard Sachar of George Washington University, Washington, D.C., who read the manuscript and made valuable suggestions; to my editors of the University of Utah Press, and Michael Pietsch of Scribner's, New York, for their patient attention to a difficult manuscript. I am again indebted to the New York Public Library, and in particular to Dr. Leonard S. Gold, chief of its Jewish Division, and to Christian Filstrup, chief of its Oriental Division, and their knowledgeable and helpful staffs; to Esther Togman, Acting Director of the Zionist Archives and Library, New York; to Myron M. Weinstein, head of the Hebraic Section of the Library of Congress, Washington, D.C.; to Madeleine Neige, head of the Service Hebraique of the Bibliothèque Nationale in Paris; to the libraries of the Hebrew University of Jerusalem and of the Tel Aviv University, for their unfailing readiness to help.

Introduction

A full treatment of Jewish-Arab relations in the course of the thirteen centuries that have passed between Muhammad's time and our own would require not one book, but a series of hefty volumes. All I intended to do in the present study was to select a number of topics that I considered important, and that had not been adequately covered before. That is to say, I understand that this book's treatment of the subject is not exhaustive but merely illustrative.

The first chapter sketches, by way of introduction, the contrasting concepts the Jews and the Arabs had of their respective prehistories: the totally negative view the Jews already had in biblical times of the religious and moral state of the world in pre-Abrahamic times, on the one hand; and, on the other, the positive view the Arabs had of the *jāhiliyya*, the pre-Muhammadan period of their past, which was, of course, coupled with a negative judgment of its paganism. Another difference between the Jewish and Arab views of their prehistory is anchored in the time period they cover. Jewish history goes back to Abraham, and therefore prehistory for the Jews in biblical times already referred to the period of mankind prior to Abraham in which Jews did not yet exist. For the Arabs, the prehistoric period prior to Muhammad lay in the recent past; it was peopled by Arab tribes, of whose mores, culture, and language the Muslim Arabs were the proud heirs.

Chapter 2 focuses on a phenomenal achievement of cultural borrowing which, despite the numerous existing studies of Jewish (including biblical) influences on Islam, has so far remained largely unexplored and, in fact, has received no scholarly attention: the wholesale appropriation by Muhammad, and his Muslim Arab scholarly heirs, of a whole gamut of biblical traditions centering on Abraham. By doing this, Muhammad, with one single master stroke, placed Abraham the *ḥanīf* at the head of pre-Islamic Arab tradition, endowed the Arabs with what to him was the noblest of genealogies, and validated the claim—invented by him—that the Muslim Arabs were the true and faithful heirs to the religion of the earliest and greatest "friend of God," Abraham. Abraham, the first great biblical founder of the Hebrew faith and ancestor of the Jews, thus became, by Muhammad's prophetic fiat, the originator of Islam and the builder of the Kaᶜba, as well as the father of all, or at least half, of the tribes of Arabia.

The story of Muhammad's disillusionment with the Jews, his growing enmity toward them, and their subsequent degradation in the lands conquered by triumphant Islam, forms the core of chapter 3. The emphasis here is on the great variety that characterized the relationships of Arabs and Jews in medieval times. The Islamic principle in dealing with the Jews (and other *dhimmīs*) was always that of *dhilla*, *ghiyār*, and *dhimma*, that is, abasement, separation, and protection-subjection. But often these Muslim obligations toward the Jews—reiterated time and again by rulers and religious leaders—were honored in the breach, so that the actual position of the Jews in the far-flung Arab lands varied widely, from degradation and misery to ease and comfort. The "Covenant of ᶜUmar," specifying the restrictions placed upon the Jews (and other *dhimmīs*) as a condition for being allowed to live in the House of Islam, was strictly applied in some places and periods, and practically disregarded in others. Thus there were times and places when and where the humbled Jews and Christians could raise their heads, although not quite as high as the Muslims.

The classical example of relative well-being enjoyed by Jews in an Arab land is that of Andalus, Muslim Spain, in the ninth to the eleventh centuries. To call Cordova, the capital city of Andalus, the "Arab Camelot" (chapter 4) may sound somewhat exaggerated, inasmuch as life there had its uncertainties, dangers, and other dark sides as well. But compared to the persecutions the Jews suffered in other lands, both Muslim and Christian, at the time, the designation is certainly not a misnomer. Viewed from a historical perspective, it can be seen that the great cultural advances the Jews were able to make in ᶜAbbāsid Iraq and subsequently in Arab Spain are evidence of a Jewish condition which was relatively favorable.

In the next two countries considered, Yemen and Morocco, the Arab attitude to the Jews was very different (chapter 5). That the Jews were able not only to maintain themselves in Yemen, but also to produce religious and literary works, as well as folk art, is remarkable in view of the relentless oppression they suffered there for centuries. By contrast, the Jewish condition in Morocco appears to have been better. The Jews of Morocco were situated between two mutually hostile Muslim ethnic groups, the Arabs and the Berbers. How they were able to turn this situation to their advantage is a most remarkable chapter in Jewish history. However, when the Muslim cultural decline set in in Morocco, it affected the Jews as well, and for many centuries now the once prominent Moroccan Jewry has produced little of real cultural significance. These two Jewish communities, the Yemenite and the Moroccan, serve as examples of the influence of the Muslim environment on the Jews and of the Jewish reaction to the treatment meted out to them by the Arab (in Morocco partly Berber) majority. The focus in this chapter is primarily on the relationship of Jews and Arabs in Yemen and of Jews and Muslims in Morocco, and on the Jewish personality that developed in the two countries as a result of pervasive environmental influences. Secondarily, it discusses the relationships that have developed in Israel between each of these two Jewish ethnic groups and the rest of Jewish Israel after their immigration, which in effect meant the transplantation of two communities, each with its own definite characteristics, into a new and very different sociocultural milieu.

In the largely illiterate lands of Islam, folk culture has played a more important role than it has in the more literate Western world. Jewish and Arab folk culture had many common features, expressed in shared beliefs, practices, and values. Chapter 6 looks into some of the salient manifestations of this phenomenon, such as the beliefs and practices connected with the jinn, the evil eye, magic, and the veneration of saints, including the worship of the same saints by both Muslims and Jews. The commonality of these and other features in Arab and Jewish folk culture seems to have militated against the efforts of the official Muslim leadership—which had their counterparts among the Jewish rabbis—to maintain an effective separation between the Muslims and the Jews. A most interesting feature in Muslim folk culture was (and still is) the appearance in Moroccan masquerades of "Jews," played by Muslim mummers and assigned important comic, but by no means villainous, roles in those performances of definitely ritual significance.

One of the psychologically most noteworthy manifestations in the realm of religion (either official or popular) is the appearance of a feminine divinity, or a feminine aspect, or a feminine manifestation, or a feminine element, in the God concept. From the point of view of the role of the feminine in the divine, Judaism stands halfway between Catholicism in which Mariolatry is a very important feature, and Islam in which the feminine is effectively excluded from an emphatically masculine divine realm. In fact, as shown in chapter 7, Islam has gone so far in masculinizing religion that it almost totally bars women from official religious practices. One of the results of this exclusion is the prevalence in several Arab countries of folk beliefs and rituals specific to women, which in most cases are frowned upon, but nevertheless tolerated, by the *ʿulamā'*, the official Muslim religious leadership. The cult of the *zār* and of other spirits (often female) is one of the most widespread manifestations of this separate women's religion within the theologically austere House of Islam. In Judaism, on the other hand, and especially as practiced by the less educated Jews of the Arab countries, the concept of a feminine aspect of God played an important role, and most religious commandments were performed (by men) with the avowed purpose of "unifying the Holy One, blessed be He, and His Shekhina." It is argued in this chapter that the exclusion of the feminine from the deity was correlated with the exclusion of women from official Islam and with the relegation of women to a lowly position in Arab (and, in general, Muslim) society, while the incorporation of the feminine into the divinity by Judaism was effective in securing women a better position in the Jewish community despite the Muslim environmental influences.

The discussion of these religious differences leads to a consideration of the position of women in general in Jewish and Arab society (chapter 8). In this respect, as in many others, the Jews were influenced by the Arab environment. One of the most painful manifestations of this influence was wife beating, which was sanctioned, in certain circumstances, by both Arab religious leaders and some of their Jewish counterparts in Arab countries. On the other hand, illiteracy among Jewish women was not quite as widespread as among Arab women, while male illiteracy was much lower among the Jews than among the Arabs in every Arab country. Nor was the segregation of women as strictly observed among the Jews as among the Arabs. The struggle for female emancipation in the modern Arab world is still going on at widely disparate rates from country to country, resulting in contrasts between, say, the position of women in Egypt and in Saudi Arabia. In those Arab cities where there was a sizable indigenous Jewish population, Jewish women were among the first to discard the veil, and their example influenced the middle- and upper-class Arab women. This move proved to be a significant first step in the liberation of the Arab women and in the modernization of Arab urban society as a whole in those countries that were exposed to direct Western influence. In recent years, however, with the upsurge of Islamic fundamentalism, a tendency has surfaced among educated Arab women to return to the veil and to demonstratively conservative deportment.

The recent developments in Arab-Jewish relations, which have culminated in the clash over Palestine, are discussed in chapter 9. Palestine, because of its Muslim religious associations, has come to mean much more to the Arabs than other parts (such as Alexandretta) of what they consider "the Arab homeland." In the course of the nineteenth century, as European influence increased, as the Jews in the Ottoman Empire and the other Arab lands began to enjoy the protection of European consuls, and as the Arabs became acquainted with what appeared to them powerful positions held by Jews in Western Europe, the traditional image of the humble Jewish *dhimmī* became gradually transformed into that of the menacing Jew. Anti-Semitic literature (such as "The Protocols of the Elders of Zion") imported from Europe implanted into some in the Arab world the image of the evil, sinister, murderous Jew. Added to this were the Zionist movement, the establishment of the State of Israel, and the repeated Arab defeats at the hand of the young Jewish state. All of these together brought about a replacement of the traditional Arab contempt for the Jewish *dhimmī* by a new hatred of the Jew, now identified with the Israeli, a Judeophobia fashioned after the European model of anti-Semitism. The first, and so far only, breach in this virulent Arab attitude came when Egypt signed a peace agreement with Israel.

The historical "anomaly" that Arabs should live under Jewish rule as they do in Israel—a situation totally unprecedented in the thirteen centuries of Muslim-Arab domination of the Jews—is something extremely difficult for the Arabs to digest; characteristically, more so for the Arab world at large than for the Arabs who live in Israel. The Arabs of Israel, despite their psychological and other problems with living as a minority in the Jewish state, are today well on the way to becoming a bicultural Arab-Hebrew community. The sociocultural configuration they constitute will be significant not only for the relationship between them and Jewish Israel, but also for that between Israel and the surrounding Arab peoples.

THE SEED OF ABRAHAM

I will multiply thy seed
As the stars of the heaven
And as the sand
Which is upon the seashore
(Gen. 22:17)

1

Jews and Arabs View Their Prehistory

In the self-image of a people, the view it has of its own origins and early history plays an important role. While in most cases popular prehistories—or ethno-prehistories, if you will—are either entirely mythical or studded with myths, the personages figuring in them nevertheless contain clues to the personality traits that the people in question considers either ideal or abhorrent. A study from this point of view of the prehistoric traditions of the great culture carriers of antiquity—the Egyptians, Sumerians, Greeks, and Romans—would no doubt yield fascinating results. As for the Jews and Arabs, the following preliminary observations can be made.

In the Jewish traditional view, Jewish prehistory ended and Jewish history began with Abraham. Prior to Abraham, events as recorded in the Bible and other early traditions had an entirely schematic course. This is best exemplified in the Genesis narrative where precisely ten generations separate Adam from Noah, and another ten pass from Noah to Abraham. The sketchy and hasty account covering these mythical prehistoric times, in which only a very few of the protagonists are given more than passing mention, shows that the impression those first twenty generations of humankind left behind in Jewish consciousness (via the brief references in the Book of Genesis and more ample aggadic material woven around it) was that they were almost to a man evil, and that they constantly disobeyed God although He made His will repeatedly clear to them.

The only events recalled from those early ages of mankind consisted of a series of human transgressions and divine punishments, and the age as a whole was one of willful human obstinacy and of recurrent divine frustration with and disappointment in mankind, barely relieved by the episodic appearance of a few pious men such as Abel, Enoch, and Noah. With Abraham all this suddenly changes. In him God finds a man who not only possessed the great virtue of absolute obedience to God, but who responded willingly to the divine challenge to be the human partner in a covenant with God, a covenant which bound him and his progeny after him for all time to God in a one-to-one relationship: He was to be forever their God, and they were to be forever His people.

Did anything survive from the ethos of the pre-Abrahamic period in the mind and mentality of Abraham's Jewish progeny? The answer to this question, I believe, is a resounding no. The memory of that period, to be sure, survived due to the Genesis narratives, which clearly served as a connecting link between the Creation of the world and the great ancestral figure of Abraham. But pre-Abrahamic human history, as reflected in Genesis and as remembered by the seed of Abraham, consisted of a series of evil deeds. Adam and Eve, the first human couple fashioned by God's own hands, disobeyed Him and transgressed the only prohibition God had imposed upon them: not to eat of the forbidden fruit of one of the many trees in the garden. Their firstborn son, Cain—whose evil was so great that post-biblical Jewish legend could explain it only by making Satan his father—killed his only brother, Abel. The next few generations, barely adumbrated in the Bible, were considered evil by the talmudic aggadists. Finally, six generations after Adam, a man was born, Enoch by name, who "walked with God," and nothing more is known or said about him. A grandson of Enoch, Lamech, became the father of Noah, the hero of the global flood. The story of the flood is introduced by a curious vignette: a brief reference to the union between enigmatic "sons of God" and beautiful "daughters of men." The mythological significance of this story is fascinating,[1] but what interests us in the present context is that the union between the divine males and the human females was evil in the eyes of God, and He punished it by reducing human lifespan to a mere 120 years. Nevertheless, man's wickedness continued, until God decided to "blot out man . . . from the face of the earth" (Gen. 6:1–7). Only Noah and his family were saved from the universal destruction. Noah, incidentally, is the only person in the twenty generations between Adam and Abraham the biblical tradition has something good to say about: "Noah was in his generations a man righteous and whole-hearted; Noah walked with God" (Gen. 6:9). However, this accolade is more than counterbalanced by the unsavory story of what Noah did and what happened to him after the deluge: he became drunk, uncovered himself in his stupor, and, according to the Midrash, was emasculated by his son Ham (Gen. 9:20–27).[2]

The history of the ten generations between Noah and Abraham is glossed over in Genesis in two short chapters of "begot"s and dry chronologies from which we learn nothing except the names and the ages of a few dozen individuals. In his impatience to reach the person of Abraham, the unknown author of Genesis 10 lists names of men and countries and peoples, almost at random, and at the end of his enumeration falls into the inconsistency of calling the "sons" "nations" (Gen. 10:32). The monotony of these lists of names and ages is broken only once, when the narrator stops to tell the story of a major debacle for mankind: the attempt to build a tower at Babel, which was punished by God with the confusion of the languages and the scattering of peoples "abroad upon the face of all the earth" (Gen. 11:9).

An overview of the story of mankind from Adam to Abraham, which at one and the same time is also the prehistory of the Children of Israel, discloses, it must be re-emphasized, that it was an almost unmitigated series of evil deeds. No wonder, then, that neither in the consciousness nor in the subconscious of the biblical Hebrews did anything survive from those early ages that would have had a positive influence on their feeling, thinking, and acting. Consequently, the folk psychology of the Israelites and their heirs the Jews reflected nothing of the pre-Abrahamic era, but was, on the contrary, totally and exclusively under the spell of the personality of Abraham and his spiritual heirs. Thus in Jewish ethos there is no trace of any survival of pre-Abrahamic traits. In the consciousness of the biblical Hebrews, and in Judaism as lived and studied by the Jews in the last two thousand years, Jewish religion and ethos as well as the Jewish people itself, originated with the election of Abraham to be God's disciple and friend. It was that great and seminal event with which Judaism originated, and everything in the realm of religion and ethics that had gone before it was effectively eliminated. Both genetic descent and spiritual origins were traced back to Abraham and no further. If there ever existed a religio-cultural heritage from the pre-Abrahamic era, it was expunged, and in effect, totally nullified. This is why the many centuries of early human history which were known to Hebrew folk tradition to have preceded Abraham were telescoped into the briefest of synopses. As for the ancestry, tribe, and paternal family of Abraham, nothing of their way of life and thought was allowed to enter into the post-Abrahamic mores of the Hebrews.

As for the Arabs, their ethno-prehistory ends with the birth, or rather the beginning of the ministry, of the Prophet Muhammad (570–632). Muhammad, the son of a poor branch of the noble Quraysh tribe, was born posthumously to his father ʿAbd Allāh, and at an early age he found employment as a caravaneer with Khadīja, a rich widow fifteen years his senior. Some time later she consented to marry him, and when he was about forty he began to have visions which, unless one accepts the traditional Muslim view that they were revelations by God, can be explained psychologically only as having been profoundly influenced by what he had learned about God, angels, and great biblical figures from his Jewish friends. His visions convinced Muhammad that he was chosen by God to be His messenger and to spread the faith in the one and only God among his fellow Arabs. With this Arab ethno-prehistory ends and Arab-Islamic history begins.

One of the most important facets of Muhammad's teachings was the rejection, not only of the totality of the religion to which the Arabs had adhered for centuries before him, but also of much of pre-Islamic Arab mores and ethos. Before long the period which preceded Muhammad's appearance came to be called *jāhiliyya*, literally "(time or state of) ignorance." This designation implied a negative view of everything that had gone before Muhammad, and was expressive of the determination to expunge from Arab memory that entire long period, of whose actual duration and historical happenings the Arabs knew almost nothing. For the believing Muslims Arab history began with Muhammad, and what preceded him was either negligible or, better, to be forgotten.

However, folk traditions are much too obdurate to be eradicated by fiats of a religious founder, and by even the strictest adherence to his teachings by his followers. In the case of the Arabs, while the appearance of Muhammad was just as great a watershed for them as was the traditionally assumed appearance of Abraham for the Jews, and while they knew next to nothing about the actual events that had taken place in the millennial history of their ancestors prior to the appearance of Muhammad, they, in contrast to the Jews, retained a rich body of lore and ethos from that period. In my book *The Arab Mind*, I called the sum total of these ancient features "Bedouin ethos," and spoke of the "Bedouin substratum of the Arab personality." I also stated there—today I think somewhat too summarily—that bedouin "society, where it still exists today, has remained essentially unchanged since pre-Islamic times in many basic aspects: it is still organized along the same structural lines, exhibits the same internal dynamics, upholds the same values, and has preserved even in its religious life many pre-Islamic features."[3]

What I would like to add here is that the Arabs in general, and not only those who represent remnants of bedouin society, are well aware of the pre-Islamic origin of the most important of their values. That is to say, in contrast to Jewish consciousness which has definitively discarded every pre-Abrahamic value, in Arab psychology the pre-Islamic values live on as a precious heritage from the *jāhiliyya*. In view of this fact, the *jāhiliyya* in Arab consciousness appeared not as an era of ignorance in general, but merely as a time of barbarism (this, indeed, is how the term was interpreted by Goldziher[4]), which, although it fell pitifully short in the only knowledge that really counts—the knowledge of God—was nevertheless rich in ethical values when it came to relations between man and man.

What, then, are those pre-Islamic values and character traits which to this day are basic ingredients of the Arab personality and which the Arabs recognize as having been the virtues of the ancient Arabs of the *jāhiliyya*? The most important among them are the five traits extolled by pre-Islamic Arab poets in their songs of praise and in the *Ayyām al-ʿArab* (literally "Days of the Arabs"), the romantic chronicles of the pre-Islamic Arabs' days of battle, to wit: *ḍiyāfa* or *ḍayf*, hospitality; *ḥamāsa*, bravery; *karam*, generosity; *muruwwa*, manliness; and *sharaf*, honor. Although these are well-known concepts in the Arab world to this day, a few words need to be said about them. But first I want to mention, even if only in passing, that also the basic forms of social organization, tribal and family structure, and the position of women are features that survived from the *jāhiliyya* in many parts of the House of Islam down to our own day.

As for the first of the five virtues, that of hospitality, in Jewish tradition it is derived from Abraham, who, according to Gen. 18, received hospitably the three visitors who turned out to be a manifestation of God in three persons. In Arab tradition, too, it is connected with Abraham, who is considered a chief knower and "friend" (*khalīl*) of God in the midst of a *jāhilī* world, but Arab legend presupposes the existence of hospitality as a value and a virtue among the pagan Arabs themselves, whom it presents as contemporaries of Abraham.[5]

In bravery, typically the emphasis is on appearance rather than essence.

A man must appear brave, must put on a brave front, however much he cringes inwardly. An Arabian folk custom will illustrate this. In the Ḥijāz and ᶜAsīr, today two provinces of Saudi Arabia, circumcision used to be a painful operation performed on the bridegroom in a public ceremony in the presence of his bride. The skin of the entire male organ was removed, together with the skin of its environs on the belly and inner thigh. While this was being done, the youth had to show unflinching courage, stand upright, shout "with a mighty joy," and brandish a long dagger. Should he as much as whimper, the bride who was sitting before him, beating a drum, and trilling the traditional shrill, sustained cry of joy, had the right to refuse to marry him.[6]

Generosity is related to hospitality but has a wider connotation. The ideal extent of generosity is illustrated by a story about Bu (Abū) Zaid, the mythical hero of the Banū Hilāl tribe, which still circulated until recently among Arab tribal elders. Bu Zaid, the story goes, slaughtered his camels one after the other to serve their meat to his uninvited guests, until he remained without any camels and faced starvation. His tribe, recognizing the great generosity of their kinsman, presented him with a few camels but only after exacting a promise that he would thenceforth curb his hospitality. Before long, however, Bu Zaid's irrepressible generosity reduced the number of his animals to one last milch camel. A few days later, as he was sitting in front of his tent, the figure of a stranger appeared on the distant horizon, and in order not to have to invite him, Bu Zaid hid in the depths of his tent. But he could not refrain from asking his wife, "Has the guest been called into one of the tents yet?" After three or four negative answers, while the stranger came closer and closer to his tent, Bu Zaid could no longer restrain himself, ran out to bid the stranger welcome to his tent, and then slit the throat of his last camel to fulfill the supreme bedouin duty of hospitality.[7]

Manliness, or manly virtue, is composed of such traits as patience in misfortune, persistence in seeking revenge, protection of the weak, defiance of the strong, loyalty, fidelity, generosity, and, of course, bravery in fighting, in the first place. The entire *Ayyām al-ᶜArab* is a paean on *muruwwa*. The *Ayyām* is a collection of legends in prose and poetry about the combats fought by the Arab tribes among themselves in pre-Islamic times. These combats were often not pitched battles but only minor skirmishes limited to throwing stones and beatings with sticks. The occasions for such encounters were disputes over borders, or insults, and if bloodshed occurred the intervention of some neutral family usually ended the strife with the payment of blood-money by the side which caused more casualties to its adversary. The *Ayyām* affords a rare insight into the chivalrous spirit, the *muruwwa*, which inspired the pre-Islamic Arab warriors. The memory of the heroes and of their *muruwwa* was kept alive for centuries, and served as examples to be emulated by the brave men of later ages. The accounts were collected in books which were lost in the course of time but excerpts from which survived to form the basis of Arab heroic tradition.[8]

The last of the five virtues, honor, is the most complex of all. Many acts are honorable, and a man can, by his behavior, either increase or decrease his honor, either "whiten" or "blacken" his face. However, the central component in the *sharaf* complex is the behavior of the womenfolk. The women's honorable comportment is called by a special term, *ᶜirḍ*, and it differs from the men's honor in that *sharaf*, the men's honor, even if lost or diminished, can be regained or restored, but the *ᶜirḍ*, once lost, can never again be recouped, resembling in this respect virginity. Much has been written on this subject, recently also from a feminist point of view represented by modern Arab women. A trenchant illustration of the traditional attitude to *ᶜirḍ* in recent times is a story about a bedouin shaykh who had to seek refuge among the Marsh Arabs of southern Iraq, who were considered less noble than the true nomads. Haddam, a young chieftain of the Marsh Arabs, fell in love with the shaykh's daughter whom he saw only from a distance, but, of course, the shaykh refused him because of his ignoble blood. One day, however, the shaykh noticed that his daughter was looking with interest toward the young chieftain as the latter passed by poling his reed boat. Thereupon the old shaykh took his daughter to a deserted place in the marshes and killed her so as to prevent her *ᶜirḍ*—and hence his *sharaf* —from being destroyed by any possible relationship with the young chieftain.[9]

The essence of this story is borne out by a historical occurrence that took place during the Mahdist uprising in the Sudan in the late nineteenth century. Some Sudanese Arabs killed their wives and daughters for fear that they could be violated by soldiers of the Mahdī's army who were considered slaves.[10]

To sum up this brief sketch of the survival of pre-Islamic attitudes in Arab mentality, one can state that several of the major components of the Arab ethical system are pre-Islamic in origin. They survive, even though occasionally at least they actually contradict the laws of Islam as laid down in the Koran and subsequently developed in the *sharīᶜa*, the traditional

Islamic law; e.g., the whole great complex of blood revenge and blood feuding has survived from the *jāhiliyya*, despite thirteen centuries of Koranic and *sharīʿa* opposition to it.

No corresponding survival of pre-Abrahamic values, or, indeed, any other pre-Abrahamic feature, is found in the Jewish mores. Quite to the contrary. All that biblical and later Jewish tradition retained from pre-Abrahamic times were memories of negative features, of man's sinful behavior. True, in the Talmud and medieval Jewish Codes we hear of the so-called "seven Noachide laws,"[11] but those laws, regarded as the minimum moral duties of all men, were believed to have been known but consistently and sinfully disregarded by mankind following the days of Noah. According to the Midrash, it was precisely because the generation of the deluge did not observe the seven Noachide laws that it was doomed to extinction. The seven Noachide laws comprise six prohibitions, that of idolatry, of blasphemy, of bloodshed, of sexual sins, of theft, and of eating part of a living animal; and one positive commandment, to set up a legal system. None of these, says the Midrash, were observed until the days of Abraham. The great religious innovation attributed to Abraham by Jewish tradition is that he managed to free himself from the moral morass of the generations that preceded him and of his contemporaries who were in violation of these elementary principles of a postulated universal human and humane law, revealed to mankind by God. The Noachide laws constitute a great chapter in Jewish legal philosophy and in the Jewish view of mankind; but all we can say about them here is that the very postulation of God-given all-human moral laws which existed but were not observed by mankind prior to Abraham is a graphic illustration of the total rejection by the Jews of the mores and behavior patterns of the ancestors and contemporaries of Abraham, that is, the period which in biblical history corresponds to the Arab pre-Muhammadan age of the *jāhiliyya*.

How can we explain this contrast between the Jewish and the Arab popular view of their respective prehistory? It seems to me that it can be traced back to the difference in the moment of ethnic history—real or legendary—in which the founders of the two religions appeared. Among the Jews, or rather the ancient Hebrews, Abraham was assumed to have been the founder of Hebrew monotheism at a time when no Hebrew people existed as yet. Abraham was a single individual whom God chose to be His friend and servant. Central to the relationship between Abraham and God was the divine promise that God would make Abraham's seed a great people and would give it possession of the Land of Canaan. The faith of Abraham in God came first; the people who became the heirs of that faith came later, when, after a number of generations, Abraham's offspring grew into the traditional twelve tribes of Israel. When Abraham accepted the divine election—and the tenor of the narrative makes us understand that he had no choice but to do so—he had to rid himself of all pagan doctrines, rites, and mores, that were part of the culture in which he grew up. An individual, and especially an exceptional one such as Abraham must have been, can achieve such a total detachment, and can transmit to his children nothing but the new faith to which he was led by God, and the mores, doctrines, and rites supplementary to it. Thus it was that it could come about that the Children of Israel retained nothing of the religion and ethos of their pagan prehistory.

The historical juncture at which Muhammad appeared in Arabia was basically different. Muhammad was not commanded by God to leave his social environment and to teach his faith in Him only to his children and children's children. God instructed him to preach monotheism to his contemporaries, the Arab tribes of which he was a part. The Arab people did not come into existence as a result of the credal heritage left behind by Muhammad. They preceded him, had existed for many centuries prior to his appearance. Hence, even though his *dīn* (religion) was powerful enough to work a radical transformation in Arab life, religion, and ethos, it was not, to begin with, taught to infants, but to adults, to thousands and tens of thousands of them, to people whose personalities were fully formed when they first heard of Muhammad's doctrines. Even though they accepted his teachings—often were forced to accept them—they could not but retain features of the culture in which they had been brought up. What these first-generation Muslims transmitted to their children was therefore an amalgam of their pre-Islamic cultural heritage, and the *dīn* of Muhammad. The same process of cultural transmission went on in all subsequent generations, so that the bedouin substratum, or better, the *jāhilī* cultural base, came to be retained among the Arabs down to the present day.

Herein lies the difference between the Jewish and Arab views of their prehistory. Hence the total Jewish condemnation of that which was retained by Hebrew folk memory of the character and deeds of the ancestors of Abraham. And hence the Arab retention of moral features which were handed down to them from the *jāhiliyya*.

2

Abraham in Jewish and Arab Tradition

THE ENIGMA OF ABRAHAM

Before embarking upon a discussion of the relationship between the children of Abraham, that is, the Jews and the Arabs, both of whom consider themselves his descendants and heirs, we should first introduce Abraham himself. This great ancestor figure, according to the Bible, was the progenitor of a surprisingly large number of peoples, tribes, and nations, and traditions about him survived among his offspring through Jacob and much later, as we shall see, were taken over by the Arabs.

The first thing to state about Abraham is that, historically, we know nothing about him. To date, no historical document, inscription, monument, or other archaeological evidence referring to him has been found. There is even doubt as to the meaning of the name Abraham (Hebrew: *Avraham*), or of its original shorter form Abram (*Avram*) (see, e.g., Gen. 11:26), although it seems that it is composed of the two elements *av*, meaning father, and *ram*, meaning exalted. But the combination *Avram* could mean exalted father, or father of the exalted, or the father is exalted, etc. What the expanded form of the name, *Avraham*, means, is even more uncertain. The biblical explanation, *av hamon*, "father of a multitude" (Gen. 17:50), is rather farfetched in Hebrew, since *raham* and *hamon* are two disparate words. However, it is supported by the fact that in Arabic *ruhām* or *rahām* means many, numerous, multitudinous, so that, in Arabic, it would have the form *Abū Rahām*, and would indeed mean "father of multitude."

While Abraham's existence is not attested by historical sources outside the Bible, the biblical narrative of Abraham fits into the life and culture of the peoples of Mesopotamia as shown by documents dating from two thousand to fifteen hundred Before the Christian Era (B.C.E.). The biblical Abraham stories are derived from three documents (designated by biblical scholars as J, E, and P), and were combined at a relatively late date, in the ninth century B.C.E. or later. However, the Abraham traditions undoubtedly go back to the very period that archaeology shows formed the background to the story of Abraham's life and his encounters with God and men. The early second millennium B.C.E. was the time when Palestine received an influx of population elements from Upper Mesopotamia—the location of the city of Haran where Abraham sojourned with his father's family (Gen. 11:31) until he received the divine command to go "unto the land that I will show thee" (Gen. 12:1). Thus, as far as Abraham's wanderings are concerned (he is called "a wandering Aramaean" in Deut. 26:5), his story could be considered a case history of the migratory movements of the period.

Also, several events told in Genesis about Abraham and his wife Sarah read as illustrations of patterns of social and familial behavior conforming to the customs and laws known to us from Mesopotamian documents found in Mari and Nuzu. Unfortunately, it has been impossible to narrow down further the gap between the generalized picture emerging from archaeological documentation and the individual life story of Abraham. For example, none of the four Mesopotamian kings who campaigned against five Canaanite kings, and were defeated by Abraham (Gen. 14), has been definitely identified. Some scholars did consider "Amraphel king of Shinar" (Gen. 14:1) to be indentical with Hammurabi king of Babylon, famous for his law code, who lived about 1728–1686 B.C.E., which would place Abraham into the seventeenth century B.C.E., but this identification has been shown by Albright, Boehl, and others to be untenable.[1]

However, this absence of historical authentication, of which traditional Judaism was blissfully unaware—and even had it been aware of it, would, in its firm conviction of the literal truth of the Bible, have remained entirely unconcerned—does not detract from the supreme importance Abraham had for the people of Israel in biblical times, and for their heirs the Jews down to modern times. The story of Abraham served as the mythical validating charter which provided the Children of Israel with a legitimization of their possession of the Land of Israel: the land was repeatedly promised by God to the progeny of Abraham (a promise God repeated again and again to Isaac and Jacob), and, by traveling across the whole length of the land from north to south, and making purchases of land in various locations, Abraham actually acquired much of it through legal transactions for his children. Moreover, by building altars and offering up sacrifices to God at Shechem and Beth-El, Abraham performed religious and ritual acts which symbolized the ideal acquisition of the land and its dedication to God (Gen. 12:6–8). The story of Abraham in Genesis made him into an ancestor in multiple meanings of the concept: he was the genetic ancestor of Israel; he was the acquirer of the land that was to be the Land of Israel; he was the founder of the religion of Israel, who initiated the unique covenantal relationship between God and Israel, and took possession religiously, juridically, and commercially, of the land which his offspring later were to conquer under Joshua by force of arms.

THE RELIGION OF ABRAHAM

A remarkable feature in the central role Abraham assumed as the progenitor of the Hebrew people and the founder of their religion is that in the entire, quite lengthy, biblical narrative about him (Gen. 21–25) there is no religious commandment associated with him except that of circumcision. In his personal conduct, to be sure, Abraham was an exemplar of what it meant to be God-fearing and God-obeying, or, to coin an expression, "God-directed." But in all his frequent contacts with God—and he was a true intimate of God from whom, God felt, He could not "hide . . . that which I am doing" (Gen. 18:17)—God gave him only two commands: to go to the Land of Promise, and to circumcise himself and his progeny. When God first addresses Abraham, He does so with what appears to be an almost frightening abruptness. Without introducing Himself in any manner, God's first words order Abraham to leave his country and go to an as yet unnamed land where, God promises, He will make Abraham "a great nation" (Gen. 12:1).

What was there in Abraham that made him worthy of such great divine distinction? What was he supposed to undertake in return for this great promise? What was his reaction when suddenly he heard or perceived the command from an unidentified voice? These and other questions go to the essence of Abraham's being as conceived in the early biblical period and remain entirely up to the reader's imagination. What we are told is only that Abraham obeys God, and that he, with Sarai his wife (who, we later find out, was his half-sister), his nephew Lot, and perhaps a considerable retinue, arrives in Canaan, the same land to which, without any divine command, Abraham's father Terah had originally intended to go when he set out from his hometown, Ur of the Chaldees, in southern Mesopotamia (Gen. 11:31; 12:5–6).

After Abraham arrives in Canaan, God, who still does not identify Himself to him, promises to give that land unto his seed (Gen. 12:7). Abraham builds an altar and calls "upon the name of the Lord" (Gen. 12:8; 13:4). Before long, God repeats the promise of the land and of numerous progeny (Gen. 13:15–16). After Abraham proves his prowess in war (Gen. 14), he is honored by "Melchizedek king of Salem . . . priest of God Most High" (*El ᶜElyon*), who blesses him in the name of that God, "Maker of heaven and earth" (Gen. 14:18–19). Thereafter, God again repeats his promise of progeny to the still childless Abraham, and Abraham, we are told, "believed in the Lord" (Gen. 15:6). Then follows the awesome scene of the nocturnal "covenant between the pieces" of sacrificial animals, and yet other repetitions of the divine promise (Gen. 15:18; 17:2).

At this late stage in the ongoing relationship between God and Abraham, God finally introduces Himself to him, and says, "I am God Almighty (*El Shaddai*), walk before me and be thou whole-hearted" (Gen. 17:1). One can only conjecture whether there was (or whether the author of this narrative assumed) any connection between *El Shaddai*, the name by which God identified Himself to Abraham, and Melchizedek's *El ᶜElyon*.

Then follows the only religious commandment God imposes upon Abraham and his offspring—that of circumcision (Gen. 17:11–14). Next, the birth of the true heir, Isaac, is foretold (Gen. 17:19), after which there is an enigmatic and vague reference to the effect that God expected Abraham to "command his children and his household after him that they may keep the way of the Lord, to do righteousness and justice . . ." (Gen. 18:19). Enigmatic and vague, because "the way of the Lord" evidently meant at this stage nothing more than righteousness and justice, that is, ethical conduct, while ritual observances are conspicuous by their absence. Throughout the lifelong close and friendly relationship Abraham had with God, the only concrete ritual demand God addressed to him (apart from that of circumcision) was the ad hoc demand that he sacrifice his son Isaac. However, as is well known, in the last moment it transpired that this was merely a test (Gen. 22).

In sum, despite the frequent contact, the working relationship, between Abraham and God, Abraham received no instruction from God as to religious conduct or ritual, and left no such rules behind for his children to follow. He walked with God, called upon God, entered into a covenant with God, bargained with God, and believed in God so much that in later biblical times he was considered to have been God's friend (cf. Isa. 41:8; 2 Chron. 20:7; Jub. 19:19), but, except for circumcision, he left behind no religious laws, doctrines, or rituals which would have been concrete and palpable expressions of his religion. This is the more remarkable since in the very midst of the Abraham narrative we come across the Melchizedek episode which tells us that Abraham was acquainted with the priestly king of Salem, who as "priest of God the Most High" was undoubtedly in charge of some established ritual in the worship of that God.

In trying to evaluate the image of Abraham as it appears in the Genesis narrative itself, that is, without the complex superstructure built upon it in later ages by the rabbis, it can be concluded that Abraham, although an intrepid warrior, was in his relationship to God an entirely passive recipient of God's grace and election. In contrast to the later development of biblical Hebrew religion and its heir, Talmudic Judaism, in which ritual occupied a central role, Abraham's religion contains—apart from the single feature of circumcision—no ritual element whatsoever. God frequently initiates conversations with Abraham, but the only thing He demands of Abraham is that he do righteousness and justice, and be wholehearted with God (Gen. 17:1; 18:19). Indirectly it is also indicated that God considered it righteousness on the part of Abraham that he believed in Him (Gen. 15:6). As for circumcision, it seems to have been considered such a fundamental ritual duty, and of such basic importance, that it was all that God was said to have asked of Abraham and his progeny as their part of the "everlasting covenant," as against which God solemnly undertook to give the Land of Canaan to him and his seed "for an everlasting possession" (Gen. 17:8, 13). Thus the religion of Abraham can be summed up as having consisted of nothing more than one credal element (the belief in God), one ethical element (righteousness and justice), and one ritual element (circumcision).

Despite this meagerness of the religious elements in the Abraham tradition which found their way into the Book of Genesis (there are indications in other books of the Bible that there existed additional old traditions about Abraham that were not included into the Genesis narrative[2]), subsequently the figure of Abraham grew in importance in biblical Hebrew religion, and was fully developed in Talmudic times. Abraham became the classical founder figure of Judaism, the path-breaker, in whose footsteps followed his son Isaac, Isaac's son Jacob, and the latter's descendants. "Abraham our father" became the most beloved ancestor figure in Judaism, and, next to "Moses our master," the most venerated one, whose life and adventures were surrounded by more endearing legendary embellishments than those of any other biblical hero, with the exception of Moses.[3]

ABRAHAM IN THE KORAN AND IN ISLAM

We turn now to a consideration of Abraham as reflected in the Koran and later Muslim religious literature. The first thing to be stated in this connection is that prior to the Koranic references to Abraham, whose name appears in it in the Arabicized form of *Ibrāhīm*, there is no mention of Abraham in any Arabic literary source or archaeological find. True, pre-Koranic Arabic sources flow very sparsely, so that the absence of any reference in them to Abraham cannot be taken as a proof that Abraham was unknown to the Arabs in the *jāhiliyya*. However, it makes such a conclusion likely.[4] When we add that the same is the case with all the other biblical figures who are referred to in the Koran and other early Arabic sources, the conclusion that the absence of any reference to them is due, not to the hazards of the preservation of documentary evidence from those remote periods, but to the fact that these figures were simply unknown to pre-Islamic Arab tradition is greatly strengthened. This holds good even with regard to Ishmael (in Arabic Ismāᶜīl), the son of Abraham, and Yoqṭan (Arabic Qaḥṭān), the two ancestor figures of the North Arabian and South Arabian peoples respectively.

The Jewish influences in the Koran are a well-known and thoroughly researched subject.[5] It is likewise well known that both in Mecca and Medina, where Muhammad lived (he was born in Mecca in 570, and died in Medina in 632), there were in his day numerous large Jewish tribes. Some of the members of these tribes were friends or acquaintances of Muhammad, and in the course of conversations with them he acquired some knowledge, albeit often a merely superficial one, of biblical laws, doctrines, and stories, as well as Midrashim (Jewish legends) woven around biblical figures, some as late as within a generation or two of his own lifetime. Thus the provenance of Muhammad's familiarity with Jewish law and lore presents no problem. Nor is there a problem in understanding that he was deeply impressed by the concept of the one and only almighty God, who is the *primus motor* and *prima causa* in all Jewish ritual and belief. What is problematic is how he went about to take the Jewish narratives, including the great Jewish foundation myth—for that is what the Abraham stories of Genesis in effect are—appropriate them, and transform them into the foundation myth of the Arab tribes and of Islam, the religion which he, Muhammad, founded. How he did this, how he took the courage to tamper with a tradition, which he, following his Jewish interlocutors, certainly believed to go back to divine revelation, is not known. What is known, because we have it in the text of the Koran, is but the end result of what must have been an agonizing and protracted inner struggle to liberate himself from the unquestioning acceptance of "The Book" of the Jews, and to get himself to the point, first to supplement what was said there with additional material, and then to introduce emendations into its narrative.

He was helped in this venture by two factors. One was that the Jewish informants who told him about what was written in the Tora (the Hebrew Bible) (Muhammad himself was illiterate) were themselves no great scholars,[6] and occasionally did not give him accurate accounts of biblical narratives. One can imagine that at times Muhammad sensed discrepancies, or even contradictions, between accounts given him by two different Jewish spokesmen.[7] This may have engendered in him the feeling, once he came to believe himself to be a prophet of God, that he had the right to reinterpret or reformulate what the Jewish informants communicated to him. The second factor was that his informants related to him not only what they remembered as being written in the Bible, but also embellishments of biblical narratives as found in the Midrash, some of which was still in the process of formation.[8] This again might have produced in Muhammad the conviction that he could furnish supplements of his own to the stories he heard from the Jews.

However that may be, the fact is that quite frequently biblical narratives appear in the Koran in a somewhat altered form, and occasionally in quite a different form. The Koranic references to Abraham contain several examples of such emendations or alterations.

Western orientalists have long ago established that there are traces of a developmental sequence in the Koran itself, that some of its *sūra*s (chapters) date from what they call the first, others from the second, and still others from the third Meccan period, while the remainder belongs to the late Medinese period, that is, to the years after 622, when Muhammad had only ten more years to live. As for the figure of Abraham, it would seem that, as time passed, it assumed greater and greater importance in the eyes of Muhammad. This may be due to the fact that he learned more about Abraham after he had settled in Yathrib (subsequently renamed Medina), or it may have been the result of an inner development in his thinking which made him attribute an increasingly significant role to Abraham as the founder of the religion of which Muhammed considered himself the full representative, the last and greatest Messenger, the "seal of the prophets."

In the earlier *sūras* Muhammad generally speaks of Abraham in terms similar to those of the Bible and Midrash. He tells how Abraham attacked the idol worship of his father, which is taken from a Midrash. In the Koranic passage (6:74) which tells of this incident, Abraham's father is not called Terah, as in the Bible (Gen. 11:27, 31), but Āzar, which seems to be an abridged form of Eliezer, the name of Abraham's servant in the Genesis story, who, in the form in which the account reached Muhammad, was mistaken for the father of Abraham.[9] The biblical story of the visit of the men (angels) to Abraham in connection with the announcement of the impending punishment of Lot's people (Sodom and Gomorrah) is recounted in the Koran, but the annunciation of the birth of Isaac is omitted. The Midrash about Abraham's miraculous rescue from the fiery furnace is repeated, as is his quarrel, likewise Midrashic, with the pagan king Nimrod. Abraham is designated as a *ḥanīf*, a true believer, or monotheist, in contrast to the idolaters among whom he lived, and, echoing the Bible, the *khalīl*, friend, of God. It is also asserted in the Koran that Abraham was neither a Jew nor a Christian. While Muhammad does not say that Abraham was a Muslim, he calls Islam "Abraham's religion" (Koran 2:135), and therewith completes the appropriation of Abraham not only as the genealogical forefather of the Arabs, but also as the founder of their religion, Islam.

In the late, Medinese, period, Muhammad liberated himself from the shackles of the biblical and Midrashic narrative, and created an entirely new Abrahamic foundation myth for the Kaᶜba. The Kaᶜba in Mecca is an old, pre-Islamic Arab sanctuary, which was so greatly venerated in Muhammad's day that he did not feel he could condemn it as a place of idolatry. When he triumphantly returned to Mecca (in 630), he removed the 360 idols which stood around the building, and purified its inside, but left the structure itself undisturbed. He declared it to be the very sanctuary which—and this was the most important part of the Islamic foundation myth he created—was originally built by Abraham and his son Ishmael. In other words, by worshiping at the Kaᶜba, restored to its pristine purity, the Muslims were directly following in the footsteps of Abraham, and serving God in exactly the same way in which "the friend of God" served him, before the Jews and Christians obscured his pure religion with their unwarranted modifications and falsifications. In fact, Muhammad went one significant step farther, and claimed that when Abraham and Ishmael built the Kaᶜba, they prayed to God that He should raise a messenger (evidently Muhammad) to teach the Arabs the ways of the Lord. Since this is the most outspoken self-affiliation of Muhammad with Abraham, it seems appropriate to quote the passage in full from the Koranic text:

> . . . We [God] made the House (at Mecca) a resort for mankind and a sanctuary, (saying): Take as your place of worship the place where Abraham stood (to pray). And We imposed a duty upon Abraham and Ishmael (saying): Purify My house for those who go around it, and those who meditate therein and those who bow down and prostrate themselves . . . Abraham prayed: My Lord! Make this a region of security and bestow upon its people fruits, such of them as believe in Allah and the Last Day . . . And when Abraham and Ishmael were raising the foundation of the House, (Abraham prayed): Our Lord! Accept from us (this duty). Lo! Thou, only Thou, art the Hearer, the Knower . . . Our Lord! And raise up in their midst a messenger from among them who shall recite unto them Thy revelations and shall instruct them in the Scripture and in wisdom . . . Lo! Thou, only Thou, art the Mighty, Wise. And who forsaketh the religion of Abraham save him who befooleth himself? [10]

For the Muslims the Koran is the word of God, so these verses establish without doubt the following points:

1. Abraham and Ishmael built the Kaᶜba.
2. The Islamic worship at the Kaᶜba was instituted by Abraham at God's commandment.
3. It was in response to Abraham's prayer that God sent Muhammad to instruct the Arabs in scripture.
4. Islam is the religion of Abraham.

The most remarkable thing in this development is that, with a stroke of true genius, Muhammad not only appropriated the Jewish tradition of Abraham, but also transformed that tradition into the foundation myth of Islam. The intent of the biblical narrative was thereby radically altered. The Bible says that the true heirs of Abraham and his everlasting covenant with God were his descendants through Isaac and Jacob, and that Abraham's other children by Hagar, his concubine, by Ketura, his wife whom he married after the death of Sarah, and by his other unnamed concubines (Gen.

25 : 1–6), had no share in the Abrahamic inheritance. Abraham gave them gifts but then sent them away "eastward, into the east country," and "gave all that he had unto Isaac" (Gen. 25:5–6). Muhammad used the biblical narrative about Abraham and his offspring, and its Midrashic embellishments, with a masterly selectivity. He accepted the election of Abraham by God, the friendship between God and Abraham, the monotheistic and antipolytheistic fervor of Abraham, and the Arab affiliation to Abraham through his son Ishmael. As for Jacob, several times when he mentions him, Muhammad mistakes him for a son of Abraham (Koran 19:49; 29:27; 6:84; 17 : 11), while at other times he correctly refers to Jacob as Abraham's grandson (Koran 21:72; 12:6, 38; 38:45–47). However, he rejects other parts of the biblical narrative, and either passes over them in silence or modifies them. Thus *sūra* 37, which retells the Midrashic story of Abraham's argument against the idolatry of his father (vv. 83–100), continues to recount the biblical story of the *ʿaqeda*, the "binding" of Isaac, but does this without mentioning Isaac by name, and referring instead to "a gentle son" (v. 101). Only after finishing that story does Muhammad mention (in v. 112) that God gave Abraham "tidings of the birth of Isaac." Hence the uninformed reader—and the few Arabs who could read were uninformed readers for several generations after Muhammad—gets the impression that the son whose sacrifice God demanded of Abraham as "a clear test" (v. 106) could not have been Isaac, but must have been the son born to Abraham thirteen years before him, namely Ishmael.

ISHMAEL

In the biblical narrative, after the story of the expulsion of Hagar and Ishmael by Abraham, Ishmael disappears from the patriarchal family history, to emerge only once again from obscurity when he and Isaac bury Abraham in the Cave of Machpela in Hebron (Gen. 25:9). In later biblical books five more Hebrew individuals having the name Ishmael are mentioned, and the name appears also in Hebrew and Assyrian inscriptions. Hence it is clear that Ishmael was a name well accepted among the biblical Hebrews, as it was also in postbiblical, Talmudic times, when one of the greatest sages was called by this name.

Most interesting for the Arab connection of Ishmael is what the Bible tells us about his descendants. His mother Hagar was an Egyptian, and so was his wife whom his mother took for him while they dwelt in the wilderness of Paran (Gen. 16:1, 3; 21:21). Twelve sons of Ishmael are enumerated in Genesis (25:13–16) and are identified as "twelve princes," which evidently means that they represented in Hebrew tradition twelve tribes, paralleling the twelve Hebrew tribes who were descended from the twelve sons of Jacob. The names of most of the twelve "sons of Ishmael" are known from other sources as well. The first two, Nebaioth and Kedar, are mentioned in Assyrian inscriptions from the time of Esarhadon and Ashurbanipal as the main tribes of the Arabs which fought against the kings of Assyria. Their territory was in the Syrian Desert between Transjordan and Mesopotamia. Three others, Adbeel, Massa, and Tema, are mentioned in Assyrian inscriptions from the days of Tiglat Pileser III as Arab desert tribes. Tema (Teyma) and Duma are the names of oases in the North Arabian Desert. The remaining sons of Ishmael are referred to in later biblical books as tribes to the south of Palestine. While the name "Arab" is conspicuously absent from the Genesis 25 list of the sons of Ishmael, it does appear, together with Kedar, among the nomadic tribes or nations in Assyrian inscriptions from the ninth century B.C.E. on.[11]

In the first century C.E. Josephus Flavius, the famous Jewish historian, writes that "the Arabians circumcise after the thirteenth year, because Ishmael, the founder of their nation, who was born to Abraham of the concubine [Hagar] was circumcised at that age."[12] This passage makes it clear that the learned among the Jews in the first century C.E. considered Ishmael as the father of the "Arabian nation," which, as Josephus states later on, consisted of twelve tribes traced back to the twelve sons of Ishmael. After enumerating the twelve sons of Ishmael in almost exact duplication of the Genesis 25 list, Josephus says that "these inhabited all the country from the Euphrates to the Red Sea, and called it Nabatene. They are an Arabian nation, and name their tribes from these [twelve sons of Ishmael], both because of their own virtue, and because of the dignity of Abraham their father."[13] Josephus also knows that the sons of Abraham by Ketura "took possession of Troglodytis, and the country of Arabia the Happy, as far as it reaches to the Red Sea."[14] In the Talmudic period (ca. first to fifth centuries C.E.), the knowledge that the Arabs were the descendants of Ishmael was common among the rabbis, who refer to them either as "Arabs" or as "Ishmaelites."

While the sources mentioned clearly show that among the Jews there existed a tradition linking Arab tribes to Abraham through Ishmael, it is more than doubtful that such a tradition existed among the Arabs themselves in pre-Islamic times. While Jews began to settle in various parts of

Arabia as early as in the first century C.E., it is unlikely that those of them who moved away from their main Palestinian, Babylonian, and Egyptian centers were knowledgeable in the esoteric subject of the genealogical derivation of the Arab tribes. And even if some of them were familiar with the tradition of the Abrahamic descent of the Arabs it is doubtful that the illiterate Arabs who lived in the Arabian peninsula at that time would take an interest in the Jewish attribution of their ancestry to Abraham and Ishmael, who certainly could not have been—Josephus' statement notwithstanding—figures of prestige for them. The absence of the names Ishmael, Isaac, etc., among the Arabs of the *jāhiliyya* is a strong indication of their disinterest in or ignorance of these biblical patriarchs.

This leads us back to the point already touched upon above. Muhammad seems to have been the first among the Arabs to become aware of the biblical tradition about Abraham and Ishmael. But he seems to have remained uninformed of the biblical attribution of Abrahamic descent to the major North Arabian tribes. This becomes evident from the Koran (19:54–55) which reads: "Lo! he [Ishmael] was a keeper of his promise, and he was a messenger (of Allah), a prophet. He enjoined upon his people the prayer and the almsgiving, and was acceptable in the eyes of his Lord." This passage attributes to Ishmael the introduction among the Arabs ("his people") of two basic religious duties (which Muhammad included among his "Five pillars of the faith"), of which no mention is made in the Bible, but makes no reference to the descent of the Arab tribes from Ishmael. On the contrary, it speaks of "the people" of Ishmael, just as elsewhere the Koran speaks of "the people" of Lot (Koran 11:78), meaning the people among whom the hero of the story (Ishmael, Lot) lived and of whom he was part, at least by adoption. That is, the passage in question actually states that Ishmael lived among the Arabs, who therefore, and evidently, could not have been his descendants.

There is one passage in the entire Koran which can be interpreted as hinting at the tradition of the Arabs' Ishmaelite descent. In *sūra* 14:37 Abraham is said to have exclaimed while he was at Mecca, "Our Lord! Lo! I have settled some of my posterity in an uncultivable valley, near unto Thy holy House [the Kaᶜba], our Lord! that they may establish proper worship . . ." However, in this utterance the words "I have settled some of my posterity" can refer only to Ishmael and his actual children, and not to the wider groups of tribes descended from Abraham according to the Bible. The definite attribution of Abrahamic-Ishmaelite descent to the (North) Arabian tribes, and the completion of the appropriation of the biblical Hebrew myth of origin for Arab prehistory was left to the early Koran commentators to accomplish.

ABRAHAM VISITS ISHMAEL

Soon after the death of Muhammad the Arab religious scholars began to collect and diligently note every word Muhammad reportedly uttered and every act he was said to have performed. They were learned men who had a much more thorough knowledge than Muhammad of the Bible and the Midrash. Thus the authors of the *Qiṣaṣ al-Anbiyā'* ("Stories of the Prophets"), the Koran commentaries, and the Arab histories, were in a position to furnish many details about the life of Abraham and Ishmael, partly adapted from Jewish sources, and partly invented in obedience to the folkloristic instinct to elaborate and embellish. In these post-Koranic sources the figures of Abraham and Ishmael are fleshed out in a manner reminiscent of what the Jewish Aggada did with the patriarchs and other biblical heroes.

Besides the one visit Abraham is said in the Koran to have paid to Mecca in the company of Ishmael, the Arab traditionists tell of several trips Abraham took from Canaan to Arabia. First of all, we learn from the Islamic elaborations of the Abraham-Ishmael story that, far from simply expelling Hagar and Ishmael, Abraham accompanied them as far as Mecca, before he felt that he had to return to his wife Sarah. Hagar, according to Muslim legend, became unwittingly the originator of one of the ceremonies of the *ḥajj*: in her desperation over not being able to give water to her thirsty son, she ran back and forth between two hills, *al-Ṣafā* and *al-Marwa*. It is in commemoration of this act that the pilgrims observe the so-called *saᶜy* ("run") rite in which they run seven times between those two hills.

Ishmael himself becomes responsible in Arab legend for the appearance of the sacred spring, Zamzam: he scratched the sand and thus enabled the waters of the spring to break through to the surface. When Ishmael grew up, he married a girl from the Arab Jurhum tribe which had settled at Mecca with Hagar's permission. It is from the Jurhum that Ishmael learned Arabic. This legend clearly shows that in Arab tradition Arab tribes antedated Ishmael and Abraham. The legend continues to tell that Ishmael's Jurhumite wife lacked hospitality, one of the basic values in nomadic Arab life, so Ishmael divorced her. His mother took him another wife, this time from Egypt. The legend of how this came about is contained in the works of Arab historians and traditionists from the ninth century on,[15] but it must have circulated earlier, because a reflection of it is found in the Targum Jonathan which dates from the seventh to eighth century. In it, Gen. 21:21 is amplified to read: "And he [Ishmael] dwelt in the wilderness of Paran, and took to wife Adisha [i.e., ᶜĀ'isha], and he divorced her, and his mother took for him to wife Fāṭima from the Land of Egypt."[16] The mention of the two typical Arabic women's names ᶜĀ'isha and Fāṭima is proof that the author of this Targum took the legend of Ishmael's two wives from an Arabic source. That legend is reproduced in full in the eighth- to ninth-century Midrash Pirqe Rabbi Eliᶜezer. I give here my translation of that version which differs only very slightly from its Arabic source.

> Ishmael sent and took a wife from the Plains of Moab and her name was Aisa [ᶜĀ'isha]. After three years Abraham went to see his son Ishmael, and he swore to Sarah that he would not dismount from the camel at the place where Ishmael dwelt. And he arrived at midday, and found the wife of Ishmael. He said to her, "Where is Ishmael?" She answered, "He went with his mother to fetch fruit and dates from the desert." He said to her, "Give me some water and some bread, for my soul is tired from the road of the desert." She answered, "There is no bread and there is no water." He said to her, "When Ishmael returns, tell him that an old man from the Land of Canaan came to see you, and he said that the threshold of the house is not good." (The Arabic version has "Tell him: Change the threshold of your house.") When Ishmael returned, his wife told him, and he divorced her. And his mother sent and took a wife from the house of her father, and her name was Patuma [Fāṭima].
>
> Three years passed and Abraham again came to see Ishmael his son. And he swore to Sarah, as on the earlier occasion, that he would not dismount from the camel in the place where Ishmael dwelt. And he arrived there at midday, and found there the wife of Ishmael. He said to her, "Where is Ishmael?" She answered, "He went with his mother to tend the camels in the desert." He said to her, "Give me some bread and some water, for my soul is tired from the road." She brought it out and gave him. Abraham got up and prayed before the Holy One, blessed be He, for his son. And the house of Ishmael became full of many good things, of all kinds of blessings. And when Ishmael returned, his wife told him what had happened, and Ishmael knew that the love of his father was still with him . . .[17]

This legend achieved something very important for the Arab claim of Abrahamic descent. The Bible, which was available to the post-Koranic

Arab scholars in one or more Arabic versions—for example, in those of the Christian Arab Ḥunayn ibn Isḥāq (ca. 800–873), and the Jewish scholar Saʿadia Gaon (see chapter 3)—says very little about the relationship between Abraham and Ishmael. All one reads there is that when he was born Abraham called him Ishmael (Gen. 16:15), and that when he was about fourteen years old Abraham cast him out, together with his mother Hagar, at the demand of Sarah, but with the approval of God (Gen. 21:8ff.). The Bible records no single word that was exchanged between Abraham and Ishmael throughout the years the lad spent in his father's house. Clearly, from the Arab point of view this account was unsatisfactory, because it made it appear that there was no fatherly love on the part of Abraham for his son Ishmael, and that there was not even any contact between them. An unloved son who is expelled by his father cannot claim to be his father's heir spiritually.

This is effectively remedied by the story about Abraham's two visits to Ishmael. From it, it transpires that Abraham did indeed love him, and was concerned about his well-being long after Ishmael had grown up, had moved to Arabia, had married, and had children of his own. (According to the *Sefer haYashar*, a twelfth-century Hebrew book of legends, Abraham witnesses how Ishmael's first wife beats and curses her children.) In fact, we are told that Abraham loved Ishmael so much that, as an old man, he undertook two arduous journeys across the desert to visit him. The story also remedies another drawback of the Genesis narrative from the Arab point of view. Esau, another ancestral figure excluded from the Israelite genealogy, received a blessing from his father Isaac. Ishmael, however, was not recorded in the Bible as having received any paternal blessing. The Arabic story fills in this hurtful omission: Abraham in fact did bless Ishmael on the occasion of his second visit to him in the desert. It also fills the time gap between Ishmael's expulsion and the Koranic reference to the building of the Kaʿba by Abraham and Ishmael, which apparently took place during a third visit paid by the father to his son.

There is only one thing this legend does not establish: the descent of the Arabs from Ishmael. On the contrary: the legend speaks about the existence of at least one Arab tribe, that of the Jurhum, at the time of Ishmael's arrival in Arabia, and states that not only did Ishmael marry a Jurhum girl, but he learned Arabic from the Jurhum tribe. How could Ishmael be the ancestor of the Arabs if he lived in the midst of an existing Arab tribe? It is at this point that the genealogical theory of dual Arab descent enters to solve the problem.

YOQṬAN–QAḤṬĀN

In the first century after the death of Muhammad *nasab* (genealogy) became an important subject of study for Arab scholars. The genealogists exerted prodigious efforts and used great ingenuity to reconcile Arab tribal traditions of descent and ancestral figures with the biblical account of Genesis 25 which enumerates the descendants of Ishmael. The family trees and genealogical lists they came up with are extremely intricate, and not without internal contradictions. We need not concern ourselves with these problems here, but can focus instead on the manner in which the various branches which figured in the autochthonous Arab genealogical traditions were grafted onto the biblical stem. In order to be able to do so, we must first briefly present how the Arabs conceived of their origin and tribal descent prior to their exposure to biblical influences.

According to indigenous Arab tradition, the Arabs descended from two original tribes or tribal groups, represented by two eponymous ancestor figures about whom nothing was known except their names. One of them, ᶜAdnān, was considered the progenitor of the North Arabian tribes, the other, Qaḥṭān, of those of South Arabia.[18] The southern, or Qaḥṭānite, tribes were considered the original true Arabs (*al-ᶜArab al-ᶜāriba*), while the northern, or ᶜAdnānite, tribes were regarded as merely Arabized peoples (*al-ᶜArab al-mustaᶜriba*). A tribal federation called Qaḥṭān or Yaman (meaning "south") actually did exist in pre-Islamic times, and tribes by this name still occupy today a considerable area southeast of Mecca. That is, the origin of southern tribes from an eponymous Qaḥṭān has some historical basis.

The genealogy of the northern tribes is more complicated and less certain. ᶜAdnān was said to have had ten sons, one of whom was Maᶜadd, and Maᶜadd's son Nizār became the progenitor of the northern tribes, most of them through his two sons Rabīᶜa and Muḍar. A son or grandson of Muḍar was Qays. A reflection of the plurality of these northern ancestor figures can be seen in the names Maᶜadd, Nizār, Muḍar, and Qays, used as alternative designations for the northern tribes.

Whether there is any historical connection between the South Arabian eponymous ancestor Qaḥṭān and the Yoqṭan mentioned in Genesis 10: 21–25 and 1 Chron. 1:4, 17–19 is a moot question. Most Arab genealogists, however, unhesitatingly assumed the identity of the two, although some of them maintained that Qaḥṭān was the father or the brother of Yoqṭan. The biblical genealogy is Noah–Shem–Arpachshad–Shelah–ᶜEver–Yoqṭan; and this list was bodily taken over by the Arab genealogists with the Arabicized forms of the names, Nūḥ–Sām–Arfakhshadh–Shālakh–ᶜĀbar–Qaḥṭān. The evident purpose of this identification was to provide the South Arabians with a respectable biblical ancestry. Although there is no further correspondence between the sons of Yoqṭan as enumerated in Genesis and as appearing in the traditional genealogy of the South Arabian tribes, it is interesting to note that modern biblical scholarship has identified several of the Yoqṭanides with South Arabian tribal or regional names. Thus Ḥaṣarmaweth son of Yoqṭan (Gen. 10:26) is found again in the name of the South Arabian Ḥaḍramawt valley; Sheba, another son of Yoqṭan in Saba; Yerah, a third son, seems to correspond to Mahra, etc.[19]

As for Arab genealogists, what they did with the biblical Sheba son of Yoqṭan (Gen. 10:27) was to interpolate two generations between them (Qaḥṭān–Yaᶜrub–Yashjub–Saba), and then made Ḥimyar and Kahlān, the two tribal groups into which the Qaḥṭān confederation is divided, the offspring of two sons of Saba. In this manner, the Ḥimyar, the progenitors of the great pre-Islamic kingdoms of South Arabia, became grafted on the biblical lineage of Qaḥṭān-Yoqṭan.[20]

The establishment of other connections with biblical ancestor figures was also attempted by Arab genealogists. Some of them made Qaḥṭān a direct descendant of Ishmael, who thereby—quite unhistorically even from the point of view of Arab traditions—became "the father of all the Arabs," the legendary Ishmael-Jurhum connection notwithstanding. Others made Qaḥṭān the son of Hūd, the earliest of the Arab prophets mentioned in the Koran, while Hūd in turn was considered either identical with the biblical ᶜEver (Arabic ᶜĀbar), father of Yoqṭan (Qaḥṭān), or a son of the same ᶜEver. Hūd is also made a descendant of Noah through Shem (Sām)–Aram–ᶜŪṣ–ᶜĀd.[21]

Biblical ancestry appears to have been the *summum bonum* of the aspirations of Arab genealogists, which they tried to claim in many different ways. Incidentally, to illustrate that these claims have survived to this day, it may be mentioned that the modern Qaḥṭān tribes in the People's Democratic Republic of Yemen (Southern Yemen) still hold that their ancestor was the son of Hūd.[22]

ᶜADNĀN SON OF ISHMAEL

Vague as the image of Qaḥṭān is in Arab tradition, the figure of ᶜAdnān, the ancestor of the northern tribes, is even more misty. Although the name appears in a few pre-Islamic Arabic inscriptions, it does not occur in pre-Islamic poetry, and nothing is known either historically or traditionally about an ancestral figure by this name.[23] Because of the uncertainty about ᶜAdnān, the descent line of the northern Arabs is traced back mostly not to him but only to his son Maᶜadd, or even only as far as Maᶜadd's son Nizār, whose two sons figure as the eponymous ancestors of the two main branches of the North Arabian tribes, Muḍar and Rabīᶜa. Finally, a son of Muḍar, named Qays ᶜAylān (who sometimes appears as Qays son of ᶜAylān son of Muḍar), or rather a tribal group named Qays, overshadowed in importance other northern tribes to such an extent that in certain parts of the Arab world, especially in Syria, Lebanon, Jordan, Palestine, and Egypt, all northern tribes were called Qays. The northern-southern antagonism that until recent times played such a crucial role in the history of this area, was commonly referred to as the rivalry between Qays and Yaman. However, despite the indefinite nomenclature, Arab genealogists agreed that the northern tribes, too, had biblical ancestry, and made ᶜAdnān a son or descendant of Ishmael.[24]

With this explanation the Ishmael-Jurhum connection was solved to the satisfaction of the genealogists. At the time Ishmael arrived in Arabia, they now could maintain, the peninsula already was inhabited by Arab tribes, the descendants of Qaḥṭān. One of these was the Jurhum tribe, under whose influence Ishmael became Arabized, and his descendants developed into the northern, *mustaᶜriba* (Arabized) tribes.

One more point must be mentioned before we can leave this subject. In Arab genealogical thinking, the older the descent line of a group, the nobler the status of that group. The identification of Qaḥṭān with a biblical figure, Yoqṭan, and the affiliation of ᶜAdnān with another, Ishmael, meant that the status and prestige of these two overall Arab moieties were determined by the position of their ancestors in the biblical genealogy. According to the Bible, Yoqṭan was a fifth-generation descendant of Noah, while Ishmael was eleven generations removed from the famed hero of the deluge. Hence the southern, Qaḥṭān, tribes were regarded the older, true, aboriginal Arab stock, while the northern, ᶜAdnān, tribes were considered merely Arabized latecomers.

ISHMAEL THE DHABĪḤ

The end result of these efforts to graft the Arab tribes upon the biblical family tree of mankind was highly satisfactory from an Arab point of view. It was somewhat akin to the emotional gratification the Christian Church must have derived from depriving the Jews of their spiritual heritage by declaring itself to be "Israel after the spirit," that is, the true Israel, the true heir to the biblical Hebrews, while assigning to the Jews the disfranchised position of being merely "Israel after the flesh." The Arabs in the days of Muhammad were a people without a history. True, there were among the Arabs some popular traditions concerning three early prophets (Hūd, Ṣāliḥ, and Shuᶜayb), one ancient wise man (Luqmān), and several old "lost" tribes, such as ᶜĀd, Thamūd, Iram, Jurhum, Ṭasm, and Jadīs, but, apart from their names almost nothing of these persons and tribes had been retained in memory by the time of Muhammad. When viewed against this paucity of the memory of indigenous Arab prophets, the fact that no less than eighteen prophets known from the Hebrew Bible (plus three from the Gospels) are mentioned in the Koran gains in significance.

What we know today about the history of the Arabs in pre-Islamic times on the basis of studies of Assyrian inscriptions, Greek and Roman authors, and Arabian archaeological work, was totally unknown to the Arabs in the days of Muhammad, and remained largely so until the onset of Westernization in the nineteenth century. Arab scholarly interest turned to history only several generations after Muhammad, and even when it did it took little or no interest in the *jāhiliyya*. Even in the eighth and ninth centuries, when Muslim historiography was well advanced, all that Arab historians had accomplished relative to the *jāhiliyya* was to divide it into two periods which were not even contiguous. The first extended from Adam to Noah, and was a mere restatement of the biblical account of the early history of mankind; the second was the time between Jesus and Muhammad. This second period of the *jāhiliyya* was termed *al-fatra*, relaxation or interval, because in contrast to the considerable number of prophets of the pre-Christian period, known to them from the Bible and the Koran, it appeared to the early Muslim historians as empty of men of God. To fill this lacuna, they searched for, found, and enumerated eight "men who had a religion before the mission of the Prophet [Muhammad]," as Ibn Qutayba (828–889) put it. Restating this tradition, al-Masᶜūdī (died ca. 956) termed these men of God *ahl al-fatra*, "men of the interval," and added several more to the list of Ibn Qutayba as men who "have believed in a single God and in the resurrection."[25] These haphazard stabs at filling a long time gap do not, of course, amount to serious attempts at studying the history of the last six centuries of the *jāhiliyya*.

In this situation it was the genealogists who, by tying Arab origins to the biblical stories and lists of ancestral figures, supplied the Arabs with a long and venerable ancestry, a prehistory reaching far back into the early days of mankind. By the end of the eighth century this artificial genealogical structure was completed, and the Arabs could boast not only of being the only true spiritual heirs of Abraham the *ḥanīf*, and of Islam being the true "religion of Abraham," but also of direct descent from the great friend of God and other biblical figures who lived generations before him. Although there are some rather vague indications to the effect that some Arab poets of the *jāhiliyya* had some knowledge of a few biblical figures and events,[26] this, even if correct, does not change the fact this masterly appropriation of a highly prestigious biblical ancestry for the Arabs was initiated by the religious genius of Muhammad.

In building up the Abraham-Ishmael connection, the Arab scholars gradually came to minimize the role played by Isaac in biblical history. During the first Islamic century, as Goldziher has shown,[27] they seem to have accepted the biblical account and considered Isaac to have been the *dhabīḥ*, sacrifice, that is, the son whom God commanded Abraham to sacrifice. The caliphs ᶜUmar and ᶜAlī still believed this to have been the case. But in the commentaries on the Koran and in the *Qiṣaṣ al-anbiyā'* ("Stories of the Prophets"), although these sources elaborate on the story of the *dhabīḥ*, the question of his identity remains open, which they could do since the Koranic text omits the name of Abraham's son to be sacrificed. Then, however, credence was given to the fabrication of a Jewish convert to Islam, who tried to curry favor with the Muslims by asserting that the Jews had substituted the name of their ancestor Isaac for that of Ishmael, the Arabs' progenitor. This view won out over those who continued to maintain that Isaac was the *dhabīḥ*, and soon became generally accepted. It is interesting to note in this connection that the Persians, who claimed descent from Isaac (and not Ishmael), maintained that he was the *dhabīḥ*; some of them even boasted that their descent from Isaac rendered them superior to the Arabs.[28] Among the Arabs only a few scholars, and they too of Persian extraction, such as Ibn Qutayba, the great Sunnī polygraph of the ninth century, and the Persian Ṭabarī (839–923), the first great compiler of a "universal" Islamic history, maintained that Isaac was, in fact, the *dhabīḥ*.[29]

For the Arab world in general, Ishmael had become the *dhabīḥ*, and the ancestor of all, or half, of the Arab tribes. Ishmael and his descendants the Arabs were effectively elevated to a position of nobility and election which could not be claimed by Isaac and his progeny, the Jews. As for Abraham, the friend of God, he became the early exponent of Islamic monotheism, and the spiritual forerunner of Muhammad, whose appearance was granted to the Arabs at the request Abraham addressed to God at Mecca. The Jews were accused of having falsified "The Book," and became, in Muslim doctrine, excluded from the true line of spiritual descent. Their subordinate status in the House of Islam could be considered a consequence of their fall from grace.

3

Jews in Arab Lands

FROM ARAB PAGANISM TO UMAYYAD CULTURE

It is difficult to imagine a greater contrast between two periods in the life of a people than between that of the *jāhiliyya*, the Arab state of pagan ignorance, which can conveniently be considered as having ended in 622 C.E., the year of Muhammad's *hijra* from Mecca to Medina, and that of the Umayyads a mere century later, when the Muslim caliphate held sway over a vast empire stretching from Spain and Morocco in the west to Central Asia and India in the east. In 622 the Arabs were nothing more than a number of disunited tribes making a living either as nomadic herders, or, mainly in the south and on the northern fringes of the peninsula, as agriculturists settled in villages, or again as traders or merchants in a few oasis towns, such as Mecca and Yathrib (later Medina) near the west coast. They were torn by centuries-old strife and feuding. They were almost totally illiterate, and the very few who could read and write had only a very defective script at their disposal which was little more than a reminder.[1] What has survived of their intellectual activity is limited to the work of a few poets, whose *qaṣīda*s were memorized by heart, and whose favorite subjects were love, camels, the desert, and, above all, self-praise, including the praise of the poet's own people, and satirical attacks on enemy tribes. Their favorite pastimes, in addition to raiding (*ghazw*), were sex and gambling.[2] Their religion was a type of pagan polytheism, or animism, taking the form of belief in and service of many gods, goddesses, and spirits. Confined to their hot and arid peninsula, whose major part was desert, the Arabs lived in the early seventh century in the same manner and fashion in which they had lived five, ten, or fifteen centuries earlier, that is, ever since the introduction in about 1100 B.C.E. of the domesticated camel, which enabled them to subsist in the desert where, without the camel, man could not survive.

A hundred years later, the Arabs were lords of an empire larger than that of Alexander and of the Romans. It included Spain and Morocco, the entire shore of North Africa to Egypt, Palestine, Syria, Iraq, Iran, Transoxiana, and the Indus Valley. In all this vast territory Arabs had become landowners, merchants, and peasants, and their numbers were rapidly and greatly augmented by converts to Islam from native populations, who, except for the outlying territories, had also become Arabized. Expressive of the degree of accomplished assimilation by the non-Arab converts to Islam and the Arabs were the reforms introduced by the Caliph ᶜUmar II (reigned 717–720), who made land and property, rather than ethnic origin, the basis of taxation for all Muslims. Less impressive than the administrative and political organization of the empire under the Umayyads (661–750) were the Arab achievements in religious and secular literature, the arts, and various sciences in that early period. Still, the Arabs had never produced a book until Muhammad's Koran, which was put in writing on the basis of scattered notes within a few years after his death in 632. Under the Umayyads, they had become a people with a considerable literary production.

Although the Golden Age of Arab letters and sciences (ca. 750–1050) was yet to come, the Koran had exerted, within a century after the Hijra, enormous influence on Arabic literature and become the central subject of study, commentary, and interpretation. Moreover, since the study of Arabic grammar and vocabulary was deemed indispensable for the understanding of the language of the Koran, those subjects were taken up, and that could be done only on the basis of the only available Arabic writings outside the Koran—those of the poets of the *jāhiliyya*. Thus came into being Arabic philology and lexicography. At the same time the science of "tradition" arose as a result of the search for guidelines for behavior in the sayings and acts of the Prophet as remembered by his companions and handed down to posterity through a chain of transmitters or traditionists. Tradition in turn gave rise to the study of theology and jurisprudence, and ultimately of history and genealogy. True, the early Arab histories, several of which were compiled by Arabs from Yemen, were nothing more than concoctions from legends, vague traditions, and Jewish sources (cf. chapter 2), with the addition of a goodly dose of invention, but they satisfied the demand for information about Arab origins and conditions of life just before and after the appearance of Muhammad. Much attention was paid also to the life of

Muhammad himself, and especially to his military expeditions (*maghāzī*), and it was out of the early works on this subject that the later Arab historiography developed. Regrettably, little of all this has been preserved, due mainly to the fact that once the material contained in such treatises was incorporated into later writings, the earlier ones ceased to attract interest.

Poetry, which was the only branch of literature to flourish in pre-Islamic times, stagnated for a while after the rise of Islam. Even those poets who had attained renown prior to the Hijra, such as the famous Labīd, author of one of the celebrated *Muᶜallaqāt*, who lived on for more than three decades after the Hijra, ceased to produce poems after converting to Islam. However, this period of silence was short-lived. Under the Umayyads (661–750) poets and poetry came to life, the classical *qaṣīda* revived, and by the end of the seventh century numerous poets sang, partly continuing the old traditions and partly adding new themes and forms to the old repertoire. Three poets stand out: al-Akhṭal, Jarīr, and al-Farazdaq, and the fact that all of them flourished in the newly conquered lands to the north of the Arabian peninsula further indicates the shift of the Arab center from the Ḥijāz to the Syria-Iraq area.

Al-Akhṭal ("the Loquacious"), as Ghiyāth ibn Ghawth (ca. 640–ca. 710) was known, was a Christian of northern Syria, a heavy drinker, who loved the company of singing-girls of easy virtue. His entire poetical career was dominated by his ongoing verbal conflict with the poet Jarīr, in which he was supported by the third of the trio, al-Farazdaq. Although the bedouin tradition is strongly evident in the poetry of all three, their themes revolve around the feuds and political controversies of their time.

Jarīr ibn al-Khaṭafa (ca. 650–729) was born in Eastern Arabia, lived in Iraq and Damascus, and was patronized by several caliphs, notably by ᶜUmar II. His lifelong verbal sparring with al-Farazdaq created keen interest even among the soldiery. One gets some idea of the role of poetry in Umayyad society from the fact that Jarīr in his *Dīwān* (collection of poems) satirized more than forty contemporary poets. He is regarded as one of the greatest Arab poets of all times.

Al-Farazdaq ("Lump of Dough"), by which name Tammām ibn Ghālib (ca. 640–ca. 728) was known, was born in Yamāma, Eastern Arabia, lived in Baṣra (southern Iraq), and became official poet of the caliph Walīd I and his two sons. He was caught up in the violent strife between the Yamanī and Qaysī factions which raged at the time in Iraq, and was consequently jailed several times. According to his biographies, which tend to exaggerate, he was an eccentric, a coward, and a drunkard, was bawdy and venal. His satirical poetry, more than that of his contemporaries, is characterized by vigor and obscenity. Further, as R. Blanchère observed,[3] in his case "the Islamic ethic has in no way enriched in depth a spirit completely impregnated with Bedouin culture." And yet he was representative of Arabic poetry at its height. Of all Arab poets he was the most prolific, his *Dīwān* alone containing no less than 7,630 verses.

A trio of Ḥijāzī poets of the same period can be juxtaposed to the above three. They were al-Aḥwaṣ, al-ᶜArjī, and ᶜUmar ibn Abī Rabīᶜa. Al-Aḥwaṣ (ca. 655–728/9) was a member of the refined society of Medina, who was whipped several times for amorous misconduct and other indiscretions, put in jail, and exiled, and who, in the judgment of posterity, had neither *muruwwa* (cf. chapter 1), nor *dīn* (religion). But he was highly praised as a poet. Al-ᶜArjī (died ca. 738) was a great-grandson of the Caliph ᶜUthman. He lived in the Ḥijāz, had a generous but violent disposition, found his pleasure in riotous or frivolous amusement, and joined the erotic poets who flourished at the time in Mecca and Medina. When he heaped insult in a poem on the mother of the governor of Mecca, he was placed in the pillory and thrown in jail where he died.

The most brilliant of the three was ᶜUmar ibn Abī Rabīᶜa (died ca. 720), a Qurayshite, whose tender poetry has been compared by Gibb to that of the English poet of love, nature and wine, Robert Herrick.[4] Like ᶜArjī, ᶜUmar scandalized his contemporaries and had to suffer more than one banishment.

We must, regrettably, stop here our sketchy evocations of the poets of the Umayyad age to avoid turning this chapter into a lengthy literary history of the period. Accounts of their lives and works, together with numerous excerpts of their poems, can be found in the incomparable *Kitāb al-Aghānī* ("Book of Songs") of Abu al-Faraj al-Iṣfahānī (897–967), whose twenty volumes are the great treasure house from which is drawn most of our knowledge of the first three hundred years after Islam of Arab society and manners, and, of course, of Arabic literature.

What triggered this spurt-like transformation from tribal anarchy to organized empire, accompanied by great cultural developments unparalleled in human history? Historians of the Arab phenomenon agree that the primary responsibility for it must be ascribed to the imposition of Islam upon the Arabs, which transformed their disunited, warring and feuding tribes into the *umma Muḥammadiyya*, the Muhammadan community, and to the ability of their religion and language to draw the conquered peoples into the magic circle of Arab culture. It was the new faith, Islam, which released Arab culture's latent potential, gave it direction, and infused it with the will to seek creative expression. If so, it is only proper that due credit be given to the influence of Judaism (and Christianity) on Muhammad, without which there would have been no Koran, no Islam, and no Arab civilization. To state this is, of course, not to deny that Arab science, medicine, and philosophy were primarily based on the achievements of the Greek and Hellenistic worlds whose works began to be translated into Arabic at an early period. I merely point out that the religious basis of Arab culture, which produced in the Arabs the thirst for knowledge and the élan to pursue it, owed its existence to the inspiration of the Koran whose religious ideas were, in turn, greatly influenced by Judaism. However, neither the Greek foundations of Arab civilization, nor the Jewish inspiration of Islam diminishes in any way the greatness of the Arab genius that went into the making of Medieval Arab culture.

THE ᶜĀSHŪRĀ *AND THE* QIBLA

While the Jews stood at the cradle of Islam, once Muhammad gave the Abrahamic creed to the Arabs, and once the Arab branches were securely grafted onto the biblical family tree of the Hebrew patriarchs, Muhammad considered the Jews as nothing more than possible and likely converts to his new faith. The story of how Muhammad tried to win the Jews, how, soon after his arrival in Medina, he became disappointed when they refused to accept him as the messenger of God, how he thereupon turned against them, fought and killed some of their tribes, forced others to convert to Islam, and then, once Islam was securely entrenched, half generously and half grudgingly allowed the remaining Jews to continue to live as Jews in the House of Islam provided they submitted to Muslim overlordship and paid a special head tax (the *jizya*), has so often been told that there is no need to retell it here. Let me instead cite two examples which show that just as Muhammad in the second half of his ministry liberated himself from following literally the biblical foundation myth of Abraham and his family (see chapter 2), so he asserted the independence of his *dīn* from Judaism by setting aside Jewish rites after having first incorporated them as elements of his religion. The two examples are those of the *ᶜāshūrā* and the *qibla*.

ᶜĀshūrā is the Arabic form of the Hebrew *ᶜāsōr*, with the Aramaic determinative ending *-a*, meaning "the tenth." In Lev. 16:29 the Children of

Israel are commanded to afflict their souls on the tenth of the seventh month, Tishri, so as to make atonement on that day for all their sins. This is the biblical origin of the Yom Kippur, Day of Atonement, the most solemn and awesome day in the Jewish religious calendar.

When Muhammad came to Medina he adopted this solemn day from the Jews, set it on the tenth of Muḥarram, the first month of the Muslim year, so as to correspond to the tenth of Tishri which, although it counts as the seventh month in the Bible, was the first month of the Hebrew year which started on the first of Tishri. At the same time Muhammad also retained the Jewish rule of fasting from sunset to sunset. By the second year after the Hijra the relationship between Muhammad and the Jews had soured, and thereupon Muhammad received a revelation in which he was instructed to make the month of Ramaḍān the fast month, and to require the Muslims to fast from sunrise to sunset on each and every day of that month (Koran 2: 183–87). Therewith the fast of *ᶜĀshūrā* was, if not explicitly abolished, made non-obligatory and merely voluntary, and was deprived of its holiness. Thus one important link between Islam and Judaism was effectively severed.

The same happened with the *qibla*, the direction Islam enjoins upon the believers to face during prayer. At first, following the ancient Jewish custom to turn toward Jerusalem when praying (cf. 1 Kings 8:44; Daniel 6: 11), Muhammad ordered his followers to face Jerusalem as their *qibla*. Whether he introduced this rule while still in Mecca is not certain, but Muslim tradition has it that he either observed the *qibla* to the Kaᶜba, or to Jerusalem, or else placed himself to the south of the Kaᶜba so that the Kaᶜba and Jerusalem were in line. Since Muslim tradition does not like to acknowledge Islamic dependence on Judaism, the very fact that the second and third traditions existed at all indicates that they must have had a historical basis. In any case, once Muhammad arrived in Medina, he firmly established Jerusalem as the *qibla* of Muslim prayer, that is the *qibla* was to the north, while Mecca lay to the south of Medina.

In the second year of his sojourn in Medina came the break between Muhammad and the Jews. His preaching had only slight success among the Jewish tribes of Medina, and, disappointed by their negative reaction to his prophetic claim, he turned away from them in more senses than one. From this time on he endeavored to substitute old Arab traditions and customs for the religious practices of the Jews. Having made Abraham and Ishmael the founders of the old pagan Arab sanctuary of the Kaᶜba, it was inevitable that the Kaᶜba which now was endowed with the sanctity of the great biblical *ḥanīf*, Abraham, should become the *qibla*. It was about the same time that the incorporation of the only pagan Arab ritual, the *ḥajj*, the pilgrimage to Mecca, took place, which, of course, was facilitated by the fact that annual pilgrimages to Jerusalem were integral parts of Jewish religion, although they were no longer observed by the time of Muhammad. The logical conclusion of this cycle of development was a new revelation Muhammad received concerning the *qibla*.

The change of the *qibla* from Jerusalem to Mecca—a turnabout of 180 degrees for the inhabitants of Medina—is perhaps the best example of an ingenious device introduced by Muhammad. He adapted his teachings to the changing conditions which resulted from the growth of his following from a small band of sectarians in Mecca to a conquering, irresistible army which they became soon after his *hijra* to Yathrib/Medina in 622. His device or doctrine was to abrogate an earlier revelation and substitute for it a later one, better suited to the new circumstances. The manner in which Muhammad handled the change of the *qibla* is so masterly that it asks for being presented in full. Koran 2 : 142–45 reads:

> The foolish people will say: What hath turned them [i.e., the Muslims] from the *qibla* which they formerly observed? Say: Unto Allah belong the East and the West. He guideth whom He will unto a straight path. Thus We [God] have appointed you a middle nation, that ye may be witnesses against mankind, and that the Messenger [Muhammad] may be a witness against you. And We appointed the *qibla* which ye formerly observed only that We might know him who followeth the messenger, from him who turneth on his heels. In truth it was a hard (test) save for those whom Allah guided. But it was not Allah's purpose that your faith should be in vain, for Allah is full of pity, Merciful toward mankind. We have seen the turning of thy face to heaven (for guidance, O Muhammad). And now verily we shall make thee turn (in prayer) toward a *qibla* which is dear to thee. So turn thy face toward the Inviolable Place of Worship [i.e., the Kaᶜba], and ye (O Muslims), wheresoever ye may be, turn your faces (when ye pray) toward it. Lo! Those who have received the Scripture know that (this Revelation) is the Truth from their Lord. And Allah is not unaware of what they do. And even if thou broughtest unto those who have received the Scripture all kinds of portents, they would not follow thy *qibla*, nor canst thou be a follower of their *qibla*; nor are some of them followers of the *qibla* of others . . .[5]

DHIMMA *AND* JIZYA

Muhammad's turning against the Jews decisively influenced the attitude of Islam toward them once and for all. Koranic criticism—embodying a Western scholarly approach to the text of the Koran—clearly discerns a change from the early Meccan *sūra*s which exhibit a more friendly position toward the Jews to the attitude manifested in the later, Medinese, *sūra*s characterized by a harsh anti-Jewish stance. The Arabs (and Muslims in general) were and remained until recently unaware of, or indifferent to, such a historical development within the Koran which in toto has been believed by them to be a divine revelation addressed to Muhammad by the angel Gabriel (Arabic *Jabrā'īl* or *Jibrīl*). The role Gabriel plays in the Koran is, incidentally, another example of the appropriation by Muhammad of biblical and aggadic concepts. In the Bible, Gabriel is God's messenger sent to Daniel (Dan. 8:15ff.; 9:21, etc.), and according to the Koran (2:97) it is Gabriel who brings the Koran down to the heart of Muhammad.[6] In any case, what determined the Arabs' attitude to the Jews was not the occasional tribute contained in the early *sūras* to the religious and moral virtues of the Jews, nor the recognition that the *Banū Isrā'īl* (Children of Israel) were God's chosen people who were admitted to His covenant and assured of Paradise. Rather the Arab view of the Jews derives from those more numerous later Koranic passages which speak of the rebellious spirit of the Children of Israel, their unbelief, their worship of the Golden Calf, their clamoring for idols, their persecution of the prophets, violation of the Sabbath, and infringement of the Law. Moreover, as already indicated, Muhammad accused the Jews of having altered or falsified Scripture, concealed it, and perverted its meaning. He also reproached the Jews with factiousness, an allegation which reads like a transference to the Jews of the conflict-prone character of the Arabs in Muhammad's time. Because of all this, says the Koran, the Jews were cursed by God, metamorphosed into apes, punished, and doomed to humiliation in this world, and destined to burn in Hell after they died.[7] One can easily recognize that this portrait of the Jews is strongly colored by Muhammad's resentment of his Jewish contemporaries who rejected his teachings and refused to recognize him as the last and greatest prophet, or, as the Arabic expression has it, the *khātim*, or seal, of the prophets. These are, very briefly and sketchily, the antecedents of the relegation of the Jews to a low-class status, as *ahl al-dhimma*, that is, client, subject people, whom to tolerate, but at the same time to humiliate and keep in subservience, became part of Muslim religious law and tradition.

As for the law, the *dhimmī* status of the Jews (and the other *ahl al-kitāb*, "People of the Book," that is, Christians and Zoroastrians) goes directly back to Koranic dispensation. When the Arabs set out on their phenomenal triumphal sweep across a major part of the world, in the course of which they conquered many peoples, they were guided in their attitude to the vanquished by the same Koranic principle which Muhammad applied to the Jews of Arabia: "Fight those to whom the Scriptures were given, who believe not in Allah nor the Last Day, and forbid not that which Allah hath forbidden by His messenger, and follow not the religion of truth, until they pay the tribute (*jizya*) readily, being brought low" (Koran 9:29). While this may seem a law prescribing harshness to the vanquished, it has to be viewed in the perspective of the Muslims' position vis-à-vis the pagan peoples whom they conquered. Pagans, if they fell into the hands of Muslims as prisoners of war could expect death, or, in the best case, slavery.[8] In theory, the heathens had to be fought, without condition, until they accepted the *dīn* of Muhammad;[9] hence the famous Arabic saying, *Dīn Muḥammad bi al-sayf*, "The religion of Muhammad with the sword."

Not only that unbelievers, other than the *ahl al-kitāb*, were not allowed to live in the House of Islam, but theoretically no dealings at all were permitted with them, and idol worshippers were considered with particular abhorrence. In practice, these tenets were not adhered to when and where Islam was weak, and Muslims lived among non-Muslims, for example in India, where the Hindus, although idol worshippers by Muslim definition, were nevertheless counted among the *ahl al-dhimma*.[10] It should be mentioned in this connection that scattered remnants of unbelievers were allowed to survive even in Arabia itself. Doughty, in his classic *Arabia Deserta*, refers frequently to the Heteym and Solubba, gypsy pariah groups who, although regarded as *kuffār* ("unbelievers"), are tolerated by the Arabs.[11] Where the Muslims had the power, as in North Africa, they proceeded ruthlessly against the idol worshippers in the conquered populations. If they adopted Islam, they were spared; if not, they were put to death. However, since martyrdom for one's faith was not a characteristic of religions outside of Judaism and its two daughter religions, Christianity and Islam, pagan rejection of Islam at the price of death was rare. It was the result of this Muslim policy that with the Arab conquests in Asia and Africa large numbers of native populations converted to Islam. Thus the *mawālī* (sing. *mawlā*) class came into being; new Muslims of non-Arab extraction who at first were treated with contempt by the Arabs. However, as time passed, the *mawālī* were gradually able to improve their position (this was most difficult for the Negroes among them), and by the ninth century they had attained a nearly equal status with the Arabs.[12]

In comparison with the fate of the heathen populations whose traditional religions were extirpated by Islam, it appears that the permission given by it to the Jews to live in their midst, even though in humiliation, but without having to give up their religion, was a great concession. The permission given to the Jews to live in the House of Islam was given to them on condition that they paid the *jizya*, and accepted their humble status. It should be pointed out in this connection that the duty to pay the *jizya* was, at least in certain times, considered by the Jews not a humiliating exaction, but an equitable, and even advantageous arrangement. It was held to be similar in kind to the *khuwwa*, the protection money, whose payment by weak social groups (e.g., vassal tribes) to strong ones was a generally accepted way in the Arab world of enhancing the safety of population elements unable to defend themselves by force of arms. When the Caliph al-Muᶜtaṣim (892–902) ordered the abolition of the poll tax payable by the Jews, Netira, a leader of the Jews of Baghdad, opposed the move and said to the caliph, "By the payment of the *jizya* the Jews become *dhimmī*s, protected subjects; were the tax to be abolished, Jewish blood would be shed freely." The story goes that the caliph entrusted Netira, one of the wealthiest Jews of the capital, with collecting the *jizya*.[13]

THE COVENANT OF ᶜUMAR

In the first few centuries after Muhammad the anti-Jewish statements contained in the Koran gave rise to a series of discriminatory regulations against the *dhimmī*, which, in turn, decisively influenced the Muslim attitude to the Jews everywhere and throughout history. However, it must be emphasized right at the outset of discussing this subject that several of the details of these early anti-Jewish or anti-*dhimmī* regulations were identical with those issued by Byzantine emperors, so that one cannot exclude the possibility that the Muslim rulers were influenced by their Christian neighbors to the north in formulating their anti-Jewish enactments.

The first caliph to issue discriminatory laws against the *dhimmī*s was ᶜUmar II, a religious fanatic, who ruled from 717 to 720. He ordered the governor of Khurasan (eastern Iran) to prohibit the building of new synagogues and churches, to compel the Jews and Christians to wear special hats and mantles so as to make them easily distinguishable from the Muslims, and to prohibit them from using a saddle and employing Muslims in their service. These items, added to the Koranic obligation of exacting a poll tax from the *dhimmī*s, and of bringing them low, had as their objective the separation or segregation (*ghiyār*) of the members of the other religions from the Muslims. This endeavor remained a basic feature of the Muslim attitude to the *dhimmī*s for all times.

At a much later date the anti-*dhimmī* regulations, which continued to be issued until the fourteenth century, were collected into a document which was given the name Covenant (*shurūt* or *ʿuhūd*) of ʿUmar, and attributed to the Caliph ʿUmar I (reigned 634–644). This document is extant in several versions, including one quoted by Ibn Khaldūn (1322–1406), the great Arab historian and philosopher of history, and another, quoted three centuries later in Hebrew by Joseph ben Isaac Sambari (1640–1703), the Egyptian Jewish chronicler. Sambari's book *Divre Yosef* (still in manuscript) contains much valuable information on the attitude of various Arab caliphs and Ottoman sultans to their Jewish subjects, including the Mameluk persecution of the Jews and Christians in Egypt in 1301.

The main points in the Covenant of ʿUmar can be summarized on the basis of the various sources as follows:

1. The *dhimmī*s are prohibited from building synagogues and churches in addition to those which had existed in pre-Islamic times.
2. They must not be taught the Koran.
3. They must not shelter spies.
4. They must not buy male or female Muslim slaves, nor slaves formerly owned by Muslims.
5. They must not sell intoxicating beverages to Muslims, nor pork, nor the carcasses of animals not ritually slaughtered.
6. They must not employ Muslims in their service.
7. They must honor Muslims and stand in their presence.
8. They must not hit or deceive a Muslim.
9. They must put up Muslim travelers in their houses for three days.
10. They must not prevent anyone from converting to Islam.
11. They must not dress or wear their hair in a manner resembling that of the Muslims. They must not wear silk girdles, nor shoes of the colors worn by Muslims.
12. They must not be called by Muslim names or appellations.
13. *Dhimmī* men while in bath houses must wear a special sign around their necks. *Dhimmī* women must not use the same bath house used by Muslim women, but special baths must be built for them.
14. The *dhimmī*s are forbidden to carry arms.
15. They must not ride on horses or mules, but only on asses, and must

not use riding saddles but only unornamented pack saddles, on which they must ride side-saddle.

16. Their houses and tombs must not be higher than those of the Muslims.

17. They must not raise their voices in their places of worship, and the Christians must not be seen in public with crosses.

18. They cannot be employed as government officials, nor in any capacity which would give them authority over Muslims.

19. If a *dhimmi* dies, his estate becomes the property of the authorities until his heirs can prove their right to it under Islamic law. If there is no legal heir, the estate remains the property of the authorities.

In the Arab world, and in the Middle East in general, clothes identify a person in a manner that has largely disappeared in the West in the last hundred years. Clothes identify the Middle Easterner with reference to his social class, but even more so with respect to the ethnic and religious group to which he belongs. In the Muslim world, where the wrapping of the head in large pieces of cloth was common, the color, pattern, size, shape of the cloth, and the manner in which it was placed around the head and the neck were the most conspicuous signs of ethnic identity. A *dhimmī* dressed and wrapped up like an Arab could easily be mistaken for one. Hence the prohibition against a *dhimmī* wearing Arab-like clothes was the surest and simplest way of giving visible expression to the *ghiyār*. In addition, the *dhimmī*s were forbidden to wear Arab military dress, and certain types of robes. Instead, the Jews had to wear yellow, and the Christians blue, clothes, although the prescribed colors changed from place to place. They also had to wear a distinguishing belt, called *zunnār* (or occasionally *minṭaq*).[14]

As for the urban women who ventured rarely out of their houses, and even more rarely out of their quarter, the principles of *ghiyār* were not as strictly applied to them as to the men. This has become recently clear from the rich data uncovered in the famous *Geniza*, the store room in a Fusṭāṭ (Cairo) synagogue, in which writings no longer in use were deposited in the twelfth to thirteenth centuries in order to prevent the desecration of the name of God mentioned in them. Numerous documents from the *Geniza* show that in those times Jewish and Muslim women dressed alike, that is to say, that the restrictions of *ghiyār* were not enforced, at least as far as women were concerned. As can be seen from the *Geniza* documents, which contain some 750 trousseau lists, the wardrobes of women contained a very great variety of dresses, head scarves, veils, belts, mantles, tunics, and undergarments made of some sixty different fabrics.[15] These lists make it evident that in medieval Egypt fashion, style, and variety in attire were a concern for middle- and upper-class women.

As for the veil, it was worn for many centuries by Jewish and Christian women who were not subject to the same strict laws of segregation as their Muslim sisters. But they wore the veil in conformity with the usage of the Muslim majority, and did so until modern times, when they began to abandon it about a generation earlier than the Muslim women under the impact of Westernization.

But to return to the Covenant of ᶜUmar, in general it constitutes serious deprivations of rights for the *dhimmīs*, and it stamps them unmistakably as second-class citizens with narrowly circumscribed acts and movements. However, it must also be mentioned that not all of its provisions were enforced everywhere, and that frequently several of its prohibitions were disregarded in practice. For instance, in several Muslim countries Jewish doctors served as personal physicians of the rulers, and Jewish statesmen rose to high positions, including that of vizier.

One must also consider that the Covenant of ᶜUmar recognizes that the *dhimmīs* have the right to security of life and property, to a free practice of their religion, and to internal autonomy. These rights were forfeited only if a *dhimmī* became guilty of transgressing the Covenant, and especially if he committed such crimes as not paying the *jizya*, refusing to submit to a Muslim legal decision, murdering a Muslim, having immoral relations with a Muslim woman, spying on behalf of an enemy, or cursing the Prophet in public. As long as the Jews submitted to the restrictions and impositions it contained, the Covenant of ᶜUmar served as a charter that defined their place in Muslim society, and, in theory at least, safeguarded their position in it. The very term *dhimma* means protection, so that the *ahl al-dhimma* were the people protected by Muslim law as far as life, safety, and property were concerned.

Until the nineteenth century the position of the Jews in the Ottoman Empire and the Arab lands outside it was more precarious than that of the Christians. Even in Egypt, where they were treated somewhat better than in other Muslim countries, the Jews were far from being equal to their Christian fellow subjects, let alone the Muslims. In fact, in many places the Jews were oppressed not only by the Muslims, but also by the Christians. In Egypt in 1664, the European Christians were exempted from paying the *jizya*. (In the remote Emirate of Bukhara only the Jews were required to pay this poll tax.) At the same time, in daily contact, the attitude of the Muslims to the Jews was less negative than to the Christians. The Christians were more of an irritant to Muslim eyes, and were more in danger of violence. The Damascus massacre of thousands of Christians by Muslim mobs in 1860 was an extreme manifestation of this Muslim anti-Christian sentiment.[16]

During the Tanzimat period, when under pressure from the European powers, notably England, France, and Austria, the Sublime Porte issued several successive firmans (in 1837, 1855, and 1856) which abolished some of the discriminatory measures against the *dhimmīs*, the position of the Jews in the Ottoman Empire improved materially. In 1859 a Jewish traveler could write, "The Ishmaelites [i.e., the Arabs] and the Jews do not hate each other; on the contrary, they love each other; but the uncircumcised [i.e., the Christians] are hated by the Ishmaelites."[17] About the same time the European consuls began to grant protection to the Jews in Palestine, which contributed to their security, and attracted Jewish immigrants to the four holy cities. In most parts of the Ottoman Empire the Jews constituted small and weak groups, had no political ambitions, and were content with their status as second-class citizens. As against them, the larger and stronger Christian minorities claimed to be equal to the Muslims, and, in view of their close links with the European powers were considered a political danger by both the Turkish authorities and the Muslim population.[18] Yet the very powerlessness of the Jews made the Muslims look down upon them more than upon the Christians. These developments have had important bearing upon the attitude of the Arabs to the Jews down to the present day.

VARIATIONS IN TOLERANCE

For thirteen hundred years the Jews in the House of Islam were always at the mercy of the Muslims. Everywhere they were small, scattered, powerless minorities whose quality of life, and even their very life itself, depended on the will and whim of their Muslim overlords. Although Islam did not implant into the mind of the average Muslim anything comparable to the deep hatred which was systematically fostered by Christianity with its myth of the Jew as the Christ killer, the Muslims, too, had strong religious motivations for disliking and disdaining the Jews. They were enjoined by the Koran to humiliate them, and this religious commandment was reinforced by the negative reaction the Muslims had when they saw that the Jews, despite living in the House of Islam century after century, stubbornly (and for the Muslims incomprehensibly) refused to accept Muhammad as the prophet of God. The Muslims, however, recognized the founders, lawgivers, kings, and prophets of biblical Israel and venerated them as precursors of Muhammad and the recipients of divine revelation. Apart from this religious motivation, the Muslims had contempt for the Jews because the Jews were weak, because they were able to survive only if they had the protection of Muslims. They similarly contemned (although not to the same degree) the weak vassal tribes among themselves which had to pay *khuwwa*, ("brotherhood money"), to the powerful, noble, warlike tribes for whom the vassals performed such necessary but degrading tasks as tilling the soil or working iron.[19]

For thirteen hundred years, while the Jews knew and kept their places at the bottom of the social ladder, the attitude of the Arabs toward them by and large remained the same: it was one of scorn and disdain. As every verse of the Koran, the injunction to bring low the "People of the Book" was subjected to the most careful scrutiny by the Muslim exegetes. They concluded from it, not only that the *ahl al-kitāb* must be made to accept Muslim overlordship by paying the *jizya*, but also, on the positive side, that they must not be killed, nor expelled, nor forced to convert to Islam, as was the case with the idolaters. The Koranic injunction epitomizes the position of the Jews in the House of Islam in normal times. Only in times of trials and tribulations, when wars or rebellions broke out, or when something caused the populace to lose self control and tempers flared, did the Arabs (and other Muslims) become guilty of violence against the Jews and other *dhimmī*s. In my book *The Arab Mind*, I attempted to portray and analyze these periodic outbursts of temper as a characteristic feature of the otherwise quiet, friendly, and courteous Arab personality. Here let me add that these flare-ups of temper, bad as they were when directed against fellow Arabs, assumed an even less restrained character when their object was a powerless *dhimmī* who could not retaliate, and assaulting, or even killing him, was considered a lesser crime than similar violence against a fellow Arab of equal standing. The sum total of all this is that while it was often neither easy nor pleasant for the Jews to live as *dhimmī*s in an Arab country, on the whole they were able to live with a modicum of security and without the fear of expulsion or other large-scale persecutions which were periodically visited upon the European Jewish communities.

Within the overall rules there were great variations in the treatment of the Jews between one Arab country and another. Two contrasting examples of these variations, represented by Yemen and Morocco, will be presented below in chapter 5. In general, one can venture to say that under the Arabs who belonged to one of the schools of the orthodox (*Sunnī*) mainstream of Islam, the position of the Jews was, as a rule, better than in lands ruled by Muslim sectarian Arabs or non-Arabs. Thus, for example, the Almohads (*al-muwaḥḥidūn*), who invaded Spain in 1136, and under whom the worst persecution of the Jews took place in North Africa and Spain, were non-orthodox Muslims, and mainly non-Arabs.

An exception to this rule is constituted by the Ismāʿīlī Shīʿī Fāṭimids, who controlled North Africa and later Egypt from 909 to 1171. They were, in general, tolerant and liberal rulers, so that under them the Jews (and Christians) enjoyed relatively favorable conditions. Several Fāṭimid caliphs even had Christian viziers, and Jews rose to important positions, but became viziers only if they converted to Islam. However, in the very midst of the Fāṭimid era, the Caliph al-Ḥākim bi-Amr Allāh (reigned 996–1021) instituted a rule of terror against the Jews and Christians. Some of the anti-*dhimmī* measures of al-Ḥākim—who became deified as the founder of the Druze religion—were to remain quasi-permanent features and were incorporated into the Covenant of ʿUmar. Thus in 1004 he ordered the Jews and Christians to wear black belts and turbans. In 1009 he extended this edict by ordering them to wear a distinctive badge hung around their necks when in the baths. Also in 1009, he had several churches demolished in Cairo and Damascus, as well as the Church of the Holy Sepulcher in Jerusalem, and tortured Christian officials which prompted many Christians to convert to Islam. In 1012–13 he forbade the *dhimmī*s to ride on horseback, and ordered the burning of a Jewish quarter. It must be added, however, that he proceeded with equal vigor against Sunnī Muslims. Thus in 1020 he ordered his troops to burn al-Fusṭāṭ because its inhabitants allegedly circulated libelous statements about him. Periodically, and quite arbitrarily, he retracted his decrees and replaced them with opposite ones. It is also remarkable and puzzling that a Jewish writer wrote a panegyric of al-Ḥākim in which he praised the caliph as a benefactor of the country and a man of justice.[20] What al-Ḥākim's rule shows is the extent to which *dhimmī* life was precarious under autocratic caliphs.

Let us conclude this section with another reference to a document attributed to ʿUmar. It is his Testament, which he was supposed to have given to his successor on his deathbed. It is of interest because it lists the classes of which society was composed in the late eighth century, and each of which ᶜUmar "commends to the favor" of his successor. The classes comprise the *muhājirūn* ("emigrants," the earliest associates of Muhammad, who left Mecca together with him in the *hijra* of 622, or rather, their descendants), the *anṣār* ("helpers," the natives of Medina who pledged themselves to Muhammad), the city dwellers, the people of the open country (the "original Arabs"), and, in the last place, the *ahl al-dhimma*, about whom ᶜUmar says: "Do battle to guard them, and put no burden on them greater than they can bear, provided they pay what is due from them to the Muslims, willingly or under subjection, being humbled . . ."[21]

This document affords an insight into the views of the Arab rulers and theologians concerning the position of the *dhimmī*s under Islam. Their tradition, going back to divine revelation in the Koran, required of the Muslims to protect the *dhimmī*s to the point of "doing battle to guard them." In exchange for this protection of life, limb, and property, the *dhimmī*s had to pay their poll tax, and occupy a humble position at the bottom of the Arab social ladder. Since they were neither Arabs nor Muslims, the position assigned to them in the House of Islam was considered by the Arabs as proper and equitable. Moreover, it took only a glance across the northern border of the Islamic realm to convince them that their treatment of the Jews was charitable compared to what was handed out to the Jews in the Christian world.

ᶜABBĀSID IRAQ: ARAB CULTURE

An important variable on which the quality of Jewish life in Arab countries depended was the cultural level reached by the Muslim majority, or, rather, the educated element in it. Generally speaking, when and where the Muslims enjoyed a higher cultural level and a better quality of life, the position of the Jews was better. A detailed substantiation of this generalization would require a vast amount of research, which would be highly worthwhile, and which, I hope, young Arab and Jewish scholars will jointly undertake some time in the future. All I can do here and now is to point to two examples, one of which will be touched upon only briefly here because it will be discussed at greater length in a later chapter, while the second example will be gone into in some detail.

One of the Arab countries in which the oppression and degradation of the Jews was the greatest was Yemen. In pre-Islamic times Yemen boasted of several flourishing cultures (the Minaean, Sabaean, and Himyarite), but after its conversion to Islam it became one of the poorest in cultural achievements despite its pleasant climate and fertility which in Roman times earned it the epithet of Arabia Felix. Throughout the thirteen centuries of its Islamic history, while it produced a number of scholars and men of letters who made themselves a name in other parts of the Arab world, Yemen itself never became a center of Arabic literature, scholarship, religious studies, or science, and, in fact, down to the present it has remained the most backward of all Arab countries. As recently as in the 1960s there were barely any literate people in Yemen: 95 percent of the male population aged 15 and over, and 100 percent of the females, were illiterate. By 1980 these figures were reduced to 82.4 percent for the males and 98.5 percent for the females. In 1974 only 4 percent of the girls of all ages were enrolled in primary and secondary school (which was the lowest ratio of all Arab countries); by 1982 this figure had increased to 10 percent. In 1980, the physical quality of life index (composed of the infant mortality rate, life expectancy at the age of one, and literacy, each indexed on a scale from 1 to 100) was in Yemen 27, the lowest of all Arab countries.[22] As for the position of the Jews in Yemen, which will be discussed in some detail in chapter 5, let me remark here only in general that it was the lowest in any Arab country.

The second example is Iraq, which in its heyday was the greatest center of Arab civilization, and which was the home of a great Jewish community for twenty-five centuries, during ten of which it enjoyed cultural predominance in the Jewish world. At the time of the Arab conquest of Iraq (633–642), the Jewish community of Bavel (Babylonia), as it was known, was twelve centuries old.

In the early ʿAbbāsid period (from 750) Iraq became the trading center of the entire Orient, and simultaneously one of the most important cultural centers of Arab arts and sciences, where poets and men of letters, scholars of Muslim law, theologians, and traditionists congregated. Baṣra (southern Iraq), the meeting place of caravans, was also the stage where the finest poets gathered to submit their work to the public in contests, competing for the honor of being recognized as the foremost defenders of their tribe, or their particular religious group (which at the time was also a political party), and the most eloquent assailers of rival social formations. It was in Iraq, in the two metropolitan cities of Baṣra and Kūfa, that the Arabo-Islamic culture, which later was to spread into the entire Muslim world, began to be developed. Several of the religious sciences, as well as Arabic grammar, lexicography, philology, and literary history (begun with the collection of ancient verse, proverbs, and traditions) were incubated in Iraq. In fact, the great branch of Arab literary culture, the *adab*, first emerged in that country.

Under the ʿAbbāsids the institution of literary patronage was developed, enabling poets and other men of letters to display their talents before an audience of select, enlightened connoisseurs. Soon literary activity in Baṣra and Kūfa, and, from the second half of the eighth century on in Baghdad, became more diversified and intense than in Arabia, Egypt, or Syria. Iraq was also the place where the *mawālī*, the Muslims of non-Arab origin, who were brought up in, or had acquired, Arab culture, adopted their conquerors' idiom, ideas, and style, and contributed significantly to the development, diversification, and "modernization" of Arabic literature. Here flourished, in addition to the satire which was old Arab heritage, also erotic, bacchic, and ascetic verse. The Shīʿites of Iraq, on their part, produced religio-political poetry devoted to the praise of the early martyrs ʿAlī and his son Ḥusayn. And it was in Iraq that Arabic literature, which had formerly consisted almost exclusively of poetry, conquered the field of prose, under the influence of Iran. The man generally credited with the creation of Arabic prose was Ibn al-Muqaffaʿ (died ca. 757) with his translation of *Kalīla wa-Dimna*, and his own didactic and entertaining writings. Many of the translations from the Greek which were produced from the eighth century on, originated in Baghdad.

Iraq was also the birthplace of Arabic literary histories, encyclopedias, inventories, and catalogues, such as the famous *Fihrist* ("Index") written by the Baghdadi bookseller Ibn al-Nadīm (died 995), which lists all the books written in Arabic, whether by Arabs or non-Arabs, and makes it possible to apprehend the richness of Arabic literature available in Baghdad in the late tenth century. Incidentally, the *Fihrist* includes a discourse on the Holy Scriptures of the Jews as well as those of the Muslims and Christians. Also, the first stories of the *Alf Layla wa-Layla* (known in English as *The Arabian Nights*), the most famous Arabic collection of fairy tales and other stories, were gathered in Baghdad. Mention must be made also of the prose of Muḥammad ibn Aḥmad Abu al-Muṭahhar al-Azdī (flourished late tenth century), who in his *Ḥikāya* ("Tale") created a new genre by painting a satirical picture of life in contemporary Baghdad.

The other cultural accomplishments of ʿAbbāsid Baghdad can be referred to only briefly. Baghdad was a city of singers, musicians, and ballet dancers, whose performances are so colorfully described in *The Arabian*

Nights. It housed the *bayt al-ḥikma* ("House of Wisdom") established by the Caliph al-Ma'mūn in 830, which was an academy, a library, and a translation office. The city itself had a network of canals, was surrounded by walls with dozens of high towers, and was subdivided into quarters, each inhabited by one ethnic group (such as Arabs, Persians, Khwārazmians, Jews) or by members of one vocation. It had numerous markets, one for each craft or trade, supervised by appointed officers. The oldest, fortified part of Baghdad was known as the "Round City," built by al-Manṣūr in 762, and was an architectural marvel.

The huge palace of the caliph was in the center of the city, which boasted also of many other magnificent palaces owned by the great potentates (e.g., those of Yaḥyā the Barmakid, and Jaᶜfar). Baghdad had a race course, a zoo with a hundred lions, lovely gardens, and its great houses were lavishly decorated and beautifully and luxuriously furnished. By the tenth century, Baghdad could pride itself of all the civilizational attainments of a great Muslim city. It had (in 993) a population of some 1.5 million, 1,500 baths, 860 licensed physicians, several hospitals, many splendid mosques, several public libraries, booksellers' markets with more than 100 bookstores. No less than 30,000 boats plied the Tigris River which was spanned by three bridges. Baghdad was the home of the Ḥanafī and Ḥanbalī schools of Muslim jurisprudence, and its men of letters enjoyed the patronage of the caliph and other potentates. And, of course, it had its complex economic structure of manufacturing, commerce, and banking, which such a great city required. To make the heat of the summer less oppressive, many houses were equipped with cool *sardāb*s, subterranean vaults, and other arrangements, and also fans were used. To the sensitive eyes of poets Baghdad appeared so beautiful that they called it "paradise on earth."

The one thing Baghdad lacked more than anything else was stability. Periods of quiescence and prosperity were frequently punctuated by social unrest and natural disaster. By the tenth century sectarian differences between the Shīᶜites and the Sunnīs erupted into frequent conflicts, and were harbingers of the decline of the greatness that was Baghdad. Fights and arson caused thousands of people to perish, and destroyed dozens of mosques and hundreds of shops every few years in the tenth to twelfth centuries. Much of the damage was caused by the *ᶜayyārūn* ("rascals," or "vagabonds"), bands of outlaws who, whenever public security slackened, attacked the rich and the rulers while adhering to such moral principles as honor, cooperation, patience, endurance, and helping the poor and women.

They both exploited political chaos and greatly contributed to it. They broke into houses at night, waylaid travelers on the roads, levied tolls on the markets, and burned many quarters of the wealthy, pillaging and murdering. To these vicissitudes were added periodic floods of the Tigris River in the eleventh to thirteenth centuries which laid waste major parts of the city. Despite occasional efforts to rebuild parts of Baghdad, general decline could not be halted. The Spanish-Jewish traveler Benjamin of Tudela, who visited Baghdad in 1171, still speaks of the greatness of some of its impressive buildings and institutions, such as the caliph's palace, the ʿAḍudī Hospital with its 60 doctors, and the mental hospital; but fourteen years later, Ibn Jubayr, in his description of Baghdad of 1185 notices the general decline, the ruin of several quarters, and the arrogance of the people.[23] Four decades later the decay had progressed to a point where western Baghdad, as described by the great Arab geographer Yāqūt (in 1226), was broken up into several isolated, walled quarters, separated from one another by broad stretches of ruins. Internecine strife intensified in the twelfth and thirteenth centuries, not only between Shīʿites and Sunnīs, but also between the adherents of the two Sunnī schools of jurisprudence, the Ḥanbalīs and the Shāfiʿīs. And there were also fights between the various quarters of the city which the government was unable to control.

In 1258 came the Mongol invasion under Hülegü, which put an end to the ʿAbbāsid caliphate, and was a major catastrophe for Baghdad from which the city never fully recovered. Contemporary and later estimates of the number of people killed by the Mongols vary from eight hundred thousand to two million; in reality, it may have been upward of one hundred thousand. However, much of the city was destroyed, and the remaining population had to pay a poll tax to the Mongols. In the thirteenth century the city gradually recovered somewhat, mosques, markets, and water systems were rebuilt, and cultural activities resumed, but the importance of Baghdad as the cultural center of the House of Islam was never again regained.

From the Mongol conquest until 1930, that is, for close to seven centuries, Iraq continued under foreign rule, first under that of the Mongols (Ilkhānids, Jalāyirids, and Tīmūrids), then under the Turcomans (Qara-Qoyunlus, Aq-Qoyunlus, Ṣafawids), followed by the Ottoman Turks (1517–1918), and lastly by the British mandate (1918–1930). Characteristic of the cultural poverty of Iraq in these long centuries is the fact that the article on Iraqi literature in the *Encyclopaedia Britannica* (vol. 3, 1971, pp. 1261–65), which devotes seven columns to the seventh- to twelfth-century period, finds almost nothing to say about the ensuing centuries.

ᶜABBĀSID IRAQ: JEWISH CULTURE

While I am unable to establish a convincing correlation between the cultural ups and downs of Iraq and the quality of its treatment of its Jewish minority, a brief resumé of how the Jews fared in that country will be suggestive, especially when contrasted with the unrelenting pressure the Jews had to suffer throughout the centuries in Yemen, which, compared to Iraq, was definitely a cultural backwater. Such a resumé will also make it appear that there is a certain congruence between three factors: the cultural level of the Arabs, their treatment of the Jews, and the cultural attainments of the latter.

The Jews of Iraq constituted one of the oldest Jewish communities in any Arab country. Apart from the fact that the legendary roots of the biblical Hebrews were said to be in ancient Mesopotamia, the first Jewish inhabitants were brought to Assyria in 721 B.C.E., and to Babylonia toward the end of the sixth century B.C.E. The Babylonian Talmud, embodying the bulk of Jewish religio-legal and literary production of three centuries (ca. 200 to 500 C.E.) was, as its name shows, compiled in Babylonia, barely four generations prior to the country's conquest by the Arabs. At the time of the Arab conquest, the Jews of Babylonia (renamed Iraq by the Arabs) were a separate, highly organized, well-to-do and well-educated community, headed by an exilarch (*Resh G'luta* in the colloquial Aramaic spoken by them). Persecuted under the Persian Sassanids, the Jews of Babylonia welcomed the Arab conquerors, and, according to Jewish tradition, the grateful Caliph ᶜUmar (reigned 634–644) honored the exilarch Bustanai ben Ḥaninai (618–ca. 670) by giving him Izdundad, daughter of the defeated Khosrau II, king of Persia, for his wife.

Under Arab rule the two great Talmudic academies of Sura and Pumbedita prospered. Their heads, known as the *G'onim* (sing. *Gaon*, an untranslatable term combining the connotations of genius and of such titles as excellency, highness) were the most outstanding Jewish religious authorities of their time, had enormous prestige, and their rulings in religious matters were recognized all over the Jewish world.

The periodic strifes which characterized Iraqi Arab life had their counterpart in the Jewish community. The Gaon and the exilarch did not always see eye to eye, and were often embroiled in sharp disagreement. The exilarch was a descendant of the Davidic line, a hereditary Jewish prince, who wielded great power over the community, and was honored by the Muslims as well. When he drove out in his carriage, horsemen rode before him shouting, "Make way to the Son of David!" Both Jews and Muslims had to stand in his presence. One of his prerogatives was to appoint or confirm the Gaons of Sura and Pumbedita; but, on the other hand, the Gaon had the right either to approve, or to refuse to ratify, the legal enactments of the exilarch.

On one occasion the disagreement between Gaon and exilarch reached a point where they mutually issued a *ḥerem* (ban) against each other, although a *ḥerem* practically amounted to excommunication. This happened between the exilarch David ben Zakkai (reigned 918–940), who occupied a respected position at the court of the Caliph al-Muqtadir, and Saᶜadia Gaon (882–942), one of the greatest scholars in medieval Jewry, of whom more will be said in the last section of this chapter. The dispute between the two Jewish leaders had to be brought before the vizier ᶜAlī ibn ᶜĪsā (according to the Arab historian Masᶜūdī), and thus an agreement was reached between the two antagonists in 937.

Conflicts between exilarch and Gaon, which occurred in later centuries as well, stemmed from the difficulty in a Jewish religious culture of separating secular matters, which were the responsibility of the exilarch, from religious issues over which the Gaon had jurisdiction. Since Judaism was (and was to remain until the Enlightenment) not merely a religion but a total way of life, it was impossible to keep religious and secular life apart. Strictly speaking there was no such thing as secular life. Every secular matter had a religious aspect, and religion had its say in all areas of life, not merely in the narrowly religious one. The problem was compounded by the tradition according to which the exilarch and the Gaon wielded comparable powers.

Arab chroniclers point out that Davidic descent was an indispensable prerequisite for the office of the exilarch, and the Shīᶜites, for whom the genetic descent of the *imām* from Muhammad was an important point in according him legitimacy, considered the exilarch comparable in rank to caliphs and *imāms*. In fact, some of them describe meetings between exilarchs and Muslim rulers as encounters between equals, and even tell of the exilarch reproving the Muslims. Such internal problems apart, at the time of the highest flowering of Arab culture under the ᶜAbbāsid caliphs of Baghdad, from the mid-seventh to the mid-eleventh centuries, also the

Talmudic academies of Sura and Pumbedita flourished, headed as they were by famous *G'onim* whose authority was recognized by all the Jewish communities in the House of Islam. Students from east and west flocked to the two great academies to study under their great masters and to carry their teachings into the far corners of the Diaspora.

The Sura academy, located in southern Iraq, was founded by Rav (full name Abba Arikha), a Palestinian sage who settled in Sura in 219 C.E. The Sura academy reached its greatest prominence in 730 when the exilarch Sh'lomo ben Ḥisdai appointed Mar Sh'muel as its Gaon. In the early tenth century, after Baghdad had developed into the metropolis and cultural center of Iraq, the Sura academy was transferred there, and remained there, with short periods of suspension, until the end of the Gaonic period (twelfth century). The sages of Sura engaged in a broad range of religious-literary activity, which duplicated in the Jewish field much of what was produced in Islamic scholarship by the Arabs. The sages of Sura wrote all their works in Arabic, apart from halakhic treatises which they wrote in Hebrew.

Sura's great rival in Jewish scholarship was the academy of Pumbedita, located in the north of Iraq. It was founded in 259 C.E. by Judah ben Ezekiel, and until the middle of the fourth century it remained the central religio-scholarly institution of Babylonian Jewry. After the death of Rava (in 352), a leading master of the academy, Pumbedita became subordinated to Sura. Following the Arab conquest Pumbedita became known as Anbar, and its school remained overshadowed by Sura until the early ninth century. Paltoi ben Abbaye (842–852), the first scholar to be styled "Gaon of Pumbedita," maintained contact with the Jews of the West, and under his son Tzemaḥ the academy surpassed in importance that of Sura. In the late ninth century the Pumbedita academy was transferred to Baghdad, which proved to be the beginning of its decline due to the reduction of financial contributions from other Jewish communities, and to internal rivalries. A period of renewed flowering followed under Sherira Gaon (968–998) and his son Hai Gaon (998–1038), during which period students of the school went on to occupy important positions in several countries.

Petaḥia of Regensburg (or Ratisbon), the German Jewish traveler, who visited Baghdad between 1175 and 1180, paints a remarkable picture of Jewish piety and scholarship on the one hand, and of Jewish power and pomp on the other, as he observed it in Baghdad. He describes that in Baghdad all the Jews walked around wrapped in woolen *talith*s (prayer shawls) and wearing *tzitzit*s (ritual fringes), and tells about the Gaon

Sh'muel haLevi ben ʿAlī that "he is a prince, full of wisdom and the written Tora and the oral Tora and all the wisdom of Egypt, and no thing is hidden from him. And he knows names [magic?], and he knows the entire Talmud . . ." Then Petaḥia goes on to describe the order of studies in the great academy:

> Among the people of the land there is no ignoramus who would not know all the 24 books [of the Bible], and vocalization, and precision, and the defective and excessive [letters], for the *ḥazzan* [cantor] does not read the Tora [in the synagogue service] but he who stands up to the Book of the Tora, he reads. And the head of the yeshiva has some 2,000 students at one time, and 500 or more [sit] around him, and all understand well, and until they know they study in the city with other scholars, and when they know they study with the head of the yeshiva. And R. Eliʿezer is the exilarch under the head of the yeshiva. And the head of the yeshiva has a big house covered with awnings, and he is dressed in golden clothes, and he sits above and the students sit on the floor, and he speaks to the interpreter (*m'turgman*), and the interpreter speaks to the students, and the students ask [their questions] from the interpreter, and if he does not know [the answer] he asks the head of the yeshiva. And one interpreter on one side says one tractate [of the Talmud], and another interpreter on the other side says another tractate. And the whole [Talmud] is studied in cantillation . . .

In the sequel Petaḥia tells of the Davidic descent of the exilarch and his power: he has some sixty servants who castigate the people with rods. But the exilarch also teaches: it is of him that the students ask about astrology and other kinds of wisdom.[24]

The end of the Babylonian Gaonate signaled also the end of the Iraqi academies and the end of the preeminence of Iraq as the intellectual center of world Jewry.

ʿABBĀSID IRAQ: ARAB-JEWISH RELATIONS

For a Jewish community to develop into an outstanding religio-cultural center several external conditions must be present. They must be living in an environment in which literature, scholarship, and other cultural attainments are appreciated among the non-Jews. They must have mastered a language with vocabularies and terminologies which render it adequate to serve as a medium for the precise expression of ideas in the varied fields of intellectual endeavor. They must have favorable, or at least equitable, living conditions, that is, must be free of oppression and harassment which rob people of the peace of mind necessary for concentration on issues other than day-to-day problems of living. And they must be part of an economically well-established society, at least to the extent that institutional and private patronage should be available for those who feel called upon to engage in literary or scholarly activity. All these conditions were present in ʿAbbāsid Iraq for both the Muslim majority and the Jewish community.

Under the ʿAbbāsids the Jews were recognized as an established minority, and the head of the Sura academy was accorded by the caliph the position of spiritual head of the Jewish community. However, since the position of the Jews at any given time depended on the attitude of the reigning caliph or his local representative, there were wide variations in the Jewish condition, swinging from good to bad or vice versa at almost every change of rulership. We have discussed above the anti-Jewish, or rather anti-*dhimmī* regulations instituted under ʿUmar II, which imposed severe restrictions on the Jews of the entire Umayyad realm, including Iraq. Of the ʿAbbāsid caliphs some actually dealt harshly with the Jews and imposed upon them strict discriminatory rules of the type listed in the Covenant of ʿUmar. Among these was Hārūn al-Rashīd (reigned 786–809) of legendary fame thanks to *The Arabian Nights* which portray him as a good and just ruler (hence his epithet *rashīd*, meaning "rightly guided"). Despite the picture *The Arabian Nights* paints of a golden age under Hārūn's rule, the fact is that his caliphate was a series of serious political disturbances and revolts, including flare-ups between the two opposing Arab moieties, the Yamanīs and the Qaysīs, the latter known in that context as Muḍarīs. A strictly orthodox Muslim, Hārūn proceeded with severity against the ʿAlids (i.e., the Shīʿites), the *zindīq*s (the revolutionaries of the poor classes), the Manichaeans, and those under their influence who were suspected of propagating false doctrines within Islam. These elements were excluded from the benefits accorded to the *ahl al-dhimma*, including the Jews. Hārūn was harsh in his treatment of the *dhimmī*s as well. In 806 he ordered churches along the Muslim-Byzantine frontier to be demolished, decreed that the *dhimmī*s of Baghdad must wear clothing different from that of the Muslims, and prohibited them from riding mounts used by Muslims. These enactments aggravated the position of the Jews of Iraq, which nevertheless remained better than in the neighboring Byzantine empire. In general, Hārūn did not oppress the Jews as such, but proceeded with equal stringency and hostility against all those population elements which did not follow his own specific variety of orthodox Islam.

Following the short reign of Hārūn's son al-Amīn (reigned 809–813), throughout which the country was torn by civil war between him and his brother al-Ma'mūn, the latter became caliph and reigned for twenty years (813–833). Al-Ma'mūn was an enlightened monarch, interested in the arts and sciences for which, despite the decline of his political power, he did more than his famous father. As already mentioned, he established in Baghdad the *bayt al-ḥikma* ("House of Wisdom"), and founded observatories in Baghdad and Damascus. In the field of religion he adopted the doctrine that the Koran was not uncreated, but created. This had the effect of reducing the authority of the Koran and of the *ᶜulamā'*, the religious scholars who relied on it. Al-Ma'mūn's attitude towards the Jews was more equitable than that of his father, but toward the end of his reign, under the influence of his advisors, it changed for the worse.

In the subsequent four centuries the ups and downs in the Jewish condition were perhaps more pronounced in Iraq than in any other Arab country. However, instead of detailing these changes of fortune, let me re-emphasize another important point: in the multi-ethnic society of Iraq, the rulers, if they were fervent adherents of their own brand of Islam, proceeded with equal vehemence against the followers of all other denominations, whether Muslim, Christian, or Jewish. To mention only one example, the Persian Shīᶜite Buwayhid *amīr*s, who reigned in Baghdad from 945 to 1055, while the ᶜAbbāsid caliphs retained only nominal rule, were generous patrons of both Arabic and Persian literature and the sciences, and builders of hospitals and founders of libraries. However, they were afflicted with typical Shīᶜite intolerance toward all other denominations and persecuted impartially Sunnī Muslims, Christians and Jews.

Some Jews attained high positions at the courts of various caliphs. One of the most important offices in the ᶜAbbāsid court was that of the court banker. In the early tenth century, two Jewish partners in banking and business, Joseph ben Pinhas (died before 928), and Aaron ben ᶜAmram, held this position under the Caliph al-Muqtadir. Their official title was *jahbadh*, and their functions included the collecting of state revenues, the issuing of bills of exchange on behalf of the court, and providing the court with long-term loans. The two also acted as bankers for the vizier and other high officials, as well as for Jewish merchants in Baghdad and other parts of the ᶜAbbāsid empire. Their firm was one of those banking houses which were used by Jewish communities all over the Diaspora to transmit by letters of credit their donations for the upkeep of the Talmudic academies of

Sura and Pumbedita. The two partners also became involved in controversies which erupted between the exilarchs and the Gaons. Aaron ben ᶜAmram's sons inherited his official position and influence, and so did Joseph ben Pinhas' son-in-law, Netira (died 916), who, for a quarter of a century, under the reign of three caliphs, was not only the principal figure of Iraqi Jewry, but wielded much influence in the caliphal court as well. In the tradition of the biblical Mordecai, Netira succeeded in preventing one of al-Muᶜtaḍid's ministers from carrying out his plan to put many Jews to death. Two of his sons, Sahl and Isaac, continued their father's work in Baghdad, while a third son, Joseph, seems to have been one of the leaders of the Jewish community in Fusṭāṭ, Egypt. In the periodic disagreements between the Gaons and the exilarchs this Jewish banking dynasty supported the Gaons, the most prominent of whom, Saᶜadia Gaon (see below), was the teacher of Sahl ben Netira. Their intervention resulted twice in the banishment of the exilarch Mar Uqva from the country. On the other hand, in a dispute between Saᶜadia Gaon and Aaron ben Meir, the Gaon of Eretz Israel, Aaron ben ᶜAmram sided with the latter, and supported his claim to supremacy in fixing the religious calendar.

SAᶜADIA GAON

There is no more suitable way of bringing to a close this brief sketch of Jewish life under the ᶜAbbāsids than presenting, in a few paragraphs, a portrait of the man who was undoubtedly the greatest intellect of all times in that community, and whose work enriched, like no one else's, the religious and scholarly life of Iraqi Jews as well as of world Jewry as a whole. His greatness and originality is in no way diminished by the fact that his entire scholarly, literary, religious, and philosophical work reflected the Muslim Arab cultural environment in which he lived, and of which he was a product as much as of his Jewish background and upbringing.

Saᶜadia ben Joseph (882–942) was born in the Fayyūm district of Upper Egypt as the son of a manual laborer. While still in Egypt, Saᶜadia began his literary and scholarly work, but apart from the fact that he wrote two books nothing is known of his youth. By 921, when he was thirty-nine years old, he was in Aleppo (Ḥalab), Syria, and next year he proceeded to Iraq where he became head of the Pumbedita Talmudic academy. In 928 the exilarch David ben Zakkai appointed Saᶜadia head of the Sura academy with the title *Gaon*, on which occasion he was required to render an oath of obedience and loyalty to the exilarch. Saᶜadia Gaon proved an able and energetic administrator, secured donations to the upkeep of the academy from as far as Spain, and won the friendship and support of the Jewish bankers Aaron ben ᶜAmram and Netira (see above). At the same time he showed himself to be a man of strong will and firm opinions, with a considerable ego, convinced that he could interpret the Halakha more correctly than anybody else, and unafraid to oppose and fight those who disagreed with him. Differences between him and the exilarch were not late to surface, until the latter finally resorted to the ultimate weapon he had by deposing Saᶜadia from his position of Gaon. Not a man to be intimidated, Saᶜadia countered this move by appointing another exilarch in the person of Yoshiya Ḥasan, brother of the exilarch David ben Zakkai. The case was presented to the caliph, Saᶜadia was forced to relinquish the Gaonate, Yoshiya Ḥasan was banished to faraway Khurasan, and the entire Jewish community was rent asunder by the great controversy. Finally, in 937, the two opponents were reconciled, Saᶜadia was reinstated as the head of Sura, and thereafter Gaon and exilarch remained on relatively good terms until the exilarch died, in 940. Saᶜadia died shortly thereafter, in 942.

Saᶜadia's versatility, productivity, and creative genius were exceeded only by those of Maimonides (1135–1204). In addition to these characteristics, Saᶜadia and Maimonides also had in common an inordinate pride, boundless self-confidence, and a disdain for those less endowed than themselves,[25] and the ability to arouse both great admiration and great opposition bordering on hatred. Saᶜadia's *Sefer haGaluy* exudes this kind of self-confidence and self importance, for which attitudes he was sharply criticized. For instance, in the book's introduction he says that in its "fourth chapter he will describe that God does not withhold from His people in every generation a scholar whom He teaches and whose eyes He enlightens, so that that scholar should instruct them and teach them, and so that they should be successful through him in their affairs. And this is the reason that I saw in my soul that God rendered favor to me and to them."[26] His opponents attacked Saᶜadia for the conceit he displayed, and cried, "See, how he boasts that God endowed him with the wisdom of knowledge about the animals, the plants, and the metals, and the stars, and the rest of the created things!"[27]

In the second version of his *Sefer haGaluy* Saᶜadia responded sharply to his opponents, referring to them with ugly distortions of their names. The exilarch David (ben Zakkai) becomes *Yidod* (i.e., "May he wander," or "May he be destroyed"); Aaron ben Sargado, known by the Arabic name Khalaf, becomes *Kelev met* ("dead dog"); Musa (perhaps a name of R. Kohen Tzedeq, head of the Pumbedita academy, becomes *M'usa immo* ("His mother despised"); Ḥananya ben Y'huda Gaon, the father of Sherira Gaon, becomes Ananya (in the meaning of *aninut*, sorrow, or perhaps an allusion to Onan of unblessed memory, cf. Gen. 38:9–10); etc.[28] Although Saᶜadia himself lists in that context such derogatory distortions of names which are found in the Bible, and, as the editor of this treatise, A. E. Harkavy, remarks, they occur in the Talmud, too, there can be little doubt that their use by Saᶜadia in heated polemical context reflects the Arab poets' and authors' tendency to resort to *hijā'*, diatribe and vituperation, which was encouraged by the caliphs who surrounded themselves with poets able to sing their praises and defend their glory, as well as to assail their enemies by hurling invective against them.[29] In such verbal assaults no holds were barred, and the opponent was accused of the most despicable things. The lengths to which writers would go to insult their opponents are exemplified by the assault Khalaf ben Sargado, the Gaon of Pumbedita (942–960), and Saᶜadia's chief antagonist, launched against him:

> O God, will You see and judge . . . for in his [Saᶜadia's] mouth there is the rod of pride, and there is deceit in him. He soils himself all day with transgressions, befouls himself all night with abominations, he rolls about in his sleep in seminal emission, and all his days lies in branches (?). Behold, he mocks Your Tora, and desecrates Your commandments, and brings disgrace on Your people like the evil ones on earth. Destroy him, and make Your servants rejoice by his ruin . . .[30]

Both unrestrained diatribes of this kind, and boundless self-praise were integral components of literary expression in the medieval Arab world. Among the Arabs, for a man of letters to praise himself to high heaven was an old poetic tradition going back to pre-Islamic days, and for several centuries after the emergence of Islam it remained a form of expression expected of poets, philosophers, and other literati.[31] As for the *hijā'*, the diatribe, since the poets' princely patrons welcomed it when directed against their enemies, it was inevitable that the poets should use the same techniques to attack their personal opponents as well. It is against this background that we must view both Khalaf's attack and Saᶜadia's self-pride, although one must also be aware of the fact that self-praise was not unknown among the ancient Hebrews either, as illustrated by the biblical admonition, "Let another man praise thee, and not thine own mouth" (Prov. 27:2).

Not as if Saᶜadia did not have much to be proud of. He excelled in all branches of religio-scholarly and literary activity which was considered the highest accomplishment among both Arabs and Jews in ᶜAbbāsid Iraq. His works are so numerous that their mere listing would be too lengthy. They can, however, be subsumed under six headings covering the main areas in each of which he not only proved himself an outstanding master but was an original innovator. They are: Bible translation and exegesis, Hebrew linguistics, halakhic writings, liturgical works, philosophy of religion, and polemics. Saᶜadia wrote almost all his works in Arabic, and the areas of research to which he devoted himself were precisely some of those whose Muslim-Arab counterpart flourished in early ᶜAbbāsid Iraq. However, since Saᶜadia's interest focused exclusively on Jewish religious subjects, he did not branch out into fields beyond the religious realm (Hebrew linguistics counted as a Jewish religious area of research, as did Jewish religious philosophy) in which the Iraqi Muslim scholar-scientists who preceded him or were his contemporaries equally excelled. The same limitation was characteristic also of the other Iraqi-Jewish scholars, who fell short of Saᶜadia in point of versatility.

In philosophy Saᶜadia was a follower of the *ᶜilm al-kalām* (literally "Science of the Word"), that influential Muslim philosophical school which developed shortly before Saᶜadia's time, became the equivalent of "theology" in Islam, and was defined as "the science concerned with firmly establishing religious beliefs by adducing proofs, and with banishing doubts."[32] Saᶜadia was the first and foremost Jewish *mutakallim* (*kalām*ist). He largely borrowed the methods and systems of argument of the Muslim *kalām*ists, but opposed them when it came to differences between Judaism and Islam. His main endeavor in his philosophical magnum opus, the *Book of Beliefs and Opinions*, which he wrote in Arabic (it was translated into Hebrew by Y'huda ibn Tibbon in 1186), was to find rational proofs for the tenets of the two Toras, the written and the oral, and to provide guidance to the Jews confused by the sectarian splits (the Karaite schism) of his day, the religious disputations, and the heretical views. While Saᶜadia took from the Muslim *kalām* the idea that it was both necessary and possible to reconcile the Bible and philosophy, that is, revelation and reason, revelation for him was the Bible and nothing else. Thus, in drawing proofs for Creation from the *kalām*, what Saᶜadia actually did was to press the results of Muslim philosophical efforts into the service of Jewish belief. Saᶜadia's work had a lasting influence in all the fields he cultivated, which was freely acknowledged by the specialists who followed him in philology, grammar, biblical exegesis, etc. Maimonides, although he disagreed with Saᶜadia's *kalām*ist philosophy, accorded him the highest praise when he wrote, "Were it not for Saᶜadia, the Tora would have well-nigh disappeared from the midst of Israel."[33]

In sum, it can be stated that an intellectual phenomenon such as Saᶜadia Gaon could not have appeared in any other environment save that of the culturally productive and receptive world of the early Islamic Arab efflorescence which, in the eighth to eleventh centuries, came to full bloom in Iraq, Syria, Egypt, North Africa, and Spain. Whenever and wherever this cultural flowering was accompanied by a tolerant attitude toward the *dhimmī*s, Jewish culture, too, burst into bloom in all or most of those fields on which the Arab intellectuals focused their attention.

4

Cordova—The Arab Camelot

The preceding chapter dealt with the relationship between Jews and Arabs in various periods and various parts of the Arab world. By contrast, the entire first half of the present chapter will be devoted to a portrayal of the Arab culture of the city of Cordova, one of the most important centers in the Arab Middle Ages, with the focus on one particular period, the tenth to eleventh centuries. Only after having painted a picture of Arab life in that great cultural center the Arabs created in an astoundingly short time in the westernmost province of their realm, will the focus of our narrative shift from them to the Jews, their culture, and their participation in the life of the Arab Camelot that was Cordova. That is to say, in the present chapter the main theme will be the Arab city of Cordova, the Arab life and culture in it, the Arab concerns which dominated it, and the Arab genius it manifested, while Jewish Cordova, its life, culture and concerns, will be dealt with only secondarily.

Devoting as much attention as I shall be to the Jews of Cordova is due, of course, to the specific focus of the present book, which is the relationship between the Arabs and the Jews through the ages. Were the subject of this chapter nothing else but the Arab city of Cordova, there would be much less room in it for a discussion of the Jewish share in its life, for, in the perspective of the life and culture of Cordova as a whole the Jews played a much less important role than would appear from this chapter.

The same observation can be made also with regard to Arab-Jewish relations. For the Arabs of Cordova the Jewish minority of the city, and the relationship between the two communities, represented a much smaller component in the totality of their life, culture, and interests than one could conclude from my presentation. A Ḥasdai ibn Shaprut or a Samuel haNagid ibn Naghrela were certainly famous personages in the eyes of Arab society and leadership as well. But it is rather doubtful whether such other major Jewish figures as Y'huda haLevi and Maimonides, who for the Jews were two of the greatest geniuses of the Middle Ages, were at all known to their Andalusian contemporaries. It is a fact that most Arab authors and scholars took little notice of the Jews and of what the Jews produced in the various fields of cultural endeavor. But precisely because this was the case, the views of those few Arab men of letters who did write about the Jews, whether in a derogatory vein as Ibn Ḥazm, or in sincere appreciation as al-Andalusī, gain added importance, because our knowledge and understanding of the Arab-Jewish relations depend to a great extent on their writings.

A GLANCE AT HISTORY

Cordova, located in southern Spain on the right (northern) bank of the Guadalquivir, at an elevation of 370 feet above sea level, is today an insignificant city of some 200,000 inhabitants. It has a few minor museums, some old churches and palaces, and boasts of a sprinkling of factories. All in all, it is of little more than limited interest to tourists, most of whom are satisfied with "doing" the Prado in Madrid, the Escorial just outside it, and the splendid Moorish palace of Alhambra in Granada. Yet in the tenth century Cordova (Arabic Qurṭuba) was a metropolis which, for a brief period, rivaled Baghdad in magnificence and as a cultural center of the Arab world.

Founded by the North African Carthaginians, Cordova was conquered by the Romans in 152 B.C.E., and became the capital of the Roman province Hispania Ulterior. In the early fifth century C.E. the Vandals devastated it, then for a brief period it was under the control of Byzantium, and from 571 it was under Visigothic rule. The Arabs, who invaded Spain in 711, took Cordova after a brief siege. When the Christians of the city surrendered, the Arabs treated them with clemency, but entrusted the guarding of the city to the Jews. In 716, the Arabs made Cordova the capital of al-Andalus, as they called the Iberian Peninsula, and embarked on rebuilding and fortifying it. Thirty years later the Marwānid prince ʿAbd al-Raḥmān I (731–788), the only scion of the Umayyad dynasty who escaped the ʿAbbāsid massacre of his family in Syria, overthrew the Arab governor of Cordova, and by utilizing with consummate skill the bitter enmity between the two Arab moieties, that of the Qaysīs and that of the Yamanīs, made himself the master of the province. In 756 ʿAbd al-Raḥmān entered Cordova, and was proclaimed *amīr* (ruler, prince) of al-Andalus.

ʿAbd al-Raḥmān had to spend much of the thirty-three years of his rule in efforts to consolidate his position. He had to put down revolts, and at one point he was almost forced to fight the invading armies of Charlemagne whose help was invoked by Arab chiefs opposed to ʿAbd al-Raḥmān. Only a sudden recall to the Rhineland made Charlemagne lift his siege of Saragossa (778). Preoccupied with problems of securing his rule, ʿAbd al-Raḥmān had little time to pay attention to matters other than military and administrative. When he died, the domain he ruled was far from secure, and the struggle he had begun had to be continued by his successors almost without surcease throughout the life span of the Cordovan Umayyad dynasty. Nevertheless, the later Andalusian Umayyads became generous patrons of literature, science, and the arts. Outstanding among them was his grandson, ʿAbd al-Raḥmān II (reigned 822–852), who was a great builder and Maecenas. Under his rule Cordova became the site of an important school of Mālikite jurisprudence, adopted much of the refined usages of Baghdad, which at the time was the undisputed center of Muslim Arab civilization, and boasted of several poets, singers, and musicians. However, it was not until another six decades had passed that Cordova entered its golden age, under ʿAbd al-Raḥmān III (born 889, reigned 912–961), the greatest and most brilliant of the Spanish Umayyads.

When ʿAbd al-Raḥmān III became master of Andalus, he was only 23 years old. Despite his youth he had been chosen to be the heir presumptive by his grandfather, the *amīr* ʿAbd Allāh ibn Muḥammad (reigned 888–912), who recognized the youth's outstanding qualities. To begin with, the young *amīr*'s rule had to be devoted largely to the traditional tasks all the Spanish Umayyads had to face: the consolidation of his rule, internal pacification, and the achievement of political unity. For decades, much of his energy had to go into subduing revolts in southern Andalus, and repulsing attacks from the Christian north. The latter endeavor was only sporadically successful; the worst setback the Arabs suffered was at the hands of Ramiro II, king of Leon, who succeeded in 939 in inflicting a serious defeat on the ruler of Cordova at the "moat" of Simancas. On the other hand, ʿAbd al-Raḥmān III was successful in several African campaigns, and occupied bases in Ceuta and elsewhere, thus establishing himself as a power in opposition to the Fāṭimids. After his victory over his Muslim opponents in 928, ʿAbd al-Raḥmān III felt justified in adopting the exalted title *amīr al-muʾminīn* ("Commander of the Faithful," the traditional title of the caliphs of the East), as well as the honorific appellation of *al-nāṣir li-dīn Allāh*, that is, "Protector of the Religion of Allah."

In the later years of his rule ʿAbd al-Raḥmān III was able to devote much of his attention to peaceful endeavors. Having pacified Andalus, made it secure from attacks from both within and without, and created a well-ordered, efficiently organized, prosperous, and highly civilized state, he set out to make his capital Cordova culturally outshine Baghdad, until then undisputed queen of Islamic learning and literature, art and architecture.

By the tenth century the Islamization and Arabization of the population of Andalus had long been accomplished. The area of Muslim Andalus, or the Caliphate of Cordova, had reached in that century its greatest extent, and comprised all of the Iberian Peninsula with the exception of its northernmost one-quarter which had remained in Christian hands. The original Arab conquest had brought into the country a relatively small Arab population contingent, numbering, in all probability, not more than a few thousand. These were later joined by successive waves of immigrants from Syria and other Asian lands, and by Islamized Berbers from North Africa. After the conquest there was a mass movement of more or less spontaneous conversion to Islam in the indigenous Christian population, which became Arabized as rapidly as did the Berbers. The Arabs, although they despised agricultural work in Andalus as much as they did in the East, nevertheless claimed ownership rights to much of the land whose actual cultivation they entrusted to crop-sharing tenant farmers. Being originally an almost exclusively male contingent, the Arabs intermarried with the native women, a practice resulting in a rapidly growing population which claimed Arab patrilineal descent and considered itself Arab. By the tenth century these neo-Muslim elements constituted by far the most numerous component of the population of Andalus. Added to these Arabized and Islamized sectors of the population were the Negro slaves with the females among whom the Arabs interbred, thus adding their share to the population conglomerate, and the Slav slaves, captured in continental Europe, who constituted a numerous and active group especially in Cordova. Thus Andalus was a veritable melting pot of numerous disparate racial stocks, held together and fused into one community by the twin forces of the Arabic language and the Islamic faith. And, of course, there was the unregenerate minority of *dhimmī*s, called *muʿāhidūn*, literally "those under a liability," protected and subject client communities, comprised of Christians and Jews, who, while adopting Arabic as their language, refused to convert to Islam.

As the process of racial amalgamation continued, the newly developed Andalusian Muslim community became differentiated within itself along class lines like other, older Muslim societies. There was on the top the elite, the *khāṣṣa*, the people of distinction, comprised of the great noble families, whose members often were hereditary grandees. There was a middle class consisting of merchants, small landowners, and the urban bourgeoisie, although the latter neither had charters nor enjoyed immunities. And there was the *ʿāmma*, the plebs, in both town and country, devoid of any legal protection, and condemned to suffer any vexation at the hand of the authority.

This was the human material which constituted the demographic base for the cultural flowering which under ʿAbd al-Raḥmān III turned Cordova into a miracle, not only of the Arab world, but of all Europe as well, into a cultural Camelot compared to whose achievements King Arthur's legendary court pales into insignificance. From the tenth century on Cordova was a center of arts, science, and literature, unparalleled in Christian Europe until the Italian Renaissance five centuries later. It was a city of general education and literacy the like of which was not achieved in the Western world until the spread of Enlightenment in the eighteenth to nineteenth centuries. If the splendor that was Andalus, with Cordova as its capital, did not last longer than some two centuries, this was to a great extent due to the Arab proneness to conflict which became the ruination of Cordova, a fate similar to that of other great Arab centers of culture.

CORDOVA OBSERVED

In the tenth century, by the latter part of ʿAbd al-Raḥmān III's reign, Cordova was a city of some half-a-million inhabitants. Physically it was unequaled and remained so for centuries in the Western world. It had miles of paved streets, illuminated at night by lights fastened to the fronts of houses, and this at a time when in Paris and London nobody dreamt of street lighting. Administratively, the city was divided into six districts, each ruled by a *walī*, a military governor. It had a well-organized and well-functioning government, with an appointed judiciary, a police force, an agency controlling trade and the markets, including weights and measures, and supervising public behavior, including gambling, sexual immorality, and improper public dress.

According to one Arabic source, Cordova had 200,077 houses inhabited by ordinary people, as well as numerous palaces of nobles, viziers, officers of the royal household, and commanders of the troops, plus 60,300 public buildings, such as hospitals and colleges, 700 mosques, 900 baths, and no less than 4,300 markets with 80,455 shops. Within its citadel there were 430 mansions belonging to the officers of the court and to public functionaries. It had numerous pleasure gardens for recreation and amusement, 21 suburbs, and several royal villas, "remarkable for the magnificence of their structure or their delightful situation."[1]

Cordova was the center of flourishing handicrafts. It kept busy 13,000 weavers and many leather workers. It was from here that the art of tanning and embossing leather spread to Morocco, and later were brought to France and England. Silk production was introduced by Muslims from China to Spain, and agricultural methods from Western Asia. Cordova had close connections with the Near East, and even with Central Asia and India. The export and import business was regulated by duties imposed on outgoing and incoming merchandise.

The largest palace, which constituted a major suburb of Cordova, was built by ᶜAbd al-Raḥmān III and called Madīnat al-Zahrā' ("City of Zahrā'"), so named for his beloved Zahrā. It had 400 rooms and apartments, and housed thousands of slaves and guards. Beautifully located at the foot of the Sierra Morena and overlooking the Guadalquivir, the palace remained unsurpassed until Louis XIV's Versailles.

The building of the great mosque, facing the lofty ancient Arab bridgehead, was begun by ᶜAbd al-Raḥmān I in 787, and was completed by his son and successor Hishām I (788–796). It was enlarged by ᶜAbd al-Raḥmān II, and overhauled by his son and successor, Muḥammad I (852–886). ᶜAbd al-Raḥmān III rebuilt the minaret and enlarged the courtyard. His son and successor, al-Ḥakam (961–976), extended the colonnades of the mosque to the south by the addition of fourteen transepts, built a new *maqṣūra* (box reserved for the ruler) and a new *sābāṭ* (arcade), and added a third *miḥrāb* (prayer niche). The last major work on the mosque was done by the regent al-Manṣūr (died 1002), the powerful vizier of Hishām II (976–1009), who added seven colonnades, increasing the number of naves from eleven to nineteen. One historian reports that the grand mosque had 280 brass chandeliers, containing 7,425 cups of oil, and was served by 159 attendants.[2] Al-Manṣūr also built a palace complex to the east of Cordova, named al-Madīna al-Ẓāhira ("The Flowering City"). In the wars which followed the end of the Umayyad rule in 1031, and especially after the conquest of the city by Ferdinand III of Castile in 1236, almost all of these splendid buildings were destroyed.

Of special interest for the cultural history of Cordova is the fact that it had a book market in which regular auctions of books were held, as well as 70 libraries. By the middle of the twelfth century writing paper was manufactured in Andalusia, the art having been introduced from Morocco. Al-Ḥakam was a great bibliophile, and he sent out agents to the great Arab cities of the East to bring books back to Cordova, which augmented the number of books in the royal library to 400,000. This library was the greatest of its time. What is even more significant is that the general state of culture in Andalus reached such a high level at that time that the distinguished Dutch Orientalist R. Dozy, followed by other scholars, could declare enthusiastically that "nearly everyone could read and write," and this at a time when in Christian Europe literacy was a privilege of the clergy.

The Spanish Umayyads did, however, much more as patrons of culture than gather books, establish libraries, and spread general literacy. ʿAbd al-Raḥmān III founded a university in Cordova in the principal mosque of the city. Under his son al-Ḥakam II al-Mustanṣir, who himself was a scholar, this mosque-university rose to a place of preeminence among the educational institutions of the world. It had departments of astronomy, mathematics, and medicine, in addition to those of Muslim theology and law. (In the university of neighboring Granada, founded in the fourteenth century, chemistry, too, was added to the curriculum.) The university of Cordova attracted thousands of Muslim and Christian students from many countries in Europe, Asia, and Africa. Al-Ḥakam invited professors from the East, and set up endowments for their salaries. Among them were the historian Ibn al-Qūṭiyya who taught grammar, and the renowned Baghdadi philologist Abū ʿAlī al-Qālī, whose *Amālī* ("Dictations") are still studied in Arab lands.

One of the results of the scientific, scholarly, and artistic advances made in Cordova was that whenever the rulers of the Christian north—Leon, Navarre, or Barcelona—were in need of the services of a physician, a surgeon, an architect, a master singer, or a dressmaker, they applied to Cordova. The fame of the city spread even into remote Germany, where a Saxon nun called it "the jewel of the world."[3]

A word, at least, is in place on the character of the Andalusians. According to one of their foremost chroniclers, Aḥmad al-Maqqarī, the dominant traits in the Andalusian Muslim personality were hospitality, courage, haughtiness of temper, devotion to friends, a keen sense of justice, generosity, readiness of wit, and poetical talent.[4] Possessed of such sterling qualities, the Arabs of Andalusia had a rather dim view of the northern barbarians. An example is worth quoting in view of the similarity between it and the negative stereotypes which have abounded in nineteenth- and twentieth-century books and reports about the Arabs written by the descendants of those same northerners. The learned Toledan Arab judge Sāᶜid ibn Aḥmad al-Andalusī (of whom we shall hear more at the end of this chapter) had this to say about the Arabs' Christian neighbors to the north:

> Because the sun does not shed its rays directly over their heads, their climate is cold, and atmosphere clouded. Consequently, their temperaments have become cold, and their humors rude, while their bodies have grown large, their complexion light, and their hair long. They lack withal sharpness of wit and penetration of intellect, while stupidity and folly prevail among them.[5]

SCHOLARS IN CORDOVA

As against the cold climate and clouded atmosphere of the north, which may or may not have been responsible for the characteristics attributed to its inhabitants by Sāᶜid al-Andalusī, the atmosphere of Cordova was, without doubt, conducive to scholarly and literary activity. The city served as a magnet which attracted intellectuals and literati from all over the Arab world, and even from beyond its boundaries. By the end of the tenth century Cordova (and Andalusia in general) boasted of so many scholars that one of them, Abū al-Walīd ᶜAbd Allāh ibn al-Faraḍī (born in Cordova, 962, studied there under local masters and taught there, and died there 1013), felt impelled to present their biographies in a volume entitled *Ta'rīkh ᶜUlamā' al-Andalus* ("History of the Scholars of Andalus"), a book of great value for the history of Arab scholarship in Spain. In the subsequent century and a half many more scholars were active in Andalus, and their biographies served as the subject for studies embracing the whole of the Iberian Peninsula. Outstanding among them is the work of another native of Cordova, Abū al-Qāsim Khalaf ibn Bashkuwāl (1101–1183), who was of Spanish origin as his surname, which is the Arabicized form of Pascual, indicates. Impressed by Ibn al-Faraḍī's opus, Ibn Bashkuwāl decided to continue the subject, and called his book *al-Ṣila*, "The Continuation." In this work, whose full title is *Kitāb al-Ṣila fī Akhbār A'immat al-Andalus* ("The Book of the Continuation in the Annals of the Masters of Andalus"), he gathered the biographies of 1,400 men of letters who had flourished in the eleventh and twelfth centuries, and it is a mine of information on the astonishingly intensive literary activity that went on in Andalus, much of it concentrated in its capital Cordova. The *Ṣila*, in turn, was continued by Abū ᶜAbd Allāh Muḥammad ibn al-Abbār (1199–1260) in his *Kitāb al-Takmila li-Kitāb al-Ṣila* ("The Book of Completion to the Book of Continuation"), which continues the story of Andalusian scholarship down to the middle of the thirteenth century. The last supplement to this series of books on Andalusian scholars was written by Abū Jaᶜfar Muḥammad ibn al-Zubayr (flourished fourteenth century), entitled *Ṣilat al-Ṣila* ("Continuation of the Continuation"). Thereafter nothing worthy of note in Arab scholarship or literature was produced in Andalus. By that time, though, only a small enclave in the southernmost corner of the peninsula, centered on Granada, had remained in Arab hands. If the last of the great medieval Arab geniuses, Ibn Khaldūn (1332–1406) did not live in Cordova, the reason for this is simply that by his time Cordova had been under Christian rule for more than a century.

IBN ḤAZM

Three men are generally recognized as the greatest minds of the medieval world; all three were born in Cordova and received their early education there, although subsequently circumstances forced all three of them to leave the city, so that their full development and flowering graced other centers of the Arab world. The first, chronologically, was Abū Muḥammad ᶜAlī ibn Ḥazm (born Cordova, 994, died Manta Lishām, 1064); the second, Abū al-Walīd Muḥammad ibn Rushd (born Cordova, 1126, died al-Marrākush, 1198), known in the West as Averroes; the third, Abū ᶜImrān Mūsā ibn Maymūn (born Cordova, 1135, died Fusṭāṭ, Egypt, 1204), better known as Moses Maimonides. The first was, in all probability, the grandson of a Spanish convert to Islam; the second the scion of an important Andalusian Arab family; the third the son of a scholarly Jewish family long established in Spain. Arabic was the language of all the writings of the first two, whose works are the central pillars of the Muslim Arab culture of the Middle Ages. The works of the third, although he too wrote practically all of them in Arabic, and only a few in Hebrew, belong essentially not to Arab but to Jewish scholarship, theology, philosophy, and science.[6] This being the case, we shall leave the portrayal of Maimonides to the latter part of this chapter which will deal with the Jewish share in the life of Cordova.

Ibn Ḥazm's father rose to high position in the administrative hierarchy of Cordova, and his son grew up in the luxurious harem of his palace in the Cordova suburb of al-Madīna al-Ẓāhira (referred to above). From the age of fourteen, however, he had to suffer from the turbulence of the times. The family was forced to leave its palace and to move to a house in Balāṭ Mughīth, which, a year after the death of the elder Ibn Ḥazm (1012) was destroyed. Ibn Ḥazm himself had his share of imprisonments, banishments, and captivity, alternating with high positions as vizier to ᶜAbd al-Raḥmān V and Hishām al-Muᶜtadd. Disillusioned with political life, the thirty-five-year-old Ibn Ḥazm withdrew to Manta Lishām, the village of his family, and devoted himself to study and writing. In the remaining second half of his life he produced, according to his son, four hundred works.

Ibn Ḥazm eagerly absorbed in his youth the teachings of a great number of the most outstanding Cordovan masters, including traditions, grammar, lexicography, rhetoric, dialectic, theology, *fiqh* (jurisprudence), poetry, and philosophy. In his own works he proved to be a veritable Renaissance man some four centuries before the type emerged in Italy. In his *Risāla fī Marātib al-ᶜUlūm* ("Letter on the Classes of Sciences"), which is a complete plan for education, he demonstrates that all sciences are related, that without renouncing mundane pleasures it is impossible to engage in the research required by the sciences, that sciences can lead man to victory and well-being in the Other World, and that spiritual education is the means of saving and promoting human (i.e., Arab) culture. He hated all falseness and deceit, but recognized that the human soul spontaneously inclines to dishonesty and vice. The only refuge from these evils, he found, was in the God of Islam, who was "The Truth and the Foundation" of all other truths. Counterbalancing his distrust in man was his belief that friendship, true friendship, was the source of truth, sincerity, frankness, and mutual understanding.[7]

Possibly as a result of his harem upbringing, Ibn Ḥazm retained a lifelong sensitivity to, and interest in, female psychology and the psychology of love. In his *Ṭawq al-Ḥamāma*, a treatise on love and lovers, he castigates the poets for their use of language in an arbitrary way, and for revelling in rhetoric. He accuses man of adopting a mask instead of showing himself as he really is. In contrast to human words which are false and deceptive, the "Word of God is the authentic Truth."

In addition to being a psychologist and moralist, Ibn Ḥazm was also a theoretician of language, in which field he opposed the search for the *bāṭin*, the hidden meaning of the Koran, and upheld the *ẓāhir*, the open, literal, apparent sense of the Word of God. He was also a logician, and, most importantly, a historian, in fact, the first historian, of religious ideas. In his *Kitāb al-Fiṣal fī al-Milal wa al-Ahwā wa al-Niḥal* ("Book of Judgment on the Denominations, Heterodoxies, and Sects") is actually an encyclopedia discussing the various religions which had any connection with Islam. His presentation is detailed, accurate, and based not only on wide reading, but also on what today would be termed field work: personal inquiries and gathering of information. It was this endeavor that embroiled him in a bitter polemic with the Granadan Jewish statesman, vizier, general, poet, and halakhist, Ismāᶜīl ibn Naghrela, better known by his Hebrew name as Samuel haNagid, who had criticized the Koran. Of this controversy we shall have more to say below.

In his *Fiṣal* Ibn Ḥazm examines and criticizes the teachings of both Christianity and Judaism, takes issue with the Christian doctrine of the Trinity, and the Jewish views on prophecy which he finds much too limited, and attacks the Christian views on Jesus. He attempts to understand the Jewish opinion on "abrogation," that is, the concept of divine substitution of a later rule or commandment to replace an earlier one, which is an important tenet in Muslim theology and Koranic exegesis. Although Ibn Ḥazm is interested in the teachings of other religions only in order to compare them with those of Islam, and to uphold the latter against them, he nevertheless presents the views of those with whom he is in fundamental disagreement fully, honestly, and accurately.

A discussion of Ibn Ḥazm's theology would lead us too far afield, but we must quote at least one of his statements which, when compared to the Christian *credo quia absurdum est* ("I believe, because it is absurd"), shows the extent of both his belief and his measured rationality. He says that one must believe in the truth of every word contained in the Koran, because *nu'minu bi-hā wa-lā nadrī kayfa hiya*, "We believe in it even though we do not understand how it is."[8]

IBN RUSHD

Much better known in the West than Ibn Ḥazm was Abu al-Walīd Muḥammad ibn Rushd (Averroes), our second great Cordovan, who was a philosopher, a judge (*qāḍī*) and a physician. He was the last, and without doubt the greatest of all Medieval Arab philosophers, whose mode of philosophizing, often referred to as "Averroism,"[9] was most influential in Western Latin thought between 1200 and 1650.

Ibn Rushd received a thorough Muslim juridical education in Cordova from the foremost scholars of the age. As a young man he left his native city, and by the age of twenty-seven we find him in al-Marrākush (modern Marrakesh), Morocco, where he enjoyed the support of the sultan Abū Yaᶜqūb Yūsuf (reigned 1162–1184), the Almohad ruler of Morocco, a great patron of philosophers, physicians, and poets. In 1169 Ibn Rushd was appointed *qāḍī* of Seville, in 1171 chief *qāḍī* of Cordova, and in 1182 he became personal physician of the caliph. In 1195 he was tried as a heretic in Cordova, condemned and exiled, but was reprieved shortly before his death. He died and was buried in Marrakesh, but later his remains were transferred to the family tomb at Cordova.

Ibn Rushd devoted much of his life to writing various types of summaries of, and commentaries on, the works of Aristotle which by that time were available in Arabic translations. Ibn Rushd's own philosophy is Aristotelian, and his great quest was to harmonize religion and philosophy, which was a dominant theme in the thought of numerous other Arab philosophers, including Ibn Rushd's great Jewish contemporary, Maimonides. His aim was to lead to a "union between the reasoned and the transmitted," as he puts it in beautiful assonant Arabic, *al-jamᶜ bayn al-maᶜqūl wa al-manqūl*.

In Ibn Rushd's perspective, Greek thought was a single coherent philosophical system, and since Aristotle's *Politics* was unavailable to him, he incorporated Plato's *Republic* (on which he wrote a commentary) in his compass of speculation. Arab philosophers were familiar with a treatise entitled *Theology*, which modern scholarship has established was fundamentally a compendium based on Plotinus' writings. The Arabs considered this *Theology* a work of Aristotle, and regarded it uncritically as the culmination of Greek thinking. They were attracted, in particular, by its Neoplatonic emphasis on the "mystical" experience as the apex of human knowledge, which signified a passing over from ordinary logical thinking to a grasp of ultimate reality. This, they felt, was closely akin to the Muslim concept of ultimate religious experience involving a passing over from individuality to an impersonal fusion with the whole Divine Essence.

Ibn Rushd viewed nature and reality as possessed of one single coherent and coordinated structure, composed of hierarchically ordered levels, but forming a harmonious whole. Following Aristotle, he distinguished between an active and a passive aspect of the intellect. God, the First Intelligence, is the unmoved mover, which is in itself pure form, operates as the source of the celestial bodies and all subordinate motions, and also is the creative originator and sustaining force behind all lower intelligences.

In his short but most important treatise, *Faṣl al-Maqāl wa-Taqrīb mā bayn al-Sharīᶜa wa al-Ḥikma min al-Ittiṣāl* ("Authoritative Treatise and Exposition of the Convergence Between Religious Law and Philosophy") Ibn Rushd set out to prove that there is but one truth, but there are several modes of access to it: the rhetorical, available to anybody through the instruction of teachers; the dialectical, accessible to some who are able to explore the probability of truths of divine law; and the philosophical, which can be attained only by those few fully competent of exercising pure reasoning. In this manner, each man, depending on his personal abilities, has within his reach the possibility of grasping ultimate realities.[10]

When confronted with discrepancies between religion and philosophy, Ibn Rushd boldly throws in his lot with the latter. His position is that only the metaphysician, employing certain proof, is capable, competent, and obliged to interpret the doctrines contained in the prophetically revealed *sharīᶜa* law. The ultimate aim of philosophy is to establish the true, inner meaning of religious beliefs. However—and here Ibn Rushd's elitism asserts itself[11]—this inner meaning must not be divulged to the masses, who must accept the plain, external (*ẓāhir*) meaning of the Koran, which contains stories, similes, and metaphors. Still, for Ibn Rushd there is only one truth, that of the religious law (*sharīᶜa*), which is the same truth as that sought by the metaphysicians. The contents of the *sharīᶜa* are the whole and the only truth for all believers. Hence the Muslims, both the elite and the masses, must accept the teachings of Islam as taught by the last and greatest of all prophets, Muhammad. Islam is the best religion, just as Christianity was the best religion at the time of Jesus, and Judaism at the time of Moses. The *sharīᶜa* cares for all believers and provides happiness to all, although there are degrees of happiness, and every believer, Ibn Rushd maintains, attains the happiness that corresponds to his intellectual capacity—a distinction in which we again perceive a note of intellectual elitism. In discussing the *sharīᶜa*, Ibn Rushd shares with the Jewish philosophers the idea that the revealed law, although it contains teachings that surpass human understanding, must be accepted by all believers because it comprises divinely revealed truths. However, he differs with his great Jewish contemporary Maimonides when he abandons the belief in creation out of nothing since

Aristotle demonstrated the eternity of matter. Maimonides parted ways in this respect with Aristotle and accorded primacy to the belief in a creative, free God.

Our framework allows us to mention only briefly Ibn Rushd's other great philosophical treatises. His *Kitāb al-Kashf ʿan Manāhij*, whose long and involved title can best be translated as "The Book of Inquiry into the Methods of Proofs Concerning the Doctrines of the Faith and Definition of that which Occurs in it of the Views of Interpretation from among the Spurious Arguments and the Erroneous Innovation," is basically aimed at the doctrines of the various Muslim sects and theological schools. It also studies the unity of God, His attributes, His incorporeality (God is the principle of all sensible experience, but is enveloped in veils of light), and the divine actions. This was followed by Ibn Rushd's *Tahāfut al-Tahāfut* ("The Incoherence of the Incoherence"), which is partly an attempt to demolish the *Tahāfut al-Falāsifa* ("Incoherence of the Philosophers") which al-Ghazālī (1058–1111) completed in 1095, and partly an attempt to reconstruct the true philosophy of Aristotle against the distortions of the Neoplatonic *falāsifa* (philosophers). It is in this highly polemical form that Ibn Rushd presents his own, original, philosophical doctrine. Creation, according to him, is eternal creation; the creative will in God is founded in His excellence, it is the method of a perfectly transcendental being. He is the metaphysical cause of the physical order.

It is difficult to make the singular greatness of Ibn Rushd palpable to the modern reader not at home in the history of philosophy in general and of Islamic philosophy in particular. For one thing, he was undoubtedly the greatest of Muslim philosophers in integrating Greek philosophy and Islamic tradition into a thought system of his own. Second, his writings, due to his immense philosophical acuity and power, greatly contributed to the rise of Scholasticism. Third, his philosophical position, which has been characterized by Stuart MacClintock somewhat narrowly as "Aristotle warped onto a Platonic frame,"[12] signified the culmination of five centuries of dynamic speculative Arab philosophy, which disappeared after him, and the beginning of a similarly energetic philosophical activity labelled Averroism in Western Latin thought between 1200 and 1650.

Ibn Rushd was unquestionably the most important link in the complex chain of transmission of classical, and primarily Aristotelian, Greek philosophy to medieval Europe. The works of Aristotle were translated from Greek into Syriac, then from Syriac into Arabic; these versions were used by

Ibn Rushd (who knew no Greek) for his Arabic summary (*Jāmiᶜ*), resumé (*Talkhīṣ*), and commentary (*Tafsīr* or *Sharḥ*). These in turn were translated into Hebrew, and finally from Hebrew into Latin, the language in which they made their impact on the schoolmen. Incidentally, only a few of Ibn Rushd's commentaries have survived in Arabic, and even these are generally in Hebrew script, which the Jews in Arab countries generally used whether writing in Hebrew or in Arabic. This little detail is an eloquent testimony to the interest Andalusian Jews took in Arab philosophy, and to their share in preserving its works for posterity.

POETS AND MEN OF LETTERS OF CORDOVA

Of the many hundreds of poets, scholars, historians, and philosophers who made Cordova the great cultural center it was from the ninth to the twelfth centuries only a very few can be mentioned. My selection, of course, reflects my own individual preferences; other reviewers would probably make other choices.

Aḥmad ibn ᶜAbd Rabbihi (860–940) was a poet laureate, or official panegyrist, of the Marwānid Umayyad dynasty from the reign of Muḥammad I (died 886) to the middle of that of ᶜAbd al-Raḥmān III (reigned 912–961). In his youth he wrote erotic poetry, in his middle years laudatory verses in honor of his royal patrons, and in his old age ascetic poems, using the rhyme and meter called *mumaḥḥiṣāt*, or "effacers of sins." The one major work that assured his place in Arabic literary history is his *ᶜIqd al-Farīd* ("The Unique Necklace"), which, after the *Kitāb al-Aghānī*, occupies first place among the histories of Arabic literature. But the *ᶜIqd* is more than that. It is an encyclopedia of all the subjects which in tenth century Andalus, and in the Arab world as a whole, were considered the components of *adab*, refinement or culture. It consists of twenty-five books which cover the following subjects: government, war, generous men, delegations, addressing kings, religious knowledge and good conduct, proverbs, homilies and asceticism, condolences and eulogies, genealogies and virtues of the ancient Arabs, bedouin speech, replies, oratory, the art of letter writing, history of the caliphs, stories of great viziers, *Ayyām al-ᶜArab* (Pre-Islamic Arab wars), virtues of poetry, metrics, music, woman, anecdotes, nature of men and animals, food and drink, diverse anecdotes. Ibn ᶜAbd Rabbihi's main purpose in this magnum opus was to familiarize the young Andalusian Arab society with the traditions and culture of the Arab East which in his days still had enormous prestige in the Arab West.[13]

A contemporary of Ibn ʿAbd Rabbihi was Abū Bakr ibn al-Qūṭiyya (died 977), a native of Seville who lived and died in Cordova, and was the first historian of Andalus as well as a grammarian. He enjoyed great prestige in his lifetime, and was considered the greatest philologist of his day.

However, the greatest medieval historian of all Spain, both Christian and Muslim, was another Cordovan, Ḥayyān ibn Ḥayyān (born 997/8; died 1076), who made a living as a letter writer in the Cordovan government chancellery. Of the many works written by him, two are of the greatest importance: his *al-Muqtabas fī Ta'rīkh al-Andalus* ("Collection of the History of the Men of Andalus") was thus named with unusual modesty by the author because in it he collected and quoted the works of others—most of them lost—who wrote about the history of Andalus. By compiling and combining numerous earlier accounts into an integral whole, Ibn Ḥayyān produced a history of the peninsula on a grand scale, painting a panorama of the unfolding events, centered on the person of the Umayyad ruler, and describing, often with bitterness, numerous personalities, their rivalries, and the anarchy in the party kingdoms.

The most important work in the Muslim historiography of Spain is Ibn Ḥayyān's original study entitled *al-Matīn* ("The Text"), which originally comprised sixty books (all of them lost) but which is nevertheless known thanks to lengthy and numerous passages quoted from it by Ibn Ḥayyān's great admirer, ʿAlī ibn Bassām (died 1147). Living a generation after him in Cordova and Seville, Ibn Bassām, in his *Dhakhīra fī Maḥāsin Ahl al-Jazīra* ("Treasury of the Qualities of the People of the Peninsula") described the lives and works of men of letters and poets of Cordova and other parts of Andalus. The basic aim of Ibn Bassām was to wean away his Andalusian compatriots from their undue adulation of everything done or produced in the Arab East. As he ironically remarked, "If a fly buzzed on the borders of Syria or Iraq, they would prostrate themselves as if before an idol." In presenting the Andalusians with the treasures produced by men of letters in their own country, Ibn Bassām could not have used a better source than Ibn Ḥayyān's *al-Matīn*. As evidenced by the ample excerpts in Ibn Bassām's *Dhakhīra*, the *Matīn* described the history of eleventh-century Andalus with, to quote A. Huici Miranda, "an admirable attention to detail and an exactitude which are highlighted by a rare political understanding of events." Or, as the most authoritative modern historian of Arab Spain, E. Levi-Provençal, put it, "Whenever one considers any particular aspect of Hispano-Umayyad history, one is nearly always obliged to revert to Ibn Ḥayyān . . ."[14]

As for poetry, Cordova was the home of some of its most celebrated masters in the Arab Middle Ages. It was an art whose practice was shared by poets whose livelihood, and often very lives, depended on their skill in it, and by the great and mighty, including *amīrs* and kings. It was practiced by historians and philosophers, such as Ibn ʿAbd Rabbihi and Ibn Ḥazm (spoken of above), to whose ranks should be added Muḥammad ibn al-Khaṭīb (1313–1375), vizier, historian, medical author, mystical philosopher, anthologist, and poet, who lived in Granada, the last remaining foothold of Arab rule in the Andalus of his day, and in Morocco.

The first Hispano-Umayyad ruler and several of his successors were poets. Also among the *mulūk al-ṭawā'if*, "the party kings," who, after the inglorious end of the Umayyad caliphate of Cordova (1031) ruled over parts of its territory, there were several who aspired to poetic acclaim. It was the fashion among the rulers to have poets laureate attached to their courts, and to take them along on their travels and to their wars. One of the most acclaimed poets was Aḥmad ibn Zaydūn (1003–1071), whose passionate love-poems were addressed to Wallāda, the daughter of Muḥammad III al-Mustakfī (reigned 1023–25). Incidentally, this last Umayyad caliph of Cordova, who was characterized by a historian as a man "whose interest in life centered on sex and stomach,"[15] met his end when, disguised as a singing girl, he tried to flee and was poisoned by one of his officers.

Poetic temperament often found expression not only in words, but also in acts of passion, and in jealous and vicious deeds as illustrated by the rivalry between Ibn Zaydūn and his younger competitor Muḥammad ibn ʿAmmār (1031–1086), the court-poet of al-Muʿtaḍid, the ruler of Seville, and chief minister of al-Muʿtaḍid's son, Muḥammad al-Muʿtamid. The enmity between Ibn ʿAmmār and Ibn Zaydūn was continued by the latter's son, who succeeded in inciting the anger of al-Muʿtamid against Ibn ʿAmmār to the point where, in a moment of rage, the ruler cut off Ibn ʿAmmār's head with the blow of an axe.

Among the many famous Andalusian poets we can mention only two more. One is Ibrāhīm ibn Khafāja (1058–1139) who was greatly admired during his lifetime. He was best known as a poet of nature, and wrote inspired and passionate evocations of rivers, ponds, gardens, trees, fruits and flowers. The son of a wealthy family, Ibn Khafāja lived on his provincial estate and did not respond to the invitations of rulers to join their entourage, although, in keeping with the customs of the times, he did sing the praises of some potentates, such as the Almoravid prince Abū Isḥāq Ibrāhīm ibn Tāshufīn. The other is Muḥammad ibn Quzmān (al-Aṣghar, died Cordova, 1160), famous as the poet who raised the *zajal* to an accomplished art form.

The eleventh-century poets of Andalus seem to have invented new forms of strophic poems; one was the *muwashshaḥ*, or "belted," the name being taken from the *wishāḥ*, the double belt worn scarflike by women over the shoulder, the other the *zajal*. Both were structured around a refrain, which, in all probability, was sung by a chorus. The *zajal* was for decades prior to the appearance of Ibn Quzmān produced by improvisation, until he, with his great artistry, secured it a place next to the classical forms of Arabic verse. Ibn Quzmān was a wandering poet, who seems to have been of Germanic (perhaps Visigothic) ancestry—he was tall of stature and had blue eyes and a red beard. He was always short of money, and lived a dissolute life. However, he was not identical with the Ibn Quzmān who is mentioned by Ibn Ḥazm, and who died of unrequited passion for a beautiful young man of Cordova, Aslam ibn ᶜAbd al-ᶜAzīz, in the early tenth century. Our Ibn Quzmān's favorite themes were the happy frolickings of gay young drinkers and beautiful maidens, singing and dancing in an enchanting setting, under shady trees, or swimming in fresh streams or in pools among flowers. Ibn Quzmān has been recognized in the history of Arabic literature as the unsurpassed master of the *zajal*, whose poems have been accepted as models of perfection in this genre.

Before concluding this section let me mention one more sparkling figure in this galaxy of talent, who was not a poet as much as he was a musician. His exploits and comportment made him much admired and emulated by the leisured classes of Cordova in the ninth century. The influence he enjoyed at the court, and his popularity in what at the time counted as "the society" of Cordova give us, incidentally, a tantalizing insight into the frivolous atmosphere of the Andalusian capital. The man I am referring to was Abu al-Ḥasan ᶜAlī ibn Nāfiᶜ (789–857), nicknamed Ziryāb (Persian "Gold Water"), who, according to one source, was a black slave. Ziryāb was at first one of the musicians at the court of Baghdad, but, having aroused the jealousy of his teacher, Isḥāq al-Mawṣilī, he had to flee, and chose to go west. What happened next is best told in the words of Philip K. Hitti, who based his account on medieval Arab sources:

> ᶜAbd al-Raḥmān [II, r. 822–52], who maintained an opulent court and imitated the lavish prodigalities of Hārūn al-Rashīd [the Baghdad caliph of legendary fame, reigned 786–809], rode out (822) of his capital

> [Cordova] in person to welcome the young minstrel [Ziryāb]. From that time on Ziryāb lived with his new patron, from whom he received an emolument of 3,000 dinars annually and real estate in Cordova worth 40,000 dinars, on terms of closest intimacy. He soon eclipsed all other musicians in the land. Besides being credited with knowing the words and tunes of 10,000 songs, which like other musicians he believed the jinn had taught him during the night, Ziryāb shone as a poet and as a student of astronomy and geography. What is more important, he proved himself so polished, witty and entertaining that he soon became the most popular figure among the smart set of the time, even an arbiter of fashion. Hitherto hair had been worn long and parted on the forehead, now it was trimmed low on the brow; certain dishes, including asparagus, had been unpopular, now those same dishes became favorites—all because of Ziryāb's example.[16]

On this note of levity we must take leave of the Muslim-Arab civilization of Cordova and Andalus, and pass on to the share of the Jews in it. In conclusion it can be stated that a unique concatenation of human and environmental factors was responsible for the outburst of Arab cultural efflorescence which took place in the tenth century in Cordova, the capital city of Andalus. The extraordinary élan which brought a relatively small group of Arab men to this farthest point west of their original homeland; their instantaneous intermingling with the local population which followed upon their rapid conquest of almost the entire Iberian Peninsula; the possibility opened up by the demographic conditions to leave what for them was the most menial and unattractive task of agriculture to the subjected indigenous population elements, thereby becoming free to devote themselves to the higher and nobler pursuits of ruling, governing, administering, and soldiering; the overall internal security which was the fruit of effective civic administration; and the economic prosperity produced by a rationally organized and hierarchically structured society—these were the major factors which, after a relatively long incubatory period of some two centuries, resulted in a splendid era of roughly the same length in which Arab philosophy, medicine, science, and literature, song and music, art and architecture reached heights unequalled in Arab history either before or after that golden age. In those two lustrous centuries the lure of the Arab Camelot was so powerful that it attracted talented individuals of the most varied backgrounds: Berbers and Blacks from the south from across the Mediterranean, Visigoths and Spaniards from the north, Slavs and Germanics from various parts of Europe. Many of these, or their offspring, having acquired the

Arabic language and adopted the Muslim religion, became significant creative contributors to the Arab culture of Andalus.

ḤASDAI IBN SHAPRUT AND HIS CIRCLE

This culture-rich environment was shared by two Arabic-speaking but non-Muslim elements. One was that of the Mozarabs (from the Arabic *mustaʿrib*, "Arabized"), as the Christian assimilants to Arab culture and the Arabic tongue were called, and the other that of the Jews who likewise had become Arabs in all but religion, which, in both cases, is a very big "but." The Mozarabs, and the neo-Muslim *muwalladūn* (lit. "adopted," or "affiliated") Christian converts to Islam frequently became discontented and staged revolts against the Muslim rulers of Andalus. These revolts, when put down, were punished by crucifixion, head down, of hundreds of their leaders. The Jews, numerically much weaker and by tradition disinclined to rebellion, remained throughout a politically reliable element whose loyalty the country's Arab overlords never had any reason to doubt. Weak as a group, the Jews were possessed by an irrepressible ambition to excel individually in the service of the Arab rulers, and in the pursuit of their own Jewish equivalents of the Arab cultural accomplishments, and especially in linguistics, literature, poetry, religious studies, and philosophy, as well as in medicine and the sciences. In doing so they not only immensely enriched their own culture and that of the Arabs, but also transmitted much of the latter to Christian Europe, assuming a crucial role in the subsequent development of Western civilization as a whole.

It took about two centuries for the Jews to recover from the trauma of Visigothic oppression, to assimilate into the newly emerging Arab society and culture, and to rise together with the Arabs to formerly unknown heights of literary, scholarly, and scientific achievements. The key role in this phenomenal development was played by Ḥasdai ibn Shaprut (ca. 905–975), a man of vast learning, who in his early years mastered Arabic, Hebrew, Latin, and the Romance vernacular of Spain. When we first hear of Ḥasdai he was a modest, though well-known physician in Cordova, which he remained until one day he announced that he had rediscovered the secret of the preparation of *theriak*, the fabulous compound remedy for all poisons and numerous diseases. Thereupon (in 1040) he was summoned to the court of ʿAbd al-Raḥmān III who appointed him physician of the royal household. From that time on Ḥasdai's rise to power was rapid. It was the custom of Arab rulers in those days to appoint their trusted physicians to high administrative positions, and this is what happened with Ḥasdai. The caliph made him supervisor of customs, and entrusted him with the diplomatic task of dealing with embassies from Byzantium and Germany.

In 958 an event occurred which greatly enhanced the value of Ḥasdai in the eyes of the king. At that time Queen Toda of the Christian kingdom of Navarre in the north of the peninsula asked ʿAbd al-Raḥmān to send her a physician to cure her grandson Sancho of his excessive obesity which had made him a laughingstock in her own court. The king entrusted Ḥasdai with the delicate mission (let us not forget that ʿAbd al-Raḥmān was almost constantly at war with the Christian north), and Ḥasdai succeeded in persuading the old queen to come with her grandson to Cordova, where the superior medical facilities would enhance the chances of a successful cure. What diplomatic skills were brought into play by Ḥasdai to persuade the Christian queen and prince to come to the capital of the Muslim enemy of Christianity can only be imagined. In any case, the Cordovan physicians' cure proved a total success, Sancho became a slender, muscular, and energetic youth, and in 960, with the help of ʿAbd al-Raḥmān's troops, he secured Leon for himself. Thus, thanks to Ḥasdai, ʿAbd al-Raḥmān was able, if not to reconquer Leon, at least to place on its throne a Christian ruler beholden to him.

Under ʿAbd al-Raḥmān's successor, al-Ḥakam II, Ḥasdai continued to fill the same trusted position, which yielded him as a fringe benefit the office of *nasi*, prince or president, of the Jewish community. His lifelong commitment to Jewry, Jewish scholarship, and Jewish culture, made this a most coveted honor in his eyes. Well known is his contact with the Jewish king of Khazaria, that remote kingdom to the northeast of the Black Sea, whose rulers and princes converted to Judaism in 730 or 740. Ḥasdai, with his extensive foreign contacts, heard about the existence of this Jewish kingdom, wrote a letter to Joseph, king of the Khazars, and received an answer from him. This correspondence is the most valuable single source on the conversion and history of the Jewish Khazars.

In his letter to Ḥasdai, King Joseph tells of a dream his predecessor, King Bulan, had, and following which Bulan invited representatives of Judaism, Christianity, and Islam for a religious debate which convinced him of the superiority of Judaism over the other two religions. Then he, and the nobility, converted to Judaism. Subsequently they established synagogues and schools, and in this manner rabbinic Judaism was introduced into Khazaria. In the second half of the tenth century Khazaria was repeatedly attacked by the Russians, and in the eleventh its end came. Some Khazar Jews fled to the West, to the Ukraine and Poland, and even as far as Hungary, while others seem to have found refuge in the Caucasus.

But to come back to Ḥasdai ibn Shaprut, it was largely due to his vision, ambition, and energy that Iberian Jewry became independent intellectually and religiously from the great and old Talmudic academies of Sura and Pumbedita in Iraq (see above, chapter 3). Ḥasdai emulated in this respect his lord and patron ʿAbd al-Raḥmān III. Just as the Andalusian caliph made his country independent religiously and culturally of the established Muslim Arab centers of the East, so Ḥasdai secured independence for Andalusian Jewry from the Iraqi Jewish centers. He brought from Iraq to Andalus a number of outstanding Jewish scholars, foremost among whom was Moses ibn Ḥanokh (died ca. 965), whom Ḥasdai appointed rabbi of Cordova and head of its Talmudic academy.

Equally important was the encouragement Ḥasdai gave to types of study and literary activity which were new to Jewish cultural development, and which emerged as a result of Arab influence. Hebrew grammar is a case in point. Despite their centuries-old preoccupation with the study of the Bible, the Mishna, and the Talmud, the Jews had not studied Hebrew grammar until they became acquainted with the results of Arabic grammatical investigations. The legendary founder of Arabic grammar, Abu al-Aswad al-Du'ilī, lived in the seventh century in Baṣra, and, according to Arab tradition, ʿAlī, the cousin and son-in-law of Muhammad, laid down for him the principle that "the parts of speech are three: noun, verb, and particle (*īsm*, *fiʿl*, *ḥarf*). In the next century Arab philologists showed that every Arabic verb is triliteral, that is, consists of three root letters.[17]

The two Jewish grammarians who attempted to apply these principles to Hebrew were both protégés of Ḥasdai ibn Shaprut. They were M'naḥem ibn Sarūq (ca. 910–ca. 970) and Dunash ibn Labrat (ca. 920–ca. 990), who were brought by Ḥasdai to Cordova, where they became competitors and bitter enemies. Incidentally, the manner in which Ḥasdai treated Ibn Sarūq shows that, once he achieved a position of prominence and power, he behaved toward those dependent on him with the disdain, haughtiness, arbitrariness, and even harshness found among the Arab rulers and powerful courtiers of the age. Although Ḥasdai made use of the services of Ibn Sarūq to compose for him important diplomatic letters (it was Ibn Sarūq who wrote for him the letters to the Khazar and Byzantine kings), he underpaid him so badly that the poor grammarian had to appeal to the generosity of others to make ends meet. Worse than that, when Ibn Sarūq's enemies denounced him to Ḥasdai, the Jewish grandee gave him no chance to prove his innocence, but sent his Jewish henchmen to Ibn Sarūq's house on a Sabbath, where they beat him severely, tore his clothes, plucked his beard, and then drove him from the city. Sometime later, when Ibn Sarūq from a safe distance wrote a letter to Ḥasdai complaining of the cruel and unjust treatment, Ḥasdai replied: "If you have sinned, I have made it possible for you to receive punishment. If you have not sinned, I made it possible for you to attain life in the World to Come." After a while Ḥasdai sent his men to the home town of Ibn Sarūq, where they ejected him from his home, put him in prison, and razed his house.[18]

It remained for a student of Ibn Sarūq, Y'huda ben David Ḥayyūj (born Fez, ca. 945–died 1000), to demonstrate that like Arabic Hebrew roots are made up of three letters—an important breakthrough against earlier views which held that there were also two-letter and even one-letter Hebrew roots. With this, Hebrew grammar became equal to Arabic in accuracy.

Ḥasdai ibn Shaprut emulated the Arab princes and viziers in more ways than one. Like them, he commissioned his subordinates to roam the towns of Italy and the Near East in search of books, and to purchase what they found and bring them home to Cordova. His men also looked, again in the manner of the emissaries of the Arab rulers of Andalus, for Jewish scholars to be invited to the court of Ḥasdai.[19] Following the examples of the Arab grandees, Ḥasdai made his house a gathering place for Hebrew writers and scholars. Poets would come and recite their verses, writers read their essays and treatises, and the halls of Ḥasdai's palatial residence reverberated with spirited debates. Among the Arabs such a gathering was called a *majlis*, meaning literally "sitting together," and correspondingly these Jewish literary salons were called *moshav*, which is the precise Hebrew translation of *majlis*.

While the Jewish grammarians wrote their works on Hebrew grammar in Arabic, as did the Jewish thinkers their philosophical works, Jewish literary production in Hebrew was also enriched under Arab influence by the transposition into Hebrew poetry of the poetic meters, forms, structures, and themes developed by the Arab poets of the age. Almost all Cordovan Hebrew grammarians also wrote poems in Hebrew. Dunash ibn Labrat was the one who introduced Arabic meter into Hebrew poetry, and he also imitated Arabic verse structure, and utilized Arabic subjects, including those of self-praise which were among the morally least attractive elements of Arabic poetry.[20]

SAMUEL HANAGID

Another native of Cordova, who became an outstanding leader of Andalusian Jewry, was Ismāʿīl ibn Naghrela (993–1056), better known by his Hebrew name, Samuel haNagid. Samuel played a role in Granada similar to that of Ḥasdai a century earlier in Cordova. His teacher in Cordova was Abu al-Walīd Marwān ibn Jannāḥ (985/90–1050), who, in turn, was a pupil of Ḥayyūj, a disciple of M'naḥem ibn Sarūq. That is to say, haNagid was the heir to three generations of Cordovan Hebrew scholars.

At the age of twenty haNagid was forced to flee Cordova, and shortly after that he came to the attention of the vizier of Granada, upon whose advice King Ḥabūs of Granada appointed him to his staff. HaNagid's rise was meteoric. He became a tax collector, the *kātib* (secretary) to the vizier, then his assistant, and finally became vizier himself, under both Ḥabūs and his son and successor King Bādis. In 1027 the Jewish community conferred upon him the title *nagid* ("prince") of Andalusian Jewry.

Granada at the time was embroiled in constant warfare with Arab Seville, and from 1038 to 1056 haNagid was the commander of the Granadan army. His poems—he was a talented poet in both Hebrew and Arabic—are the major source of information about his campaigns and numerous victories.[21] One must take into account that his poetic references to his exploits may be colored by the boasting, self-praise, and exaggeration which were common in both Arabic and Hebrew poetry of the age. He took great pride in his poems, and made sure that they were circulated among knowledgeable people. It is a fact that his war songs are unique in Hebrew poetry.

HaNagid was also a halakhist, and around 1049 in the midst of his military campaigns he found time to complete his major halakhic work, entitled *Sefer Hilkh'ta Gavr'ta*. Only fragments survive of this work, which was written in Aramaic and Hebrew, and possibly partly in Arabic. Samuel haNagid also wrote an introduction to the Talmud and a Bible dictionary (in Arabic) entitled *Kitāb al-Istighnā'* ("Book of Satisfaction"). Branching out into dangerous territory, he wrote a criticism of the Koran, which has not survived, and which prompted Ibn Ḥazm to a bitter polemic against it (see below). As a patron of Hebrew letters haNagid supported Hebrew poets, among them Solomon ibn Gabirol (1021–1053), one of the greatest Hebrew bards of all times. Like the Arab grandees, and as Ḥasdai ibn Shaprut before him, haNagid maintained a *majlis* where his poems were read to gatherings of poets, and gifts were bestowed on his favorites among them.

HaNagid maintained contact with the scholars and the leaders of Palestinian and Iraqi Jewry, among them the *Resh G'luta*, the exilarch, Ḥizqiya ben David. However, his work and activities, as the Jewish historian Abraham ibn Daud (ca. 1110–ca. 1180) remarked, contributed to the decline of the prominence of the Iraqi Gaons in Talmudic and halakhic scholarship. This, of course, is a kind of left-handed compliment to haNagid, because what it actually says is that his greatness in the Halakha eclipsed that of the Iraqi *G'onim.* As for haNagid's poetical talent, it was considered outstanding by Abraham ibn Daud as well as by the greatest Hebrew poets of Andalus, including Moses ibn Ezra and Solomon ibn Gabirol.[22]

Y'HUDA HALEVI

Of the three greatest medieval Hebrew poets, Solomon ibn Gabirol (1021–1053), Moses ibn Ezra (1055–after 1135), and Y'huda haLevi (1075–1141), only the last named lived, at least for some time, in Cordova. HaLevi was born in Toledo (or Tudela), was educated in Hebrew, Arabic, and medicine in Lucena, became a much-sought-after physician, a Jewish philosopher, and one of the greatest, if not the greatest, Hebrew poet of all ages.

By the early twelfth century Cordova had lost much of its earlier grandeur, having gone through a period of frequently changing rules. After the fall of the Umayyad caliphate in 1031, Cordova became a republic, then it came successively under Sevillan ʿAbbāsid, Almoravid, and Almohad rule, until it was conquered in 1236 by Ferdinand III of Castile. In Y'huda haLevi's time the city was under the Almoravids (from 1091 to 1148), but was still a center of Jewish culture, as can be seen from the fact that poetry-writing contests, in emulation of such meetings of Arab poets, were held there. HaLevi participated in such a contest, won it by imitating a complicated poem of his older contemporary, Moses ibn Ezra, who was at the top of his form and fame at the time. This led to a friendship between the two, and haLevi spent some time with Ibn Ezra in the latter's luxurious home in Granada, leading a life of ease and pleasures, and writing wine and love songs and paeans. After spending some years in Toledo where he practiced medicine, and also engaged in trade and was active in community affairs, haLevi took up travel, and together with his much younger friend and kinsman, Abraham ibn Ezra (1098–1164), the famous poet, grammarian, and Bible commentator, he wandered through the cities of Muslim Spain and North Africa. HaLevi loved Spain, but dreamt of Zion, and longed to see it. In 1140 he set out on his pilgrimage, embarked for Alexandria, and was induced to stay there and in Cairo. He died in Egypt just as he was about to sail for the Holy Land.

HaLevi's philosophy is set forth in his Arabic *Kitāb al-Ḥujja wa al-Dalīl fī Naṣr al-Dīn al-Dhalīl* ("The Book of Argument and Evidence in Defense of the Despised Religion"), which became famous in the Hebrew translation of Y'huda ibn Tibbon (ca. 1120–after 1190), commonly known as *The Book of the Kuzari*. HaLevi worked on this book for many years, and completed it only shortly before his death. In it he describes a religious disputation which took place before the king of the Khazars among one representative each of Aristotelian philosophy, Islam, Christianity, and Judaism (see above). His own philosophical arguments in favor of Judaism are put in the mouth of the Jewish scholar-disputant. This framework enables haLevi to refute the arguments and points of view of the three non-Jewish spokesmen, and to expand on the superiority of the Jewish faith, which is based on tradition, prophecy, and immediate religious experience. The prophet, he explains, experiences directly the Presence of God, the Shekhina, as an intermediary being between God and man. It was mainly because of this element in the *Kuzari* that it became influential in Kabbalistic circles and in Hasidism.

However, the essential greatness of haLevi lies not in his philosophy but in his poetry. Regrettably, his greatness as a poet must be taken on faith by those not sufficiently at home in Hebrew to enjoy it in the original. This, of course, is the case with poetry in any foreign language, but it is most pronounced in medieval Hebrew poetry, and especially in that of Y'huda haLevi, due to his frequent reliance for effect on a peculiar use of biblical expressions, on a subtle change he introduces into their original meaning, on his use of the same morpheme in two or even three senses, and on his unsurpassed mastery of cadence, assonance, rhyme, and strophic structure, play on sound, and depth of feeling expressed in the most appropriate choice of words. The translations of haLevi into other languages do not approximate the unique quality of the original. HaLevi's *zajal*-type poems, I am convinced, surpass in their beauty and artistry the finest *zajal*s produced by the Arab poets of the Spanish Golden Age.

In addition to love poems (some of them highly erotic), haLevi wrote poems of eulogy, friendship, and lament, opening, as in the classical Arabic *qaṣīda*s, with descriptions of nature, gardens, wine, the night, etc. He also wrote a great number of *piyyuṭim*, religious poems, often reflecting the tragic events suffered by his people. Several of these are considered the greatest in Jewish religious poetry after the Psalms. A special category is represented by his "Songs of Zion," which express his love for Eretz Israel in the form of majestic elegies. In these haLevi reveals a unique combination of poetic power, feeling, and yearning for the land of his fathers and for his people's redemption.

MAIMONIDES

It is time now to turn to the third of the three greatest sons of Cordova, the first two of whom were discussed earlier in this chapter. He was Moses ben Maimon (1135–1204), better known as Maimonides, or by the acrostic of his name Rambam (from Rabbi Moshe Ben Maimon).

The paternal ancestors of Maimonides, including his father Rabbi Maimon, were *dayyan*s, rabbinical judges, in Cordova for several generations. Maimonides was initiated into Jewish scholarship by his father, whose instruction seems to have continued even after his thirteenth birthday, when Cordova fell to the Almohads who issued an edict of forced conversion to Islam. As a result Rabbi Maimon and his family were forced to leave the city. After a period of eight to nine years spent in wanderings, they settled in Fez, Morocco, in 1160, which they probably were induced to do because at that time the aged Almohad ruler, ʿAbd al-Mu'min (reigned 1133–1163) eased his attitude toward the *dhimmī*s resident in central Morocco.

By that time Maimonides was a young scholar of outstanding accomplishments, having acquired medical education, embarked upon writing an Arabic commentary on the Mishna, written a short treatise on the Jewish calendar and another on logic, and started also on halakhic works. Muslim literary sources claim that sometime between 1150 and 1160 the Maimon family formally converted to Islam, an assertion which is, however, open to serious doubt. In any case it is interesting to note that Rabbi Maimon's attitude toward outward conversion, which at times was the only way for a Jew to save his life, was extremely liberal. In his "Letter of Consolation" he assures the many Jews who under pressure underwent formal conversion that those who recited even the shortest prayers, even in Arabic, and did good works, remained Jews. Maimonides himself took a stricter view on the matter, and in his "Letter on Forced Conversion" urged the Jews who lived in countries where they were forced to adopt Islam to emigrate rather than convert.

In 1165 the family arrived in Acre, Palestine, toured the Holy Land, and then went on to Egypt, where Rabbi Maimon died. Maimonides settled in Fusṭāṭ (Old Cairo) and devoted himself to his studies, while being supported by his elder brother David, a gem merchant. In 1169 David ben Maimon perished in a shipwreck in the Indian Ocean. The shock of the tragedy incapacitated Maimonides for a full year, and after his recovery he decided to take up medical practice for livelihood, while continuing all the time with his scholarly work. His rise to high position was slow to come. In 1177 he was elected official head of the Fusṭāṭ Jewish community, and in 1185 appointed one of the physicians to al-Fāḍil, the vizier of Saladin and virtual ruler of Egypt.

It was in the midst of these activities that Maimonides wrote his two greatest works: the *Mishne Tora* ("Second Tora"), also known as *Yad ha-Ḥazaqa* ("The Strong Hand"), which is his great halakhic compendium (completed in 1180), and his famous *Guide of the Perplexed* (in 1190), one of the greatest philosophical works of the Middle Ages, and certainly the greatest medieval Jewish work of philosophy. From a remarkable, brief description of his workday, contained in a letter Maimonides wrote to Samuel ibn Tibbon (ca. 1160–ca. 1230), the translator of the *Guide* from Arabic into Hebrew, we learn that every weekday in the early morning he rode to the vizier's palace (he calls the ruler "sultan") in Cairo, to spend most of the day administering to the health of the members of the household, then in the afternoon he returned to Fusṭāṭ where until late at night he saw patients, Jews and Arabs, until complete exhaustion overtook him. From the same letter we also learn that the "sultan" respected the Jewish Sabbath on which he would forego the services of Maimonides who spent the weekly day of rest praying, issuing instructions to the members of the Jewish congregation who would gather in his home, and leading them in religious studies.

In the midst of this overburdening daily routine, Maimonides found time and energy not only to write the two great, and quite different, works mentioned above, but, towards the end of his life when he was tired and ailing, to compose no less than ten medical books (in Arabic) on subjects such as drugs, hemorrhoids, sexual intercourse, asthma, poisons and their antidotes, maintenance of good health, etc. His fame among Muslim physicians was great, and one of his Arab patients wrote, "Galen's art heals only the body, but Abū ᶜImrān's [Maimonides'] the body and the soul. His knowledge made him the physician of the century . . ."[23] In addition to all this, he was a highly competent astronomer, and a prolific correspondent whose many letters reveal a warm, human, compassionate personality, very different from the picture of the aloof and austere rationalist conveyed by his *Yad* and *Guide*.

Of the huge and many-sided literary output of Maimonides we can dwell only on the *Guide*, and even then so briefly we can do no justice to it. It opens with a discussion of biblical expressions apt to be theological pitfalls because of their anthropomorphisms, then proceeds to discuss the nature of God, and especially the vexing problem of the divine attributes. Next follows the presentation of proofs that, despite Aristotle, the world was created by God (as stated in the Bible). After an analysis of the nature of prophecy, Divine Providence is discussed, which is followed by an analysis of the purpose of the Law in general and of individual laws in particular, whereby their educational intent is stressed. Two of the last three chapters outline the higher religion of the "perfect man," which consists of true knowledge of God, and is identical with the "Love of God." Throughout the book Maimonides stresses that he could not disclose everything, creating the impression that he possessed much additional esoteric knowledge not divulged in the *Guide*.[24]

The influence of Maimonides was so great that in his lifetime he triggered one of the greatest controversies ever to engulf the Jewish world. Seeds of a difference between rationalists and anti-rationalists among the Jewish religious scholars were present even before Maimonides, but it was the appearance of his two great works, the *Yad* and the *Guide* (the latter became accessible in 1204 in Samuel ibn Tibbon's Hebrew translation to Jews ignorant of Arabic) which brought it to the fore. Maimonides' opponents included the great sages of northern France, as well as Moses ben Naḥman (Nahmanides, 1194–ca. 1270) of Gerona, the great Kabbalistically inclined commentator, popularly known as the Ramban, who was opposed to the study of philosophy. Anti-Maimonidean feelings ran so high that his *Guide*, and even parts of his *Yad*, were put in *ḥerem* (ban), and his tomb in Tiberias was desecrated. While the ultraorthodox and Hasidic Jews still do not countenance a study of the *Guide*, the general attitude to Maimonides has crystallized in the saying, "From Moses to Moses [Maimonides] there has never arisen anybody like unto Moses."

ARAB AUTHORS VIEW JEWISH SCHOLARS

In this chapter we have spoken of Cordova and of the intellectual activities of the Muslims and the Jews centered on the city. We have also shown that Jewish literary and scholarly work reflected in many ways that which was created by the Muslims of that city and the country of which it was the capital. We have also spoken of the positions some prominent Jews achieved in the court and in Arab society as statesmen, diplomats, and doctors.[25] But we have barely touched upon the interrelationship between Jewish and Arab men of letters, and have not raised the question of whether the work done by the Jews was known to or appreciated by, the Arab literati. It is now time to fill this obvious hiatus by adducing at least some evidence to show the extent of the familiarity Arab men of letters of the period had with the work of their Jewish counterparts.

The fact is that in the Golden Age of Andalus Arab authors do occasionally refer to Jewish scholars, and quote them with approbation or criticize them. These references are in themselves sufficient to open a window from the Arab side of the intellectual give-and-take between Arabs and Jews, in which was anchored much of the literary, scholarly, philosophical, medical, and scientific achievements of that remarkable period. What the Jews learned from the Arabs has repeatedly been discussed in recent decades by Jewish scholars.[26] Less known, because less researched, is what the Arabs learned from the Jews and what they knew about the work of the Jewish scholars and writers who lived in their midst and used Arabic as their medium. The only exception is the Koran whose Jewish sources have been thoroughly researched, so that the Jewish influence on the Koran is one of the best-known subjects in the study of that unique fountainhead of Muslim religion and scholarship.[27]

Of the later Arab authors who drew on Jewish sources Abu al-Ḥasan ʿAlī ibn Ḥusayn al-Masʿūdī (died ca. 956) deserves mention. This famous Arab historian and geographer had no hesitation to seek information from Jews, Christians, Hindus, and other non-Muslims, and much of what he learned he incorporated into his works. Occasionally he supplies information about Jewish scholars not available in other sources. It is, for example, from Masʿūdī that we know that the Karaite scholar David Abū Sulaymān al-Qūmisī (died ca. 945) lived in Jerusalem and translated the Bible into Arabic, with explanations.[28]

Among the Arab scholars who entered into polemics with Jewish scholars was Ibn Ḥazm whose work we have discussed earlier in this chapter. He collected much information on the Jews (and the Christians), and was well informed on both the history and the actual state of their religions. In his *Kitāb al-Fiṣal* he outlined the various philosophical and religious systems for the purpose of criticizing them and thus to lead to the conclusion that the only true religion was Islam. He enters into sharp polemics with Samuel haNagid (see above), examines the various conceptions of prophecy in Judaism, finds the Jewish ideas of prophecy and law limited, and tries to find out the Jewish view on the doctrine of "abrogation," that uniquely Koranic concept according to which God issued commandments which He subsequently changed, that is, abrogated (see above).

However, when faced with an attack on the Koran, Ibn Ḥazm is unable to maintain the stance of the detached historian of religion, and becomes instead a vituperative polemicist. He dealt with Jews and Judaism in three works written at long intervals. When he learned that Samuel haNagid (whom he calls Ismāʿīl) had written a treatise against the Muslim claim that the Koran was of divine origin, he became virulent. Unable to obtain a copy of haNagid's book, Ibn Ḥazm used instead a treatise refuting it, written by a Muslim theologian, which quoted numerous excerpts from haNagid's argument. On the basis of these excerpts Ibn Ḥazm attacked, in the most unrestrained language, not only haNagid, but the Bible and the post-biblical sources of Judaism. He did this in several long parts of his major work, the *Fiṣal*, which was discussed above briefly. He makes sure that his readers understand why he singles out Samuel haNagid for his attack by stating that haNagid was "the most learned and most skilled in disputations" among the Jews. HaNagid had this reputation, as can also be seen from the references to him by Ṣaʿid al-Andalusī which will be presented below.

In Ibn Ḥazm's counterattack arguments against the Jews and their religious source books are intermixed. His prime purpose is not to persuade the Jews of the truth of Islam, but to undermine and demolish the reverence in which both Jews and Muslims held the Jewish Scriptures. He is at pains to prove that the biblical writings cannot be considered divinely inspired, that they abound in inconsistencies and contradictions, that they contain obvious mistakes in numbers, in geography, and in history, and that they are forgeries produced by Ezra the Scribe, an atheist and contemptible character, who lived in the days of the second Jewish kingdom. The Bible, moreover, Ibn Ḥazm argues, is replete with stories which are shocking, coarse, and immoral. Biblical characters are guilty of many sexual transgressions (e.g., Abraham marries his sister, Reuben violates his father's wife, Judah sleeps with his son's wife, Moses marries his aunt, etc.). Nor are the Talmudic sages better. Their beliefs are tainted with polytheism: Rabbi Ishmael is said to have encountered the Shekhina mourning over the destruction of Jerusalem. The "Rabbanites" among the Jews (in contradistinction from the Karaites) glorify Metatron, *al-rabb al-ṣaghīr* ("the little Lord") on the Day of Atonement; it was they who bribed Paul and sent him to mislead the early Christians by teaching them to believe in the divinity of Jesus, etc.

Ibn Ḥazm also adduces quotes from the Talmud to prove that it was compiled by atheists. In sum, Judaism is the "most contemptible of religions, the most vile of faiths."

Ibn Ḥazm's low opinion of the ancient Jews and the writings they produced is paralleled by his contempt for his own Jewish contemporaries. In writing about them he repeatedly resorts to vilification. He writes, the Jews are a "filthy, stinking, dirty crew beset with God's anger and malediction, with humiliation and wretchedness, misfortune, filth and dirt, as no other people has ever been." "Among minds, theirs are like the odor of garlic among odors."[29]

Ibn Ḥazm's venom against Jews and Judaism is, it appears, based on one of the two major factors which turned Arab religious thinkers against them. This factor was the hate-filled contempt anchored in the religious conviction that the Jews in refusing to acknowledge Muhammad and accept Islam, the only true religion, were viciously and stubbornly persisting in their sinful ways, and therefore deserved nothing but contempt and humiliation. The other factor was operative especially in places where some Jews rose to high positions. It was the rage at their affluence, dominance, and their lording it over the believers. Of the effects of this motivation we have seen some examples in chapter 3, and some more will be adduced in chapter 5. Here let me add one example from the Andalusian Golden Age.

Granada in the eleventh century had a majority of Jews in its population, and the Berber rulers of that ministate had no choice but to rely heavily on them. This situation was reflected in the Arabic designation of the city as *Gharnāṭat al-Yahūd*, "Granada of the Jews," and led to strong anti-Jewish agitation among the Arabs, and especially in the Arab states which were embroiled in armed struggle against the Jewish-commanded Granadan army. Among the most vociferous was Abū Isḥāq al-Ilbīrī (died 1067), a native of Elvira (hence his *nisba*, by-name), a jurist and a poet, whose ire was aroused by the influence of the Jews in Granada, and especially by the powerful position held by the Jewish vizier and general Samuel haNagid, and by his son Joseph, who succeeded him in the vizierate in 1056/7. It was, in all probability, due to the influence of Joseph haNagid (1035–1066) that King Bādis of Granada imposed internal exile on Abū Isḥāq confining him to forced residence in the Sierra de Elvira. In his rage, Abū Isḥāq composed a bitter and biting poem against the Jews, in which he reproaches King Bādis for having made an infidel his *kātib* (secretary), and says about the Jews in general that "the earth trembles from their immorality." He exclaims, "many a pious Muslim is in awe of the vilest infidel ape (*qird*)."[30] He reproaches the Jews in general for living in luxury, and the Jewish minister in particular for having become exceedingly rich. Therefore, Abū Isḥāq exhorts his readers, "hasten to slaughter him [Joseph] as a sacrifice, and offer him, fat ram that he is."[31]

Joseph haNagid grew up as the son of the powerful vizier and was appointed at the age of twenty-one to the position left vacant by his father's death. Although he was a man of great talents and rendered signal service to the kingdom of Granada, he lacked the wisdom of his father, indulged in luxurious living, was arrogant, disliked, and openly censured. He gave sumptuous banquets in his luxurious palace, and one of his Muslim critics told the king that "the pig [i.e., Joseph] built a palace better than yours." Joseph, in addition, was also accused of trying to establish a separate Jewish principality. All this led to great resentment among the Muslims over the suspension of the *dhull*, humiliation, of the Jews through the rise of the Jewish courtiers. However, to complete the picture, one should add that other Arab sources give due recognition to the high attainments of this same Joseph haNagid, who, in addition to being a great patron of Hebrew scholars and literati, also had an excellent Islamic library.[32]

Students of Andalusian history assume that Abū Isḥāq's anti-Jewish poem could have had a role in bringing about the 1066 Muslim attack on the Jews of Granada in which three thousand Jews, among them Joseph haNagid, were killed. Although soon afterward the Jews returned for a short time to a position of influence in Granada, in 1090, when the Almoravids conquered the city, the Jewish community was destroyed, and from 1148 to 1212 (during the Almohad regime) conversion to Islam was the price Jews had to pay for permission to dwell in the city.[33]

ṢĀʿID AL-ANDALUSĪ

A younger contemporary of Ibn Ḥazm was Abu al-Qāsim Ṣāʿid ibn Aḥmad ibn ʿAbd al-Raḥmān (1029–1070), better known as Ṣāʿid al-Andalusī (i.e., "The Andalusian"), of whose literary output only one small book survived. He was born in the city of Almeria, in his youth set out to study science in Muslim Spain, was possibly a disciple of the famous Ibn Ḥazm, and certainly of the traditionist Abū Muḥammad al-Qāsim ibn al-Fatḥ. At the age of eighteen he went to Toledo to study exact sciences under al-Waqashī and al-Tujībī. In the course of his studies he became acquainted with Jewish scholars both in Toledo and in Saragossa. He served as *qāḍī* in Toledo, and wrote a treatise on astronomy (title unknown), a universal history entitled *Compilations on the History of the Arab and Foreign Peoples*, a study on the various religions of man (title unknown), a *History of Andalus*, and a *History of Islam* (all lost). Finally, in 1068, he wrote his *Ṭabaqāt al-Umam* ("Categories of Nations"), which is extant. This book shows that al-Andalusī was burdened neither by racial nor by religious prejudices, which becomes especially evident in his impartial and objective description of the Jewish people and the work and character of Jewish scholars.

The *Ṭabaqāt al-Umam* owes its survival to the popularity it achieved. It was known under various titles, and later Arab historians quoted it in several of their works. The book opens with a discussion of the seven nations or groups of nations mankind originally comprised: 1. The Persians; 2. The Chaldeans; 3. The Greeks, Romans, Franks, Galicians, Burjan, Slavs, Russians, Bulgars, Alains, etc.; 4. The Copts, Sudanese, Abyssinians, Nubians, Zanj, Berbers, etc.; 5. The Turkic tribes; 6. The Hindus, the Sind, and their neighbors; 7. The Chinese and the peoples of the Amur, the Children of Japhet son of Noah. Next he divides the nations of the world into two categories: those who have cultivated the sciences, and those who have despised them. The first category consists of eight nations: the Hindus, Persians, Chaldeans, Hebrews, Greeks, Rum, Egyptians, and Arabs. After discussing in one chapter those nations which have not cultivated the sciences, he devotes one chapter each to science among the Indians, Persians, Chaldeans, Greeks, Rum, Egyptians, Arabs, and Jews.

What follows is my full literal translation of the chapter on the Jews, based on the undated Arabic original of the *Ṭabaqāt al-Umam*, printed in Cairo.[34]

The Sciences Among the Children of Israel

As for the eighth nation, they are the Children of Israel, and they have not become famous in the sciences of philosophy; however, their concern was with the sciences of religious law (*sharīʿa*) and the biographies of the prophets. Their scholars are the most learned of men in the knowledge of the prophets and the beginning of Creation, and it is from them that the scholars of the Muslims, such as ʿAbd Allāh ibn ʿAbbās and Kaʿb al-Aḥbār and Wahb ibn Munabbih, took it.

And behold, they have a very precise calculation of the times of their law (*sharīʿa*) and of their affairs. I do not know whether it is from the dating of their scholars or was arranged for them by some of the other scholars. And they call[35] these calculations of theirs *ʿibbur* [Hebrew: intercalation]. And their months are lunar and their year is defective and is intercalated. And the defective [year] is lunar, and the intercalation is solar. And they call every nineteen years the beginning of their dating, *maḥzūr* [Hebrew: *maḥzor*, cycle], and it is the number at which the fractions of the year become complete and in which seven months accumulate.[36] And they add from it one month to the third, eighth, eleventh, fourteenth, seventeenth, and nineteenth year of the *maḥzūr*, and these years become the seven solar intercalated years, each of them having thirteen lunar months. And the duration of their lunar year is of 354 days and eight hours and 876 minutes of the minutes of one hour which contains 1080 minutes.[37] And the duration of the solar year is for them 365 days and one quarter of a day precisely. And thus the solar year exceeds the defective lunar year by ten days and 21 hours and 204 minutes.[38] And the beginning of the first year of the 255th *maḥzūr*, [counted] from the beginning of the world, is for the Jews the beginning of the year 4827 of the date of Adam, upon him be peace, which is the year 458 of the Hijra and 1066 Masīḥiyya [i.e., of the Christian calendar].

And this nation is the home of prophecy and source of the apostolate to the children of Adam, and of most of the prophets, upon them be Allah's grace and peace. And their dwelling place was the land of Shām [Syria], and there lived their first and second kingdom until Titus, the Roman king, at the end exiled them from there, and destroyed their kingdom, and dispersed their people, and they were separated in the countries, and scattered to the four winds, and they were scattered here and there, in the regions, and there is no place in the inhabited world in which they are not present, in the east of the earth, and its west, and its south, and its north, except for the Island of the Arabs [the Arabian Peninsula], for ʿUmar ibn al-Khaṭṭāb—may Allah be pleased with him—expelled them from there, for the Prophet, may Allah bless him and grant him salvation, commanded this with his word, "there should not remain two religions in the Land of the Arabs." And after they were scattered in the countries, and entered among the nations, the endeavors of a few of them were stirred to seek the theoretical sciences and to acquire mental excellences. And a few of them obtained what they wanted in the various wisdoms.

And there was among them in the empire of Islam, of those who became famous in the art of medicine, Māsarjuwayh[39] the physician who was entrusted by ᶜUmar ibn ᶜAbd al-ᶜAzīz, may Allah be pleased with him, with the translation of the book of Aharan al-Qāṣṣ [Aaron the preacher or the priest][40] about medicine, and it is an excellent compendium, one of the finest of the ancient compendia.

And of them was thereafter among the recent ones Isḥāq ibn Sulaymān,[41] a disciple of Isḥāq ibn ᶜImrān, who is known as *samm sāᶜa* ("Instant Poison").[42] He was an outstanding physician who served in medicine ᶜAbd Allāh al-Mahdī, the master of Ifriqīyya (Africa). He, moreover, possessed knowledge in logic, and was an expert in the varieties of science. He reached a very high age, beyond a hundred years. He never took a wife, and did not acquire property. He authored excellent works, among them a book on foods and a book on fevers, which has no equal, and a book on urine, and a book on elements, and a book on definitions and prescriptions, and a book known as "Garden of Wisdom" on the questions of metaphysics. And he died close to the year 320 [ca. 932 C.E.].

And of them [the Jews] among the astrologists is Sahl ibn Bishr Ḥabīb,[43] the author of fine studies, known in the sciences, among them his book on the *mawlads* [the monthly conjunctions of the moon with the sun], and the Book of Revolutions of the Years of the World, and the Book of Questions and Choices.

And in the gate of Andalus there was of them [the Jews] a community. And of those who were preoccupied with the art of medicine was Ḥasdai ibn Isḥāq,[44] an attendant of al-Ḥakam ibn ᶜAbd al-Raḥmān al-Nāṣir al-Dīn Allāh, and he was diligent in the art of medicine, outstanding in the science of the *sharīᶜa* (religious law) of the Jews. And he was the first to open the door of their science to the people of Andalus among them [the Jews] in jurisprudence and history, and other subjects. And before him they [the Jews] were forced to depend in the law of their religion, and in the dating of their history, and in fixing the dates of their holidays, on the Jews of Baghdad, and they had to bring from them the calculation of the time of the years, and they set accordingly the beginnings of their time periods, and the start of their years. And after Ḥasdai became established with al-Ḥakam and obtained from him the utmost favor with the abundance of his skill and his utmost capability and his refinement, he was given leave to import those of the books of the Jews in the East which he wanted, and then he taught the Jews of Andalus that of which formerly they had been ignorant, and he relieved them of that of which they all had suffered.

Thereafter there was in the *fitna* (civil war)[45] Manaḥam (M'naḥem) ibn al-Fawāl,[46] an inhabitant of Saragossa. He was most distinguished in the medical art, and with it a master of the art of logic, and the other sciences of philosophy. He has a treatise titled *Kanz al-Muqill* ("The Treasure of the Pauper"), arranged in the form of questions and answers, and it contains the totality of the rules of logic and the fundamentals of physics.

And with him was in Saragossa Marwān ibn Jannāḥ,[47] of the people of interest in the art of logic and wide knowledge in the science of the languages of the Arabs and the Jews. He has an excellent treatise on the preparation of the simple medicaments and the limitation of the quantities of the weights and measures to be employed in the medical art.

And of them was Isḥāq ibn Qusṭār,[48] a servant of al-Muwaffaq Mujāhid al-ᶜĀmirī,[49] and his son Iqbāl al-Dawla ᶜAlī. He was an expert in the sources of medicine, was knowledgeable in the science of logic, a master of the doctrines of the philosophers. He was praiseworthy in his ways, most gracious in the manner in which he comported himself in society, and I never saw among the Jews one like him in equanimity and sincerity, and the perfection of his manliness (*muruwwa*). He was an expert in the science of the Hebrew language, had mastery in the law (*fiqh*) of the Jews, and was an expert in their lore. He died in Toledo in the year 448 [ca. 1056 C.E.], when he was seventy-five years old. He never had a wife.

And of them was thereafter from among the people of great meticulousness in parts of the science of philosophy Sulaymān ibn Yaḥyā, who is known as Ibn Jabirwāl,[50] of the inhabitants of Saragossa. He went to great pains in the art of logic, was refined of intellect, keen of discernment, and very guarded. He died at the age of a little over thirty in the year 450 (ca. 1058 C.E.).

And of them was in our own times Abu al-Faḍl Ḥasdai ibn Yūsuf ibn Ḥasdai,[51] an inhabitant of the city of Saragossa, of a noble house of the Jews in Andalus, from among the children of the Prophet Moses, upon him be peace. He was preoccupied with the sciences according to their grades, and the comprehension of skills through their methods. He acquired the science of the Arabic tongue, and took an ample share in the art of poetry and of rhetoric. He also excelled in the science of arithmetic and the science of geometry and astronomy, and he understood the art of music and made an effort to practice it. And he mastered the science of logic, and he pursued research and observation. Thereafter he advanced to the science of physics, and started it with the Book of Nature of Aristotle, until he mastered it. Thereafter he started on the Book of Heaven and the World. And when I parted from him in the year 458 [ca. 1065 C.E.], he had already penetrated its mystery. And if he will have enough time, and if the zeal continues to burn in him, he will become perfect in the art of philosophy and will embrace all the branches of science. And since he is still a young man he has not yet reached the pinnacle of his strength, except that Allah, may He be exalted, favors with His grace whom He wants. And these are the celebrated men of the Hebrews among us who are adepts in the science of philosophy.

And as for the scholars in the *sharīʿa* (religious law) of the Jews, they are too to be counted in the east of the earth and its west. The best known of them from among the people of the east is Saʿīd ibn Yaʿqūb al-Fayyūmī,[52] and the writer Abū Kathīr al-Ṭābarānī,[53] and Dā'ūd al-Qūmisī,[54] and Ibrāhīm al-Tustarī,[55] and those who follow their course from among the rabbis of the Jews who are engaged in arguments with the *mutakallimūn*,[56] in order to gain perfection in the art of dialectic and of discussing opinions. And of them was in Andalus Abū Ibrāhīm ibn Ismāʿīl ibn Yūsuf the secretary, known as Ibn al-Ghazāl,[57] attendant of the Amīr Bāris [read: Bādis] ibn Ḥabūs al-Ṣanhājī, king of Granada and its provinces. He was the governor of the state, and he had knowledge in the *sharīʿa* (religious law) of the Jews, and knew how to lead it to victory, and defend it, more than anybody else among the people of Andalus before him. He died in the year 448 (ca. 1056 C.E.).

Al-Andalusī's brief excursus on the Jews and their scholars is noteworthy on several counts. First of all, he gives full credit to the Children of Israel as the fountainhead of knowledge about the early prophets and the "beginning of Creation," that is, the early history of mankind, and acknowledges that this knowledge was acquired by the Muslims from the Jews. Of the three scholars whom he mentions as having "taken" their information from the Jews, the first, ʿAbd Allāh ibn ʿAbbās (619–686/8), was perhaps the greatest scholar of the first generation of the Muslims, whose teaching included frequent references to pre-Islamic history. The second, Kaʿb al-Aḥbār (died 652/3), was a Yemenite Jew who converted to Islam, probably in 638, and became the first and foremost authority on Judeo-Islamic traditions. His surname Aḥbār is derived from the Hebrew *ḥaver* meaning "scholar," a title close to that of rabbi. His original name may have been ʿAqīva (Akiba) or Yaʿaqov (Jacob). He had a profound familiarity with the Bible as well as South Arabian tradition, and introduced numerous Jewish legends into Muslim religious consciousness.

The third scholar mentioned by al-Andalusī, Wahb ibn Munabbih (flourished soon after the Hijra), was also a converted Jew of Persian descent, who was the originator of many legends on Cain and Abel, and on the angel Gabriel, God's divine messenger in revealing the Koran to Muhammad. Wahb also wrote down numerous legends of South Arabian origin about Hūd, the pre-Islamic Arab prophet. He had a thorough knowledge of Jewish traditions and of *Isrā'īliyyāt*, that is, stories of "Israelite" origin, and was the author of numerous books. He often followed the biblical sources quite closely. Although there is some question as to his original Jewishness, these facts seem to bear out the statements of the *Fihrist* (p. 22) and of Ibn Khaldūn that he was originally Jewish.[58]

Surprising is the detailed and precise knowledge al-Andalusī has of the intricacies of the Jewish solar-lunar calendar, which had received its final shape only about a century prior to his lifetime.[59] More importantly, al-Andalusī fully recognizes the Jewish nation as the originator of prophecy and apostolate to all mankind, knows of the two Jewish kingdoms prior and following the Babylonian exile, and their actual state of dispersal all over the world.

Most significant, however, is what al-Andalusī has to say about the Jewish scholars in the Arab lands of the East and the West, and especially about his contemporaries in Andalus. He mentions by name, and characterizes briefly, no less than fourteen Jewish scholars. He knows the role Ḥasdai ibn Shaprut played in transplanting Jewish scholarship from Iraq to Andalus, and in making the Jews of Andalus religiously independent of Baghdad. He is an especially great admirer of the physician and philosopher Isḥāq ibn Qusṭār, and discloses that he was a personal friend of the poet, mathematician, astronomer, musician, logician and physicist Abu al-Faḍl Ḥasdai ibn Yūsuf, whom he characterizes as already a veritable polyhistor at the young age of twenty-five. All in all, the picture that emerges from al-Andalusī's brief comments on Jewish physicians, scientists, scholars, poets, and philosophers in Arab Spain is one of a group of outstanding, creative individuals in all the intellectual endeavors the Muslims engaged in, and, moreover, is a picture painted with fairness, sympathy, and even admiration. Al-Andalusī's account shows that there were among the Muslim men of letters of Andalus at least some who looked upon their Jewish colleagues as fellow scientists and scholars, and not as members of the lowly *dhimmī* class. On the level of high intellectual activity, there was, at least occasionally, mutual recognition and cooperation between Muslims and Jews, and appreciation of each others' work.

5

Yemen and Morocco: A Study in Contrast

Glancing through the criminal statistics in Israel, made regularly available by the Central Bureau of Statistics in Jerusalem, one is struck by a remarkable set of data: of all the Oriental Jewish communities the lowest criminality is that of the Yemenite Jews, while the highest is that of the Jews originating in Morocco. While the terms "lowest" and "highest" do not say much in themselves, consider these concrete figures for 1970: of every one thousand adult Jews born in Morocco about sixteen were convicted in that year for what the Israeli statistical publications term "grievous offenses," which include murder, assault, robbery, and the like. The corresponding figure for Yemenite Jews in that year was 5.4, that is, about one-third of the former. For comparison let me add that the figure for European- and American-born Jews was 3.[1] As for juvenile delinquency, the differences between the Yemenite and Moroccan figures were (and are) even greater, and, as a matter of fact, among the Yemenites they are lower than among Israeli Jews of European extraction.[2]

These figures certainly tell us something significant about the sociocultural environments in which the two communities in question had lived prior to their arrival in Israel. The mass immigration of Yemenite Jews to Israel took place in 1949–50 when the so-called "Operation Magic Carpet" brought some 45,000 of them to Israel in what they considered a quasi-messianic flight from slavery to freedom. From Morocco 32,000 Jews came at the same time, followed by another 70,000 in 1954–56, when the imminence of Moroccan independence made emigration seem desirable in the eyes of many. All in all, from May 15, 1948, when Israel achieved her independence, to the end of 1970, 46,000 Jews from Yemen and 4,000 from neighboring Aden settled in Israel. In the same period 253,000 Jews came from Morocco,[3] making the Moroccan Jews by far the largest Jewish ethnic group in Israel from any Arab country.

Let us now have a closer look at the history and social condition of these two Jewish communities in their Arab environments, the relationship between them and the majority population, and their psychological reaction to the circumstances in which they had lived until their emigration, that is, *ʿaliya*, to Israel.

THE JEWS IN YEMEN

Yemen, or the general area in which it is located in the southwestern corner of the Arabian Peninsula, was known to the Romans under the name of Arabia Felix, or "Happy Arabia," in contrast to the northern part of the peninsula which they called Arabia Petraea, or "Stony Arabia." Since Yemen lies at the northern edge of the monsoon belt, it receives enough rain in the summer—16–32 inches annually—to make its central highlands the most fertile (happy) part of all Arabia. The low-lying coastal strip, the Tihāma, is humid and hot, and rather infertile, while in the highlands the summers are pleasantly temperate and the winters cool. Ṣanʿā', the capital of what today is the Republic of Yemen (or North Yemen), is located at an altitude of 7,260 feet. North Yemen has an area of 75,000 square miles, with a population of some 5.5 million, while Saudi Arabia, with its 873,000 square miles, supports only an estimated 8 to 10 million people.

The history of Yemen dates from the early first millennium B.C.E. Pre-Islamic Yemen witnessed the rise and fall of three major peoples, the Minaeans, Sabaeans, and Himyarites. Jews settled in Yemen, in all probability, in the first century B.C.E. In the second to fourth centuries C.E., those of the Jewish inhabitants of Yemen who had the means to do so sent their dead to be buried in the Land of Israel, in the Beth Shearim catacombs not far from Haifa. It seems that the custom was to exhume the remains about a year after burial, put the bones into ossuaries, and send them off by caravan or ship to Eretz Israel for secondary burial. In the early sixth century the Himyarite king Yūsuf Ashʿar Dhū Nuwās embraced Judaism, fought against the Christian Abyssinians, and was killed in a battle with them in 525.

The people of Yemen were converted to Islam still in the lifetime of Muhammad. A Yemenite Jew, Kaʿb al-Aḥbār, who converted to Islam probably in 638 (see chapter 4), accompanied the Caliph ʿUmar to Jerusalem in 636, and was a vigorous champion of the next caliph, ʿUthmān.

Kaᶜb was a scholar of great reputation, whose statements about ᶜUmar were accepted by Muslim traditionists without question. In later times, a great many Judeo-Muslim traditions were attributed to him.[4]

A generation later lived Wahb ibn Munabbih, a Jew of Ṣanᶜā' (born ca. 656, died ca. 732/38), who also converted to Islam, served as *qāḍī*, and became one of the most prominent early Muslim traditionists, that is, transmitters of sayings attributed to the Prophet Muhammad. Wahb was, in addition, one of the most important sources of the so-called *Isrā'īliyyāt*, tales about biblical personages mentioned, often only briefly, in the Koran, and about other events from the history of biblical Israel.[5]

From 897 on Yemen was gradually conquered by the Zaydīs, a Shīᶜite sect, whose *imāms* were to rule the country for a thousand years, until overthrown by the revolution of 1962. During the Middle Ages the Jews of Yemen maintained contact with the two great Jewish centers of Baghdad, Iraq, and Fusṭāṭ, Egypt. At the same time the Jews who lived in Aden, the port city of the southwestern tip of the Arabian Peninsula, had an active share in the trade with India. At this period, some Jews in Yemen must have been quite wealthy, as can be concluded from the fact that the Jews of a single village, Juwwa, in the Aden district, sent several hundreds of dinars to Jews in Egypt, and donated over a hundred dinars to the school of Maimonides.

Famous is the "Epistle to Yemen" of Maimonides (written ca. 1172) in which the great leader of Egyptian Jewry deals with the Jewish belief in the advent of the Messiah. This letter was written in response to an inquiry sent by the Yemenite Jewish leader Jacob ben Nethanel, who sought authoritative advice from Maimonides when the Yemenite Jews were faced with the messianic claims of a man from their own midst. Messianic expectations and movements in Yemen, as in other Jewish communities, were often the spontaneous popular reactions to persecutions. In 1165, the *imām* ᶜAbd al-Nabī ibn Mahdī initiated a campaign, led by a converted Jew, to force the Jews to adopt Islam. These persecutions resulted in the first of several messianic movements among the Yemenite Jews, which prompted Jacob ben Nethanel to turn to Maimonides for guidance.

A pseudo-Messiah appeared in neighboring Ḥaḍramawt (today part of the People's Democratic Republic of Yemen, or South Yemen) in 1495, and in the first half of the seventeenth century there were again very strong messianic expectations in Yemen itself. When the news of the appearance of Shabbatai Zevi (1626–1676) reached Yemen, it aroused an ecstatic movement, which, in turn, resulted in bloody persecution by the ruling *imām* Ismāᶜīl. The Jews were severely punished, exorbitant fines were imposed upon them, some of them died of starvation, while others converted to Islam.

In the nineteenth century no less than three pseudo-Messiahs arose in Yemen. One was Judah ben Shalom, known as Shukr Kuḥayl, whose messianic claim, based on a dream, found credence also among Muslims, with the result that he was murdered at the order of the *imām*. A few years later another messianic claimant pretended to be the resurrected Shukr, and married Shukr's divorced wife. The third was Joseph ben ᶜAbd Allāh, whose depravities and immoralities were reminiscent of those of Jacob Frank in eighteenth-century East Europe. It is not unlikely that the beliefs of the ruling Zaydī sect, which also expected the appearance of an *imām*-redeemer, created among the Yemenite Jews a particular receptivity to messianic movements, although the unrelenting oppression to which they were exposed would in itself have been sufficient to explain why messianic movements agitated the Yemenite Jews more than other Jewish communities.

For hundreds of years the fate of Yemenite Jews was to suffer periodic persecutions and constant oppression. An early fifteenth-century Arab historian supplies some data about the restrictions imposed upon the Yemenite Jews in his days:

> They must adopt an appearance by which they become distinguishable, wherein lies humiliation (*ṣaghār*), consisting of side-locks, wearing a badge, and cutting the middle of the forelock. They are not to ride an ass-saddle, but only sideways. They will not openly perform their religious rites, except in their synagogues. They will not build a new synagogue, but can renovate that which has fallen into ruin. They must dwell only in their quarters, except by permission of the Muslims, for some business . . . They must not ride horses or raise their houses over those of the Muslims. They must sell a Muslim slave they have bought or owned in any way . . .[6]

These regulations were essentially identical with those contained in the Covenant of ᶜUmar (see chapter 3), and they remained, by and large, in force until the emigration of the Yemenite Jews in 1948–49.

These rules were not the only ones the Yemenite Jews had to observe. There were several more whose intent was clearly to make sure that the Jews could never for a moment forget that they were tolerated pariah people whose life was a series of humiliations. For instance, they were not allowed to decorate their doors, to wind the turban more than threefold and to let its end hang loose, to let their hair hang down, and to wear silver and gold seal-rings. When passing a Muslim, a Jew had to get off his ass, and get the Muslim's permission to remount.[7]

After the Ottoman conquest of Yemen, and particularly of Ṣanᶜā' (1546), the Jews became victims of the conflict between the Sunnī Turks and the Zaydī Yemenites. The *imām* al-Muṭahhar accused the Jews of treachery in aiding the Turks, and persecuted the Jews of Ṣanᶜā' (1586). Among the milder rules reimposed at the time was one which provided that the Jews had to wear special garb and headgear. In South Yemen bloody persecutions and forced conversions followed in 1618, instigated this time by the Turkish governor of the province. In 1676 the *imām* Aḥmad ibn Ḥasan al-Mahdī decreed the destruction of all the synagogues and later ordered all the Jews to convert to Islam. When they refused, he expelled (in 1680) the Jews from the Yemenite highlands to Mawzaᶜ in the Tihāma, where they faced starvation and disease. A year later, when the survivors were allowed to return, they found most of their homes destroyed or occupied by Muslims, so that they were obliged to seek or build new lodgings. This was the origin of the new Jewish quarter in Ṣanᶜā' which the Jews continued to occupy until 1949.

In addition to the living quarters, this new *qāᶜa al-Yahūd* also contained the Jewish *sūq*s (bazaars), notably the silver market where the Jewish silversmiths worked and sold the jewelry they produced, the abattoir, the markets of the blacksmiths, the grape sellers, the grain merchants, the plasterers, the old-clothes sellers, and, of course, numerous synagogues.

Conditions in the provincial towns were worse than in the capital. There life proved so precarious for the Jews in 1717–25 that they either had to assimilate to the Muslim community or leave.[8]

During the drought and famine of the early eighteenth century the *imām* succeeded in inducing many Jews to convert to Islam with the promise of giving them material support. In 1762 the *imām* al-Madhī al-ᶜAbbās ordered the demolition of all the synagogues, and not until thirty years later did his son, al-Manṣūr ᶜAlī, permit the Jews to rebuild them in return for a subvention from the Jewish community.

In the late eighteenth century the Jews of Ṣanᶜā', most of whom were craftsmen, comprised three classes above those who were poor. Statistics are, of course, nonexistent, but it has been estimated that some seventeen hundred (or three hundred families) were wealthy, owners of houses, shops, and land.[9] In 1849 Turkish power was reestablished, and after the opening of the Suez Canal the powers of the *imām* were restricted to religious matters. In 1904 *imām* Yaḥyā revolted against the Turks, and conditions deteriorated to a point where people died of hunger in the streets. The number of Jews in Ṣanᶜā' was reduced to 150.

The position of the Jews in the last few decades of their sojourn in Yemen was dismal. They were considered serfs without any rights. They occupied the lowest rung on the social ladder. The testimony of a Jew was not accepted at court, and, in order simply to survive, a Jew had to find himself a Muslim patron to whom he paid a fee in exchange for his protection. The task of removing the dead animals from the streets and the excrement from the privies, imposed on the Ṣanᶜā' Jews in the latter half of the eighteenth or the first half of the nineteenth century, was especially painful. It was the most degrading demonstration of the principle of *al-ṣaghār wa al-dhilla*, that is, humiliation and abasement of the Jews, which was put into practice in Yemen with greater insistence than in other Arab countries. This onerous duty remained in force until 1950, when it was used as a pretext to prevent the emigration of those Jews who did that work, so that the community had to pay a ransom for them.

The many restrictions imposed upon the Jews, and maintained right up to the time of their emigration, include such prohibitions as putting on bright garments, wearing stockings, carrying weapons, using saddles, engaging in the same occupations as the Muslims, looking at the privy parts of Muslims in the baths, studying the Tora outside the synagogue, praying in a loud voice, blowing the shofar loudly, and lending money for interest. In the street the Jews had to walk on the left side of Muslims, and step down into the gutter when encountering a Muslim. Most painful, or tragic, for the community were the edicts of 1921 and 1925 which prescribed that Jewish minor orphans had to be taken from their relatives, converted to Islam, and raised as Muslims.[10]

In the absence of information on the psychology of the Yemenite Jews prior to their arrival in Israel one has to search for incidental indications that can throw some light on the state of mind of the last generation of that long-oppressed community. While medieval tribal law imposed penalties for calling a Muslim "Jew," or "Christian,"[11] actually, down to the present, the taunt *"Yā Yahawdī!"* ("Hey, Jew!") can often be heard in the *sūq* of Ṣanᶜā'. Shivtiel quotes a joke current among the Yemenite royalists about the one or two northern Jews serving with their forces. When addressed as *"Yā Ya-*

hawdī!" the Jew indignantly retorted, "*Mā anā Yahawdī, al-Miṣrī Yahawdī!*" ("Not I am Jew, the Egyptian is a Jew").[12] The unquestioning acceptance by the Jew of the term *Yahawdī* as a derogatory appellation speaks volumes about the Jewish internalization of the Yemenite Muslims' contemptuous attitude to the Jews. For a Muslim the term "Jew" had such unpleasant connotations that if a Muslim mentioned a Jew, he would add, as if excusing himself for doing so, the expression *ṣānak Allāh* ("God guard you"), the customary phrase appended to the mention of something unclean or distasteful.[13]

Legal documents, published by Y'huda Ratzhabi, present, in accordance with Yemenite Muslim legalism, the arguments of both the Jewish and the Muslim sides to disputes, with all gravity and full detail. Yet even in these documents, the religious obligation of the Muslims to keep the Jews in a state of abasement and humiliation is referred to again and again. For example, the *imām* al-Mahdī says in a 1919 document, "Let the afore-said [Jews] continue in that which my father established—in God's and our security, as long as they continue under our covenant of protection (*dhimma*) held in abasement and humiliation . . ." and again, "They [the Jews] have the right to erect [additional stories] . . . being prohibited only from what is inconsistent with the abasement and humiliation, such as raising their houses higher than the houses of the Muslims . . ."[14]

In some places a Jew would be forced to take a Muslim bride on his back and carry her thus over a long distance while trying to keep up with the marriage procession.[15] When writing about the Jews, the custom was to add a curse after mentioning them. Thus an Arabic manuscript from the Jarim region discussing Jewish holidays is entitled "Information About the Holidays and Fasts of the Jews, May Allah Curse Them . . ."[16] What living in circumstances such as these did to the Jewish self-image and self-esteem can easily be imagined.

All this does not mean that there could exist no kindly relations between Jews and Muslims. However, the fact is that even in friendly contact between members of the two communities the negative stereotype of the Jew intruded. Illustrative of this is a story which tells of a poor Muslim who has no means to provide the necessities for his wife after childbirth. He first goes to the *imām* al-Mutawakkil Aḥmad ibn al-Manṣūr ʿAlī (early nineteenth century), who, after listening to his tale of woe, gives him a single *riyāl*. While the Muslim ponders what to do with the insufficient amount, a Jewish merchant from Ṣanʿā' passes by, and, upon hearing of the plight of the Muslim gives him food and also twenty *riyāls*. Weighing the *imām*'s *riyāl* in his left hand, and the Jew's twenty *riyāls* in his right, the man exclaims, "I adjure you by Allāh, which one is the Jew? The one who gave me twenty *riyāls*, or he who gave me one?"[17] The term "Jew" stands, of course, for the stereotypical Jew as a "miserly person."

It is nothing short of remarkable, and it certainly testifies to the great inner strength of the Yemenite Jews, that despite these conditions they not only survived as a community, but managed to live their lives with dignity, produce a rich material culture of their own, including arts and crafts of great refinement, and even engage in scholarly activities. In contrast to the Muslims, among whom the great majority of both men and women were illiterate, most of the Jewish men were literate,[18] and throughout most of their history produced religious and scholarly works, including Midrashim, Kabbalistic writings, biblical commentaries, as well as poetry, both in Hebrew and in Arabic. Moreover, Yemenite Jewish literary and scholarly interest transcended the domain of religious writings, and branched out into such areas as travelogues and history.

The Yemenite Jews were unique among all the Jewish communities in the Arab world in that they developed a movement, called *Darda*ᶜ (from the Hebrew *dor de*ᶜ*ah*, "generation of knowledge"), which, albeit it remained limited in scope, aimed at purifying their religious life from what its adherents considered superstitious accretions of Kabbalistic mysticism, and returning to the purer Talmudic bases of Judaism. On a small scale, this movement, initiated by Yiḥya Kāfiḥ (1859–1932), was the Yemenite equivalent of the European Jewish Enlightenment, the Haskala. As the latter, so the *Darda*ᶜ movement provoked strong opposition on the part of the more tradition-minded Jews, including the chief rabbi of Ṣanᶜā'. The controversy became so heated that it had to be brought before the *imām* Yaḥyā in 1914, but it continued until the mass emigration of almost all Yemenite Jews to Israel.[19]

The oppression the Jews had to endure in Yemen for many centuries goes a long way toward explaining the modal personality of the Yemenite Jew as it became ascertainable only after their settlement in Israel. After the victory of Islam in Yemen, the Jews were reduced to the status of pariahs, whose mere touch defiled. As I put it elsewhere, "oppression, often in the most humiliating form, was their fate. In order to survive in these circumstances, they had to develop a humble, self-effacing personality. They had to learn to bear silently and without any outward reaction, the jeers of the Muslim Yemenites, their abuse, their vilification."[20]

Another factor in the development of the Yemenite Jewish personality was pointed out by S. D. Goitein. He stressed that the Shīʿites of Yemen were characterized by a particularly legalistic attitude toward religion, and that consequently they attributed great value to the study of religious law. He conjectured that in this respect "the Yemenite Jews felt themselves akin to their environment and therefore accepted many discriminatory laws affecting them with more equanimity than might be anticipated." Goitein also calls attention to the traditional Muslim interpretation of Koran 2:58 and 3:108, according to which God has ordained that the Jews be poor in Yemen (as well as in some other Arab countries). This was taken literally, and consequently Yemenite Jewish men and women were always clothed like beggars,[21] at least when they appeared in public places where they were exposed to the eyes of Muslims. These circumstances forced the Yemenite Jews to learn to be satisfied with little, to work hard in order to make a living on the bare subsistence level, to find satisfaction in interpersonal relations within family and community, and to put their trust in God and the *mori* (rabbi) and his magic. To resort to violence against a Muslim would have been suicidal; against a fellow Jew it would have been unthinkable, given the close cohesion and group identification within the oppressed community.

THE JEWS IN MOROCCO

In presenting a comparison between the conditions of the Yemenite Jews and those of the Jews of Morocco in their respective Arab environments, while I shall dwell more on differences than on similarities, I want to make clear at the very outset and very emphatically that it is not my intention to paint, for the sake of contrast, the situation of the Moroccan Jews as good in itself. The general disabilities that characterized the Jewish condition in all Muslim countries most of the time circumscribed the life of Moroccan Jews as well. But in comparison with the condition of the Yemenite Jews, the Jewish situation in Morocco was better, and, in certain periods, much better.

The authors of *Morocco: A Country Study* state categorically that, prior to the mass emigration of the Jews, "some social discrimination had existed, but it was well known that Jews received better treatment in Morocco than anywhere else in the Arab world."[22] The Jewish exodus, they maintain, was thus the result, not of government policy or severe discrimination, but rather, on the one hand, of concern over what might await them in independent Morocco, and, on the other, of Zionism, that is, the attraction of living in the independent Jewish state. The emigration of two hundred thousand Jews, many of them professional and skilled people, was an economic blow for Morocco, and in 1976 King Hassan appealed to them publicly for their return, promising them full restoration of citizenship, rights, and protection. However, despite the general dissatisfaction of Moroccan Jews with their position in Israel, very few did actually return. To this I might add that Morocco is the only Arab country in which to this day a sizable Jewish community has remained.

While in Yemen there was steady and unrelenting oppression punctuated by a few outbreaks of violence against the Jews, Moroccan Jewish history consisted of frequent oscillation between ease, security, well-being, and even prosperity, on the one hand, and misery, poverty, victimization, and even pogromization, on the other. Moreover, while in Yemen the oppression was not only steady but also general and extended evenly over all layers and parts of the Jewish community, in Morocco there were sharp contrasts in the Jewish condition from place to place, as well as class to class, with the upper-class Sephardi Jews in the coastal cities enjoying what in comparison with the sporadically harsh and brutal treatment of the autochthonous Jews of the countryside appeared as a highly privileged position. A brief sketch of Moroccan Jewish history will suffice to show the extent of these ups and downs, and the variations among places and classes.

The history of the Jews in northwest Africa begins with legends telling of expeditions of Hebrews in biblical times to Morocco to purchase gold and to fight the Philistines who had been driven out of Canaan. Historically, the first testimony consists of Jewish tombstones from the second century C.E. Jewish missionaries in pre-Islamic times converted numerous Berber tribes to Judaism, and in the seventh century Morocco served as a place of refuge for Jews who had to flee Spain where the Visigoths persecuted them. The Arabs, who conquered Morocco in the late seventh century, at first tolerated Jewish presence, but then, under Idrīs I (reigned 788–791), forced them to convert to Islam. Under the later Idrīsid who ruled Morocco until 974 with Fez as their capital, and the Berber Almoravids who held sway until 1147, the Jews of Morocco experienced their golden age, with scholarship flourishing and contact with the Jews of Spain intense. The intolerant Almohad rule, which lasted until 1269, forced most *dhimmīs* to convert to Islam, brought about the disappearance of Christians from Morocco, and visited untold hardships on the Jews. The succeeding Marīnids and Waṭṭāsids (thirteen to fifteenth centuries) were friendly toward the Jews, who gained control over the Saharan gold trade and the exchanges with Christian countries.

The decline of the Maghrib began in 1375 and affected the Jews. The first Moroccan *mellāḥ* (ghetto) was established in 1438, and a short-lived ascendancy of Jews in the court and in finances (of which more will be said later) ended when a bloody revolution terminated the Marīnid dynasty in 1465. Many Jews were killed, many others forced to accept Islam, many fled to Spain. In 1492 and 1496 Jewish refugees from Spain and Portugal were welcomed by Muḥammad al-Shaykh al-Waṭṭāsī, but, because of countrywide insecurity, disasters, famine, and disease, some twenty thousand of them perished, and many of the survivors returned to Spain.

From this time dates the tension between the native Moroccan Jews (*toshavim*, lit. "inhabitants"), and their newly arrived Spanish coreligionists (*m'gorashim*, lit. "expellees"). The latter succeeded in building up their own communities in the major cities, while keeping themselves separate from the native Jews until the great emigration of Moroccan Jewry in the twentieth century. In some north-Moroccan port cities, such as Tetuan and Tangier, the native Jews completely assimilated to the Sephardi immigrants, to the extent of adopting their disdainful attitude to the Arabic-speaking Jews of the interior, to whom they referred as *forasteros*, or aliens, in relation to the Sephardim. They themselves developed a language of their own, the Ḥakétia, which was a mixture of Spanish, Hebrew, and dialect Arabic. In other parts of Morocco the Sephardim retained the ancient Castilian dialect until the nineteenth century. This language differed from the Ladino of the Sephardi Jews who settled in Greece, Turkey, and the Levant.

An interesting development took place in those Atlantic coastal cities which were occupied in the early sixteenth century by the Portuguese. In Portugal the Jews were ruthlessly persecuted, and forced to convert to Christianity. In 1506 over two thousand "New Christians" were massacred. The Inquisition, introduced in 1531, continued to hunt for those "New Christians" who in secret observed Judaism, until it was abolished in 1821. During the three centuries of its existence the Portuguese Inquisition tried forty thousand persons, of whom twelve hundred, most of them accused of Judaizing, were burned at the stake. While this was going on in Portugal, Morocco in the sixteenth century became a haven for Portuguese and

Spanish Marranos, who were able there to reconvert to Judaism. In the Portuguese-controlled Moroccan port cities cordial relations developed between the Sephardi Jews and the Portuguese who employed them as treasurers, interpreters, and negotiators. In fact, the Portuguese kings granted the Jews in Morocco rights, privileges, and favors quite unheard of in that period. The Jews, on their part, served the Portuguese interests with great devotion, occasionally at the cost of their property and even their lives. Those Portuguese and Spanish Jews who lived in the cities of the *makhzan* (the Moroccan Muslim government) served with like loyalty the Muslim rulers (especially the tolerant Saᶜadī dynasty in the sixteenth to seventeenth centuries), as ministers, counselors, and ambassadors to the Portuguese kings, and did their best to bring about a rapprochement between the Muslim and the Christian powers. When, after the defeat of the Portuguese army in the 1578 battle of al-Qaṣr al-Kabīr, tens of thousands of Christians were taken prisoner by the Muslims, these descendants of Portuguese Jewish exiles ransomed them and treated them as friends.

The Moroccan Muslim conquests of the late sixteenth century brought prosperity to the country in general and to the Jews in particular. They established commercial relations with the east as far as India, and the north as far as the Netherlands. The Jewish courtiers and counselors of the sultan used their influence to protect the Jews, as a result of which the Jews in general enjoyed better conditions than the Muslim masses. In addition to the economic advantages, the Jews of Morocco also had considerable mobility—an outcome of their worldwide trading connections—and quite a few of them emigrated to Palestine, the Near East, Europe, and even the Americas. It is an eloquent testimony to the favorable situation of the Jews in Morocco at this time that some of the emigrés returned to Morocco in their old age.

Mūlāy al-Rashīd (reigned 1666–1672), the founder of the Sharīfian ᶜAlawī dynasty, was helped financially by the Jews, and, in turn, was favorably disposed toward them. His brother and successor, Mūlāy Ismāᶜīl (reigned 1672–1727) appointed several Jews to high court office. One of them, Moses ben ᶜAṭṭār, signed a treaty with England in the name of Mūlāy Ismāᶜīl; others served him as ambassadors to England and the Netherlands.

The death of Mūlāy Ismāᶜīl was followed by thirty years of anarchy and plunder, which impoverished the Jews, and triggered their village-to-town migration. As a result, the formerly well-to-do and well-maintained *mellāḥ*s in cities such as Fez and Meknes, deteriorated into overcrowded slums. Those Jews who were better off gravitated to the port cities which were always attractive to a commercially active element. Conditions again improved under Mūlāy Muḥammad ibn ʿAbdallah (reigned 1757–1790), who again employed leading Sephardi Jews at his court and in diplomatic service. He entrusted Jews with negotiations with all Christian countries. It was Moroccan Jews who were largely responsible for the signing of a treaty between Morocco and the United States in 1787 which provided a payment by the U.S. to Morocco in exchange for Moroccan protection of U.S. shipping interests in the Mediterranean.

With all their political know-how, Moroccan Jewish leaders committed a major blunder when they refused a loan to the rebellious son of the sultan, Mūlāy al-Yazīd. When al-Yazīd succeeded his father (he ruled from 1790 to 1792), he wreaked bloody vengeance upon the entire Jewish community. He tortured and put to death all the Jews who had been employed by his father, and sent his men to plunder, rape, and massacre several major Jewish communities. This large-scale pogrom, one of the few of such dimensions in any Muslim country, was the greatest disaster that befell the Jews of North Africa since the Almohad persecutions in the twelfth to thirteenth centuries. It ultimately aroused the Muslim notables and masses to intervene on behalf of the Jews, to many of whom they gave refuge in their homes. When Mūlāy al-Yazīd conquered Marrakesh, he had the eyes of three hundred Muslim notables put out, and had thousands massacred in the Great Mosque. He died, as a result of a wound he received in a battle near Marrakesh, before his order to massacre the Jewish and Muslim notables in several other cities could be carried out.

The situation eased again during the reign of Mūlāy Sulaymān (1792–1822), who did not engage in mass killings, but ordered the Jews to be confined in *mellāḥ*s. During his rule, two epidemics (in 1799 and 1818) depopulated the country, and destroyed its economy. A few of the Jews managed to emigrate, and settled in England where they achieved prominent positions in London Jewish society.

The nineteenth century was characterized by the growth of European pressure on Morocco and by an increase in Jewish economic and diplomatic activity. Jews negotiated treaties, served as envoys, were consuls in Morocco of European powers, and played important roles in Moroccan affairs. A large number of Jews was granted protection by European powers. Their self-confidence grew, and, in an occurrence exceptional in a Muslim country, the Jews of Mogador defended themselves by force of arms when tribal bands came to plunder the town.

The French seizure of neighboring Algeria (1830) made the Jews suspect in Moroccan eyes of treasonous activities or leanings. These suspicions were reinforced after the victory of the French over Morocco in 1844, and of the Spanish in 1860—the first inland defeats of Morocco by Christian powers. The ensuing plight of Moroccan Jewry prompted Sir Moses Montefiore's visit to the court of Mūlāy Muḥammad (reigned 1859–1873) which resulted in a temporary easing of Sharīfian restrictions on the Jews.

A relatively tranquil period in the late nineteenth and early twentieth centuries enabled Moroccan Jewry to produce a number of rabbis, Talmudists, poets, and religio-judicial scholars whose work had a positive effect on the cultural level of the Jews of Morocco as a whole, especially in the major cities. The "Westernization" of Moroccan Jewry began in 1862, when the French Jewish philanthropic organization *Alliance Israélite Universelle* established its first school, in Tetuan. In the course of the next two decades, with more and more schools opened by the *Alliance*, thousands of Moroccan Jewish boys and girls received an introduction to French culture as well as to biblical and Jewish religious studies. In 1939 there were 45 *Alliance* schools in Morocco, with 15,761 pupils; in 1952 they had 28,000 pupils, in 1959—30,123. This educational effort transformed major segments of the urban Moroccan Jewish youth into a French-educated element, at a time when general elementary education did not yet exist in Morocco. In 1960, almost all the Moroccan Jewish men were literate in Hebrew, and no less than 57 percent of all Jewish men and women aged five and over could also read and write Arabic and/or French. This represented a sharp contrast to the Muslim population of which 76 percent of those over 15 (66 percent of males and 87 percent of females) were illiterate as late as in 1974.[23] While the work of the *Alliance* resulted in a cultural uplifting of the Jews above the level of the Moroccan Muslim masses, and reinforced in them the feeling of superiority vis-à-vis their Muslim compatriots, it also brought about a resentment among the latter and a reinforcement in them of the feeling that the Jews were an alien element in their midst.[24]

These cultural improvements were to a large extent offset by the deterioration in the economic and physical condition of most Moroccan Jews in the second half of the nineteenth century. Thousands of impoverished Jews flocked from the countryside to the major cities where the *mellāḥ*s, unable to cope with this unprecedented influx, turned into slums with appalling sanitary conditions, poverty, and unimaginable overcrowdedness. The crowding in the *mellāḥ*s was much worse than in the old Muslim quarters of the cities, the so-called *medīna*s, although it was also bad in those parts. In Casablanca in the 1940s, where the average population density for the whole city was 5,993 inhabitants per square kilometer, or about 24 per acre, the density in the *bidonvilles*, the Muslim slums of the city, was 92,336 persons per square kilometer or 374 per acre. In the *mellāḥ* it was 215,095 per square kilometer or 871 per acre. In the *mellāḥ*s of the other cities of Morocco the situation was not much better. After presenting appalling population density figures, André Chouraqui remarks, "It seems incredible that entire populations should have two square meters per inhabitant as their total living space, in close quarters, without gardens, without sun, without air, without water, without roads. This is the area required for a decent grave, but for living?" And he goes on to adduce examples of families consisting of parents and six to eight children living in a single room of ten or fewer square meters.[25]

It was due, partly at least, to living in such conditions that a tough, street-wise, and ruthless type developed among the Jewish youths for whom often the habitual practice of petty crimes was the only way of keeping alive. Life in the *mellāḥ* had taught many of them to consider dishonesty and violence as inevitable means of self-assertion and even of survival.[26] Little wonder that in these circumstances morality was low, prostitution practiced, and a high percentage of the population was forced to live on alms.[27]

To make things worse, periodic epidemics decimated the population of Morocco, hitting especially hard the overcrowded *mellāḥ*s. Thus in 1900 a plague ravaged Morocco, claiming three thousand Jewish victims in the Fez *mellāḥ* alone. Compared to this mass catastrophe, the mere hundred or so Jews who were killed in Fez when a pogrom broke out in reaction to the establishment of a French protectorate over Morocco in 1912 seemed a minor incident.

In contrast to Algeria, where French citizenship was granted in 1870 to all Jews except those who lived in the deep south, in Morocco the Jews remained under the protection of the sultan as his subjects. While the distinction between the poverty-stricken masses and the thin upper crust of the rich Jewish elite continued in force, a middle class, many of them *Alliance* graduates, developed, and a certain number of youths went on to university studies in Morocco or in France. Being subjects of the sultan proved a great advantage during World War II, which the Moroccan Jews weathered with little damage apart from painful humiliations from the Vichy government. In fact, Sultan Muḥammad V declined to issue a Vichy-initiated decree aiming at the persecution of the Jews.[28] In 1948, the establishment of Israel triggered Muslim violence against the Jews: 43 were killed and 155 injured. Additional outbreaks occurred in 1953 and 1954 in the course of the Moroccan struggle for independence. These events made many Jews decide to emigrate, with most of the well-to-do going to France or to Canada, while the majority, those lacking means, went to Israel. All in all, some 200,000 Jews left Morocco, and the masses, whose transportation to Israel was financed and organized by the Jewish state, arrived there like a flock which had lost its shepherds. In the Arab-Israeli war of June 1967, King Hassan of Morocco supported Egypt. After the Arab defeat public demonstrations took place against the remaining Jews of Morocco, and acts of terrorism occurred which, however, were condemned by the government.[29]

The above brief historical sketch can be supplemented by a few vignettes centering on a number of extraordinary events which shed some light on Moroccan-Jewish relations in past centuries. Arab historical sources inform us that the Moroccan Jews, on more than one occasion, became so insolent and arrogant that their overbearing behavior aroused the ire of the Muslims, with fatal consequences for the Jews. While these accounts unquestionably manifest strong anti-Jewish bias, they must contain at least a kernel of truth as far as Jewish comportment is concerned. No similar allegations were leveled against the Yemenite Jews.

ᶜAbd al-Bāsiṭ ibn Khalīl, the fifteenth-century Egyptian traveler, reports that during his stay in Tlemcen, Morocco, news arrived of bloody events that had taken place in the capital city of Fez. The Jewish vizier appointed by the Marīnid Sultan ᶜAbd al-Ḥaqq, had been killed. The sultan himself had met the same fate, and all the Jews of the city had been massacred. All this had come about, says ᶜAbd al-Bāsiṭ, because the Jews in Fez had risen to such power that they could dominate the Muslims, oppress them, and cause them harm. They had grown in importance, especially after the sultan had made the Jewish vizier, Aaron ibn Baṭṭāsh by name, his intimate confidant, "so much so that the kingdom passed over into his hands . . . The Jew obtained the power to command and to prohibit within the kingdom of Fez, despite his continued adherence to Judaism. . . . The Jews in Fez became arrogant during his tenure—even in the provinces. They came to have authority, influence, prestige, and the power to command and be obeyed. . . . And the dominion of the Jews over the Muslims of Fez increased through him [the Jewish vizier]. The common people could not bear them . . ." The Muslims waxed furious on account of the Jews, their ostentation, and their lording it over the Muslims. Finally the patience of the Muslims ran out, they organized an uprising, and killed the sultan, the Jewish vizier, and all the Jews of Fez. When the people in the other cities of Morocco heard of this event, they too rose up against the Jews and massacred them. "This was a great catastrophe for the Jews," concludes ᶜAbd al-Bāsiṭ, "the like of which had perhaps never previously befallen them. There perished as many of them as Allah Exalted willed."[30]

In the second half of the nineteenth century a similar accusation of arrogance was made against the Jews of Morocco. Al-Nāṣirī relates in his *Kitāb al-Istiqṣā'* (Book of Research) that in 1864 the Jews of Morocco wrote to Rothschild (the Arabic text has "*Rūshābīl*") complaining about their debasement and degradation, and asking for his intervention with the sultan. This resulted in the visit of Sir Moses Montefiore to the sultan in Marrakesh who issued on February 5, 1864, a *dahir* (*ẓahīr* in literary Arabic, meaning edict) ordering considerable improvements in the Jewish condition. Thereupon, al-Nāṣirī continues, the Jews "became arrogant and reckless, and wanted to have special rights under the laws among themselves—especially the Jews of the ports," who were mostly Westernized and the least subject to the *makhzan*, because many were foreign citizens or enjoyed foreign protection. However, the sultan soon retracted his *dahir* in the form of clarifications which stated that it "had been issued on behalf of the respectable Jews and their poor, who are occupied with what concerns them. But as for their good-for-nothings, who are notorious for their depravity, for their arrogance toward people, and for plunging into what does not concern them—they shall receive the punishment they deserve."[31]

Discounting the anti-Jewish tone of these two accounts, what emerges from them is that on occasion the Jews of Morocco, or some elements among them, behaved in a manner considered by the Muslims offensive, arrogant, and overbearing. This type of behavior has no parallel among the Jews of Yemen.

THE EVIDENCE FROM FOLKLORE

An additional important source of information about the life of the Jews in Arab countries and the relationship between them and the Arabs are the folktales. The recording or writing down of Arab folktales in various parts of the Arab world is still largely unaccomplished, and, considering the rapid modernization, industrialization, and Westernization of the Arab countries, it may be too late to rescue this rich folkloric storehouse from oblivion. With regard to the folktales of Jews from Arab countries the situation is better. In the last forty years, after I first raised the issue in two programmatic articles,[32] a considerable number of Jewish folktales has been collected by individuals and institutions. Among the latter the Haifa Folklore Archives, affiliated with the University of Haifa, has an exceptionally rich collection of such folktales, told mostly in Hebrew, by Jewish immigrants in Israel from various Muslim countries. The interest of the Israeli folklorists is, as a rule, focused on the motif analysis of these folktales and their classification according to Stith Thompson's *Motif Index of Folk Literature*, and Aarne-Thompson's *Types of Folktales*. As far as I know, little has been done to date by way of utilizing these folktales as a source for the social conditions of the Jews in the countries in which the tales originated. To do this would, of course, require a major research effort, which, however, would be most worthwhile to undertake. All I can do here is to show, by presenting a few Yemenite and Moroccan examples, what type of results one can expect from this approach. I shall take my examples mostly from English and German publications so that the sources should be available to nonspecialists without a command of Hebrew.

In a true story told by a Yemenite Jew, the informant relates, quite naively, and without any resentment, that when a Jewish friend of his tried to argue with a Muslim shaykh whom he had asked to adjudicate a quarrel, the shaykh snapped at him scornfully, "Son of a dog! N. N. has given his warranty and you are still not satisfied?" At another juncture, the same shaykh turns with a snarl on the uncle of the narrator whom the latter describes as a fearless man although a Jew, "Do you want a thrashing?" The fearless uncle dares to answer not more than "If you want to beat me, you can—you are the shaykh." In another Yemenite Jewish story an irreligious Jew (a great exception among the Yemenites) transgresses the laws of the Sabbath rest by engaging in the forbidden activity of gathering locusts, which are eaten by both Arabs and Jews (the Bible permits it). When the Arabs notice this, they accost him and say, "You deserve to be killed for desecrating the Sabbath!" Thereupon "they satisfied their feelings by beating him and taking away his sacks, and then led him bound before the *qāḍi*. He put him in chains and allowed him to languish for a few months, then decided that the Jew's field and house should be confiscated because of the desecration of the Sabbath, and banished him from the country."[33] To understand the Arabs' concern with the Jew's desecration of the Sabbath, one must know that the Koran repeatedly accuses the Jews of violating their own Sabbath (e.g., Koran 7:163; 2:61; 4:50; etc.), and enjoins on them not to desecrate their religion (Koran 4:171). Thus the Yemenite *qāḍī* found in the violation of the Sabbath by the hapless Jew a ready-made excuse to deal with him summarily.

From 1957 to 1960 169 folktales were recorded from the mouth of a Yemenite Jew, Yefet Shvili, who at the time lived in Ḥolon, a suburb of Tel Aviv. This collection, which was published in 1963 in a German translation, contains several folktales which reflect the utter degradation to which the Jews were subjected in Yemen. In one of them the king of Yemen happens to pass a Jewish school and hear the children studying the biblical verse "How did one chase a thousand, and two put ten thousand to flight" (Deut. 32:30). The king becomes enraged, calls the *ḥakham*, and says to him, "What is this, you shameless one? What are you talking about? Either you strike that verse from your book, or accept Islam, or I shall kill all of you." The rest of the story revolves around the miraculous succor of the Jews from this predicament.

Another Yemenite Jewish folktale starts with a Jewish child inadvertently touching the son of an Arab *ḥājj* (a man who has fulfilled the Muslim commandment of making the pilgrimage to Mecca). The Arab child runs to his father and cries, "I have become unclean!" Thereupon the *ḥājj* comes and slaps the Jewish child. The Jewish child in turn runs to his father crying. The father says, "It does not matter." Then, with magic, by using the name of God, he brings about that there should be no fire in all Ṣanʿā' for three days. Again, as in the previous story, the predicament of the Jews described is taken from real life, the miraculous events are fabulous or magical. We are reminded, by contrast, of the Moroccan Muslim's attitude to the Jewish child who hit him with a stone.

The totally arbitrary nature of the Yemenites' treatment of the Jews is the basis of a third tale in which the king asks a Jew, "Why did you Jews lose the great kingdom you had in the past?" When the *ḥakham* of the Jews answers him that it resulted from baseless hatred, the king dislikes the answer and throws the Jew in jail. In yet another story, a Jewish boy hopes to find the fountain of youth to bring water from it to the old king of Yemen, saying, "I shall go and search for the water for the king; then I shall ask him to do good to the Jews." The Jewish youth finally finds the water, the king becomes rejuvenated, and asks the youth, "What do you want me to give you? Gold, silver, honors? Say what you want, I shall give you everything." The youth answers, "I want no gold, I want no silver, I want no honors." "What then do you want?" asks the king. "I want that my people should no longer have to do such hard and bitter work." Since that time, the tale concludes, the lot of the Jews was good under that king. Here we have a striking illustration of the *summum bonum*, the greatest good desired by the downtrodden Yemenite Jew: less of the hard and bitter work into which they were forced by Yemenite society.[34]

Another Yemenite Jewish tale starts with these words: "It happened that two hungry Arabs met a Jew on the road, caught him, and began to search his belongings. When they found nothing, they started to abuse him. When the Jew saw that he could not escape them, he asked them what they wanted, and they said, "We are hungry, and it is well known that every Jew is full of wisdom, and we shall not let you go until you provide us with food . . .[35] In this story again the same typical situation of the Yemenite Jew is reflected: he is the helpless victim of the will or whim of the Arabs. At the same time some of these stories express another feature as well in the Yemenite Jewish mentality: the conviction that the Jew was cleverer than the Arab and that he could count on divine help.

As for the Moroccan Jews, both the Muslim and the Jewish folktales show them as being much freer and more self-assured than the Yemenite Jews. One type of Moroccan Muslim folktale depicts the Jews as evildoers who seek to inflict harm upon the Muslims and Islam, but whose nefarious machinations are thwarted. Another type consists of humorous stories in which the Jew tries to get the better of a Muslim, but is outwitted by the latter. Both types of tales reflect a certain degree of freedom of action enjoyed by the Jews; they tell of conflict and contest, in which, although ultimately it is the Muslim who wins, the Jew dares to oppose him. No folktales expressing such ideas are known to me from Yemen, where conflict or contest between Jew and Arab is unimaginable because of the total subordination and oppression of the Jews.

One of the Moroccan Muslim tales tells of a Jewish tyrant in Tāzā, who annually received a tribute of beautiful Muslim maidens from Fez for his harem, until Mūlāy Rashīd (who ruled from 1666 to 1672) came to him disguised as a woman, and killed him. The story itself contains well-known folklore motifs, but what is significant for our present argument is that a Muslim folktale describes a Jew as a tyrant, so powerful that even the sultan must resort to a ruse to kill him. Another Muslim tale tells about a Muslim widow who falls in love with a Jewish friend of her deceased husband. But he will have her only if she kills her son and becomes a Jewess. The son meanwhile is studying in the mosque, and with the help of the schoolmaster it is the Jew who is killed by the boy, and the mother is tricked into eating his liver.[36] Again, what is remarkable in this story is that it can envisage a Jew in a position to demand conversion to Judaism of a Muslim woman, which is in clear violation of Islamic law.

Yet another Moroccan Muslim folktale tells of a Jew who was the supplier of jewels to the sultan, and who had brought up a young Muslim girl in order to marry her. The gist of the story is that with the help of the saint Sīdī bel ʿAbbes the girl escapes the fate of having to marry the Jew.[37] The point this story makes for us is that it depicts a social environment in which a Jew—the legal impediments notwithstanding—can plan to marry a Muslim girl, and in which the miraculous intervention of a famous Muslim saint is required to frustrate this plan.

From beyond the borders of Morocco, from the Algerian oasis of Souf, which belongs to the same culture area as the Moroccan interior, comes additional folkloric testimony as to the type of relationship between Jews and Arabs. One of the stories circulating in the towns and villages of that large oasis tells about a Jewish merchant who is defrauded by Jiḥā, the well-known jester and prankster figure of both Arab and Berber folklore, elsewhere called Juḥā.[38] The Jew summons Jiḥā to court where the shrewd prankster succeeds in convincing the *qāḍī* that he owes the Jew nothing.[39] The point interesting for us is that this folktale presents a society in which a Jew can take a Muslim to court and is given due hearing. Other folktales from the same oasis contain additional indications of the socially and legally satisfactory condition of the Jews in Souf.[40]

The Moroccan Jewish folktales present a reverse image of the Jewish-Muslim contest of wits: in them it is not the Muslim, but the Jew who wins. They tell of rivalry between a righteous Jewish and a wicked Muslim courtier, of clashes between a Jew and a Muslim in which the clever Jew triumphs over the foolish Muslim, of kings of Marrakesh favorably disposed to the Jews, of a king of Fez who has Jewish friends and plays games of draughts with a Jewish sage, of a Muslim prince who loves the Jews, of Rabbi Ḥayyim Pinto who on one occasion wonders why an Arab market inspector does not honor him as all other Arabs do, and who teaches an arrogant shaykh of Suera a lesson, etc.[41] Again what one sees in these Jewish folktales is a positive, self-confident Jewish self-image which is the reflection of the firm, and by no means helpless, position of the Jews in Morocco. Many Jewish folktales also show the Moroccan Muslims in a good light: this can be explained only as mirroring the actual good relationship between Jews and Muslims. This impression is further strengthened by those Jewish tales which speak of Muslims who come to a Jewish *tzaddiq*, holy man, to ask for his judgment, advice, help, and for his *baraka*[42] (that famous power or virtue which, in Moroccan folk-belief, distinguishes holy men of either faith). More on this subject will be said in chapter 6, which deals with the common elements in Muslim and Jewish folk religion in Arab lands.

That the Jews of Morocco dared to stand up to, and even antagonize and insult, Muslims is further attested by proverbs and sayings which were current among the Moroccan Jews. Pierre Flamand, a student of Moroccan Jewish life, collected hundreds of sayings which reflect the views of Moroccan Jews on human destiny, their moral judgments, their feelings and outlook about family, marriage, children, women, friendship, social conditions, riches and poverty, etc. Among them are several which the author groups under the heading "Sayings and Insults in Addressing Muslims." These include such invectives as carrion, bastard, and "May God take you back to the desert, stinky dogs!" In connection with this last saying the author remarks that this is "a very insulting expression used by the sedentary Shlöhs and Jews of the Sūs plain in addressing nomadic Bedouins of Mauretania and Ouad Noun (Wādī Nūn)." Other such curses are "May God cause your race to perish," and "May God curse your religion," which latter the "Muslims consider a particularly grave insult," so that a Jew who utters it against a Muslim is liable to the law court of the pasha.[43] I would add that the very fact that such curses and maledictions could at all be pronounced by Jews against Muslims is a witness to the relatively secure position enjoyed by the Jews of Morocco. No such face-to-face insults of Arabs by Jews could be imagined in Yemen.

These and other such observations on the position of the Jews in Morocco definitely give the impression of a situation very different from the steady and unrelenting pressure, the consistently inimical attitude and the degradation, to which the Yemenite Jews were exposed until the very time of their departure for Israel. The Jews were, to be sure, *dhimmī*s in Morocco as well as in Yemen; there can be no doubt about that. They were unquestionably second-class subjects with no equality and only a few rights, but—and this made all the difference—they held a position of their own and had a role to play in the power struggle and the mutual distrust which characterized the relationship between the Arabs and the Berbers.

MODERN TIMES

The Moroccan Jewish condition in modern times was the subject a few years ago of a scholarly disagreement between two groups or schools of researchers, one of which was inclined to present it as dismal, the other as rosy. The former concluded that the Moroccan Jews were a persecuted community, forced to comply rigidly with the humiliating regulations governing the status and behavior of the *dhimmī*s; the latter felt that the relationship between the Jews and the surrounding Muslim society was relatively congenial, particularly when compared with the conditions of European Jewry.[44]

Sifting the evidence, and basing himself on his own observations, anthropologist Moshe Shokeid of the Tel Aviv University concluded in a recent paper that there was in Morocco a variety of situations ranging from favorable to unfavorable, depending on the locality on the one hand, and on specific occurrences and developments on the other. After a careful review of the sources he presents, as well as of the conclusions he draws from them, my own impression is that Shokeid is inclined toward, although he does not go along wholeheartedly with, the "rosy" view. He also makes an important point when he emphasizes that the picture of Jewish life in Morocco is colored by "the interpretive element embedded" in the perception the Moroccan Jews have of their experience in Morocco.[45] Having summarized above the stormy ups and down of Moroccan Jewish history, let us now have a closer look at the contemporary and near-contemporary scene in that westernmost country of the Arab world.

The first thing to keep in mind is that the Muslim population of Morocco is sharply divided between Arabs and Berbers. The Berbers are the descendants of the native population that was present in Morocco at the time of its conquest by the Arabs. The Arabs imposed their religion on the Berbers, but the latter retained their language; they spoke, and continue to speak, many different Berber dialects. Today, the most visible difference between the Arabs and the Berbers is that the former speak Arabic, while the latter speak either Arabic and Berber, or only Berber. Also, the Berbers have retained a strong Berber ethnic consciousness, and the relations between them and the Arabs have remained tense to this very day. The central government is Arab; it has been headed for many generations by a ruler of the Sharīfian family, which claims descent from the Prophet Muhammad. Also, for many generations the control of the Sharīfian government has been confined to the major cities and their immediate environs. This is the area called *blēd (bilād) al-makhzan*, meaning "government country." However, outside the imperial cities of Fez, Meknes, Rabat, Marrakesh, the power of the *makhzan* meant little or nothing, and hence the countryside at large was referred to as *blēd as-siba*, variously translated as land of freedom, land of dissidence, land of disorder, or, as Carleton S. Coon put it, "land of insolence." The *blēd as-siba* was a patchwork of many diverse authorities, local rulers or strongmen, or tribal councils, often at odds with one another as well as with the *makhzan*, and often under the influence of *marabouts*, or holy men. In many cases such semi-independent areas were (and still are) inhabited by Berber population elements, which have retained not only their own ethnic traditions, but also an antagonism to the Arabs simmering just beneath the surface.

The livelihood of the Moroccan Jews has depended in many instances on their ability to travel from a city ruled by the *makhzan* to or through the *blēd as-siba*. In practice this meant that they had to be able to secure, either individually or as a group, protection from both the *makhzan* and the local powers that be, in return for payment in cash and/or services. While thus the client-patron relationship between the Jews and Muslims in Morocco has borne an overall resemblance to that which prevailed in Yemen, a closer look discloses significant differences and even contrasts. In Yemen the Jews were the object of constant scorn on the part of the ruling Zaydī Muslim Arab majority. The Jews themselves were a homogeneous ethnic group (although internal distinctions existed among them as well); they were the only *dhimmī*s in the country, whose entire life was confined to the locality in which they lived, or to small circles of settlements and tribes among which they made their rounds as peddlers. Almost all the Yemenite Jews were poor (we have seen above that in the eighteenth century no more than three hundred families owned houses, shops, or land), and most of them were barely able to eke out a living as craftsmen or small merchants.

In Morocco, the Spanish exiles of 1391 and 1492, and the Portuguese expellees of 1496 introduced an elite element of proud Sephardi Jews, who soon established themselves as the dominant group in the major Jewish urban communities. As mentioned before, this often gave rise to considerable tension between the newly arrived *m'gorashim*, and the autochthonous *toshavim*. In this intra-Jewish power struggle some of the Jewish leaders were as oppressive and overbearing in their relations with other Jews as any Muslim courtier might be.[46] It was mostly these Jews of Iberian extraction who became the leaders in large-scale commerce in Morocco, and controlled much of Morocco's international trade, especially with England, France, and the Low Countries. They participated extensively in government service, as customs agents, interpreters, and consuls to the sultan's court. The autochthonous Jews worked mostly in the more traditional occupations of crafts, small trade, and the like. All in all, Moroccan Jewry was engaged in a broad range of occupations, and its economic status ranged from the masses of humble means to some who had amassed impressive ostentatious wealth.[47] These differences remained apparent until well into the twentieth century, when an American consul to Morocco observed that, although "since time immemorial the Jews have been slaves in Morocco," many of them "through the influx of modern influence in the coast towns, have become independent enough to control the finance of the country," while "the old conditions of servitude still exist to a large extent in the interior. But the Jew has shown his ability to rise."[48]

Most importantly for their relations with the Muslims, the Jews occupied an intermediate position between the Arabs and the Berbers.[49] For both Arabs and Berbers to have Jews under their protection was something of a privilege, an achievement which contributed materially to the protector's prestige.[50] The protection extended by either an Arab or a Berber to a Jew was jealously guarded. As a student of Moroccan Jewry put it, "an unpunished act by a third party against a Jewish protégé (might) be taken as a sign of weakness or unreliability" on the part of the protector.[51]

This patron-client relationship was an established tradition, and in the late nineteenth century Mrs. W. B. Harris described the manner in which it functioned in the Great Atlas and in Sūs. If a Jew settled down in a Berber village, he made an *ʿār*-sacrifice, which implied a conditional curse, at the door of some influential man, who thereupon became his protector and master, expected to avenge any injury inflicted on his client, but also exacting obedience from him. The Jew rendered various services to his "lord" (*sīdī*) or "friend" (*amdakul*), as the patron was called, such as buying for him powder and ammunition when he was on bad terms with his governor, and occasionally giving him some present; but there was no real oppression on the part of the master. Since this patron-client relationship was hereditary, the great majority of the Jews in the Great Atlas and Sūs never had to resort to the *ʿār*-sacrifice in order to acquire a patron. The patron gave his client a token, such as a turban or a handkerchief, and this was sufficient to serve as a safe-conduct during the client's journeys. It was a point of honor for the patron to avenge an injury inflicted on his traveling protégé.[52] Westermarck, who quotes this account, adds that among the Ait Waráin, a patron who failed to avenge an injury done to his client was called *udei*, "Jew," an epithet of shame,[53] which, it seems, was common to Morocco and Yemen.

Other students of Morocco also report on the "terrific shame" which befell patrons who mistreated their Jewish clients, or allowed others to do so with impunity, or failed to live up to their obligations in some other way.[54] In addition to the risk of shame, there were also ritual or supernatural sanctions, especially if the protection arrangement was sealed by an *ʿār*, or conditional curse.[55] Finally, a consistently recalcitrant patron or protector could be penalized by his Jewish clients by the simple expedient of their discontinuing their services. Such a cut-off could seriously affect the patron's material well-being, since in many cases the Jews were the only traders, money-lenders, or craftsmen available.[56] Consequently, as many informers averred, "to kill or even molest a Jew was an infinitely worse offense than to kill a fellow tribesman, for the Jew's protector would show absolutely no mercy to the killer."[57] Other observers even speak of the long-term relationships that developed between Muslims and Jews, and that were "generally characterized by that kind of friendship that so often attends a clearly symbiotic relationship."[58]

These observations are borne out by those of an American anthropologist who studied the Jews of Ait Adrar, a village in the Atlas Mountains of Morocco. She found that the Jews of that community lived in virtual symbiosis with their Berber neighbors, and enjoyed excellent relations with them, as well as a high subsistence level. While it was reported to her that this was far from being the case in some other parts of the Atlas Mountains, she also learned that Jewish men in Ait Adrar often lost their temper and shouted, although they loathed being shouted at, and that they would even strike each other. Shouting and striking were not unusual also between old Jewish women. It is noteworthy that one young woman reported that even if a Jew shouted at one of the neighboring Berbers, the Berber would not shout back. This makes it appear as if the Jews were more respected by the Berbers than vice versa. In any case, reports such as this indicate that there was a familiar relationship between the Jews and the Berbers in Ait Adrar, which contrasts sharply with the Jewish experience in Yemen, where it would have been unimaginable that a Jew should dare shout at an Arab. It was also reported in Morocco that in time of need a Jew could go to a Berber and would always receive help. This arrangement was reciprocal, and Jews were expected to give Berbers money when asked. But it was never taken by force, or at least had not been since the arrival of the French. Informants frequently reiterated, "We lived like brothers, and Arab property was like Jewish property." Neighboring Berbers would be invited to Jewish weddings as guests and bring many gifts. When Jewish parents beat their children, the children might run to the Berbers for comfort. The latter would then say, "Do not hit him; he is only a child." It was also reported that on one occasion some Jewish children ran after a Berber and threw stones at him, drawing blood. The man came to the father, complaining, "Look what your sons have done." The father commiserated, but argued, "What can I do? They are only children." And the Berber was appeased.[59]

These reports give us an insight not only into Jewish-Berber relations, which appear as being those one would expect of two friendly groups on more or less equal footing, but also into the Moroccan Jewish personality: the children are undisciplined, the adults give vent to their temper by shouting and striking each other, and shouting also at Berbers. We get here a glimpse of the personality which in the Israeli context gave rise to the "Morocco-knife" stereotype. In this connection I would also like to remark, very tentatively, that reports such as the foregoing seem to indicate that the attitude of the Moroccan Berbers to the Jews was more friendly than that of the Arabs. This is certainly a subject which should be further investigated in Israel as long as the Moroccan Jewish immigrant generation is still alive, and can recall what it was like to live in a Berber and Arab environment respectively.

To the above testimony can be added the information gathered by an Israeli anthropologist who studied a village community in the High Altas, Morocco, which he calls Amran and all of whose members left for Israel by 1956. His study found that the relations between Jews and Muslims were ambivalent. On the one hand, there was cooperation to mutual advantage: the Jews rendered services to the Muslims and received protection from them, and the Muslims defended the Jews from aggression by other Muslims. On the other hand, this relationship often suffered breakdowns. The Muslims often raided and plundered the Jews, caused them injury and humiliation, so that there was a permanent feeling of insecurity among the Jews which the otherwise very religious Jewish community considered sufficient moral ground for dishonesty in its commercial relations with the Muslims. Let me interject here that this view, that dishonesty is permitted in dealing with inimical outsiders, seems to have been transplanted by the Moroccan Jews to Israel where many of them considered the entire non-Moroccan Jewish population in the same light. However, while the Moroccan Jews may have practiced dishonesty vis-à-vis outsiders, they never made it a religious tenet, as did the Druze, for whom not only is lying to outsiders permitted but dissimulation in dealings with outsiders is religiously commanded.[60]

While the Jewish immigrants from Amran did not retain in their memory too attractive a picture of their life in Morocco, they did remember that occasionally the Jews did dare put up resistance to the Muslims. One of them reminisced: "There were a few 'heroes' who tried to fight back, but once they injured or killed a Moslem they could not remain in the community. They had to escape, while those who remained had to compensate the injured Moslem family." In other words, they had to conform to the Muslim rules of behavior governing cases of murder and blood feud, which only goes to show that in this respect the same customary law applied to both Muslims and Jews. By contrast, the killing of a Muslim by a Jew in Yemen would have had terrible consequences for the entire local Jewish community of which he was a member.

Some Jews in Amran maintained relatively large partnerships in farming with Muslims whom they provided with capital. The Jews also owned large herds of sheep which were tended by Muslims, and rented nut orchards from Muslims and marketed their crops. Social control functioned well in Amran. There were order and peace, "because people were afraid of those who were either wealthier or better educated and learned . . ." When the Jews started to emigrate, the Muslims tried to dissuade them for the simple reason that they needed the Jews' services. Still, by the end of 1956 no Jew remained in Amran. They saw in their return to Israel a fulfillment of age-old messianic hopes.[61]

Incidental intelligence about the varying conditions of Jewish life in Morocco in the last few decades prior to the great exodus comes from the pens of travelers and explorers. The Polish traveler Ferdinand Ossendowski, who visited Morocco in the 1920s, comments on the contrast between the position of the Jews in most *mellāḥ*s and in the town of Debdu in the eastern Atlas Mountains:

> Whereas it is a well-known fact that Jews living in the Mellah in Moslem towns are despised as unclean and are periodically persecuted

> because of the fiery hate of the Faithful of Islam, in Debdu the situation is just reversed, for here the Jews hold the upper hand and the Moslems work for them as servants. Seeking some explanation of this, I was informed that the proximity of a tribe that is rather indifferent to the law of the Prophet [Muhammad] and regards Ben Sliman as the greatest of the saints may account for it. I feel, however, that this may not be sufficient reason for the unusual relationship between Moslems and Jews and that the real explanation may be found in the fact that the local Jews have been agriculturists for a very long time and have taught the better practice of the science to the natives of Floushe, Hassian el-Jhudi and other localities, assuring them through this a basis of existence at a time when war disrupted the regular commercial life and cut off contact with ordinary sources of supply.[62]

Thirty years later, H. Z. Hirschberg, who traveled the length and breadth of Morocco in the 1950s in the very midst of the great movement of *ʿaliya* (immigration) to Israel, found, and reported in his Hebrew travelogue, that the Jewish condition varied greatly from place to place, due to the differences in the natural environment and the social circumstances. He found especially significant differences between the Jews of the lowlands and those of the Atlas Mountains:

> The Jews of the mountains seemed to me more healthy, strong, erect, as well as freer, than those in the valley. I saw no blind persons among them. Against the background of the general poverty in the mountains their poverty was nothing unusual. One can say that they made the impression of being satisfied with their lot. On the other hand, I found in the valley many old and sick people, also some helplessness and laziness, a strong yearning for *ʿaliya*, and disappointment over the difficulties of classification and selection [for being transported to Israel]. Here the dependence on the Muslims is more apparent, externally as well. The mellāḥ constitutes part of the village within the walls, while in the mountains the mellāḥs at times are located at a distance from the village.[63]

Numerous incidents recalled by Moroccan Jewish immigrants in Israel contain clear evidence that they viewed their relationship with the Muslims as one of "mutual dependence, based on genuine mutual respect," with emphasis on "fair play and personal friendship between the Jewish trader or craftsman and his Muslim client, partner, or patron." The Jewish traders were able to travel anywhere. As one of them put it, "For us craftsmen there were no borders." An itinerant Jewish smith or craftsman would occasionally remain in the home of his Berber employer for days or even weeks, spending only the Sabbath with a nearby Jewish community. During his stay his host would see to his personal needs. In return, the Muslims too would pay visits to the homes of their Jewish partners or acquaintances, and be served food and drinks. The friendship between Jews and Muslims was at times expressed in gestures of physical contact, such as a kiss on the brow. (In Yemen the very touch of a Jew was considered defiling for a Muslim.) In any case, the Jewish craftsman, peddler, and merchant could travel in the *blēd as-siba* with little risk involved, and was welcomed, although not enjoying an honored position, in nearby or remote Berber settlements. He was even exempt from the protection fee a traveler had to pay when going from his own tribe into the territory of another.[64]

To the above features must be added that in Morocco, again in contrast with Yemen, the Jews were not the lowest, or the only lowest, status group. In addition to the blacks and the descendants of former slaves, there were, among both the Berbers and the Arabs, certain pariah elements such as the gypsies, and those *ḥarāṭīn* (sing. *ḥarṭānī*), people of mixed Arab-Negro blood, who performed such tasks as tending the herds, cultivating the palm groves, gardening, well digging, carrying water, and tanning.[65] As a result of the presence of these numerous and disparate low-class populations, the disdain often felt by traditional majorities toward low-class minorities living in their midst was diluted among all of them, and the Jews received only a minor part of it.[66] The accounts given by Moroccan Jewish immigrants in Israel of the relationship between the Jews and the Muslims in Morocco speak of both scorn and friendship, conflict and harmony, and recall Moroccan Jewish life as comprised of "circumstances of a particular mode of Jewish existence in relative safety amidst precarious environmental conditions."[67] Another observer notes that in North Africa Jews and Muslims generally maintained close neighborly relations, and ate meals together, in the course of which, when the food and drink made their hearts merry, the Jews would crack jokes about *pasūl* (meaning unfit or defective in Hebrew) which word rhymed with *rasūl* ("messenger" in Arabic), the epithet of Muhammad, or would call the Koran *qalōn* (shame in Hebrew), and the Muslims would reciprocate with similar barbs and joking expressions of derision.[68] Such familiar banter about the sacrosanct subject of religion is the most eloquent testimony to the really intimate friendships that existed between Jews and Muslims.

These Moroccan data can be supplemented by similar information concerning the neighboring Algerian Sahara which belongs to the same culture area as the Moroccan hinterland.[69] In the towns and villages of the Souf oasis, some 250 miles south of the Mediterranean and near the Tunisian border, the Jews in the main towns of Guemar and El-Oued owned one-quarter of all the houses and the best palm groves. The bedouins of Souf regularly admitted the Jews to their encampments. The Jews rendered services to them as dyers, tooth pullers, hairdressers, bloodletters, blacksmiths, armorers, and the like. In general the Jews lived on good terms with the Arabs, and were it not for their lighter skin, blond beards, and green eyes, they could not have been distinguished from them. Jews and Arabs dressed alike, Jewish women were veiled when they went out, and there were a number of conversions to Islam. The Jewish women would visit the houses of Muslim families, share with the Muslim women the use of magic, and introduce the old Arab women to the Jewish magicians. The Muslim women paid five times as much for a Jewish amulet as for one prepared by a Muslim *ṭāleb* (scholar). Although in general the two communities lived in peace, in some places the Arabs made the life of the Jews difficult. After the independence of Israel all the Jews of Souf left the oasis. In 1949, of the two thousand Jews of Guemar only one remained. Before they left, the Jews entrusted an Arab mason with the task of rebuilding their synagogue, saying, "We leave it behind as a furuncle in the heart of the Arabs," and telling the mason, "We consider you a veritable Jew, although our proverbs warn us to have no confidence in Muslims even after they had been in their graves for sixty years!"[70] These fragments of information confirm the picture obtained from the Moroccan data of relatively good relationship between Muslims and Jews, with the Jews maintaining normal social and commercial contact with the Muslims, and feeling sure enough of themselves to engage in light banter with them.

ALCOHOL AND VIOLENCE

Our necessarily sketchy comparison between the Jewish-Muslim relationship in Yemen and in Morocco must be supplemented by a few words about the consumption of alcohol and the resort to physical violence, both important features in the portraiture of any human group. While the drinking of alcoholic beverages is forbidden in Islam (see below), the Yemenite and the Moroccan Jews drank liberally. In Yemen the Jews produced and drank *ʿaragi* (i.e., arrack), a strong, colorless brandy made of grapes or dates. It was drunk by men, but not by women, and, according to one account, the quantities imbibed by the men often led to drunkenness. Erich Brauer, who wrote in the 1930s what to this day is the most thorough study of the ethnology of the Yemenite Jews, felt that this account was exaggerated, and maintained that while they drank "more than a little," they rarely got drunk, at the utmost on holidays such as Purim and Hanukka.[71]

Among the Moroccan Jews alcohol seems to have been more of a problem. In the 1880s Charles de Foucauld observed that all of the Moroccan Jews "make immoderate use of alcohol; they drink while eating, as well as between meals. A litre a day is the average for many of them. Even the women take of it more or less. Above all on Saturday they imbibe prodigious quantities: it is [considered] necessary to drink enough at lunch in order to sleep thereafter in one stretch until the four o'clock prayer." In a footnote Foucauld explains that "the Jews manufacture this brandy which they call *maḥya*. They make it, in the north, of grain or of raisins; in the mountains, of figs; in the Sahara, of dates. In the cities the *maḥya* can be bought in ewers at the market; in the country each house distills, every Thursday, the amount needed for the week."[72]

Since Foucauld had a strong anti-Jewish bias,[73] one would be inclined to take this report with a grain of salt, were it not for independent and unimpeachable corroboration provided by a number of Jewish sources. First of all there is the witness of several Jewish proverbs (in the colloquial Moroccan Judeo-Arabic dialect) which warn against the evil consequences of drunkenness.[74] Next, Hirschberg, in his travels in Morocco in the 1950s found that the use of *maḥya* was indeed widespread among the Jews. It was produced from dates, figs, or grapes, and distilled mostly by women. While Hirschberg does not mention drunkenness, his occasional remarks about the *maḥya* leave no doubt that it was indulged in frequently and copiously.[75]

A decade later, Feuerstein and Rischel inform us that:

> . . . alcoholism is widespread in certain places among all [the Moroccan Jews], adults and children alike; the inhabitants of North Africa drink a natural beverage called *maḥya*, which is a very strong brandy, made of dates, figs, or raisins. In most villages, and in particular in those of the south, they distill the *maḥya* at home. An inhabitant of the [Jewish] community of Demnat, who prided himself of this industry and of the use of the *maḥya*, explained to us that people drink this traditional beverage, and that they give some drops of it to infants as well, in order to make them stop crying and fall asleep.

The authors feel constrained to add, "One should consider this not a sign of demoralization, but a custom whose purpose is to find some respite from the stifling of the overcrowded rooms, from the annoying flies, and from sleeplessness; however, it is, of course, harmful to health."[76]

It is difficult to evaluate the role of alcohol in the relationship between adherents of Islam and Judaism. It is the only item in the diet permitted to Jews and prohibited to Muslims (cf. Koran 2:216; 4:46). One passage in the Koran (5:92) describes wine, together with *maysir* (a game of chance) as "abominations of the work of Satan," and instructs the believers to avoid them so that they may prosper. Subsequently, all the Muslim schools of jurisprudence (with the exception of the Ḥanafī) have extended the prohibition of wine to all other alcoholic beverages, and drinking was made punishable by flogging. Although transgressors were numerous, and wine was drunk at reveling parties at the courts of the caliphs,[77] the fact that the Jews were allowed officially, and even commanded by their religion, to drink wine became a source of irritation for the Muslims. In Muslim eyes the wine- and arrack-drinking Jews became objects of both overt contempt, and, one may surmise, suppressed envy. In any case, public opinion strongly condemned indulgence in intoxicating liquors, and while it was not regarded as seriously sinful by the upper classes, it was a comparatively grave offense in the eyes of the others. In traditional Muslim society it used to be the duty of the *muḥtasib*, the officer concerned with the observance of the moral precepts of Islam, to prevent wine drinking in public. If the offender was a Muslim, the *muḥtasib* admonished him and spilled the wine on the ground; if he was a *dhimmī*, he warned him not to offend again in public.[78]

The same feeling, that wine drinking was offensive in public even if done by a *dhimmī* whose religion permitted it, persisted down to modern times, and the Jews in Arab lands knew better than to become guilty of it. In the absence of hard data one can only venture to say that the Jewish indulgence in wine and liquors must have added to the social distance between Jew and Arab, which, of course, worked to the disadvantage of the minority group, the Jews.

Overindulgence in alcohol often goes hand in hand with violent behavior. This seems to have been the case among the Jews of Morocco as well. Foucauld, whom I have already quoted above, is one of the few authors who supplies some information on this subject. If one can give credence to him, the Jews in parts of the Moroccan *blēd as-siba* were even more violence prone than the Muslims.

> The country in which I saw the most maltreated and most miserable Israelites is the valley of the Wad al-ʿAbid of Wawizert at Tabia. I found there Jewesses detained for three months by their [Muslim] lord because the husband was not able to pay a certain amount. The custom there fixes at 30 francs the fine a Muslim has to pay for killing a Jew. He has to give

> the money to the *sīd* [lord] of the victim, and there is no other punishment or damage. In this region the Israelites do not engage in commerce; as soon as they possess something, it is taken away from them. They cannot be goldsmiths, they lack the money. They are all shoemakers. Treated like beasts, the misery makes them savage and ferocious. They beat one another, they wound one another, they kill one another daily. At Ait or Akeddir I saw one morning a man enter the synagogue; he had just cut the throat of his nephew in a quarrel, and boasted of it. Nobody reproached him; it was a common occurrence. I myself barely escaped being assassinated twice in this country by the Jews of Wawizert between that village and Kasba Beni Mellal, and by the Jews of Ait or Akaddir in their very mellāḥ . . . In this country, if the Jews of one village have a quarrel with those of another, both sides arm, meet, and engage in battle.[79]

Violence is especially repugnant when directed against the weak and the helpless, and, in particular, against children. Yet the fact is that the parent-child relationship among the Arabs in many countries, and among the Jews in Morocco, was characterized by frequent resort to the physical punishment of children by beating or by causing them physical pain in some other way. I have dealt elsewhere with the practice of severe corporal punishment which is (or was) frequently administered by Arab parents to their children, and which in some Arab societies takes (or took) the form of beating, whipping, or even cutting or stabbing, the misbehaving child. In addition, the children would be threatened with being killed, or with other dire punishment, without, of course, carrying out the threats of this type.[80]

In Morocco, the beating of children was a common occurrence also outside the parent-child relationship. The teachers would use ropes or whips on their pupils. Beating, in Moroccan eyes, had a comic connotation, and consequently beatings between adults often formed part of the comedies performed on the occasion of the Great Feast in various parts of the country.[81] Moreover, beatings were employed also in magic. For example, the bridegroom would try to gain power over his wife, and the bride over her husband by such means as beating, smacking, kicking, and making use of a slipper in some other way.[82]

Among Moroccan Jewish immigrants in Israel it was observed that parents would threaten their children by shouting, "I shall kill you!" or "I shall leave you!" Or they would say to the child, "You want to kill your mother!" which, of course, could create a guilty feeling in the child. When even such threats remained unheeded, the parents would administer severe beatings, until suddenly they would be overcome by feelings of compassion, and then they would hug and kiss the child in an overflow of demonstrative love.[83] What this type of treatment impressed upon the child was that physical violence was one of the normal channels of imposing one's will upon others, which lesson was retained and applied in later adult life.

Another factor which impinged upon the personality development of the Moroccan Jewish child was the lack of restraint with which his parents quarreled in his presence. The violence which is always latent in the Moroccan personality, and the Arab personality in general,[84] would often flare up into vehement altercation between husband and wife in the presence of their children whose sympathy each of them would try to enlist. When such fights or other causes led to divorce, the child, who consequently was left to live with one parent only, ran the risk of psychosocial maladjustment, or of becoming delinquent, losing his grasp of moral values, and developing other consequences of neglect. Israeli researchers found that the economic, hygienic, cultural, and familial conditions in which the children had lived in the overcrowded *mellāḥ* explained their educational backwardness, which was not confined to the school but influenced mental functioning in general and affected other areas of adjustment as well.[85] These were serious cultural handicaps which to overcome has required a sustained educational and social work effort, still going on at the time of this writing.

CULTURE LOSS

The establishment of the French protectorate over Morocco in 1912 signaled the beginning of the loosening of the communal bonds which had united most of Moroccan Jewry as long as it had lived a life circumscribed by the established traditions of many generations. The process of change actually had begun several decades earlier, with the opening of schools by the *Alliance Israélite Universelle* in the early 1860s. Up to that time there had been in Morocco a rather rigid class structure. The Jews of the hinterland, and especially of the villages, the so-called *toshavim* ("residents"), were Arabic speaking (more rarely Berber speaking) natives who formed an integral part of the native Muslim (Arab or Berber) economy, and whose material culture was, on the whole, identical with that of the Muslims. Where the two groups differed was in the higher percentage of the Jewish men able to read Hebrew, as against the higher percentage of illiterates among the Muslims. And above all, there was the insurmountable barrier of religion which separated Jew from Muslim not only in those areas of life which were the proper domain of religion, but also in the many areas which were influenced by religion. Yet, as we shall see in chapter 6, the popular dimension of religious life comprised large areas of commonality between the Muslims and the Jews.

In the cities, and especially in those along the coast, there was, in addition to the native Moroccan Jewish community, the superimposed Sephardi element which was locally called *m'gorashim* ("expellees"). They were Ladino speaking, better educated, well-to-do, influential in business and in the service of government, with international connections, and they largely held themselves apart and aloof from the native Moroccan Jews. The latter, despite their initial resentment of the Sephardim, had no choice but to acknowledge the superiority of these *m'gorashim*, as shown by the fact that in several coastal cities, such as Tangier and Tetuan, they soon began to assimilate to them. This trend, however, was superseded from the 1860s on by the influence of French culture, which was spread at first by the *Alliance* schools, and then, much more powerfully, by the French presence itself from 1912 on. As a result of these influences, gradually a new Jewish middle class came into being, composed of young people who had acquired at least a smattering of French and rudiments of French Westernization. By 1939, when the total Moroccan Jewish school-age population (the 6–14 year age group) numbered about 56,000, some one out of three of them were enrolled in *Alliance* schools or in the smaller religious Jewish school networks, in addition to those in the remote villages who continued to receive their education in the traditional *kuttāb*s (Tora schools).[86]

In the last few decades there was a continual stream of Jewish migration from the villages of Morocco to the major cities. This process gained momentum especially after the establishment of Israel, when anti-Zionist propaganda and sentiment among the Muslims made life precarious for the small Jewish groups in the villages. As a result, many small village *mellāḥ*s became abandoned, while those in the major cities grew, not in area but in density, until they threatened to burst at the seams.

Hand in hand with this physical dislocation went cultural and psychological upheavals. Attendance at a modern or semimodern school proved in retrospect to have been a mixed blessing. On the one hand, the acquisition of some knowledge of reading and writing in French and Hebrew, and of other elementary-school subjects was an important step in the mental development of the young Jewish generation. On the other, the sense of superiority this education instilled into them often led to a breakdown of paternal authority and to a feeling of disdain towards illiterate groups and individuals, whether strangers or parents, whether Jews or Muslims. The glimpse they got of French culture was often enough to alienate the adolescent or young adult boys and girls from the traditional Jewish culture of their parents. Typically, this attitude led to the desire to dissociate oneself from Morocco as a whole. The alienated young Jewish Moroccan, when asked from where he or she had come to Palestine (or Israel), would answer, "From Paris," or "From France."[87]

What the cultural and sociopsychological situation in the Moroccan *mellāḥ*s amounted to in the two or three decades prior to mass emigration was a typical illustration of the pitfalls and perils of deculturation: the abandonment of the traditional cultural values in response to the lure of the trappings of modern Western culture, but without the ability to fill the ensuing void by the values of that culture. Many years ago I commented on this phenomenon as observable in the Middle East as a whole, and remarked that in those sectors of Middle Eastern society caught up in the processes of Westernization,

> a true absorption of Western cultural patterns with their implicit ideational mainsprings takes place very rarely; and that in many cases the individual nevertheless tends to abandon his own traditional cultural values, and becomes rootless and superficial. Especially younger people often suffer serious personality damage because, having acquired the external trappings and mastered the overt mannerisms of the Westerners, they feel free to throw off the traditional restraints of their old culture without having first grasped, and often without even suspecting the existence of, the different set of restraints invisibly controlling Western behavior patterns and directing them into morally sanctioned channels.[88]

The developments in Morocco among the younger generation in the *mellāḥ*s fell into this category. As observed by Rivka Bar-Yosef several years before I wrote the above lines, "For the Moroccan community, and in particular for those who came from the *mellāḥ*s and not from the villages, there was nothing on which to draw; they had neither a sufficient Jewish tradition, nor general human Western values. They had become emptied while still in Morocco."[89] What motivated this culturally "emptied" (that is, deculturated) type, Bar-Yosef stated, was the ambition to rise to a higher economic level, to a higher class, the aspiration to achieve recognition. However, if one sees no chance to realize such ambitions, they cause tensions which, in the absence of internal controls, find their outlet in outbreaks of violence. These are signs of an internal disintegration and of licentiousness. "The tragedy is that the retreat to primitive means of release from tension only intensifies the very situation against which they rebel."[90]

These words, let us not forget, were written about thirty years ago. Since then many changes have occurred in Israel, which will be touched upon in the next section.

PROBLEMS IN THE HOMELAND

We started this chapter with a reference to the differences between the crime rates of the Yemenite and the Moroccan Jews in Israel. Our survey of the history of the two communities leads us to the conclusion that one important factor in these differences was the psychological conditioning to which the Jews were subjected in those two countries.

For the Yemenite Jews even though the new economic circumstances which they met in Israel were very different from, and at times more difficult than, those they had left behind in Yemen, adjusting to the Jewish environment and social order presented no serious problems. In fact, the very absence of abuse and degradation meant that, for the first time in uncounted generations, they were able to raise their heads, to move without restraint, and to breathe freely. For the Yemenites, life in Israel was the fulfillment of their hopes and prayers, and the predispositions which they had brought along made them feel that they had come home, and that they were an integral part of what they saw as the miraculous Ingathering of the Exiles. While I would not go as far as the author of the article on crime in Israel in the *Encyclopaedia Judaica* who opined that "these favorable circumstances are obviously the main reason for the low crime rate among them,"[91] I would certainly agree that they are among the factors making for the low Yemenite crime rate. Others, as pointed out above, are their experiences in Yemen, and their personality formation molded, in the course of many generations, by the oppressive Yemenite environment.

Much of the character traits which had developed among the Yemenite Jews in response to their oppression in Yemen persisted after their transplantation to Israel, and was transmitted there to their children, although the conditions in the Jewish state were very different from those they had left behind in Yemen. The Yemenite community in Israel has remained a closely knit ingroup, for which all other Jewish communities, and especially the dominant European Jews, constituted the new outgroup. This relationship has brought into play some of their old patterns of behavior.

In Israel, the Yemenite Jews have occupied a special position among the Jews of Middle Eastern extraction. They were the only Middle Eastern Jewish community whose folk art had a definite impact on the cultural life of the country: Yemenite embroidery, jewelry, and basketry, Yemenite songs, music and dancing, have become an integral part of the Israeli scene. More importantly, there was something in the Yemenite personality which has endeared them to the other Jewish ethnic groups. They were perceived to be devout, modest, patient, peaceable, persevering, hardworking, clean, honest, etc. In the eyes of the Jews of European extraction, the Yemenites were best liked of all Jewish communities hailing from the Middle East.

In the course of the last two or three decades the adjustment the Yemenite Jews made to life in Israel has brought about definite changes in their outlook, in their attitudes to Israeli society and their own community, and in their ethnicity. As Herbert S. Lewis, who made a special study of the Yemenite Jews in Israel, observed in 1984, their old image "should be modified to one of an increasingly sophisticated, well-educated people, well organized and proud of their history, arts, and cultural practices and values."[92]

The reaction of the Jewish immigrants from Morocco to what they found in Israel was markedly different. This was due to a number of factors. While the Yemenites arrived in Israel as total communities, complete with their communal and religious leadership, the Moroccans came to Israel as incomplete, leaderless, overwhelmingly poor, and often culturally deprived groups. Yet in Morocco they had seen themselves, despite their often precarious position vis-à-vis the Muslims, as a superior element, occupying an intermediary position between the native Muslim Moroccans and the ruling French. For them the Israeli environment into which they were transplanted, and the status to which they were assigned, comprised several disappointing features. In contrast to what they perceived to have been their position in Morocco, in Israel they found that they were considered "Orientals," and condemned by their lack of marketable skills to the low rungs of the economic and social ladder.

In Morocco, even those Jews who lived in the villages were conscious of being needed by the Muslim majority, most of whom practiced agriculture and/or animal husbandry. Although there could be no question about the low-class status of the Jews, their services as traders and craftsmen were both required and valued by the Muslims who, because of this very reason, often tried to prevent the Jews from leaving their villages or to persuade them to remain. In these circumstances it was not difficult for the Jews to maintain a sense of self-importance. To this was added the feeling of being superior to the Muslims since they were convinced that their religion, Judaism, and not Islam, was the true religion. Also the low esteem for agricultural work, in many cases the only means of livelihood for the Muslims, was common to Muslim and Jew alike. As against this, in Israel they found that they possessed no skills needed by the established population, that much in their traditional religious observances was considered superstitious by the European Jews, and that they were pressured to engage in agriculture which for a former trader or craftsman was a big step down.

In discussing the "Moroccan problem," Rivka Bar-Yosef cautioned in 1957 that what was important in dealing with such issues was not whether *objectively* the Moroccan Jews were better off in Morocco than in Israel, but what the Moroccan Jews themselves felt *subjectively* about their position in Israel. "If the Moroccans say that in Israel it is worse than in Morocco, one must not make light of this feeling by arguing that the causes of this feeling are subjective. They are objective for the Moroccans." If the Moroccans felt that they were not given the same chances in Israel as the European Jews, it was, she argued, not important whether or not this was really the objective truth. What was important was that such a feeling did exist, the feeling that it was not worthwhile to come to Israel, and that there was here no hope to realize their aspirations, that they were again second-class citizens who had no way out, and this among Jewish brothers.[93]

Added to the frustration of the Moroccan Jews caused by these circumstances was the hurtful lack of understanding for their problems on the part of the European Jews who at the time occupied the leading and power positions in the young state. The antagonism they initially encountered was quite blatant, and it contributed to the Moroccans' frustration and embitterment. In my 1953 book, *Israel Between East and West*, in which I dealt, among other things, with these problems, I reviewed some of the public statements made by Israelis of European and American extraction about the Moroccan Jews. Today, thirty-odd years later, those statements, with their bigoted ethnocentrism and lack of understanding for cultural differences, make disconcerting reading. The Moroccans were stated to be primitive to the highest degree, unable to absorb anything intellectual, completely ruled by wild passions, characterized by drunkenness and fornication, immorality and thievery. They were said to draw the knife at the slightest provocation, to hate the Ashkenazim, and to threaten, "When we finish with the Arabs, we shall go out to fight the Ashkenazim." Worst of all, the negative stereotype was made to apply even to the next generation: "There is no hope even with regard to their children." Also attributed to the Moroccans were instability, emotionalism, impulsiveness, unreliability, incompetence, as well as habitual lying, cheating, laziness, boastfulness, inclination to violence, uncontrolled temper, superstitiousness, childishness, lack of cleanliness, and, in general, "primitivity" and "lack of culture."[94]

As could be expected, the reaction to this negative stereotype was heightened embitterment and tension on the part of the Moroccans who frequently sought and found outlet in violent demonstrations and rioting. One such outbreak occurred in 1959 in the Wadi Salib quarter of Haifa in which conditions, although unquestionably much better than in a typical Moroccan slum, were still much worse than in the middle-class neighborhoods of other parts of the city.[95] Subsequently, with improvements in living conditions, with the Israeli-educated youth gradually replacing the older immigrant generation, with service in the army jointly with other Israelis, with the gradual penetration of Middle Eastern Jews into all occupational sectors, and with other improvements, both the negative stereotype of the Oriental Jew among the Ashkenazim, and the resentment of the Ashkenazim among the Oriental Jews gradually diminished, even if it did not completely subside.

In this process of change an important part was played by education, and by the understanding gained from serious studies of the psychosocial problems of Moroccan Jewish children and youth. These studies showed that the problematic features in the Moroccan Jewish personality were the result, not of genetic factors, but of environmental conditions and conditioning. One such study, for example, found no significant differences in Israel between children of the *mellāḥ* and Polish Jewish children who had suffered from severe educational neglect. Moreover, as Feuerstein and Rischel emphasized, actual experience in Israel furnished definite proof concerning the educational potential of North African youths and their ability to develop fully once they were placed into a constructive environment.[96] This was certainly a far cry from the categorical condemnation of "there is no hope even with regard to their children," made in 1949.

The decisive proof of the ultimate adjustment of the Moroccan Jews to life in Israel came in the 1970s, when King Hassan of Morocco tried to persuade them to return to Morocco with promises of equal and even preferential treatment: their response was practically nil (cf. above, p. 116).

By the 1980s, Israel's "Moroccan problem" was well on its way to being solved. More than three decades had passed since the Moroccan mass immigration to Israel, and in the course of that time a new generation had grown up. This new generation was a product of Israeli education, and it had gone through the great finishing school that the Israeli army is, in which every Israeli young man has to serve for three years and every Israeli young woman for two. The bonds between this young generation and their contemporaries from the other Jewish sectors of the population were reinforced by the Arab-Israeli wars of 1956, 1967, 1973, and 1982, each of which contributed its share to strengthening the brotherhood among them. In the light of these developments the remaining higher incidences of Moroccan criminality and delinquency appear as but the last tremors of the great social upheaval which had begun in Morocco a century ago, was carried over into Israel with the great waves of immigration in the 1940s and 1950s, and had begun to subside in the 1960s.

Although the exodus from Morocco and the arrival in Israel were not separated by forty years of wandering in the desert as was, according to the Bible, imposed by divine will on the Children of Israel who escaped from Egypt, the decades that passed since the Moroccans' arrival in Israel, were, in a sense, their time of desert wandering, which by now have come to an end. The very designations Moroccan, Yemenite, Iraqi, or, for that matter, German, Polish, Russian, have by now lost most of their original import. All the Jews of Israel, of whatever extraction, feel today that they are no longer hyphenated Israelis, but part of one nation.

6

Jewish and Arab Folk Culture

INTRODUCTION

A quotation from the incomparable Edward William Lane (1801–1876) can serve as the leitmotif of a discussion of Jewish and Arab folk culture. Lane, who lived in Cairo for several years in the early nineteenth century, and was an astute observer of life in that city, remarks in his classic *The Manners and Customs of the Modern Egyptians*, "It is a very remarkable trait in the character of the people of Egypt and other countries of the East, that Muslims, Christians, and Jews adopt each other's superstitions, while they abhor the leading doctrines of each other's faiths."[1] In the sequence Lane adduces examples of what today would be called interfaith in action, as he observed it on the popular level.

Today we don't like the word "superstition" because it implies a negative value judgment. We prefer to speak instead of popular beliefs and customs. Translated, then, into modern terminology, what Lane says is that he found that Muslims, Christians, and Jews shared each other's popular beliefs and customs, while abhorring each other's basic religious doctrines. These observations are as valid today as they were 150 years ago in Lane's Egyptian days, or if we want to be very exact, we should say that they remained valid until the mass emigration of all or most of the Jews from the Arab countries of the Middle East, which began with the independence of Israel.

The second part of Lane's observation needs little or no elaboration. The Muslims, from their dominant position as the overwhelming majority and their unquestioningly assumed superiority as the recipients of the final divine revelation contained in the Koran, have always mocked the Christians for their belief that Jesus was the son of God which was, for strictly monotheistic Islam, absurd ("How can Allah have a son?") and blasphemous idolatry ("How can there be another God next to Allah?"). They contemned the Jews for falsifying the *Tawrāh*, the Tora, which they recognized as God-given in its original form, and for not believing in the prophethood of Muhammad and the "Revealed Book," the Koran, which he received from Allah. The Christians, on their part, while fully aware of their *dhimmī* status, scorned both the Muslims and the Jews precisely for not recognizing and not understanding the great mystery of the Trinity and of the divinity of Jesus Christ. The oppression of the Copts, the native Arabic-speaking Christians of Egypt, who constitute the largest Christian minority in the Arab world,[2] is a long and inglorious chapter in the history of Arab Egypt. Some ninety-five percent of the Copts are monophysites, that is, they believe that Christ had not two natures, one human and one divine, which is the Catholic position, but only one single nature which was divine, and in which the human was absorbed. The remaining five percent of the Copts are Catholic.

As for the Jews, one can characterize briefly their position by saying that they shared the Muslims' dim view of Christianity, and the Christians' equally dim view of Islam, to which they added their own contention that Muhammad was a madman and an ignoramus whose pretensions to prophethood were without any basis or justification. Moreover, they ridiculed the Muslims who in their prayers refer to Muhammad as "our lord Muhammad, the illiterate prophet."[3] For the Jews, with the high valuation they put on literacy and learning, this was a self-contradiction: how can a person be illiterate, an ignoramus (*ummī*), and yet a prophet? For the Muslims, of course, Muhammad's illiteracy was but a further proof of his being a divinely inspired prophet, for without divine inspiration how could an illiterate and ignorant man have written the magnificent rhymed prose and used the pure and powerful language contained in the "Arabic Koran" (cf. Koran 12:2: *Qur'ānun ʿarabiyyun*), which for thirteen centuries has been regarded by the Arabs everywhere as by far the greatest masterpiece written in that tongue?

Before embarking on a brief presentation of the popular customs and beliefs—the two most important elements in folk culture—much of which was indeed shared by the adherents of the three religions referred to by Lane, a word is in place about the grammatical tense which will be used in the following pages. There can be no doubt that many of the customs and beliefs I shall discuss no longer exist, having fallen victim to the forces of modernization, industrialization, Westernization, and urbanization which have penetrated the Arab world especially since the end of World War II. In addition, the cultural symbiosis which had characterized the Jews and Arabs in the Arab lands for many centuries has come to an abrupt end in practically all Arab countries as a result of the mass emigration of the Jews in and since 1948. There are today no Jews left in Iraq, Libya, Tunisia, Algeria, South Yemen; almost none in Egypt, Lebanon, and Yemen; and relatively few in Morocco and Syria (as well as in the non-Arab Muslim countries). The uprooted Jews, whether they settled in Israel, France, or America, were exposed to stronger modernizing influences than were at work in the countries they had left behind, and therefore the old customs and beliefs have disappeared among them more rapidly.

This being the case, I shall not use in this chapter the "ethnographic present," which is, as a rule, adopted by cultural anthropologists even in dealing with a past period, but shall instead put into past tense whatever I have to say about the subject of Jewish and Arab folk culture in Arab lands. The native Christians in the Arab countries, who will be considered in the present context only tangentially, have also shared many popular customs and beliefs with the adherents of Judaism and Islam, but since they constitute largely more urbanized and Westernized communities than the Muslim Arabs, the traditional customs and beliefs among them have fallen into desuetude more rapidly than among the latter.

THE JINN

One of the most pervasive features of folk culture in the whole Middle East was the belief in, and fear of, the evil spirits, and the resort to protective measures against them. In Arab countries the most frequently encountered term among both Muslims and Jews (as well as among the native Christians) denoting evil spirits was jinn. Jinn is the collective form. The singular is *jinnī* or *jānn* or *janūn*, the plural *jānn*, *jinān*, *jinniyya*, *jnūn* (Morocco); the feminine, *jinniyya*.

According to the Koran (55:15) Allah created the jinn of smokeless fire. Iblīs, the Koranic equivalent of Satan, is, according to one passage (Koran 18:48/51) a jinn; according to another (2:32/34), an angel. Although the jinn are composed either of flame or of vapor, they are mostly invisible, hence imperceptible to our senses. But they are capable of assuming different forms and of carrying out prodigious tasks impossible for men. The jinn were created prior to man, are capable of salvation, and Muhammad was sent to them as well as to mankind. Some jinn will enter Paradise, while others will be condemned to hellfire. The world of the jinn closely duplicates that of man: there are male and female jinn; Muslim, Jewish, Christian, and pagan jinn. They are intelligent, although in some folktales they appear as naive and gullible. They are attracted to humans, in most cases with the intention of harming them, but occasionally because they enjoy human company. It can happen that a female *jinniyya* assumes human form and a man takes her to wife; the two may live together happily until something happens which makes the husband aware that his wife is of the jinn. Stories of such occurrences circulated among both Muslims and Jews.[4] In general it can be stated that belief in the jinn has assumed identical forms among Jews and Muslims down to small details. In fact, the fear of the jinn and the necessity to provide oneself with protection against them, were significant unifying factors among the Jews and Muslims in the Arab world.

There are numerous studies of the jinn in Arab countries, the most detailed and thorough of them being that of Edward Westermarck, who in his matchless *Ritual and Belief in Morocco* devotes several hundreds of pages to them, reporting in meticulous detail everything he could elicit about the jinn from his numerous Moroccan informants. While Westermarck discusses only the Muslim Moroccan beliefs about the jinn, from the works of other students of Morocco it becomes evident that, by and large, the same beliefs were found among the Jews as well. Also the various means and measures employed in order to protect oneself from the jinn's baleful power were shared by the Jews and Muslims in Morocco and other countries of North Africa. As André Chouraqui observed,

> An entire occult universe encircles man and obliges him to employ rites which render the *jnun* innocuous, or if the evil did occur, are calculated to alleviate it. One is surrounded by a whole arsenal of protection: phrases in which the number five, effective in keeping off the Evil Eye, recurs . . . figures of fish, or of Hands of Fāṭima outside or inside the houses . . . Oppressed by this mysterious world, the religious barriers are relegated to second place: it is of little importance whether the wizard or healer is Muslim or Jewish, the people, Muslims or Jews, consider only the effectiveness for which they hope. Marabouts (holy men), dervishes, *f'qih* (wise men), degaguez, walis (saints), mu'addibs (teachers), rabbis, refafas, there are legions of such persons inspired by God, men and women who can bring illusory succor to the misfortunes of the masses. If the rabbi or the refafa are impotent to alleviate the evil, if the doctor who is nowadays consulted more often was unable to bring about the rapid cure hoped for, one goes, even today, to the marabout or the local de-

> guez . . . The stall of the Jewish healer in the *mellāḥ* is often sought out by Muslims and even by Christians.[5]

Needless to say, the belief in the jinn was as deep-rooted and widespread among the Muslims and other communities in Palestine as it was all over the Arab world.[6]

As indicated by Chouraqui's remarks, the similarity between the Muslim and the Jewish beliefs in the jinn was complemented by a similarity between the preventive measures used in the two communities as a protection against the demons or as a cure in case they succeeded in doing harm.[7]

A special type of jinn is the spiritual counterpart, or double, of a person, which was believed to be born together with each child, was of the same sex as he, accompanied him or her throughout life, fell ill when the child became sick, and died at the end of the latter's life. In Syria, Egypt, and Morocco a male double was called *qarīn*, a female, *qarīna*. The same belief was found among the Jews of Morocco, who also believed that a person must not get angry lest the demon, too, get angry and cause him harm.[8]

THE EVIL EYE

Next to the jinn the most dangerous source of harm is the evil eye. Belief in the power of the eye, of a glance directed with envy or malevolence, or even innocently, at a person, was widespread all over the world.[9] In Morocco, two distinct variants of the same folk cure, based on the same belief in the evil eye, were found among the Muslims and the Jews. Among the Muslims of Tangier, if a person was suspected of having been injured by the evil eye, they symbolically burned the evil eye by burning a piece of alum and letting the stricken person inhale the smoke, and then after having everybody in the house spit on the alum, it was thrown into the drain. Among the Jews of Morocco, a member of the patient's family went about with a glass, and asked everybody who may possibly be supposed to have caused the illness to spit in it, and then the sick person was smeared with the saliva or made to taste it.[10]

Fire and water were believed to be potent purifying and prophylactic agents used against the evil eye by both Muslims and Jews in Morocco. Among the Muslims in Aglu, if somebody suspected another person with whom he was sitting of having cast upon him an evil glance, he took fire or water and spilled it on that person, as if it were accidental. The object was to make the latter angry and thereby cause his dangerous look to fall back upon himself. But the use of fire and water may also have arisen from the idea of burning or washing away the evil influence. Among the Jews of Mogador, if some misfortune befell a house soon after it had been visited by a person, an attempt was made to get hold of a little piece of his clothes, which was then burned, together with a lump of charcoal and some salt, at the precise place where he had been sitting. Then water was thrown over the ashes, and those who dwelt in the house washed their faces and hands, and subsequently also the floor of the room, with the water.[11] This procedure and many more like it were based on the belief general among both Muslims and Jews all over the Middle East that some persons had the evil eye with which they could cause untold harm to others, even without wishing to do so.

The belief in the evil eye, to which references are found in the Koran and *ḥadīth*, goes back among the Jews to Talmudic times, and beyond them, to the Assyrians and other ancient Near Eastern peoples. It was also prevalent in ancient and modern Europe.[12]

As for protective measures against the evil eye, one of the most widespread was the use of amulets in the shape of a human hand, or of drawings representing a hand. In many cases such pictures of a hand, commonly called in Arabic *khamsa*, meaning five, were painted on the walls of houses or on a door. Often these representations were so stylized or abstracted that all one could recognize in them were five elements standing for the five fingers. Westermarck reports that he saw such magic graffiti on many houses of both Muslims and Jews in all parts of Morocco.[13] For the protection of persons, especially of women and children, hand-shaped amulets, made of brass, silver, tin, iron, or even gold, in various sizes, were hung on the ears or the temples, or else symbols of "five" were tattooed on the arm, the lips, or the nose. Also animals and valuable objects were protected with these patterns. Occasionally, the metal hand-shaped amulets, made by Jews, had six fingers instead of five, or even as many as seven. The Jews of Morocco used to suspend their lamps on life-sized, or larger than life-sized, brass hands, which were a combination of charm and decoration.[14]

The verbal equivalent of the graphic or metallic representation of the hand was to utter the words "*khamsa fī ʿaynek*," that is, "Five in your eyes," accompanied by a gesture of stretching out the right hand's fingers toward the person suspected of having the evil eye.[15] Among the Muslims such a magic hand was also called "the hand of Fāṭima," and among the Jews simply "*hē*," the name of the fifth letter of the Hebrew alphabet whose numerical value is five.

Other types of charms used by both Arabs and Jews against the evil eye in Morocco were in the shape of crescents or of the Star of David.[16] The use of the Star of David (in Hebrew *Magen David*, i.e. "Shield of David") as the central decorative element in Moroccan Muslim amulets is but one example of many of the employment of the hexagram, or six-pointed star, as a magical sign in many cultures from the Bronze Age to modern times, although it was made into a national symbol only by the Jews.[17]

MAGIC

Magic was an all-pervasive element in the folk belief and custom of both Jews and Arabs in all Arab lands. While magical beliefs and practices were part of folk culture all over the world, those of the Jews and Arabs evince a particular affinity, which makes their study most rewarding within the context of an inquiry into the relationship and cultural interdependence of the carriers of the two faiths.

Magical practices in a most general way aim at influencing those forces of nature which untutored man considered intractable and mysterious, and those supernatural powers and beings with which he peopled the universe. The Jewish attitude to magic has, ever since biblical times, always been markedly ambivalent. On the one hand, there was, on the part of biblical legislators, unconditional opposition to, and total condemnation of, all magic, to the point of considering its practitioners deserving of the death sentence. As we read in Exodus (22 : 17), "Thou shalt not suffer a sorceress to live." Legal decrees such as this presuppose a belief in the reality and efficacy of magic, a belief shared by the authors of the biblical laws and by the common people. On the other hand, there existed a contrary, more enlightened view, held by several prophets, which saw in sorcery, enchantments, astrology, and related practices nothing but "vanity," that is, delusion and illusion, which had neither substance nor any power to influence events (e.g., Isa. 47 : 12–15; Jer. 10 : 2–3). In sharp contrast to this view, and in blatant disregard of the prohibition in Exodus, magic was in all ages both believed in and practiced by the people (including many leaders), with the exception of a very few rational philosophers such as Maimonides.

The belief in magic (Arabic *siḥr*) was common among the Arabs as well, as were magical practices. Muhammad himself, conditioned as he was by the Arab culture in which he grew up, believed in the reality of magic, as can be gathered from several Koranic passages. One classic example is Koran 2:102: ". . . the devils [*shayāṭīn*] disbelieved, teaching in Babel mankind magic [*siḥr*] and that which was revealed to the two angels Hārūt and Mārūt." According to the context of the passage, this event took place in the days of King Solomon who believed in God, but seems to have been unable to prevent the spread of the knowledge of magic which the devils taught men. The attribution of the origin of magic to satanic teachings in the days of Solomon indicates that this was one of the many ideas Muhammad took from his Jewish informants. Incidentally, the Arabic word *shayṭān* (Satan, pl. *shayāṭīn*) itself is derived from the Hebrew *Satan*, via the Ethiopic, but the belief in the existence and power of many kinds of evil spirits had been part of Arab folk culture long before Muhammad. From the numerous Koranic passages which tell of divine miracles being belittled by the people as "sheer magic," it emerges clearly that in the social environment of Muhammad people believed that with the help of magic it was possible to perform prodigies closely resembling miracles performed by, or with the help of, God (cf. Koran 5:110; 6:7; 11:20; 27:12; 28:36; 34:42; etc.). This view is, of course, reminiscent of the biblical story in which the magicians of Pharaoh and Moses, the man of God, perform identical feats: the former with their magic, the latter by the grace of God (Ex. 7:11).

The Talmudic legend, according to which King Solomon enslaved spirits,[18] was embellished in Arab folk tradition that knows even the names of the seventy spirits whom Solomon made subservient to him.[19] According to Arab authors, this kind of magic was licit, and contrasted with the illicit ("black") magic which was traced to Iblīs (the devil) through his daughter or his son's daughter Baydakh.[20] According to al-Ghazālī (1058–1111), the great Arab theologian and mystic, magic is a science which makes use of the properties of substances (*jawāhir*, as contrasted to form) and numbers under certain astrological conditions for the purpose of making of them a magical figure (*haykal*) in the shape of the person to be enchanted.[21] While this is but a philosophical description of one type of the many known as sympathetic or imitative magic, the use of the term *haykal*, which is of Hebrew derivation and hints at the *hekhalot* mysticism, seems to indicate that Ghazālī relies here on Jewish sources in his description of this form of magic.

Regardless of the Jewish position on magic as expressed by biblical authors, Talmudic sages, medieval Jewish philosophers, and that position's counterpart found in the Koran, its commentators, and the works of Muslim philosophers, magic played an important role in the folk life of Jews and Arabs. In Jewish society, down to the Haskala, the belief in the power of magic was practically universal both in the Middle East and in Europe. The influence of this powerful and all-pervasive folk belief on the rabbinical leaders is illustrated by the fact that Maimonides, one of the few medieval Jewish philosophers who rejected magic, was sharply criticized for this view by the thirteenth-century French rabbis (who denounced him for other reasons as well). To give even a cursory review of the attitude on magic as expressed in Jewish religious literature from Talmudic times to the age of the Haskala—a matter of some fifteen hundred years—would burst the framework of the present study. But it should at least be mentioned in a general way that most of the hundreds of Jewish authors who expressed themselves on magic took a positive view of it, and unhesitatingly provided instructions as to how to resort to the use of *s'gullot* (incantations), *r'fafot* (interpretations of itching of various parts of the human body), *simanim* (signs), *goralot* (destinies), *shimmushim* (uses), *shemot* (names of angels), etc. This is but one of the indications of the role magic played in Jewish everyday life. Although Yosef Dan may be right in emphasizing that magic literature and practices centered around private and personal concerns, he is surely wrong in concluding that therefore magic had a "relatively insignificant influence on medieval Jewish life."[22] Much of human life revolves around private and minor matters, such as aches and pains, illness and health, frustrated or unrequited love, fears of accidents, the lure of success, curiosity about the future, and, in the case of childless couples, the desire for children, and other "private" matters which have always loomed large on the horizon of each individual, and might prompt him to resort to magic. As such, a more realistic estimation of the role of magic in Jewish life up to the Haskala (and in many sectors of the Jewish community also beyond it) would be to recognize its ubiquity and the important role it played in everyday life. True, magic, as Dan put it, "did not relate to the major historical and ideological problems of medieval Jewish society," but what role did such major problems play in the everyday life of the average Jew and Jewess? An entirely negligible one. The daily events and incidents, fears and desires, formed an unbroken chain from birth to death in the life of the Jewish and gentile Everyman. And it was the firm belief in, and daily practice of, magic which smoothed that always rough, and often difficult, passage from cradle to grave.

Although the Jews were throughout their history in both Christian Europe and the Muslim Middle East much more literate than their gentile neighbors, they were as blissfully unaware as the latter of the basic discrepancy between belief in one God and belief in, and practice of, magic. The essential approach to God in all three monotheistic religions is to adore Him, to love Him, to propitiate or conciliate Him, and to appeal to His mercy in asking His help, and thus escape evil and attain good. Magic, on the other hand, as James G. Frazer long ago discerned it, is based on the belief that by performing certain acts man can coerce the supernatural forces and beings to do his will, and in this manner obtain his desire. The gap between the two approaches, the religious and the magical, was at least partly bridged by invoking in the magic incantations, or using in the other magic acts, the names of angels, some of which were of scriptural authenticity, but hundreds more of which were concocted for the explicit purpose of being used in magic. Inasmuch as angels are in the pantheons of each of the three monotheistic faiths, references to them in appropriate verbal or deedal formulae, appeals to them to perform what the magical practitioner and his client desire, gave the whole magic act or rite a sort of religious legitimacy. The use of such angelic names made it appear as if the performance of the magical act lay within the boundaries of the lawful according to the tenets of religion.

Of the many magical practices which are shared by Arabs and Jews only a few can be mentioned. In Syria, if a child was subject to fits, which were supposed to be caused by the jinn, a knife or a sword was held over his head.[23] Because the use of iron as a protection against demons is attested among the Jews since Talmudic times,[24] one may assume that this particular magical rite was adopted by the Arabs from the Jews. Another magical procedure common among members of both faiths was the custom of barren women to drink of the water in which the body of the dead was washed, in order thus to become fertile.[25] In Morocco a magic cure for a child suffering from eye ailments was to wash its eyes with water in which the child's umbilical cord (which they preserved) had been soaked.[26] In both communities they rubbed the child's body with oil three days after his birth, and sprinkled henna on his limbs as a protection.[27]

Occasionally the same customs appeared with some variations between the Arabs and the Jews. Among the Jews of Morocco, if a woman did not want to become pregnant, she wore a ring into which was set a stone called by them *ʿayn al-harr* (Arabic, cat's eye). It was a white stone with a black spot in the middle. Among the Moroccan Muslims it was the husband who wore such a ring, and if he did not want his wife to become pregnant, he turned the stone toward the next finger at the time of intercourse.[28] Sometimes one and the same custom appeared among the Jews in one locality and among the Arabs in another, remote from the first. Thus the Jews of Tunis kept the coat of an emissary, R. David Rofe ("Physician"), who had died there, and if a woman had difficulty in labor, they put this coat on her so she would deliver quickly. Similarly among the Arabs of Palestine, a woman who was in difficult labor was covered with a blanket from a saint's tomb; in Jerusalem they used a blanket from the grave of Shaykh al-Khalīlī for this purpose.[29]

THE FORESKIN IN MAGIC

Several decades ago I began to collect Jewish birth customs. After keeping at it for a few years, I gave up the effort when, having amassed a large amount of data, the sources (both oral and written) still showed no sign of drying up or even diminishing. Most of what I managed to collect takes up more than 100 pages in one chapter of my book *On Jewish Folklore*.[30] Even this is a relatively meager crop when compared, for instance, with the amount of material collected by Westermarck in one single country, Morocco: his discussion of the rites connected with childbirth and early childhood in that country alone take up sixty-four pages in his classic *Ritual and Belief in Morocco*.[31] What I regret most is that I have never made a systematic effort to compare the Jewish birth customs I collected from informants from Arab lands and from written sources with those reported by researchers specializing in Arab folk custom such as Westermarck, Doutté, and others. The identity or similarity of birth customs observed by the two communities which such a comparison would undoubtedly establish, would, I believe, be a valuable testimony to the closeness of Arab and Jewish folk life. Let me confine myself here to one single item figuring in the birth customs of both Jews and Arab, the foreskin.

Westermarck reports that among the Ait Warain Berbers it often happened that at the circumcision of a boy, his mother, immediately after the operation, swallowed the foreskin with some water. This was done because of the belief that if she did so her son would never be found out if he committed theft, adultery with another man's wife, or any other crime.[32] This was the only instance Westermarck found in Morocco of the ingesting of the foreskin by anybody. However, Françoise Legey writes that Muslim grandmothers in Morocco ate the foreskin "in order to intensify their love for the child." She also mentions that Jewish women often ate the foreskin of a newly circumcised child so as to have boys born to them, and that Muslim women ate the testicles of a rooster, and Muslim men the testicles of a sheep, in order to have children.[33] Among all the other Moroccan tribes, outside the Ait Warain, that Westermarck studied, he found that the foreskin was either buried (the most frequent form of disposal), or threaded on a string and preserved by the barber who functioned as the circumciser, so that in case the boy died, and the parents accused him of having caused his death, he should be able to prove that he had circumcised many boys who had come to no harm, and that their son must have been killed by *jnūn*.[34]

In my own inquiries I found that among the Middle Eastern Jews, as well as the Sephardi Jews in Safed and Jerusalem, the foreskin was considered a powerful fertility charm, and was therefore swallowed by barren women who desired to become pregnant. In many cases the *mohel*, the ritual circumciser, was asked in advance by the husband of a barren woman to put aside the foreskin for her in exchange for a payment. The swallowing of the foreskin for this purpose was practiced also among the Jews of Turkey, among "the uneducated Jews of Egypt," and among both Jews and Muslims in Tripoli, Libya. Also the Jews of Yemen used to preserve the foreskin as a remedy for barrenness.[35]

Several Hebrew books of charms recommend this method of obtaining fertility: "For a barren woman, so that she conceive: Let her swallow the foreskin of a [newly] circumcised child." Or: "Take the foreskin of a child and dip it in honey, and let her swallow it."[36] This custom was discussed from the point of view of its ritual permissibility for several generations, and in 1931 the Sephardi Chief Rabbi of Tel Aviv, R. Yaᶜaqov Moshe Toledano, summed up the issue in his book *Yam haGadol* ("The Great Sea"), coming to the conclusion that he was inclined to consider it prohibited by biblical law, because this act fell into the prohibited category of eating part of a living body.[37]

Also the threading of the foreskins on a string and their preservation was practiced among Sephardi Jews. I still remember how I learned about this in the late 1930s from R. David Prato (1882–1951), who was chief rabbi of Alexandria, Egypt, from 1927 to 1936, chief rabbi of Rome from 1936 to 1938, and again in Egypt from 1945 to his death. Between 1938 and 1945 he lived in Tel Aviv, where he was kind enough to let me interview him several times. On one occasion, while we were sitting in his study, and he was telling me about Jewish birth customs in Alexandria, he pointed to a large, polished wooden box which rested on top of his bookcase, and said: "That box there contains almost all the foreskins of the boys I circumcised during my stay in Alexandria." When I asked him what was his purpose in keeping them, he said: "When I die, the string of foreskins will be hung around my neck, and so I shall be buried. It will be my passport to the World to Come."

I find it most interesting that both alternative customs, that of swallowing the foreskins and of stringing them up and preserving them, existed among both Muslims and Jews, but that the motivations for doing so were so different. Among the Muslims it meant insurance against being caught if the boy in later life engaged in criminal acts, or the augmentation of love for him, or the protection of the circumciser against claims of negligence. Among the Jews it meant the achievement of fertility for barren women, and a proof of great religious merit for the circumciser.

JERBA: DEFILEMENT ANXIETY

The influence of specific Maghribite forms of Muslim religiosity on the Jews, which penetrated many areas of observance, is a very large and complex subject which has not yet been explored sufficiently. Hence a very few examples will have to suffice to illustrate the manner and extent of this influence.

The famous twelfth-century Arab geographer al-Idrīsī (died ca. 1165), who wrote a massive work of descriptive geography (completed in 1154) at the behest of Roger II, the Norman king of Sicily, expresses himself rather critically about the character of the inhabitants of the island of Jerba off the Tunisian coast in general and about what he considers their exaggerated scruples concerning ritual cleanliness in particular. They are dark skinned, he says, have a bad character, and are hypocritical. They speak only Berber. They are always ready to rebel, and submit to no authority. They belong to the Wahbī sect,[38] and they consider that their clothes will become defiled if touched by a stranger. Therefore they do not shake hands with strangers, don't eat with them, and don't use dishes which are not their own. Both the men and the women purify themselves every day, they wash in water before every prayer, and in sand after it. If a foreign visitor wants to draw water from their well, they beat him, and fill in the well which they consider defiled.[39]

We have no information as to the observance of precisely these same rules of purity by the North African Jews, but their fear of ritual defilement is attested by Maimonides who wrote in a letter to his son Abraham:

> My son, let your pleasant company be only with our brothers the Sephardim, who are called Andalusians, for they have brains and understanding and clarity of thought . . . And beware of some of the people who dwell in the West, in the place called al-Jerba, and in the Barbary States, for they are dull and have a rude nature. And beware most particularly of the people who dwell between Tunis and Alexandria of Egypt, and also of those who dwell in the mountains of Barbary, for they are more ignorant than the rest of mankind, although they are very strong in their faith . . . They have no clarity of thought at all in all their dealings, in Tora and Talmud . . . Some of them believe and behave in matters of menstruation as do the Beni Maws (?) who are a nation dwelling in the lands of the Ishmaelites. They will not look at a menstruating woman, neither at her figure nor at her apparel, and will not talk to her, and they forbid to walk on the ground upon which her foot has treaded . . . and the things are long and many more than these about which one could speak concerning their customs and acts . . .[40]

Idrīsī and Maimonides describe in the excerpts quoted what can be termed a "defilement anxiety" among the Muslims of Jerba and the Jews of Jerba and the adjoining North African territories, respectively. When one encounters such similarities between the Muslim and the Jewish views on the dangers of ritual contamination, the question of who influenced whom inevitably arises in one's mind. To my regret, I am unable to supply an answer at this time, although in view of the usually greater influence of the dominant majority on the low-status minority than vice versa, I am inclined to believe that the influence proceeded from the Muslims to the Jews.

MARRIAGE CUSTOMS

We can deal with marriage customs only very summarily. Marriage ceremonies, which constitute the greatest public celebration among both Arabs and Jews, can be expected, if for no other reason than their public nature, to manifest great similarities between the two communities. We happen to know a great deal about the Muslim marriage ceremonies in Morocco thanks to Westermarck's admirable, detailed study published in 1914.[41] Sixty years later, Issachar Ben-Ami, an Israeli folklorist of Moroccan extraction, published the results of his investigations of Moroccan Jewish marriage customs in a study based on a great number of interviews he conducted in Israel with old Moroccan Jewish immigrants, both men and women.[42] Although Ben-Ami frequently refers in his footnotes to data presented by Westermarck and others on Moroccan Muslim marriage customs, a systematic comparison of the Muslim and Jewish marriage ceremonies in Morocco (or in any other Arab country, for that matter) remains to be desired. As a matter of fact, the entire field of Muslim and Jewish folk belief and folk custom still awaits comparative investigation, and until that is done no definite conclusion can be essayed on the quality, extent, and relative weight of the mutual influences of the two folk cultures in this area.

Marriage customs have a great fascination for the folklorist, the anthropologist, and the student of folk psychology, but we cannot linger too long among their endless colorful details, since other subjects wait in the wings to make their appearance. However, I cannot resist presenting at least one example which shows a surprisingly close similarity between one particular wedding rite as practiced by the Muslims and by the Jews. In many Middle Eastern Muslim and Jewish communities it was the custom that either immediately upon the first cohabitation of bride and bridegroom, or the following morning, the mother of the bride secured the bloodstained sheet or garment, and exhibited it to the assembled guests as a proof of the bride's virginity which reflected honor upon her whole family. Among the Ait Yusi, a Berber tribe in Morocco, "a woman, who is an expert dancer, takes the chemise of the bride stained with blood . . . puts it on her head, and dances with it."[43] Similarly among the Jews of Marrakesh, on the morning after the wedding, the mother of the bride presented to the family the sheet stained with blood and put it on a tray. A woman dancer took the tray on her head, and performed a dance with it. The women used the virginal blood as a paint for the eyes.[44] Regrettably, Ben-Ami, who reports on this custom, does not say what motivation the Jewish women gave for the use of this unusual eye paint, but Westermarck informs us that the same custom, which was observed also by certain Berber tribes in Morocco, was explained by them by the belief that such blood contained *baraka*, that is, was charged with beneficial powers, and hence was good for the eyes.[45]

Ben Ami offers some general observations to the effect that the prolonged coexistence with the natives of the country, and the isolation of certain Jewish communities especially in the Atlas Mountains, have greatly influenced their physiognomy, and that the Jews, in particular those of southern Morocco, do not differ from their Muslim neighbors even with respect to clothing except for its color which had to be black.[46] A similar comment was made already by Voinot, who made a study of Jewish and

Muslim saint-worship in the 1940s, and who remarked that Moroccan Judaism has been strongly influenced by its contact with Islam.[47] More particularly, with reference to remedies taken from the vegetable kingdom, Mathieu and Manneville observed that "there are no essential differences between the Jewish and the Muslim practices which utilize common plant therapeutic knowledge."[48]

NAMING

An important feature of folk culture, which can be used as a gauge of Jewish assimilation to the Arab culture of the environment, is naming. In general one can state that the more frequently personal names are taken over by members of a certain community from the onomasticon (that is, the nomenclature) of another, the greater the cultural assimilation of the first to the second.

Leaving aside the biblical material, which is too meager to allow general conclusions, and turning to Talmudic times, we find that there was a widespread tendency among the Jews to give foreign names to their children. In fact, a Talmudic passage states that "most of the names of the Jews outside the Land of Israel are like those of the Gentiles" (B. Git. 11b). This trend to adopt gentile names was disapproved by the sages, although many of them, too, had foreign names, especially Greek and Roman names which are transcribed in the Talmud, for example, as Luliani (Julianus), Aleksandri (Alexander), Antigonos, Avdimus (Eudymos), etc. An oft-repeated statement shows that the rabbis tried to stem this tendency by asserting that the first of the four reasons the Children of Israel were delivered from Egypt was that "they did not change their names . . . they entered Egypt named Reuben and Simeon, and left Egypt named Reuben and Simeon . . ." (Lev. Rab. 32:5). The second reason they listed also testifies to their anti-assimilationist stance: Israel was redeemed from Egypt, they said, because they did not change their language. The third and fourth reason given are ethical: the Children of Israel in Egypt refrained from calumny and fornication.

When Muhammad imposed his *dīn* upon the Arabs, the Arab onomasticon underwent a fundamental change. The old pagan Arab names lost popularity, except those which could be reinterpreted in an Islamic sense, such as ᶜAbd Allāh ("Servant of Allah"), and, of course, the name of the Prophet himself, Muhammad, and its variants, such as Maḥmūd. In place of the *jāhilī* names the Arabs began to call their children by the names appearing in the Koran, many of which are biblical Hebrew names. Thus, throughout Islam, the Arabicized forms of biblical Hebrew names were among the most popular given to Arab children; for example, Ibrāhīm, Isḥāq, Yaᶜqūb, Yūsuf, Mūsā, Maryam, Hārūn (Aaron), Dā'ūd, Sulaymān, to mention only a few. While this wide utilization of Hebrew names is not an evidence of Arab assimilation to the Jews, it certainly shows the influence biblical history and heroes had on the Arabs via the Koran.

After the spread of Islam, the tendency to adopt Arabic names became common among the Jews in Arab lands. Even the classical biblical names were used, not in their original Hebrew form, but in the Arabic variants as they appeared in the Koran and were in vogue among the Arabs. Thus Jews in Arab lands were called not Avraham but Ibrāhīm, not Yitzḥaq but Isḥāq, not Yaᶜaqov but Yaᶜqūb, not Moshe but Mūsā, not David but Dāwūd, not Sh'lomo but Sulaymān, etc. The Cairo Geniza contains much information on this point, and shows that the Jewish men in eleventh- and twelfth-century Egypt and other Arab lands were, as a rule, called by biblical or other Hebrew names (mostly in an Arabicized form), while the Jewish women had typically Arabic names. Thus among the Jewish women there were those named Sitt al-Ahl ("Mistress of the Family"), Sitt al-Fakhr ("Mistress of Glory"), Sitt al-Dār ("Mistress of the House"), Sitt Ḥidhq ("Mistress of Skill"), Sitt al-Kull ("Mistress of All"), Sitt Ghazāl ("Lady Gazelle"), as well as others called by simpler Arabic names such as Khulla ("Friendship"), Fā'iza ("Favorite"), Milāḥ ("Beauty"), Mubāraka ("Blessed One"), Mawadda ("Love"), etc. Women were also referred to by Arabic terms of endearment such as Tifla ("Baby"), Ṣaghīra ("Little One"), al-Ṣughayriyya ("Littlest One"), etc.[49]

The discrepancy between the Jewish men's Hebrew, and the Jewish women's Arabic names seems to indicate that, probably, it was the mothers who named the daughters while the fathers named the sons. In biblical times the custom was for the mother to name both her sons and her daughters.[50] In medieval Egypt, under the influence of the strongly male-dominated Arab society, Jewish mothers seem to have given up the prerogative of naming their sons, but retained the right to name their daughters. Although they were undoubtedly familiar with the names of biblical heroines such as Sarah, Rebecca, Rachel, Leah, Deborah, etc., they were ignorant of Hebrew, spoke only Arabic, and were thus more exposed to and less protected from the cultural influences of the Arab environment. Hence the Arabic names of the daughters and the Hebrew names of the sons.

In sixteenth-century Jerusalem the Jewish assimilation to the Arab environment is shown by the names of the Jews to have gone a step farther. Here, not only the women, but also the men, had frequently Arabic names. Among the women we find names such as Ḥilwa ("Sweet"), Qamar ("Moon"), ʿAzīza ("Beloved"), Marḥaba ("Welcome"), Jawhara ("Pearl"), Sulṭāna or Sulṭāniyya ("Queen"), etc. These female names are paralleled by Arabic names of Jewish men such as Khalīfa, Masʿūd, Shiḥāda, Kamal, Ḥabīb, Nāṣir, Aslān, Shaʿbān, ʿAyyād, ʿAbbūd, as well as such typically Muslim Arab theophoric names as ʿAbd Allāh, ʿAbd al-Laṭīf, ʿAbd al-Karīm, ʿAbd al-Raḥīm, Faraj Allāh, to mention only a few.[51] Amnon Cohen has shown the remarkable extent to which Jewish life in sixteenth-century Jerusalem, which at the time was under Turkish rule, was intertwined with the life of the Muslim majority of the city economically, financially, and juridically. The Arabic names used by the Jews (culled from Cohen's book *Jewish Life Under Islam*) show that also the cultural influence of the Arab environment was considerable on the Jews.

DIETARY LAWS DISREGARDED

The problem of mutual influences between Muslims and Jews in any given country or locality is complicated by one additional circumstance, and that is that often the same custom which was found among both Jews and Muslims in a certain place recurred also in other places, in other Arab countries, and even in Europe among both Jews and Christians. Hence these questions are much more difficult to handle than would appear at first glance.

A particular problem within this general category is presented by those remedies and charms which are derived from the bodies of unclean (and hence ritually prohibited) animals and which folk custom nevertheless recommends to be taken internally. An example of the difficulty caused by the contradiction between folk custom and ritual law was presented above in connection with the ingestion of the foreskin as a charm against barrenness. Although Islam too places certain limitations on food intake, and requires that animals be slaughtered in accordance with a religious ritual, Islam is far less restrictive than the Jewish dietary laws. Hence the clash between religious dietary regulations and the demands of folk medicine is an almost exclusively Jewish phenomenon. In general the outcome is that folk medicine retains the upper hand, and the Jewish dietary laws are blithely disregarded in the preparation and ingestion of folk remedies. For instance, the hare, the wolf, the bear, the fox, the porcupine, the dog, the ass, the horse, the raven, etc. are all animals whose meat is prohibited by biblical law. Yet Jewish books of remedies and charms recommend the ingestion of various parts of the bodies of these unclean animals, or the drinking of their milk, in order to secure pregnancy for a barren woman.[52] Evidently, folk medicine, which thrived precisely in the most tradition-bound circles, was able to overlook and overcome religious prohibitions when it was a question of satisfying the desperate longing of a barren woman and her husband for offspring.

Were the ingestion of parts of these unclean animals confined to Jews who lived in a Christian environment, one would be inclined to assume that the practice reflected the influence of the gentiles in whose religious traditions food taboos did not figure. However, the fact is that the same or very similar folk remedies were widespread among the Jews in Muslim lands as well, who certainly could not have been exposed to the influence of Christian folk custom. One is thus driven to the conclusion that these folk remedies developed among the Jews themselves, probably as early as Talmudic times, and were carried along by the Jews to the countries in which they settled, whether in the Christian or in the Muslim world.

Among the animals enumerated above, which are ritually unclean for the Jews and yet whose flesh was ingested by them as a magical remedy, the pig is conspicuously absent. The biblical prohibition of eating pig (Lev. 11:7; Deut. 16:8) put so strong a taboo on swine's flesh that it created a deep abhorrence of the animal itself. In Talmudic times not even the name "pig" (Hebrew *ḥazir*) was pronounced, but it was instead referred to as *davar aḥer* ("another thing"). The Mishna includes a prohibition of breeding pigs (which was practiced by the gentiles living in the country) anywhere in Eretz Israel (M. Baba Qamma 7:7). Other Talmudic sources even place a curse upon him who breeds pigs. In the face of this animus, the ingestion of even a minute portion of swine's flesh as a magical remedy seems not to have been acceptable to Jews, whether in a Christian or a Muslim environment.

As for the Muslims, swine's flesh is forbidden to them in four passages in the Koran (2:168–73; 5:3–4; 4:6; 16:115–16). And yet, in contrast to the Jewish rejection of swine's flesh even as a folk remedy, Arab folk medicine did make use of it in many places, including Upper Egypt and Tunisia.[53] In Morocco, in several parts, among both Berbers and Arabs, the liver or flesh of a pig or of a wild boar was ingested as a nostrum to impart strength and to improve the health of delicate children; as a means to impart immunity from pain, even from beatings; and as a cure for syphilis.[54] The difference in this respect between Jews and Muslims can be taken as indicative of the powerful hold this millennial prohibition and the abhorrence it engendered (or of which it was the expression?) had on the Jews, even if they lived in an environment where Muslim folk custom disregarded the parallel prohibition contained in the Koran.

SAINT WORSHIP

Now we come to what can be considered the mainstay of folk religion in most places in the Middle East among Muslims and Jews, namely the veneration of saints. In both communities, saints came in two varieties: living or dead. The living saints among both Muslims and Jews were individuals possessed of a mysterious, wonder-working force, called by both *baraka* in Morocco, an Arabic term which literally means "blessing," but which has the connotation of "blessed virtue," or "beneficial power." The saint possessing this remarkable power was called by many different names in Arabic, such as *sayyid*, *ṣāleḥ*, *walī*, *fqēr* (*faqīr*); female saints, smaller in number than males, were called by the feminine forms of the same terms, *sayyida*, *ṣalāḥa*, *walīya*. The most frequently heard Hebrew designations for a saint were *tzaddiq* or *rabbi*, but he may also be called *sīdī*, *bābā*, *mūlā*, or *morī*.

One of the most important tasks fulfilled by the living saint of both religions was to write charms. The Muslim saints used sacred Arabic words and passages from the Koran, while their Jewish colleagues employed Hebrew words and passages from the Bible. Often the charm, written on a piece of paper, was encased in a small brass or silver container which was worn hung around the neck. In other types of charms the entire amulet consisted of a small metal plate, square or oblong or given a pleasing decorative shape, upon which the potent words were engraved.[55] I have in my collection several hundreds of such Hebrew metal amulets, made of iron, tin, brass, or silver, many of them having the shape of a hand, a foot, a circle, a rosette, a lock, etc., as well as several dozens of amulets inscribed in Arabic, but otherwise indistinguishable in material and shape from the Hebrew ones.

The range of the purposes for which amulets were obtained and worn encompassed all the human fears, desires, and hopes. Many of them were preventive, including protection against disease, wild beasts, scorpions, human enemies, jinn, and the evil eye. A relatively recent type of amulet is the one which was believed to make the wearer bullet-proof. Others were for good health, prosperity, good luck, safety in travel, or were aimed at exciting love in a man or a woman, bringing about the death of an enemy, making a woman dislike her husband or a man dislike his wife, securing pregnancy for a barren woman, etc. Still other charms were curative, and were believed to rid a person of diseases whether caused by the evil eye or due to other causes. An important category of amulets was that of the *maḥabba* ("love"), which made the wearer beloved or liked by a woman, a man, a ruler, etc. Others made a person feared by the government, or liked by people in general.

An important prerequisite for the efficacy of such a charm was that it had to be written specifically for the person who wished to use it. Of course, a father or a mother could have had an amulet written for a sick child, and in fact amulets for children were a lucrative branch of this customized production of means of supernatural protection. Another prerequisite of efficacy was that the saint preparing an amulet for somebody had to be paid, often quite substantial amounts, depending on the kind of the charm, the reputation of the preparer, and the ability of the customer to pay.

In writing an amulet, among both Muslims and Jews, the name of the person for whom it was written had to be mentioned, and it had to be followed by the name of his or her mother, instead of the usual patronym.[56] One of the small amulets in my possession, evidently written for a poor woman who could not afford a large and richly inscribed one, reads, "Oh, God, please heal Miriam the daughter of Sarah." Any person who knew how to write an amulet could do so, but the greater the reputation of the writer as a saintly person, the greater was the charm's efficacy.

The alternative to applying to a living saint and paying him for an amulet was to visit the shrine of a dead saint, bring him a present, and ask his help. Some saints buried in these shrines had lived recently; others, long ago; some were mythical personages. All had the reputation of having possessed a prodigious amount of *baraka*, and performed miraculous cures while alive and after their death, and it was these features which made their tombs become centers of pilgrimage, attracting many believers from near and far, who flocked to the shrines in the hope of finding succor from the many ills and fears usually besetting tradition-bound societies.[57]

When a man who had the reputation of being a saint died, he often appeared in the dreams of those who had venerated him in his lifetime, and asked or commanded them to build a shrine over his grave. Once a shrine was built, the town or village next to which it was located had acquired a new place of pilgrimage.[58] Structurally, the saints' shrines, many of which dot the countryside in many Arab lands, vary from simple tombs to imposing buildings. They are found in large numbers in all the countries along the Mediterranean, including Syria, Lebanon, Israel, Jordan, Iraq (where Baghdad used to be called "city of the saints" on account of the many holy tombs it boasted), and all along the North African coastline.[59] Even in Saudi Arabia, where the dominant puritanical Wahbī denomination did not tolerate them, saints' shrines did (and still do) exist in many places.

Visits to saints' shrines, unquestionably the most important observances on the level of folk religion, were broadly speaking of two types: they were either annual feasts or individual pilgrimages in which a person who needed the help of the saint visited his tomb at a time of his own choosing, usually on that day of the week on which the saint traditionally received his petitioners. Examples of this kind of private visitation to saints' graves were the visits paid by Jewish men and women to the tombs of the patriarchs in Hebron, or by childless Jewish women to the tomb of Rachel outside Bethlehem. In the latter shrine the women measured with a string the circumference of the tumulus under which Rachel is supposed to rest, and then wound the string around their own body. These visitations still continue at the time of this writing.

The annual feasts at the tombs of saints take place on their traditional birthday or death-day. Such celebrations are called among the Jews *hillula* (Hebrew "merrymaking"), while among the Arabs they are called *mawālid* (sing. *mawlid*, birthday). In Jewish folk tradition the *hillula* is celebrated on the anniversary of the saint's death. In Talmudic times the term *hillula* was used for the celebration of weddings (cf. B. Ber. 30b–31a), and subsequently the same term was used to designate also the joyous festivities observed on the death-days of saints. However, it was not until the sixteenth century that in Kabbalistic Safed the interpretation was put forward that the death of a saint is a kind of mystical marriage between his soul and God, and that therefore the celebration of that day is most aptly called *hillula*.[60] In the case of Moses, who according to tradition was born and died on the same day, Adar 7, the commemoration of both events coincided.

In Muslim folk tradition, as indicated by the term *mawlid*, the festivities in honor of saints generally take place on their traditional birthday. However, in case of the most important celebration of saints among the Shīʿites, that of Ḥusayn, the grandson of Muhammad, it takes place on the anniversary of his death, on Muḥarram 10 (see Saint Worship in Iraq). In

Islam there was at all times vigorous opposition to the popular folk-fests celebrating the saints' *mawālid*. They were considered forbidden *bidᶜa* ("innovation") and officially abolished. However, custom in this case, too, proved stronger than any religious decree, and the *mawālid* returned in full force. In post-Fāṭimid times they became the beloved festivals of the common people, and spread all over the Muslim world. Once the *mawālid* were accepted by the consensus of the community, opposition to them was largely eliminated.

COMMON MUSLIM-JEWISH SAINT WORSHIP

A remarkable aspect of saint worship in Arab countries was the veneration of Muslim and Jewish (as well as Christian) saints by the people irrespective of their own religious affiliation. The phenomenon did not escape the keen eye of Lane, who devoted many fascinating pages to saint worship in Egypt in general, but he commented on it only in passing:

> In sickness, the Muslim sometimes employs Christian and Jewish priests to pray for him: the Christians and Jews in the same predicament, often call in Muslim saints for the like purpose. Many Christians are in the frequent habit of visiting certain Muslim saints here; kissing their hands; begging their prayers, counsels, or prophecies; and giving them money and other presents.[61]

Half a century later Goldziher in his classic *Muhammedanische Studien* devoted more than a hundred pages to the veneration of saints in Islam, and included in it two pages of references to joint feasts, joint places of pilgrimage, and joint prayers of the three religions in Arab countries.[62] He mentions Mesopotamia, Syria, and Palestine as the countries in which this interreligious worship was most prevalent, and begins by citing Jacob of Vitry, bishop of Acre, who reported that some four miles from Damascus there was a miracle-working picture of the Virgin Mary to which "all the Saracens of that province flock in order to pray and to offer their ceremonies and oblations with great devotion." This relationship, Goldziher comments, of the Syrian Muslims to the religious traditions of Syrian Christianity has not ceased until the most recent times, and for characteristic examples he refers to Huart and other scholars.[63] Even more remarkable, Goldziher continues, is the occurrence of this phenomenon at those cultic sites which attract an even wider variety of peoples and which probably go back to pagan traditions. Yāqūt (1179–1229), the famous Arab encyclopedist, mentions a rock situated outside the Bāb al-Yahūd ("Gate of the Jews") at which the people customarily presented votive offerings. Muslims, Jews, and Christians alike would make the pilgrimage to the rock, and sprinkle rose water and other liquids over it. They believed that a great prophet lay buried under this sanctuary, which hailed from pagan times.[64] Again, near Nablus in Palestine, members of all three faiths venerated a rock to which they brought their votive offerings. The Muslims called it Sitt ("Lady") al-Salamiyya, and believed that the cave next to the rock contained the grave of this woman saint about whom they told all kinds of miracles.[65] Goldziher also quotes al-Qazwīnī and Yāqūt to the effect that near Acre, Palestine, there was a holy spring called ʿAyn al-Baqar ("Spring of the Ox"), which used to be a joint place of pilgrimage for all religions. Legends attached to the place had it that the ox which Adam first used for ploughing had emerged from that spot.[66]

At the end of his brief presentation of samples of joint saint-worship Goldziher concludes that "the veneration of saints became the cover under which the surviving remains of vanquished religions could maintain themselves inside Islam." In the sequel of his study Goldziher shows how numerous pagan elements survived in the popular religion in Muslim countries.

The Jews in various Arab countries had the reputation of being able to pray for rain with good results. Already in Talmudic times rainmaking was the specialty of certain Jewish saints, such as Ḥoni haMʿaggel ("Ḥoni the Circle-Maker"),[67] so that this ability, attributed to Jewish saints in Arab lands, had a long history behind it. Until quite recently, it was not unusual that in times of drought the Muslims would call upon the Jews, and in particular upon a Jewish saint, to pray for rain.[68] As for the preparation of amulets, while I have found no evidence of Jews applying to Muslim saints for such protective charms, the reverse is well attested in scholarly literature: it was nothing exceptional for a Muslim to ask a Jewish saint to write or make him an amulet.

Additional data about interdenominational veneration of saints come from Egypt, Tunisia, and, above all, Morocco.

Some three kilometers from Dumahou is the tomb of Abū Ḥaṣīra, an Egyptian Jewish saint, whose mausoleum was venerated by Jews, Muslims and Copts alike.[69] At Shubra, in Egypt, the feast of St. Teresa took place in October. It was a Christian version of a typical Egyptian Muslim *mawlid*. It was celebrated in the vast basilica erected in her honor, and was attended not only by members of all Christian denominations, but also by many

Muslims and Jews, who came to invoke the miracle-working saint and to bring votive offerings to her shrine.[70]

A curious case of interreligious worship is known from Tunis. The eighteenth-century chief rabbi of the Grana, the Livornese Jews in that city, called Sīdī Sifyān, or "Master of Two Swords," had converted to Islam, and after his death his tomb became an object of devotions for the Muslims. In the nineteenth century, Rabbi Uziel al-Shaykh went there to pray for the purpose of obtaining salvation for the renegade saint's soul.[71]

Morocco is the classical land of joint Jewish-Muslim saint worship. In the early years of the present century, Edward Westermarck heard there of two saints whom both the Jews and the Muslims claimed as theirs and worshipped under different names. A Berber Muslim told Westermarck that in such cases of joint worship the Jews always remained outside the *ḥawsh* (roofless shrine) of the saint, but this was disputed by a native Jew to whom Westermarck gave more credence. Sīdī Brāhīm Būᶜ Alī, a Muslim saint buried at the gate of Demnat, received offerings from sick Jews, but only when no Muslims were present. On the other hand, David d-Drāᶜ, a Jewish saint, about whom legends circulated and whose shrine was located to the west of Demnat, was visited also by Muslims. Another Jewish saint, Rabbi David ben Amram, in Tetuan, was reputed to cure Muslim children of whooping cough. Outside Sefru in the Jebel Binna, Westermarck was told that there was a cave called "the cave of the Jew," in which according to the Jews four Jewish *kohens* were buried, while according to the Muslims it was the grave of a Muslim saint.[72]

Reports about Jewish saints venerated also by Muslims in Morocco were gathered by Louis de Chenier as early as in the 1780s.[73] In the 1940s, Louis Voinot, who wrote a book on the subject, found that there were fifty-five Jewish saints whose tombs were the objects of visitation and veneration also by Muslims; fourteen Muslim saints similarly honored also by Jews; and thirty-one saints claimed by Muslims to have been Muslims, and by Jews to have been Jews. In addition to these one hundred saints, there were several others concerning whom the available information was insufficient. The tombs of most of these interreligious saints were (and are) located in the western High Atlas Mountains, just south and east of Marrakesh. However, quite a few were also in the port cities of Agadir, Safi, Rabat, Sale, Larache, Tangier, and Melilla.[74]

The favorite time among the Jews for visiting the tombs of the saints, not only in Morocco, but also in other countries of North Africa, was LaG baᶜOmer, which evidently is a reflection of the LaG baᶜOmer *hillula* of Rabbi Shimᶜon ben Yoḥai, the most popular of all Jewish saints of all ages.[75]

Voinot tried to explain the commonality between the Muslim and Jewish saint worship by pointing out that life side by side for centuries has tended to unify, to a certain extent, the aspirations and customs of the two communities. Both the Muslims and the Jews accept the holiness of saints belonging to the other faith, and when these saints have the reputation of being powerful, members of either group address their prayers and requests to them. Most interesting are those cases in which the Muslims claim that a certain saint was a renegade Jew who converted to Islam, which legitimizes his Muslim saintly status. His former coreligionists nevertheless do not disdain his *baraka*, which, they seem to believe, was not lost as a result of his apostasy. In such cases, as well as in cases in which the religious affiliation of a saint is not in dispute, but the reputation of the saint is so great as to overcome denominational barriers, members of both religions turn to him, whether he was, when he lived, a Jew or a Muslim.[76]

SAINT WORSHIP IN PALESTINE-ISRAEL

In Palestine, as one would expect it to be the case in the land of the Bible, a great many biblical figures were venerated by the Muslims, in addition to an even larger number of saints who lived in Islamic times. Taufik Canaan, a Palestinian Arab physician and folklorist, published in 1927 an excellent, detailed study of the subject.[77] He found that among the biblical saints venerated by the Muslims of Palestine were Abraham and his great-grandsons, the sons of Jacob, Simon, Zebulun, Issachar, Asher, and Joseph, Jacob's daughter Dinah known as al-Khaḍrā, as well as King David, known to Muslim tradition as Nabī Dā'ūd, "Prophet David." The traditional tomb of the Prophet Samuel near Jerusalem was another place of Muslim worship. According to Jewish and Muslim tradition, the Cave of Machpela in Hebron is the burial place of Abraham, Sarah, Isaac, Rebecca, Jacob, and Leah and the shrine built over the cave is a place of pilgrimage and worship for them. Joseph's shrine near Nablus was also venerated by Muslims, Christians, Jews, and Samaritans, as were the shrines of Job and Jonah.[78]

As for the veneration of saints by the Jews in Palestine in the past, much of which has survived into the present, the data were gathered in 1948 by Michael Ish-Shalom.[79] In addition to the biblical figures venerated by Muslims and discussed by Dr. Canaan, Dr. Ish-Shalom found several dozens of other biblical figures whose shrines were honored throughout the centuries by the Jewish inhabitants of the Holy Land, including several who, historically or traditionally, lived and died outside of Palestine, such as Queen Esther, Jochebed, the mother of Moses, Miriam, and even antediluvial heroes such as Adam and Eve, Cain and Abel, Seth, Noah, Shem, etc.

One of the most popular Jewish holy places in Israel is the Tomb of Rachel outside Bethlehem. The rites performed there by barren Jewish women to obtain offspring were referred to above. In a photograph dating from 1913, the Tomb of Rachel is shown decorated with two white symbolic *khamsa*s ("five"), apparently in order to protect the shrine itself from the baleful influence of the evil eye.[80]

Let me insert here a brief reference to another holy place, although it is not a tomb, because it shows that a place can be holy in itself, without the presence of the remains of a holy man or woman. I am referring to the holiest relic of Judaism, the Western Wall in Jerusalem, which is the outer retaining wall of the large courtyard of the Temple area, and which is the only surviving part of the ancient Temple of Jerusalem, as it was rebuilt and enlarged by Herod the Great in the first century B.C.E. It is the custom of the believers, practiced to this day, to write requests on slips of paper and to stick them into the fugues between the huge stone blocks of the wall, where God is believed to pay attention to them, and where they remain until they disintegrate.

More numerous than biblical figures are the personages from Talmudic times, whose tombs were identified and venerated by the Jews of Palestine. Most of the better known of these sages have their individual holy tombs, and so does a group of anonymous sages who are known as "the seventy members of the Sanhedrin."[81] A smaller number of tombs is attributed to holy men who lived in post-Talmudic times, in the Middle Ages, such as the tomb of Maimonides in Tiberias, the multiple tombs of Nahmanides in Hebron, Haifa, Tiberias, and Jerusalem, and of the poets Solomon ibn Gabirol and Y'huda haLevi in several places, etc.

The Israel Museum of Jerusalem has in its possession a tableau painted by a nineteenth-century Palestinian Jewish folk-artist showing several Palestinian Jewish holy places, most of them tombs of saints who had lived in biblical, Talmudic, and later times.[82] The painting is divided into five horizontal rows, the top three of which represent holy places in or around Jerusalem. The first row shows the tombs of "the kings of the House of David," of the Prophetess Hulda, of the Prophet Haggai, and of the Prophet Samuel. The second row shows the Tomb of Rachel, the "Hand" (i.e., monument) of Absalom, the tomb of the Prophet Zachariah, the "House of Study (*midrash*) of Solomon," the Temple of Jerusalem, and the Western Wall. The third row shows the tombs of the seventy members of the Sanhedrin, of Kalba Savuᶜa, of Simon the Tzaddiq, of "the Master of Miracles" (i.e., Rabbi Meir), and the Courtyard of the Marksmen. The fourth row contains pictures of the tombs of the Holy City of Shechem (Nablus): those of Joseph "hatzaddiq" (i.e., Joseph son of Jacob) and his two sons Ephraim and Manasseh, of Elᶜazar, of Itamar, of Joshua, and a picture of the Cave of Elijah. The fifth row shows the holy places of the Holy City of Hebron, including the tombs of Yishai (Jesse), the father of David, of "the fathers of the world" (i.e., Abraham, Isaac, and Jacob), of Abner ben Ner, and of several authors of religious works. Then follow, still in the fifth row, the holy places of the Holy City of Safed, namely, the tombs of R. Yose haBannai ("the builder"), R. Dosa ben Harkinas, R. Jacob Abulafia, R. Jonathan Galante, the Prophet Hosea, R. Moshe Vital, R. Sh'lomo Alsheikh, and R. Isaac Luria. These are followed in the left corner of the fifth row by pictures of the tombs of R. Yoḥanan, Rab Kahana, R. Akiba and his twenty-four thousand pupils, Maimonides, the cave of the Tzaddiqim and Hasidim, and lastly the cave of the Prophet Elijah (shown here the second time). Most of the buildings over the tombs are shown in the painting with the Turkish (Muslim) moon sickle on their top, which for the artist seems to have been simply an emblem of a holy tomb. All in all, the sites shown in the picture can be taken to be the most important or most popular of the Jewish holy places in Palestine, and the picture as a whole is an eloquent testimony to the manifold roots of holiness which nourished the love of the Land of Israel in the hearts of the simple religious Jews a long time prior to the emergence of modern Zionism.

The greatest *hillula* in Israel, in which to this day great crowds of religious Jews participate every year, is that of Rabbi Shimᶜon ben Yoḥai, the famous Talmudic sage of the second century C.E., who among orthodox and Hasidic Jews is still believed to have been the author of the *Zohar*, the holiest book of the Kabbala. His *hillula* takes place at his tomb in Meron in the Galilee, on LaG baᶜOmer, that is, the thirty-third day after the beginning of Passover. The custom is among the Hasidic Jews to bring along to Meron their two- to three-year-old sons, and to have their hair cut there for the first time in their lives. This rite is called by the Arabic term *ḥalaqa* (in literary Arabic *ḥilāqa*), "shaving." They throw the hair into a great bonfire in which they also burn (or used to burn) costly clothes, oil, and money in honor of the *tzaddiq*. In the sixteenth century, Ḥayyim Vital, the famous Safed Kabbalist, reported on this custom:

> It is a custom of Israel to go on the 33rd day of the ᶜOmer to the graves of R. Shimᶜon ben Yoḥai and his son R. Eliᶜezer, who are buried in the town of Meron, as is well known, and they eat and drink there . . . and the sage the rabbi Jonathan Sagis informed me that one year before I went to study with him, with my teacher of blessed memory, he took his little son there with all the people of his house, and there they shaved his head, according to the well-known custom, and made there a day of feasting and rejoicing.[83]

This rite had its counterpart in the Arab world as well. Lane reported in the early nineteenth century that

> it is customary among the peasants throughout a great part of Egypt, on the first occasion of shaving a child's head (which is done at the age of two or three), to slay a victim, generally a goat, at the tomb of some saint in or near their village, and to make a feast with the meat of which their friends, and any other person who please, partake. This is most common in Upper Egypt, among the tribes not very long established on the banks of the Nile. Their Pagan ancestors in Arabia observed this custom, and usually gave, as alms to the poor, the weight of the hair in silver or gold.[84]

Lane adds in parentheses that "This custom may perhaps throw some light on the statement in 2 Sam. 14:26 respecting Absalom's weighing the hair of his head when he polled it." The rite of shaving the heads of children for the first time at the grave of a saint and of placing the hair there was practiced also in Morocco among various tribes.[85]

But to return to the *hillulot* in Palestine-Israel, other tombs of famous sages which attract pilgrims are those of Maimonides in Tiberias, and of the sixteenth-century Kabbalists Joseph Caro, Isaac Luria, Moses Cordovero, Solomon Alqabetz in Safed, as well as those of numerous Hasidic *tzaddiqim*. Usually, the *hillula* is celebrated with great rejoicing, ecstatic dancing, lighting of candles and even bonfires.

In those Arab countries in which the veneration of saints played an important role in Muslim folk religion, this cult assumed the same importance in Jewish folk religion as well. Thus on the island of Jerba (Tunisia), the anniversary of the death of R. Shimᶜon ben Yoḥai was observed by the Jews with great solemnity, with a festive procession in which a richly ornamented candelabrum, called "the Menorah of Shimᶜon ben Yoḥai," was carried aloft, and which concluded with much eating and drinking and merrymaking to musical accompaniment. Also in other parts of North Africa the *hillula* of R. Shimᶜon ben Yoḥai was observed with similar colorful festivities.[86] Both in Libya and in Morocco a similar *hillula* was observed by the Jews on the first day after Passover in honor of the anniversary of the death of Maimonides. This folk festival, called Maimuna, was transplanted to Israel by the Jewish immigrants from those countries, who of course are blissfully ignorant of the dim view Maimonides had of their ancestors.

SAINT WORSHIP IN IRAQ

Among the Muslims of Iraq local cults of saints were (and still are) especially prevalent in the Shīᶜite areas. The theological difficulty of justifying saints in Islam was overcome, although not without orthodox opposition, by attributing transcendental knowledge to the saints: they were men or women who were especially close to Allah, and the miracles they performed were possible only because of the grace of God.

Practically every Shīᶜite village in Iraq boasts of a tomb of a saint, and the cults surrounding these shrines, as well as the legends told about the miracles performed by the saint in the past, give the villagers a sense of security in the face of the omnipresent jinn and other evil influences. The two major misfortunes against which the help of the saint is most frequently invoked are disease and childlessness. The shrines of the more renowned saints attract pilgrims throughout the year, and the most sacred shrines, such as that of Karbelā, some sixty miles southwest of Baghdad, where the decapitated body of Ḥusayn, the grandson of Muhammad, is buried, is a place of pilgrimage rivaling among the Shīᶜites in importance Mecca and Medina. Karbelā had become a place of pilgrimage within a few years after Ḥusayn's death (680), and it has remained a central Shīᶜite place of worship until the present, despite the fact that the tomb was looted and leveled by Sunnī opponents of the cult, or ruined by conflagration, on more than one occasion—most recently the Wahbīs destroyed it in 1801. During the Muḥarram pilgrimage tens of thousands of the faithful flock to Karbelā, whose sanctuary has the reputation of securing admission to Paradise to those buried there, for which reason many old and sick people undertake the pilgrimage so as to die on the holy spot.[87]

In contrast to the *mawālid* of Egypt and North Africa, which are gay, festive, and joyous, with occasional notes of lewdness thrown in, the commemoration of Ḥusayn's death at Karbelā is a somber, mournful occasion, in which men, stripped to the waist, march in festive procession and flagellate themselves rhythmically with iron chains, while men and women onlookers utter desperate cries such as "ohhhh—Ḥusayn, our beloved martyr, we grieve for you!" These exercises are performed by organized groups of young men, who occasionally, in their fervor, get involved in tussles with each other.[88] An important part of these mourning rituals is the performance of passion plays, called *ta*ᶜ*ziyya*, literally lamentation, mourning or consolation, while locally in Karbelā they are termed *shabiḥ*.[89] In these Shīᶜite passion plays costumed horsemen reenact the Battle of Karbelā which ended with Ḥusayn's death.[90] It has been reported that only some years ago it would happen that the man who played the role of the leader of the Arab army who killed Ḥusayn would, after the death scene had been finished, be attacked and torn to pieces by the enraged mob.

Such passion plays are still being performed in Iran and in the Shīᶜite regions of Iraq of which Karbelā is the focal point, as well as among the Muslims in the Indian subcontinent. It is remarkable, and typical of the folk character of these plays that side by side with the deepest grief expressed in desperate wailing, outcries, and self-flagellation, they have room also for hilarity: clown-like figures play parts in them and provide comic relief. In Karbelā the spectators are given *muhr*, cakes of earth from the sacred tomb steeped in musk, which they press to their foreheads in abject grief. The passion plays themselves are performed in Arabic in Iraq, and in Persian in neighboring Iran. In addition to the major figures—the martyr Ḥusayn, the man who killed him and cut off his head (Sinān ibn Anas)—several actors represent angels who, according to legend, wept when Ḥusayn was killed and carried his head to Damascus. Also biblical figures appear, among them Jacob and Joseph, who admit that Ḥusayn and his children suffered more than they themselves did when Jacob was made to believe that his beloved son Joseph was killed, and when Joseph was sold into slavery in Egypt. A contrapuntal element is provided by the scene which shows the wedding of Ḥusayn's son al-Qāsim, and right after it by the scene in which he is murdered by the treacherous enemy. Contrary to historical fact, all the enemies of Ḥusayn are portrayed as Sunnī Arabs. Several scenes show Christians, Jews, and pagans, who are so shaken by seeing the severed head of Ḥusayn that they pronounce the confession of faith, that is, convert to Islam, then and there. In the closing scenes the severed head is the principal speaker and actor. The plays have a strongly mystical element in that the martyrdom of Ḥusayn is presented as the price for which Allah forgives the sins of the Muslims (i.e., of the Shīʿites who believe in Ḥusayn), which is reminiscent of the Christian doctrine of salvation brought to man through the death of Jesus. I should add that the Muslim clergy have from time to time voiced strong opposition to the performance of these passion plays, but to no avail. The plays evidently satisfy a deep-seated religio-emotional need which simply could not be ignored.

Among the Jews of Iraq (all the 120,000 of whom were evacuated in 1950–51 in a major airlift via Cyprus to Israel) there was no counterpart to the violent Shīʿite Muslim Muḥarram performances and passion plays, but the veneration of saints nevertheless played an important part in their religious life. The most famous Jewish saints' tombs in Iraq were those of the Prophet Ezekiel near the city of Hila, of Ezra the Scribe near Baṣra, and of Joshua the High Priest in Baghdad on the west bank of the Tigris River. Pilgrimages to these holy tombs took place throughout the year, although the preferred season for visiting the shrines of Ezekiel and Ezra was at Shavuʿot (Pentecost), while the grave of Joshua the High Priest used to be visited during Hanukka.[91] These visitations were not called *hillula*, as in Palestine, but by the Arabic name ʿĪd el-Ziyāra, that is, "Feast of Visitation." The ʿĪd el-Ziyāra of the Prophet Ezekiel took the form of a festive procession in which a flag was carried, held aloft on a long pole the top of which was decorated by a large metal hand with an engraved inscription to the effect that it was the donation of Joseph ʿAbd al-Eliyahu in 1827, and "May the merits of the Prophet Ezekiel protect us. Amen."[92]

THE JEW IN MOROCCAN MASQUERADES

An intriguing manifestation of the relationship between Muslims and Jews in Morocco is the role assigned to Jews in Muslim Arab and Berber masquerades or mummers' plays, which fulfill in traditional Moroccan culture the important role of folk entertainment with some popular religious overtones. Westermarck and others have described these masquerades—performed on the ʿĀshūrā and/or on the Great Feast—in considerable detail,[93] so there would be no point in giving here their full description interesting though they are in themselves. However, a few general observations as to the role of Jews in them are in place.

First of all it has to be made clear that all the "Jews" appearing in these Arab and Berber mummers' plays were not real Jews but Muslims dressed up as Jews and Jewesses, to whom certain stereotypical roles were assigned in practically all the masquerades. Even more interesting is the light in which these "Jews" are shown in the plays. We shall recall that in the *taᶜziyya* mystery plays performed in Iraq and Iran the portraiture of the Arab enemies of Ḥusayn is calculated to evoke strong hostility to Sunnī Muslims. In contrast to these plays, the "Jewish" personages in the Moroccan mummers' plays are throughout comic or amusing figures who engage in banter, badinage, and friendly interaction with the audience. Thus in a village of the Sahel, a mountain tribe in northern Morocco, Westermarck observed in 1900 a performance in which a "Jew" amused the audience with his twaddle.[94] In the village of Dār Fellaq in the mountain tribe of Jbel Ḥbīb, the mummers' group included a "Jew" who pretended to sell goods and was made fun of, while in Andjra the company included a "Jew" with his wife ᶜAzzūna and his "mule."[95] Among the Ulād Bū ᶜAzīz, at the performance on the second day after the Great Feast, one of the bachelors was dressed up as a Jew, with his face covered with a crude mask to which was attached a long beard of wool, while his head was covered with a blue kerchief (*qazza*) in the Jewish fashion. He carried a stick and led a camel, walking with the others from tent to tent in their own and neighboring villages. The "Jew" asked for fodder for his camel, and the people gave him eggs. He was addressed as *shekh l-geddīd*, "Chief of the strips of dried meat." On the following evening a young man again simulated a Jew, and the tour was repeated. On the evening of the fourth day the Jew was in a like manner accompanied by an *nmer*, "leopard."[96]

In many other masquerades mummers were dressed up as a Jew and a Jewess, or several Jews and Jewesses, and performed lewd or obscene mimicry in the same fashion as was done by the other participants. In the Ḥiaina a mummer played an old Jew named Bashshekh. His face was covered with a mask made of the skins of a sacrificed sheep, with the wool turned outward. A long beard was attached to it, and two side-locks were hung over his temples. His wife was called Sūna. A third person played the stepson of the Jew. Sūna danced, Bashshekh pretended to have intercourse with her on the ground, and the stepson washed him with earth. While this was going on, they were surrounded by a ring of musicians who played on tambourines. This performance was repeated in all the villages visited by the group, until the seventh day of the feast inclusive, and everywhere Bashshekh was presented with money, eggs, and dried meat.[97]

Similar masquerades were performed among various Berber groups. Among the Ait Warain, the star of the performance, called Buiheḍar

("Dressed in skin") had his face and whole body covered with skins of sacrificed sheep. His wife, called *Tudeit* ("Jewess"), was nicely dressed in a woman's costume. Two "Jews" (*udein*) with long beards and teeth of pumpkin seeds, accompanied them. Buiheḍar, who was of a most indecent appearance, mimicked intercourse with Tudeit. Tudeit danced, and the people stuck coins on her forehead, while the "Jews" collected money for Buiheḍar.[98]

Among the neighboring Ait Sadden Berbers, one or several "Jews" and "Jewesses" (called ʿAjjūna, the name by which every Jewish wife was called by the Berbers, and by the Jews themselves if the real name of the woman was unknown to them), were parts of the mummers' groups going from house to house and from village to village. The "Jews" had in their hands papers from which they read out fictitious claims to get a little money from the people, while others in the party, dressed up as sheep and goats, amused the public with the grossest obscenities.[99]

Among the Ait Ndēr the masquerade included two "Jews" with sidelocks made of goattails and long beards of white wool fastened to their faces. They carried a long stick and a basket supposed to have contained goods which they sold to the people, receiving in return a little money, meat, and eggs. The "selling" of goods by "Jews" was a feature of masquerades in other villages as well, and it clearly was a reflection of the actual role played by the Jews as peddlers in the country places.[100]

In Fez, in the course of quite an elaborate mummers' play, "Jews" went from house to house, played on instruments, danced, and sang some nonsense in imitation of the Arabic idiom peculiar to the Jews. Then the masked "Jewesses" danced, first alone, then with their "husbands." A "Jew," carrying on his shoulder a bamboo cane with a basket which was supposed to contain fish, entered and danced. The other "Jews" and "Jewesses" gathered around him to "buy" fish. One of them was pushed and "died." His "wife" wept over him, scratching her face in the usual manner of mourning women. The "Jews" asked the owner of the house to give money for the funeral, telling him that otherwise they would leave the body where it lay. The money demanded was paid, and given to the manager.[101]

Several scholars have tried to explain the meaning of these mummers' plays (of which I mentioned only the "Jewish" features, omitting the many others). The results of their efforts seem to me to be less than completely satisfactory. All I can do here is to state in very general terms that there can be no doubt but that the purpose of these masquerades was to secure some benefit or benefits, such as purification, driving away evil influences, securing good crops, health, and the like. Most frequently they were performed at, or immediately after, the Great Feast (ʿĪd al-Kabīr, or ʿĪd al-Aḍḥā), which falls on the tenth day of the month of Dhū al-Ḥijja, and on which the sacrifice of an animal, usually a sheep, is obligatory. This feast is soon followed by the Muslim New Year (first day of Muḥarram, the next month), so it is the appropriate time for the performance of rites aiming at securing benefits for the coming year.

The important part played by Jews (as represented by Muslim mummers) in these masquerades allows us to draw certain conclusions with reference to the role of the Jews in the life of Muslim Moroccans as perceived by them. First of all it shows that the Jews were neither despised nor hated, and that they had their traditionally assigned niches in Moroccan economy and society. Inasmuch as all the mummers, whether acting the roles of Jews or of Muslims, usually engaged in comic, gross, and exaggerated representations of sexual intercourse, this part of the masquerade could not have had any special Jewish significance. The representation of sexual acts seemed to have to do with fertility magic. The special feature typically assigned to "Jews" in the mummers' plays was the carrying and selling of imaginary merchandise for which they received actual gifts of money and/or food. There can be little doubt that this mummery was performed in imitation of the actual role the Jews played in Moroccan life: making the rounds of the villages with their wares, and thereby satisfying the need of the villagers for consumers' goods not produced by them. One could even argue that, since the masquerades as a whole served the purpose of making sure that the requirements of the people would be met in the coming year, the participation of "Jews" in them must also have served the same purpose: to make sure that during the coming year the Jewish peddlers would unfailingly appear in the villages at the customary intervals, so that the villagers would not remain in want of the many items which they could obtain only from them. If so, the simulated sale of merchandise by the "Jew" and the payment given him in exchange was a simple rite of sympathetic magic just as was the make-believe enacting of sexual intercourse which served the purpose of ensuring the blessings of fertility. In brief, the mummeries of "Jews" in the Great Feast and other masquerades expressed figuratively and confirmed ritually the role played by Jews in Moroccan life. They also show that the Moroccan Muslims clearly knew that they were in need of the services performed for them by the Jews as itinerant peddlers.

I am fully aware that the above interpretation of the role of "Jews" in the Moroccan mummers' plays leaves many details and features contained in them unexplained. In the present context I can try to explain only two more features of these masquerades: the wearing of ample wooly and furry coverage by the mummers representing "Jews," and the surprisingly generous donations of money, eggs, and meat given to them by the people.

In addition to fulfilling the function of peddlers supplying consumers' goods to the tribes and villages, the Jews played an important role in Moroccan Muslim folk belief and custom as rainmakers. Thus, for example, a folktale current in Morocco tells of a severe drought in the lifetime of Muhammad. The Prophet and his disciples entreated God in vain to put an end to it. Then an old Jew went to a Jewish grave, took from it a bone, and keeping it in his hands prayed for rain together with the other Jews. Two hours later plentiful rain began to fall.[102] This folktale had its counterpart in folk custom among the inhabitants of Urfa (in Turkey, close to the Syrian border), who dug up the skull of a Jew, and cast it into the Pool of Abraham, in order to produce rain.[103]

In Morocco the Muslims attributed special rainmaking powers to the Jews, and would ask them to pray for rain.[104] To the same context belongs the custom of the Ait Yusi and the At Ubakhti to make a Jew walk about in their vegetable gardens, and flick the plants with his finger, in order to ensure their growth, evidently because the Jews, whom the Muslims considered a fertile race,[105] were believed to be able to endow the gardens with the requisite fertility.[106] In the light of these beliefs and practices, the bizarre hairy and wooly coverages worn by the mummers who personified Jews could perhaps be explained as symbolizing clouds whose appearance is a prerequisite of rainfall. The imitation of rain clouds was part of rainmaking rites in various places in Morocco. Several types of masquerading for rainmaking were reported by M. Bel from neighboring Algeria, e.g., from the region of Palikao, where "the men dress up as women and perform women's dances to the accompaniment of flutes and tambourines; others wrap themselves in old pieces of tent cloth. In most cases they blacken their faces with soot or coal."[107]

In Morocco, the women uncovered their heads and dishevelled their hair as part of a rainmaking rite. The fluttering of the loosened hair was believed to produce rain. In Dukkala, women used to dress up a ladle as a woman and take it about from tent to tent, dancing and singing, "Taghenja has loosened her hair, O God, wet her earrings." In contradistinction, the uncovering of a bald head was believed in Tangier to produce a cloudless sky, characteristic of the east wind.[108] These customs make us suspect that the hairy and wooly coverings worn by the supposed Jews in the Moroccan masquerades were intended to produce rain which would be well in accord with the special rainmaking ability attributed to Jews.

The money, eggs, meat, etc. given by the people to the "Jews" can be seen as yet another rainmaking rite. Since Islam, like Judaism, considers drought a punishment inflicted by God upon those who have transgressed his law,[109] almsgiving—a great commandment in both Islam and Judaism—is resorted to in order to regain his favor and to induce him to let rain fall. Thus the Ait Yusi gave money and food to the women and children who were walking from village to village with a doll for the purpose of obtaining rain. Similar customs were practiced among the Ait Ndēr and the ʿAbda.[110] These customs make it likely that the money and food given by the people to the mummers playing the role of Jews were also intended to serve the same aim: to induce Allah to let rain fall. Even though there is no overt or direct reference to rainmaking in the role of the "Jews" in the masquerades, the hirsute appearance of the mummers personifying Jews, and the gifts given to them indicate that they were performing that traditionally assigned function.

CONCLUSION

In conclusion, a few general observations are in order on the historical basis of the close similarity between Jewish and Arab folk culture as expressed in popular belief and custom in the Arab countries.

In seeking an understanding of this phenomenon one must first of all take into account that in each of the Arab countries in question the Jewish presence preceded its conquest by the Arabs by several centuries. Some of them, such as Iraq and Egypt, had a Jewish population for more than a thousand years prior to the Arab conquest which resulted in the Islamization and Arabization of the majority of the inhabitants. In others, such as Syria and the North African lands, the presence of the Jews anteceded that of the Arabs by at least five hundred years. In any case, the long pre-Islamic Jewish presence had a certain impact on the local pagan populations. If nothing else, they had at least an awareness of the existence of a monotheistic faith, so that the religion of Muhammad, which the Arabs imposed upon them "with the sword," as the Arabic saying goes, did not strike them as quite so strange and alien as it would have had there been no Jewish population elements living among them.

Jewish presence before and after the Arab conquest also meant that the popular beliefs held, and folk customs practiced by the Jews were at least known to the local population in the pre-Islamic and the Islamic stages of their history. We have no way of gauging the extent of this influence or familiarity, except by an admittedly dubious extrapolation from the few cases in which the folk customs and/or beliefs of the non-Jewish populations coincided with those recorded in the pre-Islamic Jewish literary sources.

One must not lose sight of an alternative possibility in explaining the similarity between the Muslim and the older Jewish folk customs and beliefs. Such similar features could also have originated in an ancient pagan culture and then could have survived, first the arrival of the Jews on the scene, then the successive conversions of some of the natives to Judaism and Christianity, and finally the conversion of their great majority to Islam. The Talmudic sages observed at an early date that, in a clash between *minhag* (custom) and *halakha* (religious law), it is the custom which prevails,[111] and the same observation can be made in regard to the popular beliefs and customs which, all over the Arab world, succeeded in surviving official conversions of the population to monotheistic religions. The belief in the evil eye, dealt with above, is one example of the survival of such a feature from pre-monotheistic times. Another is the veneration of those saints who lack any proof of historicity, and are to all appearances mythical figures—such saints were (and still are) found in numerous Arab countries. Their worship was equally disapproved, or at least disliked, by the Muslim *ʿulamāʾ* (religious scholars) and the Jewish rabbis or *ḥakhams*, but the prevalent popular sentiment made it impossible for either group of religious authorities to proceed energetically against it. What the religious leaders instead did was to proceed to give these beliefs and practices a Muslim, or Jewish, veneer or coloration, and thus to incorporate these originally pagan cults into the confines of orthodoxy.[112] Once Islam was established in what today are the Arab countries, the mutual influences between Jews and non-Jews continued. Such influences in general tend to be stronger from the majority population to the minority than vice versa, if for no other reason than because of the fact that practically all the members of a minority—and especially of a small and scattered minority such as the Jews—necessarily have contact with members of the majority, while many or most members of the majority may live out their entire lives without ever encountering any member of the minority groups. Accordingly, one would expect a priori Muslim folk culture to have had a stronger influence on the Jews than vice versa, and in fact observations made, and studies carried out, in Arab countries actually show this to be the case. In addition to the numerical imbalance, the legal and social inequality of the Jews in Arab countries also facilitated the Muslim-to-Jew, and hindered the Jew-to-Muslim direction of cultural emanation. The contempt the Muslims had for the Jews as *dhimmī*s created a strong predisposition among the former against accepting Jewish cultural features whether on the official religious or on the popular level. However, the Muslims could, and occasionally actually did, simply impose certain features upon the Jews. Although in most cases they did this in order to create a *ghiyār* ("separation") between themselves and the Jews—this was the basic purpose of the Covenant of ᶜUmar (cf. above chapter 3)—at times what they imposed upon the Jews resulted in the introduction into Jewish life of certain Muslim cultural traits or items. Thus, for instance, the Jews were forced to use a certain kind of packsaddle, originally developed in Muslim culture; certain types of clothes which differed from those used by the Muslims but still were in conformity with the styles in use among the Muslims; and Jewish women had to adopt the use of veils in response to Muslim social pressure.

More frequently, Muslim cultural features were adopted by the Jews as a result of their inevitable tendency to emulate traits and items which formed parts of the culture of the dominant Muslim majority. In my book *The Jewish Mind* I devoted a whole chapter to the manifestations of this voluntary adoption and emulation by the Jews in the medieval Arab world of such features of the great Arab tradition as linguistic studies, poetry, science, medicine, philosophy, and mysticism. In chapter 4, I added a detailed case history, that of ninth- to eleventh-century Cordova in which this cultural adoption, and resulting symbiosis, were especially pronounced. "Adoption" in this context does not mean mere copying; rather, what happened among the Jews who lived in the orbit of the great Arab cultural flowering in Andalus was creative assimilation and incorporation of Arab cultural features into the body of the existing Jewish tradition.

As for a similar process on the folk culture level, the present chapter contained a number of examples. One is the *khamsa*, the hand emblem, whose wide distribution among both Jews and Arabs in Arab countries, and absence among the Jews in Christian environments, seem to indicate that its use was the result of diffusion from the Muslims to the Jews. Another, more localized, example is the great emphasis placed on ritual purity among the Jews of the island of Jerba and other parts of North Africa, which appears to have been the reflection of similar attitudes among the Muslims of those lands. A third group of examples is presented by the veneration of Muslim saints by Jews and vice versa, which can be explained only as the adoption of the beliefs of one community by the other. In the area of material culture, the list of feminine apparel contained in the Cairo Geniza documents (discussed in chapter 3) indicates that in the Middle Ages Jewish women in Arab lands wore largely the same clothing as their Arab sisters, which can be explained only as due to the voluntary adoption by the women of the Jewish minority of the fashions developed among the women of the Muslim majority.

The total picture one gains from an overview of the relationship between Jewish and Arab folk culture is one of considerable similarity despite all the efforts exerted by the Muslim rulers and religious leaders to impose a *ghiyār*, separation, between the two communities, which efforts were duplicated on the Jewish side by those of rabbis and *ḥakham*s. There was, of course, throughout the thirteen centuries of Jewish sojourn in Arab lands, a vast difference in power position between Arabs and Jews. While the Arabs frequently issued explicit prohibitions to prevent the Jews from transgressing the rules of *ghiyār*, all the Jewish leaders could do was to admonish the members of their own community not to adopt foreign customs. For the Jews this was as much a Scripture-based religious requirement as was the humbling of the Jews for the Muslims (based, as already pointed out, on the Koran). The Bible contains the commandment, "Ye shall not walk in their statutes" (Lev. 18:3), which originally referred to the Canaanites, and which was interpreted already by the Targum Onkelos and early Midrashim as meaning, "You shall not follow their customs."

Maimonides, who lived in an Arab environment, enumerated in detail the customs of the non-Jews covered by this prohibition, as he interpreted it. According to him, one must not: 1. Wear apparel special to the non-Jews; 2. Let one's hair grow as they do; 3. Shave the sides of the head and let the hair grow in the middle, as they do; 4. Shave the beard from ear to ear; 5. Build places similar to the buildings of the heathens.[113] At first glance, one is struck by the apparent triviality of the prohibited customs as enumerated by Maimonides. The first four of the five seem to touch upon rather superficial matters of appearance, but only until one realizes that the clothes a person wore, and the manner in which he cut his hair and beard were in Arab lands the signs most visibly identifying him as belonging to a certain religio-ethnic group. So that what Maimonides actually says in these four points is that a Jew must make himself readily identifiable as a Jew by wearing clothes, hair, and beard in a manner which clearly differentiates him from the non-Jew.

Due to the differences in apparel and haircut, Muslim and Jewish men were certainly easily distinguishable. With women the situation was less clear-cut, especially once the Jewish women took to wearing the veil in public as did their Muslim sisters. (This subject will be discussed further in chapter 8.) In many other respects, however, the coincidental efforts of Muslims and Jews to maintain *ghiyār* were less than successful. Folk custom managed to override all such efforts. No prohibition could alter the fact that the material component of folk culture was practically identical in the two communities: the architecture, shape and size of dwellings; the furnishings contained in them; the cuisine (except for the differences demanded by the Jewish laws of *kashrut*); the cut, style, and material of the clothes (the Muslim-imposed differences were usually in color only); the jewelry and decorative objects worn by men and women (in many places, e.g., in Yemen, only Jews were jewelers)—all this, with the exceptions noted, were the same among Jews and Muslims. The overall similarity in folk belief and custom has been dealt with in some detail in this chapter. As for language, the Jews in all Arab lands spoke Arabic, as did the Muslims; true, there were dialectal differences, but then so were there between the Arabic spoken in one locality and the other by the Arabs themselves. Folk poetry and other forms of oral folklore (in Arabic) were in many places shared by Jews and Muslims. This leaves official religion (as contrasted to folk religion) as the main area in which most of the differences between the two communities were concentrated. Of course, since religion was an all-pervasive force in the traditional life of both Arabs and Jews, one must in no way belittle the extent of separation this factor created between them. Yet, one can state in general terms that there was for many centuries a great commonality between Jews and Muslims in Arab lands, the like of which developed in Ashkenazi Jewry, living in Christian Europe, for the first time only after the

Enlightenment, and even then only in the circles of the enlightened Jewish assimilants. The great majority of the Jews in Arab lands remained untouched by the Enlightenment, and their relationship to the Muslims remained, until their immigration to Israel, the same as it had been ever since the Middle Ages: religious separatism, coupled with great cultural congruence, especially on the level of folk culture.

7

The Feminine in the Divine

DEITY AND GENDER

In both Hebrew and Arabic all nouns and adjectives are either masculine or feminine; a very few nouns can be either. The neuter gender does not exist, nor does the concept it denotes—an entity or object which is neither masculine nor feminine. The English "it" must be translated into Hebrew with "*hu*" and into Arabic with "*huwa*," both meaning "he." Moreover, all adjectives, too, have either the masculine or the feminine form. Thus far Hebrew and Arabic are like French. However, unlike French, in Hebrew and Arabic the pronouns, with the exception of the first person singular and plural, are also either masculine or feminine. The same holds good for verbs: only the first person singular and plural in past and future are identical whether the speaker is male or female. All other verb forms, that is, first, second, and third person present tense in singular and plural, and second and third person past and future in singular and plural have separate masculine and feminine forms.

This grammatical characteristic means that in Hebrew and Arabic one cannot formulate a sentence, with the exception of such brief first-person verbal statements as "I wrote," or "we shall write," without identifying the subject, the predicate, the object, and the adjective as either masculine or feminine. In English one can say, "Come to the big house," without conveying any grammatical clue to any gender in any part of the sentence. In the same sentence in German there would be some gender identification (italicized here and in the subsequent examples): "Kommen Sie in *das grosse Haus*." In French likewise, "Venez à *la grande maison*." In Hebrew and Arabic each and every word in such a sentence is gender identified. In Hebrew: "*Bo labayit hagadol*"; in Arabic: "*Tadkhul al-bayt al-kabīr.*"

What this means, of course, is that in Hebrew and Arabic gender identification is ubiquitous, and that the masculine-feminine dichotomy of all persons, things, and actions is omnipresent in language, and must hence be omnipresent in thinking as well.

With reference to the God-concept this gender-emphatic nature of Hebrew and Arabic has as its consequence that no statement can be made about, and no name given to, the deity without simultaneously designating the divine person referred to as either masculine or feminine. In European languages, the term God has either a masculine denotation, as in English (one speaks of "Him"), or the masculine gender as in German *Gott*, French *dieu*, Italian *dio*, etc.; Still when one says "God is great," this statement carries no explicit, or even implicit, identification of God as a male deity. The uninitiated outsider, who hears this English sentence, or the German "*Gott ist gross*," gets from this statement alone no clue as to any gender identification of the deity referred to. Only in the Romance languages does the masculine form of the adjective betray the notion that the God spoken of is grammatically masculine. Whether as a result of this characteristic of the Romance languages the people speaking them are inclined to imagine God more in masculine terms than do the English speakers, is a psycholinguistic question which still awaits investigation. In any case, a similar statement in the Arabic, *Allāhu akbar*, "God is great," or the Hebrew *haEl hagadol*, "the Great God," instantly conveys through the masculine form of the adjective "great," which is not separated from the noun "God" by a genderless "is," that, at least as far as language is concerned, the reference is to a masculine deity.

To this must be added the fact that neither in the idolatrous periods of the biblical Hebrews, nor among the Arabs of the *jāhiliyya*, did sexless or genderless deities ever exist. All the deities they worshiped were either male of female. And when they adopted monotheism, the one and only God whom they accepted remained, because of the grammatical characteristics of their respective languages, at least vaguely, male. I make this statement while fully cognizant of the Jewish and Muslim theological doctrines which deny God all corporeality and never tire of emphasizing His purely spiritual nature. What I am speaking of is linguistic formulation and the interdependence between it and popular thinking. Let us now have a closer look at the question of the gender of the divine in Judaism and Islam.

IN THE BIBLE AND THE TALMUD

In biblical Israel there were two mutually antagonistic and competing religions. One was the religion of the masses and their leaders, including kings, princes, and priests. This religion was replete with gods and goddesses whose worship had been adopted by the Hebrews from the Canaanites and the neighbors of Israel. Foremost among these deities were Baal, the male weather-god, and the goddesses known by the names Asherah, Anath, Astarte, Queen of Heaven, each with his or her realm, function, and mythical ambiance. The other was the religion of the prophets, who taught an uncompromising monotheistic Yahwism, which, although from time to time it was adopted by a king whom the biblical chroniclers subsequently designated as pious and God fearing, remained until the very end of the Israelite and Judahite monarchies, and for a time even after their demise, the faith of but a small minority.[1] However, soon after the destruction of Jerusalem (586 B.C.E.) the polytheistic cults declined and died out among both the Palestinian and the Babylonian segments of the Jewish people, and Yahwist monotheism, as preached by the prophets and codified by the authors of the biblical books, became the basis for the postbiblical development of Judaism.

In the Bible itself, the God of Israel has a distinctly masculine character. His names, Yahweh (later pronounced Adonai), Elohim, El, Shaddai, are of the masculine gender. He is addressed in second person masculine singular, and references to Him are in third person singular masculine, as are all the adjectives used by the biblical authors in describing Him. In addition, toward the end of the biblical period He is referred to by Deutero-Isaiah as *Avinu*, "our Father" (Isa. 63 : 16; 64 : 7), and the author of Chronicles puts these words in David's mouth, "Blessed art Thou Yahweh, the God of Israel, our Father, from eternity to eternity" (1 Chron. 27 : 10). In a prophecy of Jeremiah a personified Israel addresses God as "my Father" (Jer. 3 : 4, 19). In the Psalms David calls God "Thou art my Father, my God, and the Rock of my salvation" (Ps. 89 : 27).

In postbiblical Jewish literature the appellation "our Father" became a fixed ritual phrase: God is addressed as "Our Father in Heaven," and "Our Father, our King." But even apart from the fatherhood attributed to God, His masculinity is pronounced and made emphatic in Jewish liturgy by the use of the masculine gender in the nouns, adjectives, and verbs relating to Him. Thus the first sentence in the Eighteen Benedictions, the central prayer in Jewish worship recited three times every day, reads (I put the God-related words which have the masculine gender in *italics*):

> *Blessed art Thou our God* and *the God* of our fathers, *the God* of Abraham, *the God* of Isaac, and *the God* of Jacob, *the great, mighty, awesome God, the supreme God,* who *performs* good charities, and *creates* everything, and *remembers* the charities of the fathers, and *brings* the Redeemer to the children of their children, for the sake of *His name* in love.[2]

Elsewhere in this prayer God is addressed as "our Father," "king," "shield," "hero," "master of heroic deeds," "strong Redeemer," "shatterer of enemies and subduer of evil ones," "the Rock of our life,"—all designations with a definitely masculine connotation.

This prayer (also called *T'filla*, "Prayer," and *ʿAmida*, "Standing," because it is recited standing and facing the direction of Jerusalem), which by the first century C.E. had assumed more or less the form in which it is still recited today, testifies to the male-oriented character of the Jewish God-concept as reflected in Jewish liturgy in and after that period. But we encounter in it, albeit in a subordinated and passive form, the Shekhina: God, the prayer states, will bring her back to Zion. This is one of the earliest references in Jewish sources to the Shekhina, who in the Talmud and Midrash, and even more so in the Kabbala, was destined to play an increasingly important role as the feminine manifestation of God's presence on earth. The Shekhina ultimately was seen as the consort of God, styled the "Matron," and the countervailing feminine divinity balancing the masculinity of "God the King." More will have to be said in the sequel about the feminine Shekhina and the feminine element in general in the Jewish God-concept as it developed in the Kabbala from the thirteenth century on. But first, in order to adhere to a chronological sequence, we shall have a look at the gender aspect of the Islamic God-concept.

ALLAH AND GENDER

Islam, it can be stated outright, is the only one of the three major monotheistic religions from whose divine realm the feminine was totally and definitely excluded. This was not always the case among the Arabs. Quite the contrary. In the *jāhiliyya* they worshipped both gods and goddesses, among whom the three goddesses Allāt, al-Manāt, and al-ʿUzza were the most widely venerated deities. The information on their worship, and even on their identity, is woefully inadequate, but it is at least known that according to one version they were considered the daughters of Allah, while according to another, one of them, Allāt, was held to be the mother of the gods. In a third view she was the consort of Allah, who was one of the Meccan male deities, and possibly the supreme god in the pre-Islamic Arab pantheon.

With Islam all traces of these indigenous Arab goddesses were eradicated. The religious triumph of Muhammad was the recognition of only one single God, Allah. Whether Muhammad, and even more so his contemporaries, recognized any connection between the Allah of the *jāhiliyya* and the Allah whose messenger Muhammad was, is a moot question, although the identity of the names of the two deities must have carried in itself the kernel of a certain identification. In any case the name itself must have created in the mind of Muhammad's followers the image of a masculine deity, not unlike the manner in which Yahweh of the Hebrews was tacitly assumed to have been a male God.

The persistent masculinity of Allah in popular Arab thought remained unaffected by the doctrine of divine attributes (*ṣifāt Allāh*), developed by Muslim theologians on the basis of the Koran. The attributes included not a single one which could have indicated that Allah was believed to be a masculine divinity. They described Him typically in terms such as *malik* (king), *wāḥid* (only one), *ẓāhir* (manifest), *bāṭin* (hidden), *al-ḥaqq* (the truth), *al-ᶜazīm* (the sublime), *al-badīᶜ* (the creator), *al-ᶜalīm* (the knower), *al-baṣīr* (the seer), etc. But they could not get around the linguistic given which determined that all these divine attributes had to be cast in the masculine gender. Thus when Allah is described in Arabic as *al-raḥmān al-raḥīm* ("the beneficent, the merciful"), the masculine forms are used. In English this everpresent grammatical masculinity cannot be reproduced, since in English the adjectives have no gender. Hence one simply cannot convey in English the feeling of masculinity an Arabic speaker gets when he hears or reads that Allah is great, omnipotent, the seer, and the hearer. The extent to which the masculinity of God, due to the character of the Arabic language, permeates Arab consciousness can be grasped by a non-Arab only if he masters Arabic sufficiently to understand its all-pervasive gender dichotomy. As an example, let me give here my translation of the *Fātiḥa*, the "Opening," the first *sūra* of the Koran, which in the original consists of a mere twenty-nine words. I italicize all the words which in the Arabic original carry a gender identification, all masculine:

In the *name* of *Allah* the *beneficent*, the *merciful*.
Praise be to *Allah*, *Lord* of all the *creatures*,
The *beneficent*, the *merciful*,
The *king* of the *Day* of *Judgment*.
Thee we serve and *Thee* we ask for help.
Lead us on the *straight path*,
The *path of those* whom *Thou hast favored*,
Not *of those on whom is wrath*,
Nor *of those who go astray*.

I may add that in the Arabic original twenty-six of the twenty-nine words of this *sūra* have the masculine gender, and twelve of them refer to Allah.

The same is the case with all Arabic statements about God, all prayers addressed to God, etc. Thus all Muslim theological assertions about the incorporeality of Allah notwithstanding, in Arab popular consciousness God is nevertheless an unmistakably male deity.

Although the maleness of Allah is never explicitly stated in the Koran, there are indications in it to show that Muhammad considered Him to be masculine. In one Koranic passage Muhammad ridicules the polytheists for ascribing daughters to Allah (the three pre-Islamic Arab goddesses), while they themselves only want sons, and castigates them for calling the angels by feminine names (Koran 53:19–22, 27–29). While Muhammad flatly rejected the idea that God could have any children (*sūra* 112:3 says, "He [Allah] begot not, nor was He begotten"), his objection to giving female names to angels must stem from his conviction that the angels were male (an idea which he could have got from Judaism), and that therefore only masculine names were proper for them. And if so, the notion that God himself was of a male character could not have been foreign to him, despite the absence from the Koran of all but the mildest anthropomorphisms (e.g., God sits on His throne, descends towards the earth, has eyes, has a hand, speaks, etc.).[3] I would even dare go so far as to say that while Muhammad conceived of Allah as incorporeal, the image which emerged in his mind when he emotionally turned toward God was that of a male father figure.

The question as to what extent the maleness of Allah was derived from the biblical and Talmudic tradition of a masculine Yahweh with which Muhammad was well acquainted, and to what extent it was a reflection of the maleness of the pagan Arab creator god Allah, is a major problem which we cannot come to grips with in the present context. But it should be mentioned at least briefly that several verses in the Koran leave no doubt as to the importance of the male creator god named Allah who was worshipped by the pagan Arabs. Muhammad's quarrel with his pagan contemporaries was not over the power and acts they ascribed to Allah, but over their belief in other gods as well. He was convinced, and preached, that Allah was the one and only God (cf. Koran 13:16; 29:61, 63; 31:25; 39:38; 43:87). When Muhammad declared this, in doing so he did not alter the features already attributed to Allah by the pagan Arabs, but asserted in effect: The god Allah, whom you have worshipped until now as the creator god, the giver of rain, the lord of heaven and earth, is not merely the chief god among many, but the one and only God. This promotion from chief god to only God must have meant that the maleness of Allah remained untouched. Muhammad's Allah remained essentially the same as the Allah of the *jāhiliyya*, except that He was now recognized as being the one and only God, which meant that all the other gods were but idols. In trying to understand what went on in Muhammad's mind in developing his own concept of Allah, it should be emphasized again that while his contemporary disciples probably continued to see in the new Allah a male god, Muhammad tore himself away ideationally from this pagan concept, even though in his feeling he was probably unable to liberate himself from the traditional male idea of Allah.

The tacitly assumed maleness of Allah, and the male-oriented nature of Muhammad's teachings are affirmed and confirmed on every page of the Koran in which a male God, surrounded by male angels (Koran 53:27–29), addresses through the intermediacy of a male chief angel, Gabriel, a male prophet, Muhammad, and through him a male-dominated Arab society. True, several *sūra*s, which contain religious generalities, address the "believing men and believing women" (*al-mu'minūn wal-mu'mināt*, e.g., Koran 9:72, 73, etc.), but this in no way alters the fact that in general the Koran speaks to men alone, and it is men whom it instructs as to what to do, what not to do, how to behave in general, and how to relate to women. A typical example is *sūra* 4, titled "Women," which prescribes what men must and must not do with respect of orphans and women. Considering the male-dominated character of Arab society in the days of Muhammad (and thereafter), it is not a surprise that no comparable (or, indeed, any other) instructions addressed to women are contained in the Koran. In sum, Islam was from its very inception, and has remained to this day, an exclusively male-oriented religion, centered on an all-powerful incorporeal deity, who nevertheless was imagined and spoken of as a male god. It was not until our own days that a few modern Arab authors, influenced by Western feminism, have begun to raise their voices and give expression to their feelings that there are not a hundred million Arabs, but only fifty million, since women are not part of the Arab body politic, and "Allah does not talk to them."[4]

SHEKHINA–SAKĪNA

Characteristic of the consistent Muslim exclusion of everything feminine even from the vicinity of manifestations of God is what happened to the Jewish Shekhina in Islamic context.

Shekhina (literally "[act of] dwelling"), a feminine abstract noun, is a Talmudic concept developed from the biblical idea that God occasionally dwelled on earth where His presence was manifested in a cloud or in a visible "glory" filling the Sanctuary. In Talmudic and Midrashic literature the term came to denote the visible and audible manifestation of God's presence on earth. According to a Talmudic statement the Shekhina was contained in a casket the Children of Israel carried with them out of Egypt. The Temple of Jerusalem served as the abode or resting place of the Shekhina. After the destruction of the Temple she went with the Children of Israel into exile, and dwelt in various synagogues in Babylonia. She also rested on the pious, the wise, the sick, the modest, the valiant, as well as on married couples, and was present whenever ten men gathered. That is, the Shekhina was not merely the presence of God on earth, but also the inspiration emanating from God and gracing men who deserved it. She also was, on the one hand, the love aspect of God, and, on the other, His punitive power. While the Talmudic and Midrashic sources state nowhere explicitly that the Shekhina was a female entity, this is implied in the feminine gender of the name, and also in the role assigned to the Shekhina as the personification of the community of Israel, whose relation to God is likened to that of a wife to her husband. Also, the behavior of the Shekhina is typically feminine and emotional: she is said to have cried, and caressed and kissed the walls and columns of the Sanctuary.

Even before these ideas about the Shekhina developed, the two cherubim whose intertwined golden statues stood in the Holy of Holies of the Temple of Jerusalem were considered as symbolizing the marital union between God and the community of Israel. The male cherub represented God, and the female cherub the community of Israel. In the first century C.E.

Philo of Alexandria, the famous Hellenistic Jewish philosopher, gave a different interpretation to the two cherubim. According to him the male cherub represented the fatherly and husbandly aspect of God, referred to also in the name Elohim, while the female cherub represented the motherly and wifely aspect of God, referred to also in the name Yahweh (usually translated as Lord).[5] That is to say, according to Philo, God had both a male and a female aspect, and both were symbolically present in the Temple in the form of the male and female cherubim.

Philo's interpretation is, at least partly, reechoed in the Midrashic view which considers the Temple the earthly abode of the Shekhina, the feminine manifestation of the presence of God on earth. The Shekhina, as Midrash tells us, loved the Temple dearly, was deeply attached to it, and "would kiss its walls and caress its columns, and say, 'Be in peace, my house, be in peace, my palace.'" According to R. Jonathan, sometime prior to the destruction of the Temple the Shekhina left it:

> For three and a half years the Shekhina dwelt on the Mount of Olives [which faces the Temple], and cried out three times every day, "Return, ye backsliding children, I will heal your backsliding" (Jer. 3 : 22). And when they did not return, the Shekhina began to flutter about in the air, and she recited this verse, "I will go and return to my place, till they acknowledge their guilt and seek my face; in their trouble they will seek me earnestly" (Hos. 5 : 15).[6]

In an earlier and briefer version of this legendary vignette, transmitted in the name of R. Yoḥanan bar Nappaḥa (died 279 C.E.), "the Shekhina withdrew for six months from the Children of Israel [and dwelt] in the desert, and when, despite this, they did not repent, she said, 'Let them perish!'"[7]

After the destruction of the Temple, the Shekhina, although she continued to dwell in certain synagogues in Babylonia, ceased altogether to address her children, and made her presence known only by making a noise, apparently like unto the tinkling of a bell.[8] This reticence of the Shekhina to speak contrasts with her loquaciousness in the days of yore, when she spoke to Adam, the Serpent, and the fishes, and conversed with Moses many times. However, even in later times she would join the sick and comfort them, and help those in need.[9]

As to a differentiation between God and the Shekhina, its beginnings are discernible in the Talmudic period. It was done with hesitation, and gradually. When R. Y'hoshuᶜa (end of the first century C.E.) says that God "let His Shekhina dwell among" the Children of Israel,[10] this can only be understood as presupposing that the Shekhina was either an emanation of God, or a hypostasis (as in several passages in the Targum Onkelos), or a separate divine person. The last-mentioned interpretation is the only possible one of those sayings which speak of a confrontation between God and the Shekhina. A synonym for the Shekhina in the Talmudic period was the "Holy Spirit" (Hebrew: *ruaḥ haqodesh*, feminine), and R. Aḥa, a Galilean sage who flourished about 300 C.E., is quoted in a fifth-century Midrash as saying that "the Holy Spirit comes to the defense of Israel by . . . saying to God, 'Say not: I will do to him as he has done to me (Prov. 24:29).'"[11] That is to say, the Holy Spirit admonished God not to punish Israel. A later Midrash (from the ninth century) has the Shekhina address God in defense of King Solomon whom God intended to exclude from the world to come. God listened to her, and allowed Solomon to have a share in the otherworld.[12]

The little that has been said so far about the Shekhina suffices to show that from the point of view of Muhammad here was a so to speak ready-made Jewish feminine divine concept, endowed with all the prestige which features of the ancient Jewish religion had in his eyes. He could have easily incorporated into his Islam the idea of the feminine Shekhina as a complement to the many other ideas he took over from Judaism. He even could have identified the Shekhina with one of the goddesses of the pre-Islamic Arab pantheon.

That Muhammad was acquainted with the Jewish concept and the Hebrew name Shekhina is amply attested by the frequent occurrence of it in the Koran in the Arabicized form of Sakīna. In discussing the Koranic references to Sakīna, Goldziher observed that Muhammad "seems, in using the word Sakīna, to follow information which was not thorough and pertinent," that "he only casually snatched it up, as he did all sorts of things, and connected with it totally unclear notions which did not harmonize with one another." And, Goldziher adds, "only in the later Ḥadīth, whose authors allowed themselves to be influenced by quite specific Jewish teachings, do the notions about the Sakīna return to their original source."[13]

While Goldziher is undoubtedly correct in observing that the exact meaning of the term Shekhina seems to have eluded Muhammad, the lack of harmony among the various Koranic passages mentioning the Sakīna can be readily explained by analogous contradictions in the Jewish sources which seem to have been communicated to Muhammad by his Jewish informants.

Thus in Koran 2:249 Muhammad clearly considered the Sakīna as something concrete which was contained in the Ark of the Covenant in the same manner as the relics of Moses and Aaron. This is clearly a reflection of the Talmudic passage, according to which, when the Children of Israel wandered in the desert, they carried with them two caskets: one contained the bones of Joseph, and the other the Shekhina, who in this context is conceived of as having the shape of the two stone Tablets of the Law.[14] An echo of this Talmudic-Koranic association of the Shekhina-Sakīna with the Ark which contained the Tablets of the Law was preserved among the Arabs of Jerusalem until the eleventh century. The Persian poet and traveler Nāṣir-i Khusraw (1003–1060–61) mentions that one of the gates of Jerusalem was called Bāb al-Sakīna ("Gate of the Shekhina"), and that according to local legend next to this gate was found "the *tābūt Sakīna* ("Ark of the Shekhina"), which, according to the words of the Almighty revealed in the Koran, was brought here by the angels."[15]

In other passages of the Koran and in the Jewish sources which they reflect both in terms of content and stylistically, the Sakīna appears as the manifestation of divine inspiration or spiritual presence on earth. In them the Shekhina-Sakīna is spoken of as "His [God's] Shekhina," or, when God himself speaks, as "My Shekhina." For example, in Koran 48:26, "He [God] sent down His Sakīna upon His Messenger and the faithful"; or 9:26 and 40: "Allah sent down His Sakīna upon His Messenger and the believers." These passages correspond closely to the Targum Onkelos in Ex. 29:45–46, which reads, "Let them make before Me a Sanctuary that I may let My Shekhina dwell among them"; or the same Targum *ad* Deut. 32:10: "He [God] filled their needs in a desert land . . . He let them dwell around His Shekhina." Similarly R. Y'hoshuᶜa, the first-century C.E. Talmudic sage, is quoted as having said that God liberated the Children of Israel from Egypt "only in order that they build Him a Sanctuary, so that He can let His Shekhina dwell among them . . ."[16]

To this context belongs also the saying of R. Ḥama bar Ḥanina, the third-century C.E. Palestinian Amora: "When God lets His Shekhina rest, He will let her rest only on the noble families of Israel"; and of his contemporary R. Yoḥanan bar Nappaḥa: "God lets His Shekhina rest only on him who is heroic, rich, wise, and modest."[17] Compare with these sayings Muhammad's utterance, "He [God] sent down the Sakīna into the hearts of the faithful so that their faith might grow stronger" (Koran 48:2). One may also add that in stating that God sent down the Sakīna upon him, Muhammad intended to claim a status similar to that of Moses about whom several Talmudic passages report that the Shekhina frequently spoke to him.[18]

These Koranic-Talmudic parallels make us suspect that Muhammad was better informed of the Jewish traditions about the Shekhina than Goldziher assumed, and that the apparent contradictions between his views on the Sakīna as expressed, on the one hand, in Koran 2:249, and, on the other, in Koran 9:26, 40, and 48:4, 18, 26, are probably due to his recollection of disparate Jewish beliefs and traditions about the Shekhina of which he learned from his Jewish informants.

Muslim traditionists made repeated attempts to explain the Koranic term Sakīna. Among them was Wahb ibn Munabbih (flourished ca. 740 C.E.), whose explanation is: "Sakīna is a spirit from God which speaks whenever a difference of opinion arises in a matter, advising them with clarity concerning that which they seek."[19] The role Wahb here assigns to the Sakīna is identical with that of the Bat Qol (literally "Daughter of a voice"), the heavenly voice, which in Talmudic sources is often said to have intervened in scholarly disputations and decided in favor of one of the opposing opinions.[20] Wahb must have been acquainted with these Jewish traditions, and, although he confused the Shekhina with the Bat Qol—which are two different concepts in the Jewish sources—he at least attributed to the Sakīna a role which closely corresponds to that attributed in Jewish tradition to a divine manifestation on earth. In contrast to Wahb, most Arab traditionists understood the word Sakīna to mean something like patience, repose, calm, composure, or else courage, compassion, generosity, dignity, and the like, that is, emotional states or character traits.[21]

According to some *ḥadīths*, the Sakīna manifested itself on occasion in the form of a cloud or in a cloud. According to al-Azraqī, the Sakīna, in the shape of a cloud, and endowed with the power of speech, directed Abraham to the right place where he was to build the Kaᶜba.[22] These explanations equate the Sakīna with the biblical "cloud of glory" or "cloud of Yahweh," in which God was believed to descend into the Sanctuary.[23] According to another *ḥadīth*, "People do not gather in one of the houses of Allah [i.e., mosques] and read the book of Allah and study it among them, without the Sakīna descending upon them, compassion covering them, and angels surrounding them."[24] This tradition, again, has its origin in the Mishna which quotes R. Ḥanina ben Teradyon to the effect that "Two who sit together and occupy themselves with the Tora, the Shekhina descends among them."[25] Also Bukhārī (810–870), the famous Muslim traditionist, asserts in his

Faḍā'il al-Qur'ān ("The Excellences of the Koran") that the Sakīna comes down benevolently when the Koran is recited.[26]

These statements, and several others gathered by Goldziher from Muslim traditional literature, show clearly that the Arab scholars were well acquainted with the Jewish Shekhina concept, and that they accepted the Shekhina-Sakīna as a manifestation of God's presence on earth in a manner closely duplicating that of Jewish tradition. What they did not accept was the feminine role ascribed to the Shekhina in the Jewish sources. This is the more remarkable since the form Sakīna, given in Arabic to the Hebrew term Shekhina, has the feminine gender, and as such is exceptional in the rich Arabic terminology relating to Allah, His attributes, and His manifestations. Goldziher, regrettably, did not consider this aspect of the term Sakīna in his paper. To me it seems that the masculinity of God and of His divine retinue (the angels) was such an ingrained tenet, such a self-evident fact, for Muhammad and his scholarly followers that they had little choice but to ignore the femininity of the Shekhina. To acknowledge it would have been a serious disturbing element in their picture of the exclusively male company of the heavenly hosts. Thus while they incorporated the Shekhina-Sakīna in their imagery of divine manifestations, they made of her either a physical object contained in the *tābūt* (the Ark, Koran 2 : 248), or else an incorporeal and hence sexless presence of a divine spirit or influence in the minds or emotions of men.

THE HOURIS OF PARADISE

My foregoing comment on the exclusive maleness of the heavenly cohorts in Muslim thought calls for at least a brief digression on the houris, the heavenly maidens, the lure of whose pleasurable company Muhammad held out to the believers as their reward after death (Koran 55:56–58, 70–74; etc.), and whose presence in Paradise seems to contradict my statement. It seems to, but actually it does not. A closer look at the Koranic passages in question will show what I mean. The most detailed of them describes the pleasures of the "two gardens" (i.e., of Paradise) which await the believers as follows (in my literal translation, with the omission of the refrain "Which of the favors of your Lord do you deny?" which punctuates the original after each sentence):

46. But for him who fears the place (*maqām*) of his Lord [there are] two gardens
48. With shady trees.

50. In them are two springs flowing.
52. In them is of every fruit a pair.
54. [The God-fearing will] recline on couches lined with silk brocade, with the fruit of both gardens near at hand.
56. In them are maidens of modest gaze, not touched by men nor by jinn before them.
58. Like unto rubies and pearls.

. . . .

62. And next to them are two gardens,
64. Dark with foliage.
66. In them are two abundant springs.
68. In them are fruit trees, date palm and pomegranate.
70. In them are good maidens, beautiful
72. Houris, closely guarded in tents,
74. Whom neither men nor jinn touched before them.
76. They [the God-fearing] will recline on green cushions and rich carpets . . .

The dictionary definition of houri (Arabic *ḥūriyya*, pl. *ḥūriyyāt* or *ḥūr*) is a virgin of Paradise having eyes with a marked contrast of white and black—evidently an Arab ideal of beauty. The context in which the houris are mentioned shows that they were considered by Muhammad as mere appurtenances meant to serve the pleasure of the men who feared God in their lives, as were the luxurious couches, shady trees, rich fruits, and abundant springs. They certainly were not imagined as belonging to the divine personnel surrounding Allah. The entire paradisiacal scene described by Muhammad in the quoted passage and elsewhere in the Koran indicates that he imagined life after death in Paradise as a quasi-physical existence in which the believers would be rewarded with all the luxuries and pleasures which most of them missed in this world. The houris were simply part of that idealized physical environment, and their only function was to add the pleasures of sex to those of rest, shade, and delicacies. The houris, we read elsewhere, were created by God "in perfection," and kept by Him virgin, to serve as "loving companions for those of the right hand," that is, the pious believers (Koran 56:34–35). What paradisiacal rewards awaited the pious women is not stated, except indirectly, in those passages of the Koran which specify that the elect will rejoice in Paradise in the company of their parents, wives, and children who were faithful (Koran 13:23; 36:56; 40:8; 43:70). The houris, also called "pure consorts" and "chaste virgins," are promised to the faithful (Koran 2:25; 3:15; 4:57) in addition to the company of their pious earthly wives.

The *ḥadīth*, in general, dwell on the subject of Paradise in exaggerated and even extravagant detail. One *ḥadīth* states that the carnal pleasures the houris will give the believers through their perpetual virginity are "a hundred times greater than earthly pleasures." Another asserts that the female believers, whose merits and good deeds have secured them admission to Paradise, will rank 70,000 times higher in the eyes of God than the houris. The *mutakallimūn* (kalāmists), who discussed the pleasures of Paradise in especially great detail, held that the sensual delights of "the Garden" must be taken literally. This literal interpretation has remained standard in Muslim thought down to modern times, although some of the recent commentators have argued that the realities of Paradise, and hence its delights, are intrinsically different from those of this world.[27] In view of the male-centeredness of Islam and Arab culture it is perhaps superfluous to point out that Arab fantasy has not peopled Paradise with male equivalents of the houris who would provide augmented and intensified pleasures to the pious believing women in that garden of bliss.

ṢŪFISM

The most significant development in Islam, which has put the seal on the exclusion of women from the realm of religion, is the masculine character of the great Muslim mystical movement known as *taṣawwuf*, or Ṣūfism, which flourished from the twelfth century on. The Ṣūfī orders, which were very popular in Iraq, Egypt, and North Africa, as well as in non-Arab but devotedly Muslim Turkey and Iran, were fraternal associations of men, with their own buildings, ecstatic rites (*dhikr*, literally "remembrance," so called for the frequent mentioning of the name of Allah in their rites), garb, doctrines, and way of life. Asceticism, emphasized to varying degrees by various Ṣūfī orders, did not include celibacy, except for some members of the Turkish Bektāshī order, which was a latecomer on the Ṣūfī scene, having made its full appearance only in the sixteenth century. In the Bektāshī rites also unveiled women participated, and in their major *tekke*s (monasteries) there were also women's quarters.[28] Nothing remotely similar by way of the participation of women in Ṣūfī rites has ever existed in Arab lands.

Eloquent testimony to the maleness of Allah, or at least to the total absence of any feminine element in Him, in Ṣūfī thinking, feeling, and fantasy is presented by the great Ṣūfī Arab poets. They clothed their religious experiences in the language of human love, yet the theme of human rapture in the love of God is never carried to the point where God, the object of the poet's love, would be described or conceived as feminine, or where the Ṣūfī adept, in relation to God, would assume a quasi-feminine role. True, ᶜUmar ibn al-Fāriḍ (1181–1235), universally acclaimed as the greatest Arab mystical poet, in trying to make his love of God palpable, addresses God the beloved under many names, including that of a heroine of an old Arab love song, or simply speaks of Him as "She." On one occasion he refers to Him as "disdainful charmer."[29] But these appellations are nothing more than poetic devices employed in order to give tangible reality to a feeling almost impossible to express or describe, just as in other poems he speaks of God as a gazelle, a camel driver, an archer shooting deadly glances from his eye, or simply as "He." All these images of traditional Arabic love poetry are used without, of course, the slightest intention on the part of the Ṣūfī poet of equating God with any of these colorful metaphors, or of implying that one of the aspects of God is being a gazelle, a camel driver, or a delectable damsel.

In one of his finest poems, the *Khamriyya* ("Wine Song"), Ibn al-Fāriḍ writes: "In memory of the Beloved we quaffed a vintage that made us drunk before the creation of the wine." This, according to Nicholson, means that the soul was intoxicated with the wine of divine love (i.e., rapt in the contemplation of God) during its preexistence in the eternal knowledge of God before the body was created.[30] The imagery is rather confusing, but its basis undoubtedly is the application of the term "Beloved" to God: the very thought of God is enough to make us (men) intoxicated. There is certainly no intention here of making any statement about the nature, let alone the sex, of the deity.

Similarly absent is the feminine element in the thought of Ibn al-Fāriḍ's great contemporary, the Spanish Arab mystic Ibn al-ᶜArabī (1165–1240). This almost incredibly prolific author of some 240 works, and most influential mystical teacher, professed that through silence, withdrawal from men, hunger, and wakefulness, if observed with sincerity, there will be awakened in the heart of the "traveler" (i.e., the seeker of God) a love, which grows to be a passion and which brings men to God, until the veil which hides God is removed, the "traveler" is granted the manifestation of God, and finally a union with God is achieved.[31] In this prescription of the mystical path which can lead man to God through a crescendo from love to passion and from passion to union, no place is allowed to any feminine aspect of the deity, despite the language which, without any change, could be used for the description of man's love and passion for, and union with, woman.

In Ibn al-ᶜArabī's Ṣūfism the mystical trinity of love (*maḥabba*), the lover, and the beloved plays an important role. But both he and other Muslim mystics operating with the love concept speak only of the love between God and man: the object of God's love is man, and man's love directed to God is the gateway leading from the ascetic and contemplative life to the unitive life. In one his poems Ibn al-ᶜArabī calls the Divine Wisdom, Bilqīs, the name by which the biblical Queen of Sheba (1 Kings 10: 1–10, 13) is known in Arabic literature. Bilqīs, according to Arab legend, was the daughter of a male jinn and a human female, and thus was both spirit and flesh and blood. Such being her nature, Bilqīs is well suited to represent Divine Wisdom which is the child of theory, which is subtle and spiritual, and of practice, which is gross.[32] Needless to say that by using the feminine image of Bilqīs Ibn al-ᶜArabī did not intend to introduce a feminine element either into Divine Wisdom or into the deity himself.

These examples, which could be multiplied, indicate that in the ideational world of Arab thinkers, poets, and mystics concepts such as those of a feminine element, or of a feminine aspect, or even of the faintest feminine traits, in the deity simply could find neither a place nor an echo. The Muslim God-concept, from Muhammad on, was, in each of the many disparate trends and schools of Islam, that of a purely incorporeal God on the philosophical and mystical levels, and of a masculine God on the emotional and popular levels.

THE MATRONIT

While Islam throughout its history continued to exclude the feminine from the realm of the divine, to the extent of disregarding its possibilities even in its great mystical trends of Ṣūfism, in Judaism the feminine element of the godhead acquired added importance with the flowering of the Kabbala in thirteenth-century Spain. With this development the feminine in the Jewish God-concept came to occupy an even more important place than it did in Christianity. The Christian yearning for the feminine in the divine expressed itself most poignantly in the mystical and popular forms of Mariolatry—the worship of Mary as a divinity—yet Mary has never attained in Christianity the position of a veritable goddess, although as "the mother of God," the "coredemptress" with Christ, and "Queen of Heaven"[33] she came quite close to it. Since Muhammad refers with disapproval to a Christian doctrine according to which Mary and Jesus were "two gods beside Allah,"[34] one can assume that such a view, assigning Mary an equal place with God the Father and God the Son, did exist among the Christian Arab tribes of his day.

The Kabbala, while it did not represent a schismatic deviation from traditional Judaism, emphasized the feminine aspect of the deity to a much greater extent than was the case in Judaism prior to its emergence. We have spoken above about the Shekhina in Talmudic and Midrashic literature, and also referred to Philo's discernment of paternal and maternal features in the godhead. However, Philo's thought never became a part of normative Judaism—in fact, his very existence remained unknown to Orthodox Jews. The Shekhina, despite the significant role assigned to her in the traditional sources from which Orthodox Jews drew their religious ideas, remained a vague, indistinct spiritual image, that is, something quite different from a palpable (if one is allowed to use this adjective in speaking of a divinity) divine being. For one thing, no prayers or supplications were ever addressed to her (as they were so amply to Mary in Christianity). For another, among all the Talmudic and Midrashic legends about the Shekhina there is not a single one which would record a dialogue between her and a human being, while such dialogues between God and men are a characteristic and recurring feature of both biblical narrative and later Jewish legend. Thus the Talmudic-Midrashic Shekhina was characterized by what can best be described as a great passivity; although she "dwells" in the Temple, she rarely communicates with her children, the Children of Israel; even in the hour of their greatest tragedy, the destruction of the Temple of Jerusalem and the exile of Israel, she does not address a single word of consolation to them.

Following these Midrashic beginnings, the role of the feminine in the Jewish God-concept reached its culmination in the Kabbala, in thirteenth-century Spain, and again in sixteenth-century Safed, when and where the Shekhina was developed, or transformed, into a veritable separate and discrete divine entity, acting independently of God, and, on occasion, even opposing Him. In Kabbalistic mysticism the central position in its extremely complex theosophy is occupied by the divine couple consisting of God the King, and His spouse the Shekhina, most frequently referred to by the name Matronit. The term Matronit, borrowed from the Latin *matrona*, is used in the Talmud and Midrash in the sense of lady, noble woman, but it was not until the *Zohar* that it came to designate the "Lady of God," that is, the feminine aspect or counterpart of "God the King." In the mystical God doctrine of the *Zohar*, the chief opus of the Kabbala, written in the late thirteenth century by Moses de Leon in Spain, which is replete with mythological imagery, the tragic love relationship between God the King and His consort the Matronit plays a central role. The mood and the atmosphere permeating these theosophical myths require to be exemplified by a few summarized or fully translated passages from the Zoharic literature.

One of them describes that while Solomon labored on the construction of the Temple of Jerusalem, the Matronit made her own preparations for her union with God the King. She prepared a house in which He could take up joint residence with her, and which, in a mystical way, was identical with the Jerusalem Temple. When the great day arrived, her father and mother adorned her so that her bridegroom should become desirous of her.[35]

After the destruction of the Temple, the Matronit remembered the marital happiness she had enjoyed with her husband, God the King, while the Temple stood and served as their bed chamber. The following is my literal translation of the passage describing her remembrance and lament.

> At midnight she [the Matronit] enters that point of Zion which is the place of the Holy of Holies. She sees that it is in ruins, and that the house of her dwelling and her couch are defiled. She cries and laments, goes up and down, and looks at the place of the Cherubim. She cries in a bitter voice, lifts up her voice, and says: "My couch, my couch! The Place of the house of my dwelling! . . . My bed! The couch of the Matronit!" She moans and sobs, and cries: "My couch! The place of my sanctuary! The place of precious pearls! The house of the [Holy] Curtain and the lid of the Holy Ark, which was studded with sixty thousand myriads of precious stones arranged in row after row and line after line, facing one another. Rows of pomegranates were spread over you toward the four winds. The world existed because of you. In you the Master of the World, my husband, would come to me, and would lie between my arms, and everything I wanted of Him, and all my requests, He fulfilled. At this time He would come to me, put His dwelling in me, and play betwixt my breasts. My couch, my couch! Do you remember how I came to you in joy and with gladness of heart, and those youths [the Cherubim] were coming to meet me, beating their wings in joy to receive me. [And now] the dust in you has risen from its place, and, see, how forgotten is the Ark of the Tora which was here. From here issued sustenance for the whole world, and light and blessing for all. I am looking for my Husband, but He is not

> here, I am looking everywhere. At this time my Husband would come to me, surrounded by many pious youths, and all the maidens [36] were prepared to meet Him, and we would hear from afar the tinkling of pairs of bells between His legs, so that I should hear His voice even before He came to me. And all my maidens would praise and exalt the Holy One, blessed be He. And then all of them would go to their house of dwelling, and we would embrace [and exchange] kisses of love. My Husband, my Husband! Where did You go? This was the time when I would look at You. [But now] I look in every direction, and You are not there. Where can I see You, where have I not searched for You? This is Your place, to come to me at this hour. Behold, I am ready here. Woe, You have forgotten me! Do You not remember the days of love when I was lying in Your bosom, and I was impressed into Your form, and my form was impressed into You. Like unto this seal which leaves its imprint upon a page of writing, so did I leave my impress upon You, so that You play with my form while I am in the midst of my fort." [And] she bursts into tears and cries: "My Husband, my Husband! The light of my eyes has become dark! Do You not remember how You would extend Your left arm under my head, and I would enjoy Your strength, and Your right arm embraced me with love, and kisses, and You vowed to me that You would never forsake my love, and said to me, 'If I forget thee, O Jerusalem, let my right hand be forgotten!' And, woe, You have forgotten me!" [37]

In view of such beautiful, sensuous, mythological passages, of which there are many in the Zoharic literature, it is futile to maintain, as the commentators of the Zohar do, that the Matronit who remembers the pleasures of her nightly unions with God the King, and so bitterly laments their loss, is in the mystical thinking of the author (and perhaps also of his most erudite readers) nothing but a *sefira*, an emanation of the deity, or one of His aspects, and that the "pious youths" are unborn souls, etc. Whatever the original intention of the author of this and other such passages was, what he actually put on paper is a fully developed and very explicit myth about the love and union of the King and His Matronit, and about the tragic end of their marital happiness which came about when the Temple, their splendid bed chamber, was destroyed. It must also be added that in these Zoharic passages God the King appears far from being omnipotent. The destruction of the Temple, and the consequent separation between Him and the Matronit, did not come about as a result of God exercising His limitless will. In that great tragedy, both God and the Matronit were passive sufferers, and its consequence was, as one Zoharic passage puts it, that God "lost stature and power, was no longer king, was neither great nor potent."[38] Certainly no omnipotent deity can be imagined to have willed, or have been subjected to, such a diminishing of his stature, let alone caused such misery to his fervently beloved spouse, the Matronit. What brought about the earthly and heavenly catastrophe of the destruction of the Temple and the disruption of the love relationship between God the King and His Matronit were the sins of Israel. Incidentally, nowhere else in Kabbalistic mythology is the power of the female deity as clearly manifested as in this myth of the separation of God the King and the Matronit. The degradation the King suffered through losing the Matronit emphasizes His dependence on her, which becomes even clearer when we read that after that tragedy God the King let the slave-concubine-demoness Lilith become His consort, and that this act, more than anything else, caused Him to lose honor. Let me present here, in my literal translation, the passage in question:

> R. Shimᶜon [ben Yoḥai] said: "We see that all the nations are high up, and Israel is down below all of them. Why? Because [God the] King sent away the Matronit from Him, and took the slave-woman in her place . . . Who is that slave-woman? She is the alien crown [i.e. Lilith] . . . At first she used to sit behind the hand-mill, and now this slave-woman inherited [the position of] her mistress." R. Shimᶜon cried and said: "The King without the Matronit is not called king. The King who cleaves to the slave-woman of the Matronit, where is His honor? . . . He lost the Matronit and cleaved to the other place, which is called slave-woman . . . And this slave-woman is destined to rule over the Holy Land of below, as the Matronit formerly ruled over it . . . [But] the Holy One, blessed be He, will return the Matronit to her place as before . . . [And then] the King will rejoice because He will return to her and separate Himself from the slave-woman, and the Matronit will rejoice because she will return to couple with the King . . ."[39]

In Kabbalistic thinking there is a close correspondence between the divine love relationship of the King and the Matronit on the one hand, and the human relationship between man and wife on the other. Just as God the King is at the height of His power, dignity, and status only when He is together with the Matronit, so the human being is complete only when man and wife are together. Moreover, the coupling between man and wife, which in Kabbalistic tradition is supposed to take place during the night between Friday and Saturday, is believed to exert a mystical influence on the divine realm, and bring about, or promote, the union between the King and the Matronit.[40]

The notion underlying the above belief, that the King and the Matronit are engaged in constant or frequent copulations evidently contradicts the idea that the destruction of the Jerusalem Temple, their bed chamber, disrupted the love relationship between them, and that the handmaid Lilith has taken the place of her mistress as the consort of the King. However, since the Zohar has no coherent and logically consistent system of theology, but is a huge and complex compendium presenting often disparate and mutually contradictory concepts, the question of consistency cannot and must not be raised. The fact simply is that, in addition to the notion of the definite disruption of the marital relationship between God and the Matronit by the destruction of the Jerusalem Temple, there are passages in the Zohar which speak of daily copulations between the divine couple, others of weekly couplings, and still others of an annual separation and reunion between them.[41]

YIḤUDIM (UNIFICATIONS)

The notion that man's behavior influences the love relationship, the union or separation, of the King and the Matronit, placed an awesome responsibility upon the Jews learned about the Kabbala. They were convinced, to put it in the simplest possible terms, that the completeness, even the happiness, of God depended upon their behavior, their relationship with their wives, and in particular their performing the great and mysterious commandment of coupling with their wives at the traditionally prescribed times, and with the proper *kawwana*, concentration on its mystical significance. The term *kawwana*, an important concept of Lurianic Kabbala, is difficult to translate. Its primary meaning is "intention," but in Kabbalistic context it signifies intense concentration on a sacred mystical purpose while performing a commandment or reciting a prayer or benediction. Isaac Luria (1534–1572), the great Safed Kabbalist, recommended many such *kawwanot*, concentrations, which were collected and published in a book titled *Sefer haKawwanot* ("Book of Concentrations").[42] He recommended, for instance, that the pious should study from midnight to dawn, so that the Shekhina (identical with the Matronit), personified as Rachel, should "ascend together with the ascent of the morning prayer, and have union with her husband (i.e., God) through the power which you added to her during the night. And then you will be called Groomsmen of the Matronit . . ."[43] He also suggested that, prior to beginning to study either the Midrash or the Kabbala, the pious student recite the sentence, "For the unification of the Holy One, blessed be He, and His Shekhina, in fear and trembling to unite the *Yah* with *weh* [the two halves of the divine name Yahweh], in a complete union, in the name of all Israel, [and] to raise up the Shekhina from the dust, behold, I study this and this Midrash (or: this and this Kabbalistic treatise)."[44]

However, Luria went an important step further and ruled that the fulfillment of all commandments should be preceded by the expression of one and the same intention, and that before and during their performance one should concentrate on, and intend to bring about through it, the unification of God and the Shekhina.[45] He proposed the observance of the following "Rules of Prayer in the Synagogue": "One must be careful always to say before everything, 'For the unification of the name of the Holy One, blessed be He, in fear and trembling and awe, in the name of all Israel,' for one must always unite the male and the female . . ."[46]

These Lurianic *kawwanot* rapidly spread all over the Jewish world, and until the onset of the Haskala, the Jewish Enlightenment, they were regularly recited by all observant Sephardi as well as Ashkenazi Jews. Prayer books with Luria's annotations, or containing his *nusaḥ* (version) of the prayers, or identified simply as following the Sephardi *minhag* (custom), were published in dozens of editions all over the Ashkenazi diaspora, while in the Jewish communities in the Arab lands they were practically the only ones used. Ashkenazi prayer books, even if the Lurianic or Sephardi provenance of their *nusaḥ* or *minhag* remained unstated, often bore the distinct marks of Lurianic-Kabbalistic influence. A typical example is the *Seder T'filla Derekh Y'shara* ("Order of Prayer Straight Path") of the German Rabbi Yeḥiel Mikhael Epstein (died 1707), published in Frankfurt in 1697 (and also in later editions), which presents detailed information on what the Kabbalists' intentions were in connection with various prayers. For example, it says, "the Kabbalists wrote: If a man prepares his body for the performance of a commandment, he should say explicitly (*b'fe male*) that he does it for the unification of the Holy One, blessed be He, and His Shekhina. Then, instantly, out of that word a holy angel is created who will help him fulfill that commandment leisurely and easily, and who will become an honest advocate for him before the Holy One, blessed be He . . ." According to another Kabbalistic view quoted in the same prayer book, "by putting on the *ṭallit qaṭan* (the square undergarment with the four *tzitzit* fringes) one's body becomes a vehicle for the Shekhina, after the manner of the Holy Beasts which carry the Throne of Glory" (cf. Ezek. 1).[47] Although

R. Epstein himself was of the opinion that only those who had penetrated the gates of the Kabbalistic mysteries should recite these "unifications," he considered them so much part of the prayers and other religious ritual that he felt constrained to devote considerable space to them in his prayer book.[48]

Even more characteristic of the hold the "unifications" had on the religious life of the Jews even in a country as remote from Kabbalistic Safed as anti-Hasidic Lithuania is the fact that they were printed many times in the *Siddur Ishe Yisrael* ("Prayer Book Fires of Israel"), which follows the rite of the Gaon Elijah of Vilna (1720–1797). In this *siddur* formal obeisance is paid to the views of the Gaon of Vilna by the addition of a footnote to the effect that "According to R. Elijah of Vilna one should not recite any unifications prior to the performance of a commandment."[49] However, this footnote cannot obliterate the fact that even in this prayer book the unifications have an important place.

Also the *Siddur Otzar haT'fillot* ("Prayer Book Treasury of Prayers"), which contains the comments of both Elijah of Vilna and R. Akiba Eger (1761–1837), another most prestigious exponent of strictly orthodox halakhic Judaism, prints several times the "For the unification . . ." formula.[50]

The "unifications" constitute a recurring refrain in the prayer books in use to this day among the Hasidic, Sephardi, and Oriental Jews, which testifies to the widespread and persistent influence of Lurianic Kabbala with its emphasis on the need to concentrate on the secret, inner meaning of both prayers and commandments. Prayer took up a considerable part of the everyday life of the ordinary pious Jew in each of these three major divisions of the Jewish people, so the most direct way of acquainting oneself with the force of the Lurianic traditions in these communities is to have a closer look at some of the most popular prayer books used by them. A quick rundown of the references to the Shekhina found in these prayer books follows.

I possess a much thumbed-through old prayer book which belonged to my grandfather, R. Moshe Klein of Pata, Hungary, and which he used until his death in Jerusalem in 1928, when it passed into the possession of my father from whom I, in turn, inherited it. It is the *Siddur Bet Yaʿaqov heḤadash* ("The New House of Jacob Prayer Book"), published in Vienna by H. Ziegelheim (no date), which follows the Sephardi *minhag*. It is a late version of the prayer book of the Sephardi Jews which was edited in the sixteenth century in accordance with the *kawwanot* of Isaac Luria. On the very first text page of the copy I have, the worshiper is instructed to recite, prior to wrapping himself in the *ṭallit*, the unification formula quoted above, with the appropriate ending, ". . . behold, I wrap my body into the *tzitzit*."[51] The very next page contains instructions to recite the same formula in connection with the tying of the *tefillin* (phylacteries) on the left arm and around the head, again with the appropriate changes in the closing part. This means that the only two ritual acts, which introduced the daily prayers, were explicitly stated to be performed for the purpose of bringing about a union between God and the Shekhina.

If I may digress for a moment to another prayer book, I would like to mention that the most elaborate description of the "unificatory" purpose of the ritual of putting on the prayer shawl and the phylacteries is contained in the *Siddur T'filla k'Minhag S'farad* ("Prayer Book According to the Sephardi Custom") which contains the commentary of R. Moshe Cordovero (1522–1570), another leading Safed Kabbalist and contemporary of Isaac Luria. Prior to putting on the tefillin, this prayer book states, one must recite the following:

> For the unification . . . and so as to provide, through the tefillin of the hand, brains for the Female of the Small of Face [i.e., the Shekhina of God], and, through the tefillin of the head, brains for the Small of Face [God], so that the bridegroom [God] embrace the bride [the Shekhina], His left arm under her head and His right arm embrace her . . . And the straps [of the tefillin] should be bonds of love between the bridegroom and the bride, and let not the sins bring it about that the straps be tied to Samael [Satan] and his female [Lilith], and all their retinue . . . Behold, I put on the tefillin of the head so as to bring all the idolaters under the hand of the Lower Shekhina, and the tefillin of the hand so as to bring all the other gods under the dominion of the Upper Shekhina . . .[52]

An explanation of each of the concepts appearing in this *yiḥud* would require pages and pages, but the intention of the passage is to state that one of the purposes of putting on the tefillin is to bring about a unification between God and the Shekhina by tying them to one another with the straps of the tefillin.

But, to return once more to the *Siddur Bet Yaᶜaqov heḤadash*, it contains instructions that one should recite the "For the unification" formula on the following occasions: Before beginning the morning prayer, in connection with the sanctification of the new moon, when performing the *tashlikh* ceremony on the afternoon of the first day of New Year, prior to performing the *kappara* rite on the eve of Yom Kippur, before observing the commandment of the *lulav* on the Feast of Sukkot (Tabernacles), and before entering the *sukka* (booth) on that feast, and on many more occasions throughout the liturgical year in connection with all kinds of holiday rituals.[53] It also contains Isaac Luria's erotic Sabbath-eve poem about the union of the divine bridegroom and bride.[54] In connection with the *kappara* rite it prescribes the recitation of the following *kawwana*:

> . . . for the unification of the Holy One, blessed be He, and His Shekhina . . . behold, I come to perform this *kappara* [atonement], to perfect [the Shekhina's] root in the supernal place . . . and through the power of the virtue of the slaughtering of this cock may the five stern judgments be softened . . . And rebuild the Sanctuary quickly in our days, and there we shall perform before You the rite of the Scapegoat and the he-goats . . . to soften the power and the severity of the Queen [the Shekhina] . . .[55]

On Sukkot, when the worshiper enters the booth, he is advised to recite:

> Be it the will from before You, O Lord, my God and the God of my fathers, that You let Your Shekhina rest among us, and spread over us the booth of Your peace, by virtue of the commandment of the *sukka* which we fulfill to unite the name of the Holy One, blessed be He, and His Shekhina, in fear and trembling, to unite the *Yah* with *weh* in complete union, in the name of all Israel . . .[56]

Among the *Hoshanot* (songs for the Feast of Booths) printed in the same prayer book, one reads: "*Hoshaᶜna* (help us) . . . for the sake of Your Shekhina . . ." and another mentions "the Holy of Holies, paved with love, the Shekhina of Your glory, O help us!" One of the prayers recited on the day of Hoshaᶜna Rabba includes this:

> On this day give the Shekhina of Your Strength five powers softened through the beating of the willow branches, according to the custom of Your holy prophets. And may love arise between them, and kiss us with the kisses of Your mouth which soften all the severities and all the judgments. And light up the Shekhina of Your Strength in the name of *yod*, *he* and *waw* [the first three letters of the tetragrammaton] . . .

Pious Jews used to make vows to fast on Monday, Thursday, and again on Monday, and to recite *s'liḥot*, penitential prayers, on those days. Among those to be recited on Mondays, according to the prayer book we are discussing, is one in which the worshiper entreats God to have mercy for the sake of many divine attributes, such as glory, kingship, holiness, and also "do it for the sake of Your Shekhina." On the second Monday they recite a prayer which contains the words, "Return Your Shekhina to the bosom of my palaces . . ."

On the fast day of Tammuz 17 one of the *s'lihot* recited states, "Our enemies destroyed the Sanctuary, and the Shekhina fled from a corner of the Sanctuary . . ."

On a Sabbath which falls on a new moon, a brief prayer is inserted into the Eighteen Benedictions, in which the Community of Israel (personified as the Shekhina) voices her complaint: "In my vineyard, the lodging between my two breasts, I made the Almighty [*Shaddai*] rest 410 times . . . Blessed be, O Lord, who brings back His Shekhina to Zion." This is followed by another poetic insertion which begins, "O kid (*g'di*), tied to the hands in order to receive blessings, the Shekhina delighted in the love of the skins of his kids . . ." The allusion is, of course, to the story in Genesis 27, according to which Jacob tied the skins of kids to his hands so as to be mistaken by his father for Esau, and thus receive the blessings.

In a *yotzer* (liturgical poem) for one particular Sabbath is found the following statement: "He [God] will contact His Shekhina inside the New Gate, and He will be called by a new name, as the name of the city from the hallowed day."

At the time of burning the *hametz* (leaven, in the morning of the day before Passover) the following plea is addressed to God: "May it be the will from before You O Lord, our God and God of our fathers, that just as I remove the *hametz* from my house . . . so You should remove all the oppressions of the Shekhina." And after the Passover seder (festive meal) the Song of Songs is recited, which is understood to speak about the love of God and the community of Israel, that is, the Shekhina.[57]

The above survey of one of the most popular prayer books suffices to demonstrate that the concept of the Shekhina permeated the religious life of the Hasidim and the Oriental Jews, and that they observed a great many commandments with the avowed purpose of bringing about the unification of God and the Shekhina. A rapid count indicates that in the course of the year an observant Hasidic, Sephardi, or Oriental Jew stated close to two thousand times that he carried out a commandment or recited a prayer "for the unification of God the King and His Shekhina." It is only in the modern Ashkenazi prayer books that these references to the Shekhina have been excised with the exception of one which occurs in the ʿ*Amida* or Eighteen Benedictions, recited three times every day, which reads: "May our eyes see when You [God] return to Zion in mercy. Blessed are You, O Lord, who brings back His Shekhina to Zion."

A glance at the other prayer books which were, until one or two generations ago, in use in most Jewish communities in the Arab world, shows that they contain the "For the unification" formula as often, or even more often, than the *siddur* we discussed above.[58] These prayer books, and their counterparts used in Ashkenazi communities, are striking concrete illustrations of the general observation made by Scholem almost fifty years ago: "The Lurianic Kabbalah was the last religious movement in Judaism the influence of which became preponderant among all sections of the Jewish people and in every country of the diaspora, without exception."[59]

To come back now to the mystical significance of the relationship between man and wife in Kabbalistic doctrine mentioned in the beginning of the present section, the practical outcome of that doctrine was to endow the wife with a special aura in the eyes of her husband. She was his partner in a mystical spiritual sense just as the Matronit was of God the King. Especially in the festive atmosphere of the Sabbath eve, the mistress of the house became associated in her husband's thoughts and emotions with the Shekhina and with Sabbath the queen and bride, and thus represented for him the earthly counterpart of the divine consort of God. Hence to relate to one's wife with love, tenderness and respect was, in the circumstances, natural and inevitable. It was in sixteenth-century Safed that the custom arose to recite Friday night Proverbs 31:10–31, which is a paean to "the woman of valor." Originally this was meant to be a praise of the Matronit-Shekhina, but eventually this original intention was forgotten, and the text was understood to refer to the mistress of the house in its literal meaning. The respect paid to women in the Hasidic communities was in no way diminished by the Kabbalistic doctrine that they represented the "Left Side," that is, the side of judgment and severity, or even the cruel and the demonic, in the divinity or the divine scheme of things. On the contrary, one suspects that such ideas may have contributed an element of awe, of apprehension, to the attitude of love and respect the women enjoyed.

The attitude of men to women was also influenced by the figures of the great women of the Bible, the four matriarchs, the prophetesses Miriam, Deborah, and others, Esther, the heroine of the Purim story, etc., who have always occupied an important place in Jewish consciousness. Especially Rachel, the tearful mother of Israel, who weeps over the bitter fate of her children, and is addressed by God with words of consolation (Jer. 31:

15–16), has become a classic image of the compassionate Jewish national *mater dolorosa*. In Kabbalistic doctrine Rachel became identified with the Matronit, so that her grief was not only about the fate of her exiled children, but also about her own cruel separation from her beloved husband, God the King. Her tomb near Bethlehem is to this day a place of pilgrimage, especially for women, all year round, and in particular on the new moons, during the month of Elul, and on the 14th of Heshvan, the traditional date of her death.

It is the great merit of Scholem that he has made historians of religion recognize the Kabbala as a great religious movement in Judaism. I would like to add that one of the great merits of the Kabbala was that it secured women a place of honor and respect in the Jewish family and community. Although from a religio-legal point of view the Jewish woman was certainly not equal to man either before or after the emergence of the Kabbala, it was due to the Kabbala that she became highly regarded by her husband, honored as his life partner, and considered the helpmeet without whom not only would his life be lacking, but he himself would not be a complete human being. As the Zohar puts it:

> It is written, "Male and female created He them" (Gen. 1:27). Hence any image in which male and female are not found is not an image of the Supernal . . . Come, see: Any place in which male and female are not found together as one, the Holy One, blessed be He, does not set His abode in that place, and blessings are not found except in a place where male and female are found . . .[60]

The Kabbalistic view that only man and wife together form a complete human being became accepted among Jews everywhere. It spread from the Kabbalistically learned to the ignorant, and was found equally in Kabbalistic and non-Kabbalistic circles, among Ashkenazi, Sephardi, and Oriental Jews. In a Muslim environment, the persistence of this tradition made all the difference between the Muslim and the Jewish attitude to women, and between the status of the Muslim and the Jewish women. While the position of the Jewish woman in Arab lands was deeply influenced by that of her Muslim sister, this Kabbalistic tradition functioned as an effective barrier against the penetration into the Jewish *mellāḥ* of the Muslim, Koran-based view that women were inferior to men. In the Ashkenazi world, the Jewish emancipation and the Haskala, the Jewish Enlightenment, resulted in a rapid disappearance of traditional Jewish learning and outlook, including the Kabbalistic teachings which assigned an equal place to man and woman in the divine mystery of the creation of the human being, and an equal task in bringing about the unification of God and the Shekhina. In Arab lands, as has repeatedly been stated, the Jews experienced neither Haskala nor emancipation, which meant that until their emigration to Israel the old traditions remained alive among them, and those old traditions were always Kabbalistically colored to a considerable extent. Thus the old doctrines about man and woman remained a living heritage in the Oriental Jewish communities, and continued to secure for the Jewish woman a better position than the one had by her Arab sister. And even though most of the Jews in Arab countries had only a faint idea about the teachings of the Talmud and the Kabbala, in each community there were rabbis and learned men who were the repositories of Talmudic and Kabbalistic knowledge, and whose comportment, including their relationship to their wives, was the example the others tried to follow. In this manner the respect the learned men showed toward their wives as the earthly counterparts of the Shekhina influenced the general attitude of the men toward the women in all Jewish communities in the Arab lands.

WOMEN'S RELIGION

In this chapter so far, we have spoken only of those religious beliefs and practices which were prescribed or approved by the official religious authorities of the various sects, trends, or schools within Judaism and Islam. However, as we have seen in chapter 6, in addition to these official forms of religion, there were also manifestations of popular religion in both Judaism and Islam; in these, in contrast to the official religion, the participation of women was generally as great as, or even greater than, that of men. What remains to be done in the present chapter is to provide a brief overview of those specific forms of religious beliefs, customs, and cults, which were either the exclusive domain of women, or in which the participation of men was rare and unusual.

In general it can be observed that the greater the exclusion of women from the official religion, the stronger the tendency among them to develop, adhere to, believe in, and practice a special "women's religion," whose tenets and rites either remain unknown to the men, or are disapproved by them, and especially by the spokesmen of the official religion. As we have seen, the participation of women in the official cult is more limited in Islam than in Judaism. Consequently, if our above generalization is correct, we shall expect to find that a separate "women's religion" is a more widespread phenomenon among the Muslims than among the Jews. A closer look at the religious life of the women in both communities will show that this, indeed, is the case.

In Judaism, definite, albeit limited, functions have been assigned to women within the framework of official religion. To mention only a few of these: the observance of the complex rules of *kashrut* (dietary laws) has been the almost exclusive domain of women. Women were obliged to observe the laws of sexual purity, the setting aside of the *ḥalla* from the dough they kneaded, and the lighting of the Sabbath and holiday candles with their appropriate benedictions. Although the Halakha (religious law) does not command women to pray and to attend synagogue services, in traditional Jewish circles they were expected to do so, and unfailingly did. In the synagogues separate galleries or sections were built to enable women to pray without mixing with the menfolk. At home women were expected to recite the varied benedictions prior to eating and drinking, and the after-meal grace. The wearing of various, locally sanctioned, types of head coverings was considered a definitely religious duty for married women. As formulated in the Mishna (Qid. 1:17), Jewish women had to observe all the laws of religion, except the positive commandments whose performance was tied to certain times. In sum, the numerous religious observances imposed upon her by Halakha and custom, imparted to the Jewish woman the feeling that she had an important role to play in the religious life of her family and community.

This being the case, the Jewish woman's need for religious expression was, by and large, satisfied by officially prescribed observances, and consequently she turned to popular religion to a not much greater extent than did the men. The veneration of saints is a case in point. Although undoubtedly more Jewish women than men used to take part in the *ziyāra*s (visitations of saints' tombs), those folk-fests have always attracted large numbers of men as well, so that they were not manifestations of a separate women's religion. Likewise the folk customs connected with childbirth, although they centered on the person of the barren wife, the expectant mother, and the woman in childbed, they were observed with the participation of men, and the various remedies, prophylactic measures, charms (*qameᶜot*), etc., were as a rule prescribed and supplied by men, including rabbis. Neither in the Arab lands nor elsewhere were there among the Jews beliefs, rites, or cults which were the exclusive domain of women, let alone adhered to and observed by the women contrary to the wishes of the official religious leadership, or clandestinely, without its knowledge.

The situation was very different among the Muslims. Official Islam, in a development that began several generations after Muhammad, has become a religion of and for men only. In general, Islam demands the performance of much fewer ritual observances than Judaism; and it is only men who are expected to follow them. In recent times, practically the only commandments Islam addresses to women pertain to modesty in dress and comportment, which in many segments of Arab society has taken the form of veiling and seclusion. Yet this was not always the case. Muhammad himself, in a significant passage of the Koran (33:35) expressed the expectation that men and women would equally follow his *dīn*:

> Lo! Men who surrender unto Allah, and women who surrender, and men who believe and women who believe, and men who obey and women who obey, and men who speak the truth and women who speak the truth, and men who persevere (in righteousness) and women who persevere, and men who are humble and women who are humble, and men who give alms and women who give alms, and men who fast and women who fast, and men who guard their modesty and women who guard (their modesty), and men who remember Allah much and women who remember—Allah hath prepared for them forgiveness and a vast reward.[61]

This passage shows unmistakably that, apart from matters of belief and morality, Muhammad wanted women to give alms, to fast, to guard their modesty, and to call upon God, that is, pray. Of these duties only the guarding of modesty (i.e., veiling), and fasting survived the subsequent Islamic developments. Later Muslim traditionists and Koran interpreters maintained that, as against many pious men who attained paradise, only a very few (according to Bayḍāwī, a leading Koran commentator, not more than four) women were able to do so.[62] While Muhammad, according to an early tradition, allowed women to pray in his company and in the mosque, in fact women were soon excluded from attendance in mosques.[63] By the thirteenth century, Bayḍāwī stated categorically (*ad* Koran 4:38) that prophecy, religious leadership, sainthood, the pilgrimage rites, giving evidence in law courts, the duties of the holy war (*jihād*), and worship in the mosque on Friday were all confined to men.[64] This being the case, women in Muslim society were left literally starving for religious expression and experience, and it was inevitable that they should turn to folk religion to satisfy that hunger.

A feature which takes an intermediary position between official and folk Islam is the *qraya* (in literary Arabic *qirā'a*), or "reading," which plays an important role among the Shīᶜites in Iraq. *Qrayas* are held separately for men and for women, and are attended with greater enthusiasm and ecstatic excesses by women than by men. The *qrayas* are held on Ramaḍān nights, in some places on every night of the fasting month, as well as on Muḥarram, and are presided over by a male *mullah* for the men, and a female *mullah* for the women. The female *mullahs* are literate women who have received training in their youth from older *mullahs*. They learn to recite the Koran, memorize *sūras* from it, and stories about the tragic events of Muḥarram, and eventually write them down in their own book of *qrayas*, which they then use to conduct their readings. For the women who attend these *qrayas* they constitute rare occasions on which large groups of them can gather, and engage in unrestrained, and even violent, behavior in public. The proceedings begin with loud responses to the reading of the *mullah*, then advance to rhythmical breast-beating, baring the breast, nodding the head, weeping at the story of the martyr Ḥusayn told by the *mullah*, and wailing aloud. As Dorothy Van Ess, who attended many of these sessions in Baṣra in the 1910s, put it, "Women find in these gatherings a social satisfaction, dramatic gratification, and emotional release, all bound up with religious fervor." As can be gathered from Elizabeth Warnock Fernea's description of the *qrayas* in the 1950s in a village in southern Iraq, the ritual had lost nothing of its power to produce religious ecstasy in women in the ensuing half century.[65]

But to return to Bayḍāwī, of the items enumerated by him only one, that of sainthood, came to play a role in popular Islam. As is typical of folk religion in general, in this case too the official attitude of the religious authorities was disregarded, and, as we have seen in chapter 6, female saints thrived in Arab countries, although their number remained everywhere much smaller than that of male saints. As far as the participation of ordinary people in the veneration of saints was concerned, the picture presented by the Muslims and the Jews was largely identical—this too emerges clearly from the preceding chapter. The only palpable difference in this respect between the two communities was that the proportion of women in the groups who flocked to the *ziyāras* was greater among the Muslims than among the Jews.[66] But, in addition to these rites, grudgingly tolerated by the religious authorities, Muslim women, especially in the southern tier of the Arab lands, were addicted to religious practices strongly disapproved by the official religious leadership. Foremost among these practices were those based on the belief in all kinds of demons, spirits, and quasi-deities, who often took possession of human beings. A great majority of these cases were of women, who experienced pain and states of disorientation, and behaved in a manner contrary to accepted norms. Once a person was thus possessed by a spirit, it became necessary to exorcise it, which was done in complex rituals, handed down by folk tradition, performed by a female mistress of ceremony, and attended almost exclusively by women.

Most typical of this type of veritable cult was that of the *zār*, which seems to have penetrated the Arab world from Black Africa. The *zār* had (or still has) devotees in various parts of Negro Africa, in Ethiopia, Somalia, Sudan, Egypt (both Upper and Lower), Southern Arabia, including the former Aden Protectorate (today the People's Democratic Republic of Yemen), the Ḥijāz province in Saudi Arabia, including the holy city of Mecca, and certain tribes between Ḥijāz and Nejd. In all these places, the person possessed had no recourse but to seek out the help of an expert, a woman who knows the ritual of exorcism, called *shaykhat ez-zār* ("mistress of the *zār*") in Mecca, *umm az-zār* ("mother of the *zār*") in Southern Arabia, *ʿālima* ("knowing woman") in Egypt, *shaykha* ("sheikess") in the Sudan, and *umm j-jnūn* ("mother of the jinn") in Morocco, where similar exorcisms are performed but the spirit is not called *zār*, but jinn.[67]

Snouck Hurgronje, who studied life in Mecca in the late nineteenth century, found that each of the ethnic groups of the city had its own variety of *zār* ritual: thus there was a Maghrebite (Moroccan), Sudanese, Abyssinian, Turkish, etc. *zār* exorcism. However, basically all these rituals were identical: they were always performed by an elderly woman, whose first task was to elicit from the *zār*, speaking through the mouth of the possessed person, what gift he (the *zār* was as a rule believed to be a male) wished to be given in exchange for leaving the body of the possessed. The usual answer was a new dress or some kind of jewelry. Once the gift was procured and handed to the *zār*, that is, to the possessed person, the *zār* was supposed to leave. In many cases the *zār* ceremony went on for hours, throughout the night, or even for more than one day, and involved much drumming or other rhythmical music, bloody animal sacrifices, ecstatic behavior, erotic dancing, etc.[68]

Although the name *zār* is of non-Arab origin, the nature of the spirit designated by this name is very similar to that of indigenous Arab spirits, whether called jinn, *ghūl*, or *ᶜafrīt*. Nor are exorcisms foreign to Arab folk tradition, so that the African *zār* cult could easily gain acceptance in the Arab world. As for the feminine character of the cult, it is readily explained by the position of the Arab woman in Islam. Her exclusion from what I called elsewhere the Apollonian orthodox Muslim ceremonies, as well as from the Dionysian Muslim brotherhoods,[69] left a void in both the religious and social life of the Arab woman, and this void was filled by the *zār* cult which afforded women an opportunity to congregate, to participate in an exciting group event, to act out unconscious stirrings, to establish contact with powerful spirits, to be the center of group attention, to manifest aggressive behavior, to feel that they were powerful, to indulge in a degree of nudism (e.g., in the so-called "cannibal *zār*" ceremony), and to dance in a highly erotic and suggestive fashion. In addition to the psychological satisfactions derived from all this, the *zār* cult was the basis for a kind of women's association in a community in which they were only marginal participants, and which recognized only men's associations. Thus, as Barclay put it, the *zār* cult "may be viewed as a functional counterpart to the men's religious brotherhoods."[70] Thus both psychologically and socially the *zār* cult fulfilled an important function.

Since the turn of the century Arab literati and religious leaders have repeatedly expressed their strong displeasure at the *zār* cult, and published treatises condemning it.[71] Yet the cult continued to flourish among the women in the southern sector of the Arab world outside the cities which in recent decades have become foci of modernization.

The Moroccan equivalents of the *zār* cult of the eastern Arab world are the fraternal associations and their beliefs and rituals which aim at serving or propitiating certain spirits, curing ailments believed to be caused by them, and establishing a quasi-institutionalized relationship between them and individuals who have attracted their displeasure or merely their attention. Among the spirits on whom is centered much of Moroccan folk religion important roles are played by individualized female demons (sing. *jinniyya*), called by such personal names as Lalla ("Lady") Malika, Lalla Mimuna, Lalla Mira, Lalla Jwimᶜa, La-Khraja, Tajnnisht, Gōla, Tagznt (or Taguznt), Tamza, Tayu, Shbuha, Tabᶜa, etc. These *jinniyya*s share a number of common physical features and personality traits: they often appear either in the form of a beautiful young woman or in that of an old hag with pendulous breasts, and are highly libidinous. Their counterparts are well known in the eastern Arab world as well, such as in Egypt, Sudan, and Ḥijāz.[72]

The most famous of these *jinniyya*s all over northern Morocco is Lalla ᶜĀ'isha, whose full name is ᶜĀ'isha Qandisha, and who is an evil, dangerous, fear-inspiring, oversexed she-demon. She is said to enter into marriage with men by seducing them before they discover her identity, and to appear in dreams and visionary experiences. The members of the Ḥamadsha brotherhood, who consider themselves special devotees (*muḥibbīn*) of ᶜĀ'isha Qandisha, specialize in the trance cure of her victims. Those in a trance mutilate themselves by cutting their foreheads with knives, in order to please the *jinniyya*, and to force her to leave them.[73]

Westermarck conjectured some sixty years ago that the cult, or at least the name, of ᶜĀ'isha Qandisha was of ancient Canaanitish origin. He suggested that the name Qandisha was derived from the term *q'dēshā*, the Hebrew-Canaanite-Phoenician name for a temple harlot.[74] Westermarck's conjecture is strengthened by the fact, unknown to him at the time, that there was in the Canaanite-Syrian pantheon a goddess named Qadesh or Qedesh, who was worshiped also in Egypt and styled "Qedesh, the Lady of Heaven and Mistress of All the Gods."[75] The cult of Qedesh (the name means something like "[Her] Holiness"), could have spread, together with the worship of other Phoenician deities, to the North African Phoenician colonies, and it is definitely possible that, as Westermarck put it, "ᶜA'isha Qandisha is the old goddess of love degraded to a Moorish *jenniya* of a most disreputable character."[76] Even so, legends current in Morocco about ᶜĀ'isha Qandisha suggest a Sudanese origin, and, in fact, one of her names is Lalla ᶜĀ'isha Sudaniyya, that is, "Sudanese Lady ᶜĀ'isha."[77]

However, the origin of the cult of ᶜĀ'isha Qandisha is of lesser importance for our present considerations than an actual description of it as a phenomenon. ᶜĀ'isha Qandisha is a she-demon whose propitiation is effected by established cultic procedures which serve to save or to protect those afflicted by her. She is, as it clearly emerges from Vincent Crapanzano's research (although he himself does not draw precisely these conclusions), an objectification of the Moroccan male attitude to women, a personification of those features of the female which make men desire, but at the same time fear, her. The female, as Crapanzano put it, is stereotyped as weak, inadequate, defenseless, treacherous, untrustworthy, and inferior, as well as sexually insatiable, by Moroccan Arabs, at least by those of the Ḥamadsha milieu. The fear of adultery by women is rampant. Lone women are always fair game. "Men must demonstrate no overt emotional dependence upon women . . . they must strive continually to live up to the ideal of male behavior: domination; extreme virility; great sensitivity to matters of honor, independence, and authority . . ."[78] The view of the opposite sex in primarily sexual terms is an old Arab tradition that goes back to the ancient Arab belief that demons lived in the desert and assumed the shape of women to lead travelers astray, while appearing to women as male seducers.[79] The seductive, and therefore dangerous, woman is "the image of ʿĀ'isha Qandisha and must be pacified and controlled." She, "and the other female jnun are, at least for the majority of Ḥamadsha, the cause of their illnesses; they must be placated and transformed. This—the cure—is accomplished by means of the saints' baraka."[80]

While several men believed themselves to be the husbands of ʿĀ'isha Qandisha, few of them were members of the Ḥamadsha brotherhood. Two of the many *zāwiya*s (lodges) in the city of Meknes belonged to the Ḥamadsha; their adepts (*foqra*), about fifteen in each of the two, comprised the core of the brotherhood. Much more numerous were the devotees (*muḥibbīn*), men, women, and children, attracted to the *ḥadra* (ecstatic dance) of the Ḥamadsha, who would attend the performances whenever they could, some three or four times a week, others once or twice a year. The Ḥamadsha fell into two groups: that of the followers of the saint Sidi ʿAlī ben Ḥamdūsh (who gave the name of the brotherhood), and that of those who follow the saint Sidi Aḥmed Dghughi. Members of both groups are also devotees of ʿĀ'isha Qandisha. Most of the Ḥamadsha are illiterate and belong to the lowest end of the Meknes social spectrum.[81]

The basic triangular relationship between the saint, the *jinniyya*, and the follower seems to revolve around attempts to strengthen the beneficial influence the saint has or can have over the follower, and thus to cure him of the ailment caused by the she-demon. This ongoing struggle takes place on a level far below that on which the sublime powers of Allah function. In fact, the very name Allah is conspicuously absent from the Ḥamadsha world, except for the *aryāḥ* (sing. *rīḥ*), the musical phrases played and sung during a dance, which are said to be the favorite of a particular jinn, and send a follower into a trance. In the *aryāḥ* of Lalla ʿĀ'isha, Lalla Malika, Lalla Mira, and of the male *jnun* Sidi Mimun, Sidi Musa, etc., the word "Allah" does, in fact, appear, but in a disjointed form, without any syntactical or ideational connection with the invocation of the demon which is the context of each *rīḥ*.[82] It is clear that the *jnun* of both sexes live in, and form, a world thoroughly apart from the divine realm of Allah. This world of demons has no relationship to Allah, is not part of the heavenly realm peopled by angels, but is strictly an aspect, a very painful one, of human life in the here and now.

As for the role of men and women in the Ḥamadsha and other rites associated with the *jnun*, it is difficult to generalize. In the major Friday afternoon ceremonies of the Ḥamadsha most of the visitors are women who come to obtain some of the *baraka* of the place, or to ask for something—a child, relief from pain, the preservation of a marriage, or simply good luck—and leave a small offering, such as candles, bread, sugar, or couscous. Also many of the *ṭallāᶜ*s, the exorcist-seers who identify attacking *jnun* and prescribe the appropriate cure, are women. The leaders and members of the adept group, the inner circle, of the two Ḥamadsha lodges, however, are all men.[83] Possibly, the Ḥamadsha represent a transitional stage from the type of folk-cult which is led by women and is attended mostly by women (as is the *zār* ritual in the Arab East) to a male-dominated cult: the attendants and exorcists are still mostly women, but the cult leadership has been taken over by men.

A similar process of takeover by men of the leadership in rites of exorcism could be observed in Egypt in the 1960s. In an Egyptian village the regular public Friday ceremonies of curing the possessed by exorcising the evil spirit (called here not *zār* but *ᶜafrīt*) were attended, either regularly or occasionally, by many women and only a few men; but they were conducted by a male *shaykh* who specialized in magic and charged an admission fee. Another type of ritual, held in the home of the possessed person as the need arose, was called *ṣulḥa* ("reconciliation"), and was conducted by a woman, but with the participation of the *shaykh*. While there were thus definite indications of male takeover, most men, in contrast to most women, were ashamed to admit publicly that they believed in the possibility of spirit possession, yet that deep down they did believe in it was evidenced by the fact that they feared to disobey the commands given by the spirit to their wives.[84]

In Jewish folk religion the belief that spirits can enter the bodies of persons, take possession of them, and cause them pain and harm dates from antiquity. According to the Hellenistic Jewish historian Josephus Flavius (first century C.E.), King Solomon was enabled by God to

> learn the skill which expels demons, which is a science useful and sanative to men . . . [Solomon] left behind him the manner of using exorcism, by

> which to drive away demons, so that they never return, and this method of cure is of great force unto this day; for I have seen a certain man of my own country, whose name was Eleazar, releasing people that were demoniacal in the presence of Vespasian, and his sons, and his captains, and the whole multitude of his soldiers. The manner of the cure was this: He put a ring that had a root of one of those sorts mentioned by Solomon to the nostrils of the demoniac, after which he drew out the demon through his nostrils; and when the man fell down immediately, he adjured him to return to him no more, making still mention of Solomon, and reciting the incantations which he composed. And when Eleazar would persuade and demonstrate to the spectators that he had such power, he set a little way off a cup or basin full of water, and commanded the demon, as he went out of the man, to overturn it, and thereby let the spectators know that he had left the man; and when this was done, the skill and wisdom of Solomon was shown very manifestly; for which reason it is that all men may know the vastness of Solomon's abilities . . .[85]

This report shows that by the first century C.E. exorcism was an established practice among the Jews of Palestine, and was believed to go back to a Solomonic tradition. The same conclusion can be reached from Matthew 12:22–29 which tells that Jesus engaged in exorcising demons, and that, according to contemporary view, demons could be driven out by invoking either the power of Beelzebub, the prince of the devils, or else "by the spirit of God."

In the pseudepigraphic Testament of Solomon (of uncertain date, but possibly from the second or third century C.E.), there is the story of the demon Ornias plaguing the overseer of the construction of the Temple, and then being exorcised by King Solomon with the help of a ring the king received from the angel Michael.[86]

Ever since those early days exorcism has remained an integral part of Jewish folk religion, which meant that on the part of the Jews there was an a priori readiness to adopt features from the demonology and exorcisms of the gentiles among whom they lived. The influence of Arabs on Jewish demonology was touched upon by Scholem who stated that, "Among North African and Near Eastern Jews elements of kabbalistic and Arabic demonology were combined even without literary intermediaries."[87]

Among the sixteenth-century Safed Kabbalists, who lived in an Arab environment, both the belief in spirit possession and the practice of exorcism were widespread. The literature produced by them contains numerous detailed instructions of how to proceed, and eyewitness accounts of actual exorcisms.[88] The Hebrew term for such an invading spirit or demon is *dibbuq* (literally "cleaving," i.e., a spirit which cleaves to the body of a person). The theory was that if a person committed a secret sin, thereby he became vulnerable to a *dibbuq*. The *dibbuq* would enter his or her body, take possession of it, speak through his or her mouth, force the possessed to do things he would not do in normal circumstances, and cause him pain and illness. As for the character of the *dibbuq* himself, he was considered to be the soul of a person who, while alive, committed great sins, for which he was punished after his death by being denied permission to transmigrate into the body of another person. Such a sinful soul could find momentary rest or refuge only by entering the body of a living person. Many Kabbalistic masters undertook the dangerous task of forcing the *dibbuq* to leave the body of the possessed, and to do so without killing him in the process. Part of the exorcism was to redeem the *dibbuq* by providing a *tiqqun* ("restoration") for him either by transmigration, or by causing him to enter hell and receive there the statutory punishment of the sinful.

While *dibbuqim* and *dibbuq* possession were parts of Jewish folk religion in both the Muslim and the Christian orbits (in the latter especially from the seventeenth to the nineteenth centuries), both the belief and the practice received the sanction of *ḥakhamim* and rabbis, quite a number of whom engaged in exorcisms. Those who did were frequently styled *ba'ale shem* ("master of the Name [of God]"), because they engaged in their magic activities by invoking the holy names of God in their incantations. In Europe, the spread of Enlightenment largely put an end to these beliefs and practices in the nineteenth century, although it was not until the early 1900s that S. An-Ski's play *Der Dibbuk* (1916) made the concept popular outside Hasidic circles. In the Arab lands, exorcisms continued in the Jewish communities well into the twentieth century. Thus in Baghdad, in 1903, Judah Moses Fetya exorcised the *dibbuqim* of the false Messiah Shabbatai Zevi and his "prophet" Nathan of Gaza, who took possession of men and women. In the following year, R. Ben-Zion Ḥazzan exorcised in Jerusalem the *dibbuq* who had entered the body of a woman.[89] In general, the victims of *dibbuqim* were women rather than men; but, in contrast to the Arab *zār*, which was always exorcised by a woman, in Jewish folk religion the exorcist was invariably a man, a *ba'al shem*, a man qualified by his great piety and expertise in sacred names, to function as an exorciser. This difference in the sex of the exorciser also indicates a basic difference in the relationship between the exorcism and the official religion. In Islam, the *zār* ceremony definitely stands beyond the perimeter of official religion; in Judaism, the *dibbuq* exorcism has been tolerated, albeit rather unwillingly, by the rabbis among the Hasidic Jews, and the *ḥakhamim* of the Jewish communities in Arab lands.

The foregoing discussion of the emphatic masculinity of Islam was, I believe, required as a preamble to a presentation of the woman's position in the Arab world. The exclusion of the feminine from the realm of the divine is unmistakably the theological counterpart of the social doctrine and practice which have relegated women to a subordinate position in the House of Islam. Just as Islam did not give the feminine a place in the world of the divine, so it did not give women a public place in Muslim society which was (and largely still is) the domain of men only. This had far-reaching consequences for the quality of the male and female mentality in the Arab world, by which the outlook of the Jewish men and women who lived for many generations in an Arab environment could not remain entirely untouched. This is the subject to which we turn in the next chapter.

8

Women: Jewish and Arab

In the foregoing chapter we dealt in some detail with the issue of the feminine in the deity, and saw that, in Jewish religion as practiced down to the present century especially in the Arab world, the Shekhina-Matronit played an important role, while Islam, even in its Ṣūfī form, comprised no concepts of any feminine element in the divinity. As already indicated above, it seems to me that one is justified in assuming that the presence of the feminine in the Jewish God-concept contributed to an attitude of respect and regard for women among the Jews, while its absence in the Muslim God-concept may have had a share in the exclusion of women from the official Muslim worship and in the relegation of women to a subordinate position. What follows is a rapid survey of the position of the women in the two communities, beginning with biblical times and concluding with the latest developments.

IN BIBLICAL AND TALMUDIC TIMES

There can be no argument about the subordinated position of women in biblical times. Ancient Near Eastern society as a whole was essentially male dominated in the age in which the stories of the patriarchs are set, that is, around the seventeenth to fifteenth centuries B.C.E. All the subsequent ages of the biblical period, in which the great milestones were the exodus from Egypt, the revelation on Mount Sinai, the conquest of Canaan, the rule of David and Solomon, and the teachings of the great Hebrew prophets, present the same picture. The Bible, to be sure, has preserved traces of matriarchy in family, society, and the realm of the divine, but the evidence is inconclusive, and no hypothesis of an early "matriarchal age" can convincingly be based on it. Even the early biblical myths have a distinctly patriarchal, male oriented, coloring. A typical mythical projection of patriarchy back into the days of creation is the reversal in Genesis 2 of the everyday reality in which man is born out of the body of woman, and the ascription of the origin of women to being fashioned by the Lord God out of an insignificant part of the body of man. Incidentally, the parallel creation story, contained in Genesis 1, assigns man and woman an equal place as far as their God-made origin is concerned: it says, "God created man (*ha'adam* in Hebrew whose meaning approximates that of "the human being") in His own image, in the image of God created He him; male and female (*zakhar un'qeva*) created He them" (Gen. 1:27).[1] As for the religio-legal position of woman in ancient Israel, it can be summed up in a few brief statements: She was subordinated to man ("he shall rule over thee" says God in Gen. 3:16 in cursing Eve for her disobedience); man had the right to marry more than one wife simultaneously (Deut. 21:15) and also to have concubines; a wife could be divorced by her husband at will (Deut. 24:1–4); she was given in marriage by her father, who could also sell his daughter in payment of debt (Ex. 21:7); and there were several religious duties, such as the annual pilgrimages to Jerusalem (Ex. 23:17; 34:23; Deut. 16:16) which did not have to be observed by women. Very onerous, at least from our modern point of view, were the laws of impurity which imposed severe restrictions on women during their menses, as well as for seven deys thereafter (Lev. 15:1ff.), and for much longer periods after giving birth to a child (Lev. 12:2–5).

Despite these legal restrictions, many biblical stories tell of the leading roles women played in their family and society, beginning with Sarah, the importance of whose position vis-à-vis that of her husband Abraham has only recently been pointed out in a study on Sarah the priestess.[2]

In view of the widespread Muslim custom of veiling it needs to be pointed out that among the biblical Hebrews and the Jews of Talmudic times, the women were neither veiled nor segregated. The only reference to veiling in the Bible occurs in connection with Rebecca (Gen. 24:65), and Tamar (Gen. 38:14, 19), and in both cases the women in question covered their faces with a veil temporarily and on a special occasion only.

In Talmudic times, on the basis of their close scrutiny of the biblical references to women, the sages established the principle (already referred to above) that women were exempt from all those positive commandments which are tied to definite time periods (M. Qid. 1:7). This principle, which is the law for observant Jews to this day, meant that women were, for example, not obliged to pray; for the duty of prayer, a positive commandment, a "do," must be performed at certain definite times of the day, the week, or the year. They don't have to go to the synagogue, for the same reason. They don't have to study the law (i.e., the Bible and the Talmud), because that too is tied to certain times, as it is written, "Thou shalt meditate therein day and night" (Josh. 1:8; cf. Deut. 6:7). Although women, either frequently or occasionally, undertook voluntarily to observe one or the other of these commandments—for instance, they quite generally attended synagogue services—these legal exemptions from basic religious duties imposed upon the men had dire consequences for the Jewish women, especially in Arab countries. In the Jewish communities of the Arab world generally the women remained uneducated, illiterate, even in societies in which most of the Jewish boys were taught to read Hebrew so as to be able to peruse the Bible, the prayer book, and the other holy books of Jewish religious literature.

In the Talmud and the Midrash literature, some of which was composed or compiled after the emergence of Islam, there are about as many negative as positive opinions about women. The misogynist view is expressed in statements such as "Women are light minded" (B. Shab. 33b), that is to say, unreliable, flighty, and frivolous; or "Ten measures of talk descended to the world; women took nine" (B. Qid. 49b), which means that women were regarded as querulous and garrulous. Woman was considered a source of sexual temptation, and especially her legs, hair, and voice, but even her finger, were termed "*ᶜerva*" (lit. "shameful nakedness"), that is, sexually exciting (B. Ber. 24a). According to one opinion, a man is forbidden even to look at a married woman (Tanh. Buber 1:170), and some rabbis held that a woman should not go out to the street because people would look at her (ibid.). One especially harsh statement about woman describes her as "a pitcher full of filth, with its mouth full of blood, yet all run after her" (B. Shab. 152a). An aggadic explanation of why God created woman from man's rib expresses a rather dim view of woman's character:

> God said: "I shall not create her from the head [of Adam], lest she hold up her head too proudly; nor from the eye, lest she be a coquette; nor from the ear, lest she be an eavesdropper; nor from the mouth lest she be too talkative; nor from the heart lest she be too jealous; nor from the hand lest she want to touch everything; nor from the foot lest she be a gadabout; but from a part of the body which is hidden" so that she be modest.

And yet, all these precautions notwithstanding, women turned out to be characterized by all the enumerated traits: they are greedy, eavesdroppers, lazy, and jealous.[3]

These dim views of woman are, however, more than counterbalanced by statements that show a deep appreciation of woman and of what she meant in the life of man, and some of which are expressions of great tenderness. Israel, we read in the Talmud, was redeemed from Egypt by virtue of its righteous women (B. Sota 11b). Women have greater faith than men (Sifre Num. 133), and greater powers of discernment (B. Nid. 45b). They are especially tenderhearted (B. Meg. 14b). A man without a wife has no joy, blessing, and good in his life; a man should love his wife as himself, and respect her more than himself (B. Yev. 62b). The Tora, the greatest treasure of the rabbis, is frequently personified as a woman (e.g., B. Yev. 63b), and is represented as God's daughter and Israel's bride (Ex. Rab. 41:5). Especially idealized is the woman as mother. Of one Talmudic sage, R. Yosef, it is reported that, when he heard his mother's footsteps, he said, "Let me rise before the approach of the Shekhina" (B. Qid. 31b).

In sum, the Talmudic and Midrashic literature presented the tradition-directed Jews with a wide range of opinions from which to choose when it came to finding hallowed views after which to mould their own attitudes to women, from the most positive to the most negative. However, the balance between the two was definitely tilted toward the positive by the existence of a feminine aspect of the deity whose earthly counterpart was the mistress of the house. These traditions assured the Jewish woman in the Arab countries a position better than the one into which Arab culture and Muslim tradition placed the Arab women.

IN THE JĀHILIYYA *AND UNDER ISLAM*

In speaking of the position of women and of male-female relations in the Arab world, it is important to distinguish between the traditional situation and the new developments whose thrust has been to introduce modern, Western features into Arab life in general and the man-woman relationship in particular.

In the traditional outlook, the segregation of women, the overvaluation of female chastity and modesty, and the conviction that the men's honor depended on their women's impeccable conduct in relation to men, has resulted in what appears to Western eyes as well as to the eyes of modern Arab students of their society, as an obsession with sex. Woman has become, above all, a sexual object. Both men and women are believed to be unable to resist the temptation of sex; the upbringing they receive makes them assume unquestioningly that if a man and a woman find themselves alone, without the restraining influence of the presence of others, sexual engagement will inevitably take place. Hence precautions must be taken to prevent even the remotest possibility of such an encounter, including, in certain sectors of Arab society, as little as a chance glimpse a man may have of a woman's face.

As a consequence of these taboos, traditional Arab society consisted of two separate sectors, that of the men and that of the women, and the two shall never meet. The typical urban Arab above the poorest class practically never spoke to or even saw a woman except for his own wife or wives, mother, sisters, and daughters. The same held good for the Arab woman, with a reversal of the sexes: she could never speak to, or allow to be seen by, any man, except for her husband, father, brothers, and sons. Perhaps the only exceptions to these narrow rules were the shopkeepers in the bazaars, who could conduct business with veiled women doing their shopping, and that was that.

In addition to the above, men in most Arab cities did have the opportunity to have sex with prostitutes, and to enjoy the performances of female singers and dancers, whose reputation was always doubtful, to say the least. Only in the nomadic encampments, in some villages, and among the city poor was there a relaxation of the rules of male-female segregation. This, of course, meant that statistically segregation was either absent or else limited among the majority of the Arab populations. But precisely in those sectors of the population which counted, which were influential, to which the "notables" belonged, and in whose hands was concentrated the political, administrative, economic, religious, and cultural leadership in every country, segregation and veiling were strictly observed. Segregation and veiling were therefore considered marks of elite status by both men and women, and a manifestation of Muslim Arab moral superiority over the nations whose culture lacked these traits.

In pre-Islamic Arab society, upon which Muhammad imposed his religion, women enjoyed considerable freedom. Although veiling was sporadically practiced, there was little segregation between the sexes. The wearing of the veil (*naṣīf*, *sitr*, *sijf*, etc.) was, far from being an imposition, a prerogative of women of a certain rank. In some cities, such as Yathrib (later called Medina), it was very little practiced. Also the fact that three important deities worshiped by the pagan Arabs were female (cf. Koran 4 : 117) can be seen as a reflection of the strong position women occupied in pre-Islamic Arab society. Robertson Smith, in his classic *Kinship and Marriage in Early Arabia*, concluded that among many tribes in the *jāhiliyya* there existed a form of polyandry, and that tribal government was by matriarchy.[4] It is also possible that the sexual hospitality (i.e., putting women of the tribe at the disposal of visiting strangers), traces of which have been found until recently in isolated localities in the Arab world,[5] was a survival of a pre-Islamic condition in which women enjoyed great sexual freedom. Muslim apologists for the inequality of women in Islam often argue that the introduction of Islamic law pertaining to women represented a marked improvement in their position compared to their status in the *jāhiliyya*. Historical research bears out this claim only partially.

There was, for instance, the practice of female infanticide engaged in by the pagan Arabs, for which there were several motivations: poverty, fear of disgrace and loss of prestige in case a girl married a stranger, the danger that a girl may be carried off in a raid and become the wife or concubine of an enemy, and the anxiety over being dishonored by her conduct. The last-mentioned factor is explicitly stated in a saying to the effect that the grave is the best bridegroom, and that the burial of daughters is demanded by honor.[6] A Koranic passage (6 : 138) outlaws the killing of children (Arabic *awlād*, masculine plural), because it was part of the worship of idols. Another passage speaks specifically of the killing of daughters who were unwanted, and condemns it. It reads, "When one of them is informed of the birth of a daughter, his face darkens, and he is filled with gloom. He hides from the folk because of the evil he was told: should he keep her in disgrace, or should he bury her under the dust? How evil is their judgment!" (Koran 16:58–59). It is somewhat puzzling that such an inhumane practice should be dismissed in a brief general condemnatory statement, instead of being explicitly prohibited. Still, Islam succeeded in largely—not totally—eliminating female infanticide. However, the larger concept of which this practice was one of the expressions, namely that the individual (whether male or female) was subordinated to the family and hence remained even in adulthood under the rule of the *patria potestas*, was not only not opposed by Islam but became the cornerstone of Muslim society.

Muslim Arab mores have less regard for individual human life than for the honor of the family, the prestige of the family, the interests of the family to which the individual belongs. The killing of daughters among the pre-Islamic Arabs was an extreme case of the disregard of the individual human life for the sake of the family; but the same tendency, expressed in less blatant forms, has remained a feature of the traditional Arab family, that is to say, in all sectors of the society except those which have become Westernized. While in principle both sons and daughters are to an equal degree subject to the will of the father (who acts in his capacity as family head and guardian of the interests and honor of the family), in practice it is the women in particular whom this system places in dependence and subservience. In the traditional Arab environment the woman was under the authority of her father in her childhood; under that of her husband in her womanhood; and under that of her son in her old age or in widowhood.

Many features in the position of the woman in the Arab (and Muslim) world go back to the Koran which assigns to women a position inferior to that of men. The key passage is *sūra* 4:34–38 which reads in Dawood's translation:

> Men have authority over women because Allah has made the one superior to the others, and because they (the men) spend their wealth to maintain them. Good women are obedient. They guard their unseen parts because Allah has guarded them. As for those from whom you fear disobedience, admonish them, and send them to beds apart, and beat them. Then if they obey you, take no further action against them. Allah is high, supreme.

The extent to which this Koranic passage still influences the thinking of men and women in the Arab world today was strikingly illustrated by a TV film aired by PBS in New York on July 15, 1984. The film, made with the participation of anthropologist Elizabeth Warnock Fernea and dealing with women's life in Morocco, had a scene I found especially moving. It showed how five- to six-year-old girls in a classroom were made to memorize the foregoing Koranic passage. The girl reciting it by heart stumbled over the more difficult words, and had to be helped out by the teacher, but the scene was a clear demonstration of how the doctrine of the inferiority of women (together with other Muslim teachings) is impressed into the uncritical and malleable minds of small girls even today. Small wonder that only a very few exceptional individuals can, when they grow up, demand and work for the liberation of the Arab woman (see below).

As a consequence of such teachings, and of the tradition-directed nature of Arab society in general, the position of women in the Arab world has changed little ever since it was circumscribed by the Prophet Muhammad partly in the Koran, and partly in the *ḥadīth*, the Islamic tradition which is attributed to him. One *ḥadīth* quotes Muhammad as having stated that Allah said, "I have left no calamity more detrimental to mankind than women." Another quotes Muhammad as follows: "Do not follow up one look at a woman with another; for, verily, the first look is excusable, but the second is unlawful." A third *ḥadīth* which, incidentally, shows that Muhammad was acquainted with the biblical myth of the creation of Eve, puts this statement in his mouth: "Admonish your wives with kindness, because women were created from a crooked bone of the side; therefore, if you wish to straighten it, you will break it, and if you let it alone, it will always be crooked." The fourth and last *ḥadīth* I shall adduce here, admonishes: "Not one of you must whip his wife like whipping a slave." *Ḥadīth*s such as these create the impression that Muslim tradition took a harsher attitude toward women than the Jewish as reflected in Talmudic and Midrashic stories and sayings.[7]

In considering the traditional position of the Arab woman—a subject about which there exists a sizable and still growing literature—one must keep in mind two things. One is, that the women's position has always varied greatly from place to place, and from one class, social or ethnic group to the other. Take, for instance, veiling, to which two brief references have already been made above. Until the onset of the recent feminist movements in Arab lands, Muslim women have always *wanted* to wear the veil, because it was a mark of, not restriction, but privilege: to wear the veil was for a woman the most visible sign of membership in the well-to-do class, the elite. The veil covering the face of a woman proclaimed that she was a lady of leisure, who had servants (or slaves) to relieve her of the work women had to do in and out of the house. The majority of urban women, comprising all those who had to perform personally the many onerous daily feminine chores, could not and did not veil. And as for the villages and the nomadic tribes, while it is difficult to generalize, the impression is gained that in most of them there was no veiling.[8]

The situation was quite similar with regard to polygyny. Although the Koran (4 : 3) allows men to marry up to four wives simultaneously, polygyny was always and everywhere a privilege of which very few men could avail themselves. Because of the institution of bride price, that is, the rendering of a considerable payment by the bridegroom (or rather his family) to the father of the bride, the general rule always was that only the well-to-do men could afford to marry more than one wife. In modern times the number of men who had more than one wife has been estimated at not more than five percent of all married men in most places. Therefore, to be the wife of a man who had a second (and even more so a third or fourth) wife, meant to belong to the privileged few, to be envied by the great majority of women who lived in monogamy with a poor husband and had to work hard to make ends meet.

A psychological analysis of the reaction of women to polygyny would require too much space, but consider the following brief scenario. A girl is brought up in a family in which from early childhood on she hears that if she is lucky, a rich man, who may have one or two other wives, will marry her; or, she will be his first wife, but after a few years he will be able to afford marrying a second wife. The girl is lucky, and she is married to such a man, at the tender age of, say, thirteen. Whether she is his first or second wife, whatever feelings of jealousy she may have toward her cowife (or cowives) will be amply compensated for by the satisfaction she will derive from being one of the wives of a rich and respected man who in all probability is a leader in the society of which the family is a part. What troubles her most as a wife is not that she has to share her husband's affection with another woman, but the ever-present danger that he may find some reason to divorce her, which he can do by simply pronouncing the traditional words in the presence of two witnesses. All in all, such a girl stands as good a chance to find happiness in her married life as a woman in the Western world. This is borne out by reports such as that by Elizabeth Warnock Fernea who spent two years in an Iraqi village. On one occasion, when she was chatting with a group of local women about their polygyny versus her monogamy, all unanimously agreed that their way was better.[9]

One of the most serious handicaps women suffered in traditional Arab society was lack of education. Schooling was restricted to boys, and even among them only a minority was sent to school. Up to some two generations ago, even among the urbanites only the relatively prosperous could afford to send their boys to the *kuttāb*, the mosque-affiliated Koran school, in which they were taught to read and write Arabic, to memorize the Koran, and some rudimentary arithmetic. In many cases the boys attended these schools for no more than two or three years, after which they were required to help their fathers in whatever manner they made a living. In the villages, schooling was even more sporadic, and in the nomadic tribes it simply did not exist.

As for the girls, it was in general held that the knowledge of reading and writing was not for them. Although in the early history of Islam it was possible for a *ḥadīth* to be recorded to the effect that it was incumbent on every Muslim man and woman to seek learning,[10] in practice this injunction was not followed. Among the wealthy who could have afforded to educate their daughters segregation was strictly observed, so a girl could not be sent to a school attended by boys. Even at home she could be tutored only by women. These external obstacles facilitated the disregard of the *ḥadīth* just referred to, and made it easy to follow the custom which denied education to girls. Thus women generally remained illiterate, and learned women were very rare exceptions.

One of these exceptional learned women was the poetess Wallāda, daughter of the Caliph al-Mustakfī, who was renowned alike for her charm and her literary ability. Andalus in its golden age represented an exception in this bleak picture of female illiteracy. Among its women there were many who were highly educated, and several who manifested talent for poetry and literary creativity. The literary historian al-Maqqarī (early seventeenth century), one of the chief sources of the history of Arabic literature in Andalus, devotes a long section of his *Nafḥ al-Ṭīb* ("The Fragrance of the Perfume") to these women authors in whom, as he puts it, "eloquence was a second instinct." He sings the praises of Wallāda, whose home in Cordova was the meeting place of savants, poets, and wits. She was also a great beauty who inspired Abu al-Walīd Aḥmad ibn Zaydūn (1003–1071), considered by some the greatest poet of Andalus, to write beautiful love poems to her. But she was an incurable flirt who caused both happiness and misery to Ibn Zaydūn, and his poems express his joy when she granted him her favors, and his deep unhappiness over her inconstancy.

We have already mentioned above that women did not take part in official communal religious activities, and were, in effect, excluded from the mosques in which the men regularly gathered for the Friday noon communal prayers. Exceptions from this rule were a few popular festivals in certain countries, such as that of the ʿĀshūrā in Egypt, so colorfully described by Lane.[11]

The other factor which one must take into consideration when viewing the position of women in Arab lands is the pronounced traditionalism which, until the mid-twentieth century, was a general characteristic of the Arab world. The West, as already mentioned, had its great religious and cultural upheavals as it passed from the Middle Ages into modern times. It had its Renaissance, Reformation, and Enlightenment, to name only the most important three. Nothing of the sort was experienced by the Arab world. What happened there, most broadly speaking, was that at first the incredibly powerful Arab élan, set in motion by Muhammad, produced the Arab golden age between the eighth and twelfth centuries, during which the Arabs spearheaded the cultural, scholarly, and scientific achievements in the Mediterranean area. Then, in the middle of the thirteenth century, the Arab lands were devastated by the Mongol invasion, and in the fourteenth they were swept twice by the Black Death and by a renewed attack of Mongol hordes. These catastrophes not only put an end to their golden age, but, before they could recover from these blows, Spain was lost to the Christians, and the other Arab lands were conquered by the Ottoman Turks who held them in oppressive serfdom for the next four centuries. As a result, as Faris and Husein put it, "until the closing years of the eighteenth century the Arab world was in a state of near stagnation, ingrown, content with its prevailing conditions, resigned to its fate, and blissfully ignorant of the events unfolding around it."[12] Other Arab students of Arab history have also commented upon, and bemoaned, the "drying up of the creative and adventurous spirit" of the Arabs, which was replaced by a "hard crust of dogma and fundamentalism."[13]

In these circumstances it is not surprising that the position of the women in Arab society should have remained practically the same until the nineteenth centuy as it had been in the Middle Ages. One of the most typical manifestations of cultural stagnation is the freezing or encrustation of societal conditions, and, in the first place that of the position of women. The more remarkable it is that at least one of the great minds of the Medieval Arab world was able to look at the position of women in Islam and find it wanting.

Ibn Rushd, one of the great geniuses of the Middle Ages, whose works we discussed in chapter 4, spoke out about the Islamic tradition of confining women to what was no more than a biological function. In his commentary on Plato's *Republic* (extant only in a Hebrew translation by Samuel ben Yehuda of Marseilles [born 1294] from the lost Arabic original) Ibn Rushd expresses his regrets over the position of women in Islam as compared with their civic equality in the *Republic*. Women in Islam, he observes, are used only for childbearing and the rearing of children, and this limitation is detrimental to the economy and responsible for the poverty of the state. The passage is so important, because of its exceptional nature, that it must be quoted in full:

> In these [Arab] States, however, the ability of women is not known, because they are only taken for procreation there. They are therefore placed at the service of their husbands, and [relegated] to the business of procreation, rearing, and breastfeeding. But this undoes their [other]

> activities. Because women in these States are not being fitted for any of the human virtues, it often happens that they resemble plants. That they are a burden upon the men in these States is one of the reasons for the poverty of these States . . . They should be educated in the same way [as men] in music and gymnastics."[14]

Six centuries had to pass before this solitary voice calling for the education of women found an echo in Arab society. When it did, it was not due to a sudden discovery that Ibn Rushd may, after all, have been right in his unorthodox evaluation of the position of women in "these States," but to the impact of the West. What happened then will be discussed later in the present chapter.

JEWISH WOMEN IN ARAB LANDS

The status of the Jewish woman within her community was in every Arab land decisively influenced by that of her Arab sister, and yet was nowhere identical with it. This is, of course, precisely what one would expect, considering, on the one hand, that it was practically impossible for the small Jewish minorities tolerated in the House of Islam to avoid being influenced by the pervasive culture of the dominant Muslim majority, and, on the other, that the religio-cultural differences between the two communities prevented the Jews from totally adopting Arab mores and behavior patterns in place of their own traditional customs and rules of conduct. A result of the interplay of these two forces was that, in contrast to the post-Emancipation European Jews who, as their self-critical adage had it, were like the gentiles only more so, in Arab lands the Jews were like the Arabs only less so. While I would certainly not go as far as S. D. Goitein, who termed the Arab influence on the Jewish women's position within rabbinical Judaism "unfortunate,"[15] it is an undeniable fact that the position of Jewish woman as it developed in Arab lands was similar to that of the Muslim women. However, one must never lose sight of the complementary fact that the Jewish women's lives were, as a rule, not circumscribed by restrictions and limitations to the same extent as were the lives of the women in Muslim society. I inserted the qualification "as a rule," because, as we shall see, occasionally at least the segregation of women was as rigorously insisted upon among the Jews as among the Muslims.

Among the inhabitants of Arabia, as we have seen, the veiling of women when they went outdoors was, although far from general, an established custom prior to the appearance of Muhammad. One of the testimonies to pre-Islamic veiling happens to be a brief statement in the Mishna (second century C.E.) discussing what a Jewish woman can take along when leaving her house on a Sabbath, on which day the carrying of anything at all in the public domain was prohibited. The Mishna in question states that the Jewish women of Arabia are allowed to go out veiled on the Sabbath (M. Shab. 6:6). This brief ruling (only three words in the Hebrew original) opens a window on the life of Jewish and Arab women in Arabia—that is, the lands to the east and south of Palestine—in the second century C.E. It allows us to conclude that for the Jewish women of Arabia it was of considerable importance to cover their faces with a veil when leaving the home; had it not been so, the sages would not have permitted them to put on, that is, to carry, on the Sabbath something that was not an essential part of their clothing. It also allows us to conclude that in countries other than Arabia the Jewish women did not wear veils, for otherwise the ruling would not have specified that this permission applied only to the Jewish women in Arabia. One can, furthermore, also infer that the mandatory custom of veiling must have been adopted by the Jewish women of Arabia under the influence of the general custom of the women of the land of wearing a veil when going out of the house. Thus this Mishna is perhaps the earliest testimony as to veiling among the Arabs [16] and the adoption by Jewish women of an Arab custom, supplying the earliest example of Jewish assimilation to Arab mores.

After Muhammad, once veiling spread to the countries conquered by the Arabs, also the Jewish women living in those lands adopted it. This immediately raises the question: to what extent was veiling considered mandatory in the Jewish communities in the House of Islam, and to what extent was seclusion practiced by them? In effect, only two generalizations can be made which contain only partial answers to these questions. One is that these practices were, on the whole, adopted by the Jews from the Muslim Arabs; the other is that neither veiling nor seclusion was, as a rule, as stringently applied to Jewish women as they were to their Muslim sisters.

As for the Arab origin of veiling and seclusion among the Jews, this conclusion is supported by two sets of facts. First, as we have seen above, neither in biblical nor in Talmudic times were the Jewish women veiled or secluded, with the exception of those of the Arabian Jewish communities. Second, it was directly after the Jews of the Middle East had come under Muslim Arab rule (i.e., from the seventh century on) that both practices began to spread among them. The evidence relating to the issue is meager but it is sufficient to lend support to both the above generalizations, and to show that by the twelfth century segregation of women was observed by the Jews in a manner closely corresponding to the Arab custom.

Petaḥya of Regensburg, the German-Jewish traveler who between 1175 and 1180 visited the eastern Arab countries and whose notes were written up in a fascinating travel book by unknown authors, reports about the Gaon Sh'mu'el ben ʿAlī (died 1194) that "he had no sons but only one daughter, and she was well versed in the Bible and the Talmud, and she taught the young men Bible—while she was shut up in the building—through a window, and the students were outside, below, and could not see her . . ."[17] The arrangement made for the Gaon's daughter to be able to speak to students while remaining unseen by them conformed to the Muslim custom which permitted a man to speak to the wife of another as long as she remained separated from him by, and hidden behind, a curtain (Koran 33:53).

If I may digress here for a moment I would like to mention that learned women, who were able to, and did, teach children Hebrew and Bible, were known to have done so in the Jewish communities in the medieval Arab world. The mother of Samaw'al al-Maghribī (a Jewish scholar who lived in Syria, Iraq, and Iran, and converted to Islam in 1163) and her two sisters, who grew up in Baṣra as daughters of a scholarly rabbi, were well versed in Tora studies and Hebrew writing.[18] And the Cairo Geniza contains documents relating to women who assisted their male relatives in tutoring children in Hebrew and the Bible.[19]

But to return to Petaḥya, he reports in general terms about the Jews and Arabs in Baghdad that "one sees no woman, and no man goes to the house of a friend, lest he see the wife of his friend. He [his friend] would instantly say to him, 'Shameless one, why did you come?' Instead, he [the visitor] beats the tin [i.e., uses the door knocker], and he [the host] comes out and speaks to him."[20] This procedure was, again, in strict conformity with Koranic law which warns, "O ye who believe! Enter not houses other than your own without first announcing your presence and invoking peace upon the folk thereof" (Koran 24:27).

More information about the seclusion of Jewish women comes from the seventeenth and subsequent centuries. In the early seventeenth century the Spanish priest Pedro Cantera Vaca visited the Algerian coastal town of Wahrān (Oran) and described the Jewish community he found there. According to him, the Jewish women were extremely modest. They never left their houses except in order to visit women neighbors, including Christians, and even on such occasions they did not go alone. On the Sabbath they would visit the cemetery. As against this, Cantera Vaca refers with indignation to the immorality of the Christian and Moorish women of Wahrān.[21]

In the eighteenth century, according to Alexander Russell, the Jewish women of Aleppo, Syria, did not eat at the table together with the men, except on holidays, and when no strangers were present. In the presence of strangers they were always veiled.[22] In the late eighteenth century William Lempriere informs us that "like the Moors, the Jewish men and women of Morocco eat separate; and the unmarried women are not permitted to go out, except upon particular occasions, and then always with their faces covered."[23]

In the early nineteenth century Lane reports that the rule for the Jewish women of Egypt was to "veil themselves and dress in every respect, in public, like the other women of Egypt." However, at home, the Jews were "not so strict as most other Orientals in conceiling their women from strange men, or, at least, from persons from their own nation, and from Franks [i.e., Europeans]: it often happens that a European visitor is introduced into an apartment where the women of the Jew's family are sitting unveiled, and is waited upon by these women."[24]

Lemprière, in speaking of Morocco, and Lane in reporting of Cairo, mention "intrigues" which allegedly were common among Jewish women.[25] It is difficult to know whether these statements owe their origin to the actually greater relaxation of sexual mores among the Jews than among the Muslims in the two countries, or should rather be attributed to the misleading impression outsiders got when they noted nothing more than a lesser degree of segregation of Jewish women, which may have appeared to them as license due to the contrast it represented to the strict seclusion of Muslim women. The latter alternative is made probable by the comment of yet a third nineteenth-century student of the Middle East, William C. Prime, in whose eyes the very fact that a Jewish woman appeared unveiled in front of visitors to her home seemed indicative of lack of "scruples." Writing about the home of a wealthy Jew in Damascus whom Prime visited, he says: "The lady who presided in this palace, and who, being a Jewess, had no scruples about being seen by strangers, received us in a dress of calico, outrageously dirty . . ."[26]

From accounts such as these it appears that in the eighteenth and nineteenth centuries the Jews in Arab lands no longer observed the medieval custom reported by Petaḥya of Regensburg of not allowing strangers to see the faces of their womenfolk, while still insisting on the women being veiled when going out of the house. Yet in some places the old custom persisted; for example, in Rabat, Morocco, some Jewish women covered their faces even at home, and even in the twentieth century.[27]

Veiling and seclusion, whether observed as stringently as was the custom in certain sectors of Muslim urban society, or with some relaxation as among the Jews, were but the tip of the iceberg as far as the position of women in both communities was concerned. Hidden by the closed doors of the houses and their latticed windows was the complex cultural configuration of the woman's position in her family and the wider society, the relationship between her and her menfolk on whom she was dependent all her life, her rights and obligations, and the emotions whose threads ran invisibly but powerfully back and forth between the two parallel worlds of the men and the women.

We have seen above that the framework within which the Arab woman lived her life was once and for all fixed by the Koran, which taught that the inferiority of women to men was established by Allah's creative will. The Arab attitude to women—reflected in the Koran, and, in turn, further reinforced by it—influenced the Jewish views of women, and the position of the Jewish woman, in Arab lands. One has to face the fact that in Arab lands, among both Muslims and Jews, women were considered lesser human beings than men, beings who in certain respects fell short of the mental development attained by men. This position is poignantly expressed by Maimonides (1135–1204) who speaks of women in a manner which provoked sharp criticism on the part of Jewish legal authorities who lived outside the House of Islam and thus were not influenced by Muslim ideas. In his law code, the *Mishne Tora*, Maimonides frequently refers to "women and the ignorant" in one breath, and rules that women cannot be appointed to communal office.[28] His views in this area parallel those of the thirteenth-century Koran commentator al-Bayḍāwī, one of the leading authorities of the Shāfiᶜī *madhhab* (school of jurisprudence), which we had occasion to refer to in the preceding chapter. The view that women are incapable of public duties has remained the official position of the *ᶜulamā'* of al-Azhar University down to the mid-twentieth century.[29]

In connection with the position of the Jewish woman in Arab lands, it is instructive to consider the areas in which Muslim influence made itself felt, and those in which the Jews resisted such influence. Under Muslim influence the bride price the husband was supposed to pay to his bride was divided into two parts: one part was paid out at the time of the wedding, while payment of the other part was deferred and effected only if and when the husband divorced her, or she became a widow.[30]

Muslim-Arab influence can be felt also in the presence of male and female slaves in Jewish households, which often caused problems in the sexual area. In Muslim society the destiny of every slave-girl was to serve as a concubine of her master, in accordance with the Koranic pronouncement which allowed men to have sex "with their wives and those whom their right hands possess" (Koran 70:30), that is, their female slaves. While slavery as such was not questioned by the rabbinical authorities in Arab lands—it would have been impossible to question it in view of its biblical approval and its wide incidence in Arab society—the Gaons did the best they could to prevent or limit sexual relations betwen master and slave-girl. They flatly forbade Jewish men to have sexual intercourse with slave-girls in their possession, and ruled that if a man was caught violating this prohibition, the slave-girl was to be taken from him and sold to somebody else, and the money thus obtained distributed among the poor, while her master was to be flogged, his hair cut, and he was to be excommunicated for thirty days. Or else, the slave-girl was set free. If a man had relations with the slave-girl of another man, he had to buy her from him, set her free, and marry her. Of course, if the slave-girl was a consenting partner in such an illicit master-slave relationship, which gave her an advantageous position in the household, and the master recognized as his the children born of such a union, there was little the authorities could do about it.[31]

Remarkable is the opposition Jewish leadership put up against the custom of polygyny, which was an accepted and approved feature of family life among the Muslims. One of the Gaonic *responsa* states explicitly that a man can marry a second wife only with the consent of his first wife. If he married a second wife without the consent of the first, the rabbinical authorities forced him to divorce his first wife, and to pay out to her the deferred part of her bride price. Also, it became customary to include a codicil in the *k'tubba* (marriage contract) to the effect that the husband obliged himself not to marry a second wife, nor to take a concubine, as long as his first wife lived, except with her consent.[32] These Gaonic rulings were based on Talmudic precedents (cf. B. Yev. 65a), and they bear witness to the persistence of Jewish custom in the face of Muslim-Arab influence.

The degree of assimilation of Jewish women to the Arab environment, though, is also amply documented in historical records, particularly in those which were preserved in the Cairo Geniza. For one thing, the general rule was that the Jewish women, like the Arab members of their sex, did not go to school, could not read and write either Hebrew or Arabic, and spoke only Arabic. Of the tens of thousands of pieces of Hebrew liturgical poetry found in the Geniza, not a single one was written by a woman. Jewish women, when going out of the house, dressed exactly like the Arab women, and could not be recognized as being Jewish. The same was the case with the Jewish men. Jewish women had, as a rule, Arabic names, while Jewish men had biblical and other Hebrew names.[33] Since it is unlikely that it was the fathers who gave their daughters Arabic names while calling their sons by Hebrew names, it seems probable that the naming of daughters was left to the mothers, which would be in conformity with the old biblical custom of letting the mother choose the names of her children.[34]

While with respect of clothing, language, names, and illiteracy the Jewish women were largely assimilated to the women of the Arab majority, there were certain differences between the women of the two communities in addition to the lesser Jewish insistence on veiling and seclusion. Among the Muslim women, attendance at the public Friday prayer in the mosque (as already mentioned) was exceptional. Jewish women, however, attended the synagogue regularly, sitting in the special galleries built for them. They also met frequently in the bathhouse, the bazaar, in gatherings on happy or mournful occasions, and often visited female friends and relatives.[35] In evaluating this situation, one must take into account that in medieval Egypt women enjoyed much more freedom than, for example, in Morocco, and the adherence to the rules of Muslim orthodoxy was generally more relaxed. The Muslim traveler Muqaddasī (ca. 946–ca. 1000) went so far in his disapproval of the mores of the Egyptian women that he wrote that in Egypt "every wife had two husbands."[36] For another thing, in the Middle Ages wine was sold publicly in Egypt, which would have been unimaginable in more conservative Muslim countries, such as Morocco. While in modern Egypt, even prior to the onset of Western influence, many Muslims drank wine and hard liquor in secret, and some did it even in public, although in moderation.[37]

It is in this general relaxation of Muslim religious strictness that the explanation must be sought of the greater freedom enjoyed by Egyptian Muslim women than by women in other Arab (and Muslim) countries. For the position of the Jewish woman in Egypt, this meant that the still greater freedom allowed them by Jewish tradition was not curtailed by the influence of the Muslim mores in Egypt to the extent it was in countries such as Morocco, Iraq, or Yemen. In an overview of all Muslim countries, I suspect that, if the requisite studies were carried out, it would be found that the restrictions imposed on Jewish women in each of them were closely correlated to those imposed by the local variety of Islam and folk custom on the Muslim women, but were in every country somewhat less stringent.

Of course, such a correlation between the position of the Jewish and the non-Jewish women was not confined to the Arab or Muslim world. In the Christian world the gentile environment exerted its influence on the Jewish attitude to women in the direction of the Christian mores. The outlawing of polygyny by Rabbenu Gershom (ca. 1000) is perhaps the most conspicuous example of this development. In Europe, whatever modicum of female seclusion had been practiced in Talmudic times and brought in by the Jews, disappeared. By the time of the Enlightenment and emancipation, the Jewish woman occupied the same position in her community as the gentile women did in theirs—mutatis mutandis, of course.

In the Muslim world the influence of the environment worked in the opposite direction. It introduced, or reinforced, the wearing of the veil and the seclusion of women, and their relegation to a subordinate position in relation to men. However, since the Jewish tradition did not allow these features to become as prevalent or as entrenched among the Jews as they were among the Muslims, when the modernization of the Middle East began in the nineteenth century, the Jews were more receptive than the Muslims to changes in the position of their women.

WIFE BEATING

Tradition-bound cultures, whose ethos, values, doctrines, and mores crystallized many centuries ago, inevitably retain in their orthodox forms features which are at variance with modern outlook, and some of which may appear in modern eyes as primitive, backward, and even barbarous. Certain items in the position of women in both Judaism and Islam seem to belong to this category, especially if considered in isolation instead of parts of a broader picture. Since Judaism and Islam, despite the great age difference in the periods of their emergence and formation, assumed much of their final configuration in the early Middle Ages in Arab lands, they carry the imprint of that time and that environment in their attitude to women, view of women, valuation of women, and the place they give to women in family and society. Because of the absence in Arab lands of great, revolutionary cultural upheavals like those which shook Europe, Arab culture remained static or even stagnant, and this meant, among many other things, that the position of women among both Jews and Arabs in the Middle East remained until the twentieth century by and large identical with their position in the early Middle Ages. Therefore, in order to understand the situation of the Jewish and Muslim women in the Middle East as it was on the eve of the onset of Westernization, it is necessary to view it within the context of the mores which dominated medieval Jewish and Muslim-Arab society. It is from this perspective that I want now to have a look at the painful subject of wife beating.

The Koran (4:34–38), as we have seen, permits, and perhaps even recommends in certain circumstances,[38] that a man beat his wife. Inasmuch as the word of the Koran is the sacred law of Islam, a Muslim husband was considered entitled to administer physical punishment to his wife whenever he felt that she deserved it. In some traditional sectors of Arab society the practice has remained alive until modern times, and European visitors who witnessed it have repeatedly reported about it.[39]

In modern American society wife beating exists, and is considered a very serious social and psychological problem. One of the factors which makes wife beating appalling and revolting in the American social context is that it is completely out of line with accepted behavior in all walks of life. The wife beater would never dream of beating his secretary; or, if he is an officer in the army, his subordinates; or if he is a foreman in a factory, his workers. In most cases he does not beat his children either. He singles out his wife as the sole object of his physical brutality. The singularity of wife beating in a culture in which the beating of anybody by anybody is legally outlawed, culturally condemned, and psychologically considered a manifestation of serious emotional disorder, makes it a traumatic experience for the wife, and a degrading one for the husband. It turns her into the victim, and him into the perpetrator, of a crime.

In sharp contrast to this situation, in the traditional Arab family and society the beating of people was, so to speak, part and parcel of everyday life and a common daily occurrence. Within the family, among the Rwala bedouin in northern Arabia, for instance, not only the father and the mother, but also the male and female slaves would beat the recalcitrant child with a stick, and the father would punish an adolescent or young adult son for disobedience by cutting or stabbing him with a saber or dagger. In Iraq, too, corporal punishment was frequently administered, more often in the urban than in the rural families. In Egypt, slapping or beating or striking a child with a stick or whipping him with a rope was nothing unusual. The same was the case in the Sudan, in Algeria (where an observer stated that the Arabs "were comparatively brutal to their children"), the Teda of Tibesti, etc.[40] In the traditional *kuttāb*, the Koran school, the beating of the children with a stick was part of the educational routine. The *falaqa* (beating) was administered by the teacher on the naked soles of the child culprit, while other pupils, or the teacher's assistants, immobilized his feet with the help of an apparatus, also called *falaqa*, which consisted either of two poles, or of a stout pole with a rope tied to it, or of a plank with two holes in it. There were detailed scales of *falaqa*, commensurate with the severity of the offense. In some Arab countries, especially in North Africa, the use of the *falaqa* "is still very much alive, not only among the Muslims, but also in the Talmudic schools."[41]

Beatings administered to adults were less common, but still a frequent occurrence. Slaves were beaten by their masters, soldiers by their officers, subordinates by their superiors, and even ministers or viziers by the king or at the king's behest. All this was neither exceptional, nor did it arouse moral indignation. In the streets, too, beatings were a part of daily life. When a potentate rode through a street, his henchmen who ran in front of him would beat the people with sticks to make them move aside and let him pass without obstruction. When children or beggars would tug at the sleeves of an effendi in order to extract baksheesh from him, they were driven off by his servants with the generous use of sticks.

The beating of both children and adults was practiced by the Jews as well as by the Arabs. The reference to "Talmudic schools" quoted above should actually read *ḥadarim*, elementary Tora-schools in which the teachers introduced small boys into the mysteries of Hebrew reading and the translation of the Bible with the generous use of the rod. That Jewish adults, too, were beaten whenever their leaders had the power to do so is illustrated by an incidental comment of the twelfth-century Jewish traveler Petaḥya of Regensburg, who reports that in Baghdad "the head of the [Talmudic] academy has many servants. They flog anyone not immediately executing his orders; therefore people fear him."[42]

The sum total of these references, which could easily be multiplied, is that among both Arabs and Jews beating was a frequently applied form of instant physical punishment, which precisely because of its frequency was considered neither particularly insulting nor degrading.

When viewed against this background, wife beating appears as but one variety of the customarily meted out treatment by superiors of inferiors who for some reason incurred their displeasure. One must also take into account that in tradition-bound communities in Arab lands the girls at marriage were little more than children, whom therefore their husbands were inclined to discipline in the same manner in which they treated their own children. While this, of course, in no way excuses the practice, it puts it in a different light from wife beating in the Western world.

The official religious permission given by the Koran (4:34–38) to a man to beat his recalcitrant wife is, on the one hand elaborated in the Muslim religious literature, and, on the other, paralleled by Arab folk custom down to modern times. Alois Musil, who studied the inhabitants of Transjordan and the Syrian desert in the early 1900s, says that

> Among the fellahin, where one cannot speak of marriage out of love, the wife receives often beatings which she must accept as long as no blood is drawn and no bone is broken. For "the flesh of the woman belongs to her husband, her bones to her family,"—laḥm el-mara li-zawjhā wᶜaẓāmhā lahālhā.[43]

The same proverb was heard by Hilma Granqvist in Palestine, and although she adds that she does "not know if it is to be taken too seriously," she herself states that in the village of Artas, near Bethlehem, which she studied in the 1920s, "There are men who are praised for never having struck a woman, neither wife nor daughter,"[44] which clearly indicates that such men were exceptional. These illustrations could easily be multiplied.

As can be expected, the Jews living in an Arab environment adopted this permissive attitude to wife beating. R. Yehuday Gaon, who lived in the ninth century in Iraq, wrote: "A wife should never raise her voice against her husband, but should remain silent even if he beats her—as chaste women do."[45] The Geniza documents, testifying to the exigencies of Jewish life in Egypt and other Arab countries in the eleventh and twelfth centuries, provide numerous examples of wives lodging legal complaints against their husbands because of being beaten by them.[46] On the basis of the Geniza material Goitein concluded that wife beating among the Jews in Arab lands occurred, but only rarely, and added (on what basis?) that it was not more rampant in the Mediterranean Islamic countries than in medieval Europe. The rabbinical courts invariably reprimanded the husband, and occasionally fined those who were recidivists. That the possibility of being beaten loomed large on the horizon of Jewish brides is proven by those marriage documents, also found in the Geniza, in which the bridegroom undertakes not to beat his wife-to-be, not to misbehave toward her, and to pay her a fine of ten dinars "whenever any revolting behavior on his part is established," and even promises not "to enter the house of frivolous and licentious persons."[47]

Maimonides, who lived in Egypt in the same period, describes the circumstances in which a man is justified to administer physical chastisement to his wife. He says: "The woman washes the face, hands, and feet of her husband, and mixes his drinks, and makes the bed for him, and stands before her husband to serve him by such acts as giving him water or a vessel, or taking them from before him, and the like . . ." A few paragraphs later he specifies the punishment to be administered to a disobedient wife: "Any woman who refuses to perform one of the labors which she is duty bound to perform, they force her until she does it, even with a whip."[48] These rulings reflect not only the Koranic punishment of the recalcitrant wife, but also the traditional Muslim view according to which a wife must perform certain services for her husband. These wifely duties were summed up by Khalīl ibn Isḥāq (born 1374) in his *Mukhtaṣar* ("Abstract"), which became one of the most popular manuals of Muslim ritual, personal law, etc. In it, he states that a wife, who has not been accustomed to the help of a servant, is expected to look after the cleanliness of the home and to prepare meals for her husband, as well as to perform other tasks according to the customs of the country.[49]

When the European Jewish halakhists learned about the ruling of Maimonides which gave permission to a husband to whip his wife, they were scandalized. His contemporary, the Provençal authority Abraham ben David of Posquieres (ca. 1125–1198), who was his leading opponent, wrote in his *Hasagot* ("Objections") to the Code of Maimonides: "I have never heard of chastising women with whips. But the husband can reduce [the satisfaction of] her needs and her food, until she submits."[50] In the next century R. Meir of Rothenburg (ca. 1215–1293) went so far as to recommend that the hand of a husband who habitually beats his wife be cut off.[51] Three centuries later, R. Moshe Isserles (1525 or 1530–1572), in his emendations to Joseph Caro's great law code, the *Shulḥan ᶜArukh*, objects to wife beating even more vehemently. He writes:

> If a man beats his wife, it is a transgression, just as if he would beat his fellow man. And if he is in the habit of doing so, the *Bet Din* (rabbinical court) can chastise him, and excommunicate him, and flog him with all kinds of castigations, and force him and make him swear that he will not do it again . . . for it is not of the way of the Children of Israel to beat their wives, and it is an act of Gentiles . . . And some say that it is forbidden to beat even an evil wife . . ."[52]

The foregoing references to wife beating among the Arabs and the Jews in Arab lands can be taken in toto as an illustration of the manner in which the Arab environment exerted its influence on the Jews. The Jews were influenced in this respect, as in many others, by the culture and mores of the Muslim Arabs. But this influence was limited because it was blocked whenever it ran counter to traditional Jewish mores and values. Wife beating occurred in both societies. But among the Muslims it was, once and for all, sanctioned by the Koran, while among the Jews, although it was a form of castigation permitted in principle by such halakhic authorities as the Iraqi Yehuday Gaon and the Egyptian Maimonides, in practice it was considered such an inexcusable behavior that wives treated in such a way could initiate legal steps against husbands who physically abused them, and rabbinical courts invariably took action against the offending husbands. Still, among the Jews who lived in a Muslim environment we find no general statement of principle against wife beating, similar to those issued by the leading rabbinical authorities of Europe. This difference, one might add, can be considered an initial manifestation of the disparate religio-cultural trends which were to result within a few centuries in the relative cultural stagnation of Middle Eastern Jews as against the successive waves of cultural and social transformations experienced by European Jewry from the Renaissance on.

ILLITERACY: MALE AND FEMALE

One of the most direct ways to evaluate the position of women in relation to men in any country is to have a look at the statistics of literacy. Comparatively low female literacy is as a rule a manifestation of the low position of women as compared to that of men. In utilizing this approach in Arab countries, one has to take into account the centuries-old Muslim tradition in which even male literacy was a prerogative of but a thin upper layer of society, while the idea that women too should be literate was foreign, and occasionally even repugnant, to Muslims. Among the Jews in Arab lands the situation was different inasmuch as the majority of the men was, as a rule, able to read (although not necessarily to write). As for female literacy, its almost general absence was, by and large, as characteristic of Jewish as of Muslim society.

The notion that literacy should be general, and should extend to women as well as men, was introduced into the Middle East only with its Westernization. The history of modern education in the Arab lands does not belong in the present context, so it should be enough to state that by the mid-twentieth century even the most conservative Arab states had in principle accepted the Western premise that general literacy was basic and culturally desirable. In practice, however, historical, religious, and organizational factors influenced the speed and extent of the movement toward the achievement of this goal. Thus while in the less tradition-bound Arab countries literacy had made considerable headway, in the conservative Arab countries it had barely begun to make a dent in the solid wall of general, and especially female, illiteracy. A few examples will serve as concrete illustrations.

In Lebanon, one of the most Westernized Arab states, in 1970, only 21.5 percent of the male, and 42.1 percent of the female population over the age of ten was illiterate. In more conservative Syria, in the same year, the corresponding percentages were 40.4 percent for the male, and 80.0 percent for the female population over fifteen. In Egypt they were 43.2 percent and 71.0 percent for those aged ten and over. In Tunisia, in 1975, they were 48.9 percent and 75.2 percent for those aged fifteen and over. At the lower end of the literacy scale, of those aged fifteen and over, in Morocco, in 1971, 66.4 percent of the male, and 90.2 percent of the female population were illiterate; in Algeria, in 1971, 58.2 percent of the males and 87.4 percent of the females; in Iraq, in 1965, 64.5 percent of the males and 87.2 percent of the females; and in both Saudi Arabia and the Republic of Yemen in 1962, 95 percent of the males and 100 percent of the females were illiterate.[53] In each of the countries mentioned, while the male illiteracy figures showed the general state of education, the gap between them and the female illiteracy figures is an indication of the position of the women: the greater the gap, and the lower the percentage of literate females in a country, the lower the status of women.

By the same token, the differences between illiteracy among the Muslims and among the Jews can be taken as illustrative of the differences in the educational level between the two communities. Precisely analogous figures are not available for Jewish literacy in Arab countries, but some data exist which are instructive. Thus in Egypt in 1927, when the Muslim male illiteracy of those of five years and over was 79.7 percent, the Jewish illiteracy of the same age group was 18.3 percent. The corresponding figure for Muslim females was 97.5 percent and for Jewish females 36.0 percent.[54] This surprisingly wide gap between Muslim and Jewish illiteracy in Egypt—which subsequently was to narrow considerably—was due partly to the fact that urban illiteracy was always lower than rural and that practically all the Jews lived in the two major cities of Cairo and Alexandria; partly to the European extraction of a sizable proportion of the Egyptian Jews; and partly to their readiness to send their children to the available non-Arab, European-sponsored schools. The corresponding figures for the Jews from all Asian and African countries who had immigrated to Israel (most of whom came from Arab and other Muslim countries) after 1948, were only somewhat less favorable for the men, but considerably less so for the women: 22.5 percent of the males, and 57.8 percent of the females had never attended school.[55] After their arrival in Israel, the female illiteracy rate was gradually reduced, so that by 1961 of all the Israeli Jewish females born in Asia and Africa only 44 percent were illiterate.[56]

Due to the absence of data, comparisons between Jewish and Muslim school attendance can be made only in a very few Arab countries. One of the countries from which information is available is Tunisia, where in 1946 there were 2,919,860 Muslims, and 71,543 Jews, and where in 1949 71,404 Muslim, and 10,964 Jewish children attended primary schools.[57] That is to say, while the proportion of the Jewish to the Muslim population was about one to forty, that of Jewish children attending primary school to that of Muslim children was about one to seven. In other words, proportionately almost six times as many Jewish as Muslim children attended primary school. In Morocco in 1953, 80 percent of the Jewish boys and girls of primary school age attended school, while only 6 percent of the Muslim children did the same,[58] so that here proportionately thirteen times as many Jewish as Muslim children attended primary school. Moreover, and this is important for our present considerations, while the number of Jewish girls in school was about the same as that of Jewish boys, among the Muslims only one out of five of the pupils were girls.

The above data, meager though they are, are concrete numerical illustrations of the differences between the Muslim and the Jewish educational level in general, and between the educational status of the women in the two communities in particular. These data are, of course, but the manifest latter-day reflection of the differential cultural traditions which had dominated the two communities for centuries. The one or two or even three generations that have passed since the adoption by the Arabs of the Western ideas of general literacy are too short a time to result in more than a beginning in the elimination of the almost general illiteracy which had been part of the Muslim tradition since the Middle Ages. Among the Jews the requirement that men should be able to read has been an even older tradition, sanctioned and made necessary by the Jewish religion for the observance of whose commandments by men a knowledge of reading was an indispensable prerequisite. As for Jewish women, they were not required to be able to read in order to fulfill their more limited religious duties, so they remained generally illiterate, approximating in this respect their Muslim sisters. Hence the gap between male and female illiteracy was, until the onset of Westernization, greater among the Jews than among the Muslims.

Nevertheless, since even in the most tradition-bound Jewish communities there was a lesser emphasis on the veiling and the seclusion of the women than among their Muslim urban neighbors, when Westernization began in the Arab countries the Jews were more receptive than the Muslims to the idea of formal schooling for girls (the Alliance Israélite Universelle schools played an important role in this respect), and this resulted in a rapid increase in the literacy of Jewish females, which development was not at the time paralleled among the Muslims. In the Muslim population it was only after Westernization and modernization had progressed, and especially after World War II, that the education of the Arab girls began to advance apace, albeit at rates greatly differing from country to country. Thus in the 1960s and 1970s, as we have seen, the female illiteracy rates were still rather high. As for the next decade or two, the school enrollment indicates an improving situation. By the early 1980s the primary school enrollment of girls of all ages was reported by Arab countries to UNESCO to have reached the following percentages of girls aged six to fourteen: Yemen 17, Mauritania 23, South Yemen 34, Sudan 43, Saudi Arabia 54, Oman 57, Morocco 62, Egypt 65, Algeria 81, Syria 90, Kuwait 91, Bahrain 95, Tunisia 98.[59]

Thus while female illiteracy in the Jewish communities from Arab countries, most of whom have been transplanted into Israel, will be a thing of the past in another ten or twenty years at the utmost, it can be foreseen that in the Arab countries the elimination of female illiteracy is still a long-range problem whose solution will require great educational efforts for another one or two generations.

WOMEN IN THE MODERN ARAB WORLD

What remains to be discussed before concluding this chapter is the advancement in the women's position in the Arab world in the last decade or two. I have focused on this subject in several chapters of my book *The Arab Mind*,[60] so that what I intend to do here is to summarize what I said there, and to add some new observations and conclusions.

The Arab awakening started in the nineteenth century and reached its full extent after World War II, and brought in its wake (as far as the conservative circles were concerned, rather disconcertingly) the special awakening of the Arab women. Gradually more and more Arab women became aware of what they considered anomalies and indignities in their position, began to demand improvements in it, and organized in order to achieve them. Today, in countries in which direct contact with the West is new or limited, such as those of the Arabian Peninsula, women's movements either do not yet exist at all or are in their infancy. In those Arab countries that can look back on two or three generations of contact with the West, such as Lebanon, Egypt, or Algeria, the first feminist stirrings took place several decades ago, and, following them, certain early demands for female betterment have begun to be met.

One expression on the part of modern Arab governments of the willingness to accommodate some of the demands of the new Arab woman is found in the national charters and constitutions promulgated by progressive Arab states since the 1960s. Several of them include statements deploring the existing conditions of women, and expressions of the intention to ameliorate them. Examples of such proclamations can be found in President Nasser's 1962 National Charter for Egypt, in Iraq's National Charter of 1971, and in Syria's Permanent Constitution of 1973. Another important achievement for Arab women was the creation in 1971 by the Arab League of a Commission on the Status of Arab Women with the primary objective of eliminating discrimination against women, and realizing equality between them and men in all walks of life.[61] Although these and other such resolutions and measures have often remained unimplemented, they must be considered, and are considered by Arab feminists, significant achievements for countries in whose traditional culture the inferiority of women had for centuries been both a religious doctrine and a social practice. Arab feminists see in these proclamations, and rightly so, important expressions in principle of a daring doctrinary innovation in a culture whose religious tenets include the prohibition of all innovation (*bidᶜa*) relative to established religious doctrine.

Today, the social structure of each Arab country is composed of a broad spectrum of strata ranging from ultra-conservative to ultra-modern. Where the countries differ considerably is in the proportion between the various sectors. A socially modern Arab state is one in which the religiously liberal population element is relatively strong. Lebanon, until the dislocation and devastation caused by a decade of civil war, was such a country. The Arabs of Israel also stand close to the modern end of the range. The most conservative Arab states (if we disregard the selective and dictatorially imposed conservatism of Libya under the Qadhdhafi regime) are located in the Arabian Peninsula, although even within its confines there are considerable variations. In Saudi Arabia, the largest and by far most important of them, conservative Islam is the law of the land, and women, at least in public, must conform to rules of behavior which have historically dominated Islam. The situation is similar in the other political entities of the peninsula with the exception of the People's Democratic Republic of Yemen (Southern Yemen), where special efforts have been made to increase education (which includes Marxist teachings), especially for girls. In the peninsula in general emancipation of women lies still far in the future, and so does any loosening of the Islamic code of male and female comportment.

And yet, there are signs that even in Saudi Arabia, that stronghold of Muslim conservatism and puritanism, the winds of change have begun to blow since the oil boom has transformed it from one of the poorest to one of the richest countries of the world. The reforms in the position of women are being introduced with great caution, occasionally by royal fiat, in the face of conservative resistance by the *ᶜulamā'* and the people of some localities. At times the efforts to make concessions demanded by the modernists and at the same time to avoid offending the tradition-bound, lead to peculiar situations. Thus, for example, in Saudi Arabia women are admitted to some universities, but they may hear lectures given by male professors only in separate rooms over closed-circuit television. Some women are allowed to study religion, but they are taught by blind *shaykhs*. Since women do have control over their own finances, which in modern circumstances requires the use of banking services, special women's banks have been established, staffed by women only. The strict rule that even engaged couples cannot see each other has been relaxed to the extent of permitting the young man to call his fiancée over the phone, and thus chat with her from a safe distance. In a neighboring Gulf state, a university admits boys and girls to the library on alternating days.[62]

Serious social studies of this transformation and its effects on the way of life and outlook of the people are not yet available, but impressions of the changes and their concomitant problems have been conveyed by journalists and television reporters. The interviews these outsiders conducted with local men and women in what the media like to call the Arab "oil kingdoms" are, of course, in English, which means that the people interviewed belong not only to the educated class, but to that sector within it which had acquired a certain fluency in English—a feat impossible to accomplish without absorbing a certain amount of Western influences. Thus the picture these interviews give is not that of the average peninsula Arab but of the Westernized or partly Westernized layer of its society which is still rather thin. Despite these limitations, what I found striking in these interviews was the sense of unease that came through in the views, opinions and value judgments of the people interviewed, whether government officials, businessmen, teachers or students, whether men or women. The untenability of the old Islamic urban way of life with its ultra-conservative posture, its veiling and seclusion of women and their relegation to the home was a foregone conclusion for all those interviewed. That changes have taken place, and are continuing to take place, leading society away from the old, which traditionally was always considered identical with good, and toward the new, which in traditional thinking used to be regarded bad, is likewise recognized by all. Unease and confusion enter in when individuals try to find their place in that rapidly changing world, and when they try to make up their minds as to how much of the old ways they should retain and how much of the new they should allow into their lives and the lives of those dependent on them. The old solid frameworks which had for centuries defined and delimited life have become irreparably shattered. This holds good especially with reference to the man-woman relationship. The two traditionally separate worlds of men and women, which used to meet and mingle only within the narrow confines of family and home, run into and impinge on each other more and more, and there is no longer avoiding the worrisome question, "where will all this lead?" and the problem, "where shall I take my stand?"

Thoughtful men and women seem equally troubled by these phenomena and questions. Many of both sexes have opted for modernism, which the new mentality unhesitatingly equates with improvement, but very few would subscribe to the idea that their social environment should become a mere Arabic-speaking version of a prototypical Western society. The solution, envisaged hazily if at all, is in most cases a combination of the basic and still highly regarded old Arab-Islamic values with certain elements of Western culture, and especially its material and technological manifestations that, once people are exposed to them, are generally considered beneficial and hence desirable. But a host of problems arises in connection with the decisions which have to be made as to what precisely to retain from the old, and what to admit from the new. And even if these issues are resolved, as they often are on a pragmatic, day-to-day basis, there remains the equally grave difficulty of the how: how to unite or combine in the life of one individual, of one family, the often contradictory elements of the old and the new? These problems have burdened the new Arab not unlike that particular type of jinn which in Arab folklore was said to jump on the back of the unwary passer-by, bestraddle him, lock him in an iron grip with his legs and arms, so that from that time on the poor human victim of the demonic embrace is but a beast of burden for his invisible rider. Something like this is the impression one gets from interviews with Westernized Arabs in the "oil kingdoms" (and, to a lesser extent elsewhere too): they are carrying the burden of new problems which they do not know how to solve, and in the center of which is the relationship between man and woman.

Arab feminists, both male and female, are fully aware that the transformation of Arab women from a still largely illiterate into a largely literate part of the population is a primary prerequisite of any betterment in the women's status. The magnitude of the task does not have to be reiterated. What its advocates are only now beginning to envisage is that female literacy, once achieved, will have a number of consequences whose importance for the Arab world as a whole cannot be overestimated. In the first place, literacy will be the door through which modernism will make its triumphant entry into the female half of the Arab world. Beyond that, it will open up to the Arab woman the rich storehouses of Arabic literature and

Arab culture which she had been excluded from for centuries. This, in turn, will inevitably mean a certain loss of the folk traditions and folk culture the Arab women have transmitted from generation to generation.

The education, and with it the broadening of the mind, of the Arab woman will redound as much to the benefit of the men as of the women. This will become self-evident if one considers that the Arab child is in its early years almost exclusively under the tutelage of its mother. One is reminded of the oft-quoted Jesuit saying, "Give me the child in his first seven years; thereafter you can do what you want with him." The first seven years of life, during which the Arab mother alone is in charge of the shaping of her children's mind, leave their imprint on them for the rest of their lives. This means, if I may be permitted to quote what I wrote two years ago, that

> as long as the mental faculties of the mother are hemmed in, encysted, and stunted by the illiteracy, ignorance, and superstition in which she is kept by the male-centered ethos of Arab culture, she will go on instilling into the minds of her sons and daughters the very same character traits, values, concepts, and ideals that have been so bitterly excoriated by Arab critics of the Arab personality.[63]

I may add that the indignation which male Arab critics, such as the Moroccan sociologist ᶜAbdelwaḥad Radi, the Lebanese Lutfy Najib Diab, and the Iraqi Ayad al-Qazzaz bring to the subject is quite mild compared to the vehemence with which Arab women feminists attack the Arab men for keeping the Arab woman in what they perceive to be a state of indignity. The Moroccan social psychologist Fatima Mernissi, for instance, says that "the traditional family mutilates the woman by depriving her of her humanity," and the Egyptian woman physician and health official Nawal el-Saadawi, who excoriates her society for fostering genital mutilation (clitoridectomy) of women and subjecting young girls to various forms of sexual abuse, says, "the education of female children is . . . transformed into a slow process of annihilation, a gradual throttling of her personality and mind."[64]

Slowly, these voices are becoming heard all over the Arab world, and even more slowly they produce action leading to the spread of female education and other improvements in the women's status. It is this gradual progress that holds out the hope for a reinvigoration of the Arab mind and a recapturing of that creative spirit that in the Middle Ages made the Arabs the torchbearers of great cultural developments.

Appendix

WOMEN IN SAUDI ARABIA: AN EGYPTIAN VIEW

During a visit to Egypt in 1984 I had an opportunity to get a glimpse of the reaction of modern Egyptian women to the position of their sisters in ultra-conservative Saudi Arabia. I met in Cairo a Muslim woman member of the faculty of one of the Egyptian universities, who had just a short time previously returned from a visit to Saudi Arabia, where her brother was working. She insisted on anonymity, but once I promised that under no circumstances would I reveal her identity, she spoke openly about what she saw during her visit and how she reacted to it. The interview took place partly in English and partly in Arabic. The following is a condensed and rephrased version of it.

Question: Coming from Egypt, how did Saudi Arabia strike you?

Answer: I had a mixed reaction. The many new, ultra-modern buildings, along the broad, beautifully laid out streets, the utilization of modern technology, in all this Saudi Arabia is far ahead of Egypt. But as far as social conditions are concerned, and especially the relationship between men and women, Saudi Arabia is still in the Middle Ages. It is a great pity that Westerners are often inclined to judge the Arabs, that is, the hundred million or more Arabs who live in many different countries, on the basis of Saudi Arabia.

Question: To what do you attribute this generalization which, I take it, you consider unwarranted?

Answer: The reason, I think, is that Saudi Arabia is the original Arab country, and the religious center of Islam. Also, the Saudis with their flowing robes and picturesque headdress are the most conspicuous, and most romantic looking of all the Arabs. And they are, of course, the most influential in the world due to their prominent place as investors, and the most visible as great spenders in fashionable places.

Question: Do you think that the Westerners also confuse Saudi women and Arab women in general?

Answer: Yes. The average Westerner believes that the position of the Arab woman in general is identical with that of the Saudi Arabian women, which, of course, could not be farther from the truth. In fact, the difference between the position of women in Saudi Arabia and most other Arab countries is very great. Coming as I was from Egypt, when I arrived in Saudi

Arabia it was quite a shock for me to see with my own eyes how the Saudi women lived, how they dressed and behaved in public, and how they were limited in their movements and deprived of what we here in Egypt consider the natural freedom of every human being. The first thing that, so to speak, hit me was the insistence of my brother that I put on a veil so as not to be too conspicuous. Imagine, I, a Muslim woman, actually had to disguise myself in order not to damage my brother's reputation, or perhaps even jeopardize his position. I was really shocked. I think that the Saudi treatment of women gives the whole Arab world a bad name in the West, and even in several countries of the Third World.

Question: Can you give me some examples of the restrictions imposed upon Saudi women?

Answer: Easily. Take the question of freedom of movement. A Saudi woman is not allowed to drive a car. She can travel only if her husband, or father, or whatever other man is in charge of her, gives her his permission. I find it abhorrent that every woman, throughout her life, is something like an appendage of a man. A woman is not an independent human being. As far as self-determination goes, she remains a child all her life, under the control of a man. She cannot even undertake any work outside the home without his permission.

Question: What kind of work can Saudi women do?

Answer: Their choice is very limited. The overall principle is that in work they can be in contact only with other women. This means that they are excluded from private and government offices, businesses, industrial plants, banks, institutions, etc. What is left are such jobs as teaching in girls' schools, nursing in women's departments of hospitals, or working as women's physicians, as midwives, and very little else.

Question: It seems to me that this means that the female half of the Saudi population constitutes a large untapped work-force potential.

Answer: It does. I think that the absence of women workers greatly aggravates the labor shortage from which Saudi Arabia suffers. I understand that there are one and a half million foreign workers in the country, who do all the heavy manual work required by the rapid industrial development. Were it not for them, the whole country would grind to a halt. As it is, the Saudis themselves constitute an elite upper layer, enjoying economic advantages totally unknown, even unimaginable, in Egypt.

Question: In what way do women benefit from these advantages?

Answer: Well, first of all, thanks to generous government subsidies, the average Saudi family has a lot of money to spend, and inevitably part of this spending is done by women. One can see women, with their whole body, including head and face, wrapped in black, in supermarkets, clothing stores, dry goods stores, in the bazaars, and so forth. It struck me that there was something symbolic in the all-black clothes worn by women and the all-white robes worn by men—as if they were two entirely different species. At home, upper-class women wear Western dresses, often from fashionable houses of *haute couture*.

Question: Speaking of the black wrap, are there attempts made by women to discard the veil?

Answer: There are two opposing trends. One is toward modernization and the loosening of the shackles in which Saudi tradition keeps women. Of this trend very little can be actually observed outside the home, because any modernization of female apparel in public is prohibited by Saudi law. The other is the opposite of it: a return to old-fashioned rigorism, a demonstrative adherence to the rules of segregation, including the wearing of the veil, and public behavior in the most orthodox manner. This trend has become especially noticeable since the Khomeini revolution in Iran, despite the generally negative feelings the Sunnī Saudis have toward the Shīᶜa in general and its new Iranian fundamental variety in particular.

Question: What do you personally think of veiling?

Answer: I find it a horrible custom. A woman brought up in a society where veiling is practiced, a woman who can go out of her house only if wrapped from head to toe in a black, voluminous, billowing robe, looks like a walking . . .

Question: Zombie?

Answer: Yes, or at least like a person deeply ashamed of herself. She seems, how shall I put it, to consider her face an obscenity, which must be carefully hidden from view. The men in such a society, on their part, consider a woman's face the height of eroticism. A veiled woman is, above everything else, a sexual object, a walking advertisement which shouts, "Look, under this veil is an irresistible sex object!" What veiling and segregation achieve is to sexualize and eroticize men and women in each other's eyes, to create the impression that they have to be kept apart, because, should they be given the opportunity, they would fall upon each other in a sexual frenzy.

Question: Is the actual number of sex offenses in Saudi Arabia greater or smaller than in a less restrictive Arab country?

Answer: I don't know of any statistics of sexual offenses, or, for that matter, of any types of crimes in Saudi Arabia. But I believe that the great severity of the punishment that would be meted out to the offenders if caught is a powerful deterrent, and therefore I would guess that such transgressions are less frequent there than in other countries.

Question: Are the women very unhappy as a result of the severe restrictions placed upon them?

Answer: This question is even more difficult to answer than the previous one. From what I could observe and find out in conversations with women, there seems to be quite a variety of responses. For most women the traditional framework in which they live is the only one they know. In Saudi Arabia there are no cinemas, TV is strictly controlled by the government, imports of foreign books and magazines are also controlled and practically nonexistent. All this means that the average Saudi woman who, of course, speaks only Arabic and is illiterate, has no opportunity to learn that outside Arabia there is a world in which women live as freely as men, and in which there is a society composed of both men and women.

Then there are the few women who know about the West, or at least about other Arab countries such as Egypt, have visited it or spent some time there. Some women, especially those of the most affluent layers of society, accompany their husbands on trips abroad, and a very few privileged ones can even spend some time in a European or American university. Some of these find what they see in the West so strange, so frightening and confusing that, upon their return home, they are happy to resume their places in the Saudi women's society in which they feel sheltered, protected by father, brother, and husband, and are totally contented to continue to live the life of the traditional Saudi woman. Others, of course, have precisely the opposite reaction. The freedoms they find Western women enjoy make the life imposed upon Saudi women appear in their eyes little better than slavery. These women feel—and some of them told me so—that women are treated in Arabia either as children or as chattel, or as a combination of the two. Some of them become so embittered that they are filled with a virulent hatred against all men . . .

Question: What do you think will happen to the women of Saudi Arabia in the future?

Answer: I have no doubt that they will achieve emancipation, but only very slowly, very gradually. There are signs that point in that direction. One is that in recent years a few schools for girls have been opened, while only some years ago such a step would have been considered a forbidden innovation. A woman able to read and write is a very different person from one who is illiterate. Another sign of the changing times is the fact that, despite all the traditions to the contrary, there are today women in Saudi Arabia employed outside the home, even if for the time being only in a very few occupations. As more and more girls graduate from school, the number of such women will grow. This too is inevitably a sign of things to come. But it may take another ten, twenty, or even more, years before Saudi women will attain a position similar to that of the women in Egypt today.

On this guarded note of optimism we concluded our conversation. The woman I had interviewed asked me again to make sure never to divulge her identity. I reiterated my promise.

What I found most interesting in this interview was not so much the picture it presented of the life of women in Saudi Arabia as the distance it revealed between the position of the Saudi and the Egyptian women. The woman's reaction to what she saw in Saudi Arabia did not differ substantially from what an American woman would have felt had she been given the same opportunity to gain an insight into the life of her Saudi sisters. What this means is that the life of women in the modern sector of Egyptian society is today more similar to the life of women in the West than to the life of women in Saudi Arabia.

Saudi Arabia is, of course, one of the most conservative Arab countries. At the same time, it is the only Arab country which for centuries has not tolerated Jews within its boundaries.[65] Thus Saudi Arabia (that is, the central part of the Arabian Peninsula) was not exposed to the socio-cultural leaven, or irritant, if you wish, which the presence of Jews meant for other Arab countries. Whether the absence of a Jewish element in the country had anything to do with the phenomena which set Saudi Arabia apart from other Arab countries is a moot question. But it is a fact that Saudi Arabia has been characterized, and still is in the 1980s, to a greater extent than any other Arab country by the following traits: religious and social conservatism, puritanism, traditionalism, cultural quiescence (or, if one prefers a stronger expression: cultural stagnation), and the seclusion of women. True, geography and history conspired to isolate inner Arabia from both the West and other Arab countries, and this fact undoubtedly had something to do with the phenomena referred to. Yet I cannot help feeling that they must also be related to the absence of the Jewish leaven.

Take, as an example, the process of cultural change manifested in discarding the veil. In all the Arab countries in which Jews lived, it was first the Jewish women who, soon after the onset of Westernization, began to appear in the street unveiled. About a generation or more had to pass before the Muslim Arab women did likewise.[66] Historical research has not established whether or not in undertaking this step the Arab women were influenced by, and followed the example of, the Jewish women. But it stands to reason that the mere phenomenon that native Jewish women (in contradistinction from resident or visiting European women) began to appear unveiled in the streets, bazaars, and stores, must have served as an encouragement to those Arab women who were inclined to do likewise. And, as we all know only too well, once a thing becomes fashionable, official ukases, whether issued by religious or secular authorities, can do little against it.

In Saudi Arabia there were no Jewish (or other *dhimmī*) women to spearhead the adoption of Western ways and to induce the *mu'mināt* (the believing Muslim women) to emulate their example. The old, religiously approved, custom of veiling remained unchallenged, and with it the entire great chapter of life which is composed of the seclusion of women, the position of women, and the relationship between men and women.

9

Arabs under Jewish Rule: A Historical Anomaly

In the course of their many centuries of historical contact with the Jews, the Muslim Arabs always had the upper hand. Leaving aside the *jāhiliyya*, from which we have only a trickle of historical sources, a review of Muslim-Arab history shows that in Arabia itself, as well as in each and every country conquered by the Arabs from the seventh century on in which Jews lived or subsequently settled, they were subdued by the Arabs and continued to remain in submission under them without ever even attempting an uprising. For thirteen centuries this was the iron rule from which there was not a single deviation, and which therefore became ingrained in Arab consciousness as the unchangeable norm for Arab-Jewish relations, the charter for which was contained in the Koran. This having been the case, it was inevitable that the new Arab experience with and in Israel, where since 1948 Arabs have lived under Jewish rule, should have struck them as a historical anomaly which, even several decades after its inception, they were psychologically unable to accept.

Not as if the Arabs had not had their share in experiencing life under non-Arab rule. As a matter of fact, after the decline of the ʿAbbāsid caliphate in the ninth century, Arab history comprised a series of armed struggles in which one Arab territory after the other was overrun by, and came under the dominion of, outsiders—foreign Arabs from other countries, non-Arab Muslims, Christian Crusaders from Europe, Seljuks and Mongols from Central Asia, Mameluks originating in Turkey, and finally Ottoman Turks. This went on for some six centuries, after which the European powers began their penetration of the Middle East with the French invasion of Egypt in 1798 and of Algeria in 1830, which opened an era of increasing European domination of Arab lands. The defeat of Turkey in World War I ushered in the establishment of European rule over all Arab lands with the exception of the central part of the Arabian Peninsula. The common feature of all these conquerors was that they were powerful outsiders who, when their historical moment arrived, appeared from beyond the local Arab horizon, and with their superior arms and military capability overwhelmed whatever resistance the local Arab regimes were able to put up. The blow these defeats meant for the Arabs, and the indignity of being consequently forced to bend under a non-Arab yoke, were mitigated by the awareness that with Turkey and the European states which replaced it, the Arabs faced conquerors greatly superior to them as military powers.

The defeat the Arabs suffered in the 1948 Arab-Jewish war, the establishment of the State of Israel in part of Palestine, and the subsequent repeated victories of the fledgling Jewish state over several Arab states many times more populous could in no way be fitted into this familiar pattern.

ALEXANDRETTA: A CASE IN COUNTERPOINT

A brief review of the Alexandretta conflict and the Arab response to the 1939 annexation by Turkey of that Syrian province can serve as a counterfoil to the Arab reaction to the establishment of Israel.

Alexandretta (Arabic name Iskandarun, renamed Hatay by the Turks) is a province at the northern corner of the east-Mediterranean shoreline which, as all lands of the Levant, was part of the Ottoman Empire until the end of World War I. Its land area is 2,205 square miles (or 5,402 square kilometers). In 1936–37 its majority population consisted of 103,500 (or 47.07 percent of the total) Arabic-speaking people, who by religion were divided into 62,000 ʿAlawīs, 22,500 Sunnī Muslims, and 19,000 Greek Orthodox Christians. The next largest population group was that of the 85,000 (38.9 percent) Turks, all of them Sunnī Muslims. There were also 25,000 (11.37 percent) Armenians who were Christians, and 7,000 (2.66 percent) others, including 4,831 Kurds and 954 Circassians (both Muslims), and 474 Jews.[1]

Under the Ottoman Empire Alexandretta was part of the *vilayet* (province) of Aleppo, while the later Palestine, also part of the Turkish realm, comprised the *sanjak*s (districts) of Acre, Nablus, and Jerusalem to the west of the Jordan River, and parts of the *sanjak*s of Ḥawrān and Maʿan to the east of it. After the war, when the victorious allies carved out several Arab states from the provinces of the Ottoman Empire, Alexandretta became part of French-mandated Syria. Although Alexandretta was accorded special status within Syria on account of its large Turkish population, there is ample documentary evidence to the effect that France considered it an integral part of Syria.[2] As for Syria, it naturally embraced the same position.

In 1936, international political exigencies induced France to accommodate Turkish demands and to enter into negotiations with Turkey as to arrangements to be made for Alexandretta. The negotiations went through several stages, and resulted in 1939 in the annexation of Alexandretta by Turkey. The League of Nations, which had awarded the mandate over Syria to France, never gave formal consent to the cession of the territory to Turkey. Some years later, M. Georges Scelle declared that "France committed an illegal act by disposing of territory in which she had not a free hand."[3] Syria refused to recognize the loss of Alexandretta, and for several years continued to consider it part of its own territory.[4]

At this juncture the first differences between Alexandretta and Palestine become manifest. First, Alexandretta, although it had an autonomous regime, was for two decades part of Syria, an Arab country, before it was annexed in 1939 by Turkey. Palestine, on the contrary, was not part of an Arab country prior to Israel's establishment in 1948 in the western part of it. Second, the annexation of Alexandretta by Turkey was never recognized by the League of Nations, while the establishment of a Jewish state in Palestine was decided upon by the League's successor, the United Nations. This means, that while Syria had a legal claim to Alexandretta, no Arab country had a similar claim to Palestine. Further significant differences emerged in the Arab reaction to the two events.

The years following Syria's independence (1945) were a turbulent period for the country. There were several coups d'état in Damascus, and violent overthrows of government, which meant, among other things, that there was no consistent Syrian policy toward Turkey, nor on the problem of Alexandretta. A Committee for Defense of Alexandretta was set up, but remained rather ineffectual. In August, 1945, the Syrian and Lebanese governments issued a joint communiqué refusing to renounce Syria's rights to Alexandretta. This remained the only action any Arab state took in support of Syria's claim. Of the other Arab states, Iraq was the most open in its opposition to Syria. Among the steps Iraq took was the signing of a Treaty of Friendship and Good Neighborly Relations with Turkey (in March, 1946), which was promptly renounced by Syria as "treason." In January, 1947, Jordanian King Abdallah came out in support of the Iraqi-Turkish alliance by declaring that a Turco-Arab bloc was a necessity, and by announcing his support of Turkey in its dispute with Syria over Alexandretta. Similar pro-Turkish sentiments existed even inside Syria. In April, 1949, Ḥusnī al-Zaᶜīm, who had seized power in a coup d'état in Damascus only a month earlier, told journalists that he wanted close friendship with Turkey. In July the Syrian minister in Ankara announced that Syria had, in effect, renounced its territorial claims on Alexandretta.[5] A month later Zaᶜīm was captured and executed by Col. Sāmī al-Hinnawī, and in December of the same year he, in turn, was ousted in a coup led by Col. Adīb Shishaklī, who remained in power until February, 1954, when an army revolt forced him to flee. Both the Hinnawī and Shishaklī regimes were anti-Turkish, but, remarkably, their recriminations against Turkey focused more on the diplomatic recognition Turkey extended to Israel than on the Alexandretta issue.

After the overthrow of Shishaklī the new Syrian Foreign Minister Faydī al-Atāssī, defending the pro-Turkish policy of his government, went so far as to argue that there was nothing wrong in trying to improve relations with Turkey, since, "If one has an enemy such as Israel, one prefers to have one enemy only." At the same time Syrian Prime Minister Fāris al-Khūrī defended the political legitimacy of the projected Baghdad pact in which Turkey was the leading member by asserting that "the intended pact is directed against Israel." When Turkey, on her part, protested the proposed Syria-Egypt-Saudi Arabia pact, Syria assured Turkey that the "tripartite Arab alliance was directed solely against Israel."[6]

Statements such as these are clear manifestations of the political and emotional tabling of the grievance Syria had against Turkey over Alexandretta under the impact of the greater injury Syria felt was done to her and the other Arab states through the establishment of Israel. As a student of the Alexandretta issue put it, "Syrian resentment of Turkey's ties with Israel and with the Western Powers has extended so far as to overshadow their grievances over the lost territory . . ." Moreover, "there has been no effective organization within Syria for the recovery of the district . . . no [Arab] separatist tendencies have developed within Hatay itself . . ." and the whole *sanjak* issue has "become one of secondary importance to Syria in comparison with more important domestic and foreign matters."[7]

If this was the case in Syria which had directly sustained the loss of Alexandretta, it could be expected that the other Arab states, which were only indirectly affected by the Alexandretta affair as an infringement on the territorial integrity of the theoretically and emotionally upheld entity of "the Arab nation," would take even less notice of it. And this was what transpired. The Arab world became so preoccupied with the remaining survivals of colonialism in the Arab lands, and, in particular, with the creation of Israel in their midst, which they regarded as a threat to themselves, that the issue of Alexandretta became all but forgotten. The fact is that neither Syria herself nor any other Arab country has ever taken the Alexandretta issue before the United Nations, nor has any Arab state asked officially the Arab League to pursue the matter. Consequently, the Arab League, which has so vehemently fought for the rights and interests of the Arab countries and peoples, and has been so consistent in its denunciations of Israel (the "Zionist entity," as they prefer to call it), has evinced no active interest in the Syrian loss of Alexandretta.[8] This, and the absence of any activity for the recovery of the *sanjak* for Syria represent a sharp contrast to the energetic and unceasing Arab work in the UN and other international bodies against Israel. In April, 1975, Syria, and in July of that year other Islamic countries, called for the expulsion of Israel from the UN, and later that year the Arabs initiated the resolution which defined Zionism as a "form of racism and racial discrimination," and which was adopted on Nov. 10, 1975, in the UN General Assembly by a vote of seventy-two for, thirty-five against, with thirty-two abstentions.[9]

Nor was this by any means all. The entire Arab League often created the impression as if its sole purpose was to combat Israel. The League was organized in March, 1945, with strong British encouragement, by the seven Arab states of Iraq, Syria, Lebanon, Transjordan, Egypt, Saudi Arabia, and Yemen. From 1953 on its membership was gradually augmented by the admission of other Arab states, until, by 1977, it comprised twenty-one states plus the Palestine Liberation Organization as the representative of Arab Palestine. Throughout the history of the League, while in nonpolitical fields, such as cultural and technical cooperation, it could pride itself of considerable accomplishments, in the political area major achievements eluded it. The only political issue which produced solidarity among the members of the League was the Palestine problem. However, even this held good only as long as it was a question of passing resolutions and making diplomatic representations. As soon as action was required, even the common agreement in principle on the opposition to Israel and support of the Palestinian Arab cause could not overcome the basic differences which existed among the members of the League.[10] They were unable to put aside their rivalries and suspicions even during the crucial armed confrontations between several of their member states and Israel in 1948, 1956, 1967, and

1973. During the quiescent intervals between these four wars the Arab League was torn by deep internal conflicts that, however, did not prevent the member states from exhibiting political and psychological solidarity whenever the issue was Arab struggle against imperialism and external threats. And the one issue with which the League was most frequently and most vehemently seized, and that led to general unanimity in motions and speeches at the UN, in meetings of the League itself, and in summit meetings of Arab leaders, was the Palestine problem. Thus the issue of Palestine became the most important focus for collective Arab pronouncements, verbal protests, and threats of action. The contrast between this almost obsessive Arab preoccupation with Palestine and the rapid disappearance of the Alexandretta issue from the Arab horizon in general and from Syria's national endeavors in particular is nothing short of conspicuous.

Why this striking difference in the Arab reaction to the two cases? Why the relatively quick acquiescence in the loss of Alexandretta which for almost two decades had been part of Syria, and the continued and vehement all-Arab wrath over the "loss" of Palestine, which had never been an independent Arab state and had not been under Arab rule since the Middle Ages? The answer, I believe, must be sought in two separate factors.

One is that Palestine, with its many biblical and Koranic associations, has always meant, and still continues to mean, much more to the Arabs than the obscure northwestern corner of Syria. Most Arabs certainly have never even heard of Alexandretta, whether under that name, or under its Arabic name Iskandarun, or its Turkish name Hatay. Its loss to Turkey may have been painful for the Arabs inhabiting the district itself, or even for all Syrians, but it could not arouse strong feelings in the Arab world as a whole. The situation with Palestine, precisely because of its biblical and Koranic associations, and because of the Ḥaram al-Sharīf ("Noble Sanctuary") of Jerusalem, was very different. Just as the Arabs appropriated Abraham from Jewish tradition and made him their ancestor, so they emotionally appropriated Jerusalem, the Holy City of the Jews and Christians, and made it their own al-Quds, "The Holy," the third holiest site of all Islam after Mecca and Medina. To give up Palestine with its Holy City would have been contrary to age-old Muslim religious traditions and convictions.

The second factor is the differences, already hinted at in the introduction to the present chapter, in the Arab attitude to the two opponents who, in their view, robbed the Arab nation of Alexandretta and Palestine, respectively. The Turks, who took Alexandretta, had been for four hundred years

(1517–1917) the masters of most territories inhabited by the Arabs. They were the overlords of Iraq, Syria, Lebanon, Palestine, Transjordan, of major parts of the Arabian Peninsula, of Egypt, and of parts of North Africa. Their rule over their Arab subjects was always harsh, and often cruel. The memory of the cruel Turkish rule has remained alive among the Arabs for decades since it ended. Hitti, in his *History of the Arabs*, speaks of the Turkish "terror which still haunts Syrian memory."[11] In Jerusalem, in the early 1930s, my friend Shaykh Aḥmad Fakhr al-Dīn al-Kinānī pointed out to me the spot in front of the Jaffa Gate where the Turks used to string up the Arabs they found guilty of even minor infractions.

Not as if the Turks, with all their ruthlessness, had been able to impose a *Pax Turcica* over the Arab lands they ruled. The Ottoman system allowed wide latitude to the pashas, the Turkish governors appointed over the provinces, and it was largely left to these potentates, who often clashed among themselves, to get along as best they could with the support of whatever power their Turkish-officered garrisons provided. Nevertheless, they were able, as a rule, to manage and to fulfill their major, and often only, assignment, which was to collect taxes. Arab uprisings against the Ottoman presence were rare, and in most cases limited and short lived. Most often, in the Syria-Palestine area, Arab and Druze bellicosity exhausted itself in internal fights between Qaysī and Yamanī Arabs, Qaysī and Yamanī Druze, Christian and Muslim Arabs, Kurds and Druze, or any other combination of opposing parties lined up against each other on the basis of religious or ethnic affiliation. These internal conflicts constituted no threat to the Turkish authorities; on the contrary, it repeatedly happened that the Turks fomented internal strife in order thereby to weaken the local population elements and strengthen their own position.[12]

Even in World War I, when a weak Turkey was in serious trouble, the Arabs, although they were by then familiar with the European idea of nationalism, and hopeful that the defeat of Turkey would lead to their liberation, did not organize any anti-Turkish military action except for guerrilla attacks. These actions were led by T. E. Lawrence (1888–1935), the famous "Lawrence of Arabia," who described them in highly dramatic colors in his *Seven Pillars of Wisdom* (first published in 1926). However, neither those guerrillas nor any other Arab military formations dared to engage the Turks in pitched battle. It would seem that the hundreds of years of subjection to the Turks had instilled into the Arabs a respect for Turkish power which persisted long after Turkey had become weakened to the point that had any sizable Arab force risen up against her she would have been unable to put it down.

Now, almost twenty years after the Allies had dismembered the Ottoman Empire and carved out several Arab states (temporarily under mandates) from the former Arab provinces of Turkey, the new, republican, rapidly modernizing Turkey felt again strong enough to initiate steps to regain a small area of her former empire, the *sanjak* of Alexandretta. These Turkish efforts provoked Syrian protests, which, however, remained ineffective. Turkey, this time with the help of France, again had the upper hand in her relations with the Arabs, and the latter had no choice but to acquiesce and accept the loss of Alexandretta.

Psychologically, such acquiescence was facilitated by the fact that, not having been able to resort to arms to begin with, the Arabs suffered no military defeat in the Alexandretta affair. They were defeated in the political and diplomatic arena. The annexation was prepared by elections held in the disputed territory in which a majority (in whatever way it was achieved) of Turkish representatives was returned. While the loss of Alexandretta was a defeat for Syria (and the Arabs), it was not a humiliation. In general, to be defeated by a patently stronger adversary is in the Arab code of honor not a humiliation; in particular, to be defeated by Turkey was nothing new for them, it was as it always had been, and as it was almost expected to be in any renewed Arab-Turkish clash. To have to cede Alexandretta to Turkey was but another loss in a long series of losses that the Arabs had sustained at the hand of Turkey in the course of centuries, and to which they had become psychologically inured.

The "loss" of Palestine was a different matter altogether. The victors in the struggle for Palestine were the Jews, who had been, as pointed out earlier in this book, for thirteen centuries weak, scattered, humiliated, and despised. Therefore, there was nothing in the millennial Arab experience with the Jews which could have prepared the Arabs for the victories of Israel. Those victories, and the resulting strengthening of Jewish Israel's grip on part of Palestine and its Arab inhabitants constituted for the entire "Arab nation" not only an unprecedented reversal of a long-established historical experience, but also a violation of the religious duty imposed upon it by Islam to "bring low" the *dhimmīs*, that is, the Jews, and keep them in a state of humble subservience. This is why the existence of Israel and its domination of even a minuscule part of the Arab nation is a historical anomaly in Arab eyes. To get used to it is very difficult for all Arabs, but especially for those who were rendered homeless and who were forced by the Arab states surrounding Israel to live in refugee camps almost within sight of their former towns and villages.

The Palestine problem is important, not only in the eyes of Israel and the Arab states, of Jews and Muslims all over the world, but also in international perspective. A closer look is warranted at its antecedents, present state, and emotional ramifications.

FROM HUMBLE DHIMMĪ *TO MENACING JEW*

Having described in sufficient detail the Arab view of the Jew as *dhimmī*, I wish to make here a brief presentation of the Jewish psychology which enabled the *Yahūd* to endure their humble state in the House of Islam. The first thing to note in this connection is that despite their lowly position, internally the Jews were able to preserve their own convictions of superiority. Every Jew knew from his reading of the Bible that the Arabs were the descendants of Abraham's son Ishmael, born to him by his lowly concubine Hagar, while they themselves were the children of Abraham's son Isaac, who was born by Abraham's legitimate wife Sarah, the "Princess," and called by God Himself Abraham's "only son whom thou lovest" (Gen. 22:2). They disparaged the Muslim assertion, stamped false by the explicit biblical text, that it was Ishmael whom God commanded Abraham to sacrifice, and for such reasons, as well as numerous others, they rejected the Arab claim that Muhammad was the prophet of God. Instead, they considered him a "madman," and held the Koran to be a book full of follies.

There were several other religious and nonreligious reasons which made the Jews feel superior to the Arabs. The Jews accorded (as we have seen in chapter 8) a much better position to their women than did the Arabs to theirs. They had the Sabbath, their sacred weekly day of rest and elevation of the spirit, devoted in its entirety to the service of God, while the Muslim Friday, the *yawm al-jumʿa*, or "day of gathering," was only a day of special communal prayer and preaching in the mosque with everyday work performed before, and continuing after, the relatively short religious services. And, above all, they knew, because it was laid down in the Bible and etched into their consciousness throughout the centuries, that, despite all their trials and tribulations, they were God's own "Chosen People." They believed that, sooner or later, the Messiah would come, and with him redemption, kingship in the Land of Israel, and a time of happiness.

The Jews, of course, took good care not to let any of this become known to the Arabs. What they truly thought and felt about the Arabs, about the relative value of their own religion versus Islam, remained carefully guarded secrets which a Jew would never dream of divulging to an Arab. Only after the immigration of Jews from Arab lands to Israel did it become known, to the surprise of the Ashkenazi Jews, how heavily loaded on the negative side was the image of the Arab carried about in the mind of the Oriental Jew. While living in Arab lands, they had no choice but to remain silent. This was facilitated by the fact that, in contrast to Christian Europe where the Jews were often forced to engage in public religious disputations, in Muslim countries they were pressed into no such public presentation of their religious views or their arguments against Islam. There were, it is true, some discussions between Jews and Muslims, for instance, about anthropomorphisms in the Talmud, but, by and large, whatever interreligious disputations did take place in the House of Islam were between Jews and Christians, against whom the Jews could, of course, argue much more forcefully in a Muslim than in a Christian country. Still, to be on the safe side, Maimonides forbade even the instruction of Muslims in Jewish religion.[13]

In any case, as far as the Arabs perceived it, the Jews were not only brought low, as the Koran commanded, but were resigned to their inferior position, and had actually become a humble people who recognized and accepted that they were a low-class community, enabled to exist only by the grace of the Muslims. This long-established relationship pattern between the Arab masters and their Jewish *dhimmīs*—psychologically satisfactory for the Arabs and tolerable for the Jews—began to undergo a serious dislocation only in modern times when Christian European powers started their penetration of the Arab world. As they occupied Arab countries and established themselves as the controlling powers, the Arabs could not help noticing, to their considerable surprise, that the Europeans exhibited towards the Jews a type of conduct which was radically different from the Arabs' own traditional attitude to the *dhimmīs*. At the very least, the European consular and other officials in the Arab lands did not treat the Jews worse than they did the Arabs, and in some cases even did, or seemed to, treat them better.

Prior to the European penetration of the Middle East, anti-Jewish attitudes, as shown in preceding chapters, frequently surfaced in all periods of Arab history, including even the famous Golden Age in Andalus. But until the nineteenth century these anti-Jewish attitudes among the Arabs were anchored primarily in the Koranic injunction to keep the *dhimmīs* low, in the traditional duty of *ghiyār*, separation, between Jews and Muslims, in the religious conviction that the Jewish refusal to accept the prophethood of Muhammad was reprehensible, and in the Arab experience that the Jews were willing to accept their lowly status in the House of Islam. In Arab eyes the Jew had no honor because he was either afraid or unable to stand up to the Muslim, and instead swallowed insults silently, without any manifest reaction. For these reasons the major ingredients in the traditional Arab anti-Jewish attitude were contempt and scorn. The Jews were weak and defenseless, servile and obsequious, deferential and unresisting, and therefore contemptible. But the Jews were not hated—that feeling was reserved for enemies—only despised.

That this indeed was the case in the past is confirmed by the nature of the misconduct with which the Jews were reproached, and which occasionally triggered, or was used to incite, violence against them. The Jews were not accused of such crimes as rebelling, conspiring against the authority, desecrating the holy places of Islam, defaming the Prophet Muhammad, defrauding Muslims, committing violence against Muslims, defiling Muslim women, or any of the other many allegations whose counterparts were the stock in trade of Christian anti-Semitism for centuries. Instead, as shown by several examples in this book, they were accused of having become overbearing, of lording it over the Muslims, of aspiring to, or having attained, power over them—in short, of having forgotten or disregarded that by the traditional definition of their status they had to be meek, humble, and obsequious, and had to lead lives inferior to the lives of the Muslims. If they actually, or allegedly, became overbearing, that was considered intolerable and was punished by severely chastising them, attacking their quarters, and in some cases killing a number of them. This, in addition to the basic religious resentment, was the typical pattern of anti-Jewish sentiment in the Arab world until the onset of Westernization.

This classical relationship of the Arabs to the Jews began to change in the nineteenth century. To begin with, among the increasing numbers of Europeans who appeared on the Arab horizon—strange but powerful people who, even if disliked, had to be approached with prudence and caution—there were also Jews. The Europeans, *al-Ifranj*, were treated by the Turkish and other authorities which held sway over the Arab lands, with respect, more so even than the Arab notables and effendis. To mention one example, when Sir Moses Montefiore (1784–1885), who paid several visits to Palestine and the Near East from 1827 to 1874, arrived with his entourage, he was received as a celebrity and a potentate by the rulers of Turkey, Egypt, and Morocco, and obtained from them what at the time were considered important benefits for the Jews of the Orient. Gradually, the Arabs learned that the Jews in Western Europe were socially and juridically equal to the non-Jews, which made the Jews of those "Frankish" lands appear unduly powerful in Arab eyes. The *firmān* of the Sublime Porte known as *Khaṭṭ-i Humayun* (dated February 18, 1856) was seen by the Muslims as having made the Muslim and non-Muslim subjects of the Sultan equal in all rights, and this made many Muslims grumble.[14]

In 1864 Montefiore appeared before the Sultan of Morocco and asked for the emancipation of the Jews in his country. The result of this intervention of the powerful English Jew was the *dahir* (literary Arabic *ẓāhir*, edict) which prohibited hostile acts against the Jews, whereupon, as a Muslim historian put it, "The Jews . . . became arrogant and reckless."[15] That is, the Arab reaction was cast in the mold of the old traditional Arab indignation at seeing the Jews transgress the limits of the humble demeanor imposed upon them by Islam.

Similar developments were the interventions of British, French, Prussian, and other consuls and representatives in the interest of the Jews in the Ottoman Empire, the protection these powers extended to Jews resident in Turkey and her Arab provinces, and the occasional appointment of resident Jews as consular representatives of European powers. The work of the French-based Alliance Israélite Universelle for the benefit of the Jews in Arab lands began soon after the middle of the nineteenth century, and was followed by the Crémieux Decree of 1870 by which the Jews of Algeria received French citizenship en masse. That Isaac Adolphe Crémieux (1796–1880), minister of justice of France, was a Jew did not remain unknown to the Muslim leaders and literati of Algeria and other Arab countries. It was also well remembered that in 1840 Crémieux had accompanied Sir Moses Montefiore on a delegation to the East which secured the release of the Jews imprisoned in Damascus in connection with the blood-libel known as the Damascus Affair. Incidentally, the nineteenth-century blood-libels in Arab lands originated not among Muslim, but among Chistian Arabs, who were better acquainted with European anti-Semitic manifestations. In this respect, just as in the introduction of modern European-style nationalism into the Arab world, the Christian Arabs played a crucial role. The granting of

French citizenship to the Jews of Algeria contributed to the image of the powerful European Jew who was a creature quite different from the Arabs' own *dhimmīs*.

This image was further strengthened by the issuance on November 2, 1917, of the Balfour Declaration which promised the help of the British government in the establishment of a Jewish national home in Palestine, and the subsequent appointment (in 1920) of a Jew, Sir Herbert Samuel (1870–1963), as the first British High Commissioner of Palestine. All these events, the Arabs felt, could not have come to pass except as the result of European Jewish power.

These and other such developments brought about a shift in the Arab perception of the Jew, from being based on their experience with the indigenous Jews of their own countries to a new view, based partly on fact, but mostly on rumor and fantasy, of the Jews as powerful people, who can work their will in the councils of the mighty, and who, with their money (the Rothschilds!) and their influence, can sway the decisions the European powers were making in the years following World War I about the fate of the Muslim peoples of the Middle East. Thus the contempt for the weak local Jews was first supplemented, and then gradually supplanted, by a fear and a hatred of the powerful Western Jews, an entirely new experience for the Arabs in their millennial relationship with the Jews.

When the Jews succeeded in establishing a state of their own in western Palestine, this was for the Arabs nothing less than a traumatic experience. During the preceding two generations, in which the number of the Jews in Palestine grew, largely through immigration, from 24,000 (in 1882) to 650,000 (in 1948), the Arabs became increasingly apprehensive as to the fate of Palestine, but in the Arab world at large the problem was still seen as a local one which to solve was best left to the leadership of the Palestinian Arabs themselves. Moreover, during that period Palestine was ruled first by the Turks, and then, from 1918 on, by the British. After the end of World War I most of the other Arab areas were also under European rule, so that the attention of the emerging Arab states was directed almost exclusively to the problems of their nationalism and liberation. Thus, concerning Palestine only a few, and rather ineffective, protests were mounted by the Arabs against the policies of Britain (the mandatory power in Palestine), while the Jewish community in Palestine grew apace. When, however, the State of Israel became a reality, the entire Arab world, which by then had largely achieved independence and had thoroughly absorbed the Western doctrine of nationalism, reacted vehemently. They felt that drastic action, which could not be left to the Palestinian Arabs alone, must be taken.

There followed the repeated Arab-Israeli wars, whose disastrous outcome for the Arabs gradually convinced them that as of then it was no longer the humble *dhimmī* who dared to oppose them, but a new breed of Jew whose very existence they considered a menace to the Arab world. First came the attack of five Arab states on the very day after the Jewish community of Palestine, in accordance with the November 29, 1947, resolution of the United Nations General Assembly, declared its independence and assumed the name of Israel. The outcome of that war, known in Israeli history as the War of Independence, was the first severe jolt sustained by the old Arab stereotype of the Jewish *dhimmī*. Before they attacked, the Arabs were so sure of their superiority, and so convinced of the weakness of the Jews, that they felt it was unnecessary to make serious preparations, and to throw into battle all their strength. They spoke boastfully of the ease with which they would "deal with a few Jews" in Palestine, of "a few brooms" which was all they needed "to drive the Jews into the sea," and of the facility with which they would throw out the Jews once they got "the green light from the British."[16] Elsewhere I attributed the Arab failure to follow up such verbal threats with commensurate military efforts to the Arab proclivity to substitute oral statements of intention for action.[17] I want to add now that, in this particular case, the relatively limited Arab war effort against the Jews may have been also an expression of the traditional Arab view of the Jews as *dhimmī*s, and of the inability of the Arabs at that early juncture of their confrontation with Israel to envisage a strong, resolute, fighting Jew. In any case, the total of all the invading armies put into the field by five Arab states and including contingents from several others, amounted to only about 23,500, and, according to another estimate, to 35,000 men. President Chaim Herzog of Israel estimated that Jordan and Iraq fielded each 10,000 men, Syria 8,000, Egypt 5,000, and Lebanon 2,000. As against them, the Israeli forces numbered 17,000 to 19,800, of whom only 3,000 were well-trained troops. However, the Arabs had overwhelming superiority in firepower, were better equipped and supplied, and had the strategic initiative.[18] These advantages, when brought to bear upon the extremely thin lines of Israeli defense, enabled the Arabs to gain several local victories before their general defeat on all fronts.

The Arab reaction to the 1948 defeat, conditioned by the old stereotype of the Jews as *dhimmī*, was that this simply could not happen. It was not possible that the Jews should be able to defeat the Arabs. The same reaction recurred when the Arabs suffered defeat in the Six-Day War of June, 1967. Among the many manifestations of this reaction one of the most telling was supplied by the Fourth Conference of the Academy of Islamic Research, held in September, 1968, that is, about fifteen months after the Arab debacle in the June, 1967 war. The conference, held in Cairo, was an international event, attended, in addition to twenty-one members of the Academy, also by invited delegates from twenty-four Muslim countries, as well as numerous guests. It differed from the previous conferences, which were devoted to various issues of Muslim scholarship, in that it consisted almost exclusively of a series of virulent verbal assaults on Israel and the Jews. The welcoming address, in the name of President Nasser, was given by Egyptian vice-president Ḥusayn al-Shāfiʿī, which meant that the conference was held under the aegis of the Egyptian government. The conference lectures, delivered by Islamic scholars from many countries who represented a cross section of the religious leadership in the Arab-Islamic world, including several heads of Islamic religious institutions of higher learning, exhibited total unanimity in discussing again and again the same basic themes with numerous but minor variations. The thrust of them all was that the Jews were enemies of God and of humanity; that there was a historical continuity in the evil qualities of the Jews from biblical times down to the present; that the Jews were a riff-raff and did not constitute a true nation; that the State of Israel had to be destroyed; that Islam was superior to all other religions and hence would ultimately triumph; and that it was "outrageous for the Jews who traditionally were considered to be of inferior status and were characterized by cowardice, to defeat the Arabs, have their own state, and cause the contraction of the Abode of Islam"; and that all these events contradicted the march of history and God's design.[19]

In his opening address, Shaykh Ḥasan al-Ma'mūn, identified as "His Eminence the Grand Imām Rector of Al-Azhar," said:

> I am in no need to make a diagnosis of the misfortunes and sufferings that had befallen the Arabs and Muslims. Every soul has been moved by the shock, and minds are still taken by surprise, because of the anomaly of this frustration. The bitterness was further intensified by the fact that the unexpected event occurred before a roguish Zionism whose adherents had

> been destined to dispersion by the Deity. "And humiliation and wretchedness were stamped upon them and they were visited with wroth (sic) from God" (Koran 2:61) . . . It is inconceivable that God would grant Unbelievers a way to triumph over the Believers."[20]

Another speaker expressed the Arab reaction to the anomaly of Jewish victory from a historical-traditional point of view. Shaykh Nadīm al-Jisr, a Lebanese member of the Islamic Research Academy, stated that when the Muslims

> neglected compliance with these [Islamic] principles, they became analogous to the wreckage swept down by a torrent. Other nations united against them; even the weakest and most submissive among these, like the Jews . . . [Islamic] tradition never implies any possible outbreak of contest between Muslims and dispersed bands of Jews, living as "Dhimmis," or "People of the Covenant," under Muslim rule . . . because fighting against such powerless and scattered bands of people was not so significant an issue as to require an announcement of glad tidings to Muslims by the Prophet—peace be upon him . . .[21]

What Shaykh al-Jisr says boils down to this: the sins of the Muslims caused them to be attacked by other nations, among whom "the weakest and most submissive" were the Jews. Islamic tradition has never envisaged the possibility that the "dispersed bands of Jews living as Dhimmis" under Muslim rule could rise up against the Muslims. Any fight that possibly could have taken place between Muslims and Jews would have been so insignificant that it required no reference to it in the Koran. Then Shaykh al-Jisr went on to add that now that, contrary to all tradition, a serious struggle was taking place between the Jews and the Muslims, "relinquishing the fight against the Jewish aggression is tantamount to unbelief and renunciation of Islam."[22]

If the victories of Israel over the Arabs were an "anomaly" and "inconceivable," how could they nevertheless take place? The explanation found for the clash between the immutable belief and the irrefutable fact was that the Arabs were defeated not by Israel, but by the great powers who helped her in secret. On the very second day of the June war President Nasser and King Hussein, in the course of a telephone conversation, decided, at Nasser's suggestion, that each of them would publish a communiqué to the effect that American and English aircraft were attacking Egypt from their aircraft carriers.[23] Whether King Hussein, and Nasser himself, actually believed that this was indeed the case, is unknown, but the communiqué found ready credence all over the Arab world. Thus, after the war, the League of Moroccan Scholars issued an appeal denouncing "the treacherous Zionist aggression, backed by world imperialism in general, an Anglo-American imperialism in particular."[24]

This explanation of Israel's victory as due to the help given to her by the great powers was the perfect face-saving device, but it was more than that: it enabled the Arabs to continue to believe in the weakness of Israel and the Jews, as laid down in their religious traditions. Incidentally, the credibility of this explanation for the Arabs was enhanced by the fact that in the 1956 Sinai campaign France and England actually did cooperate with Israel in military action against Egypt. The explanation did not alter the fact of the defeat, but it made it more easily bearable. For the Arabs to be defeated by a powerful opponent, and especially by powers generally recognized as superior, although painful, is not a loss of face, not a devastating shame. But to be defeated by the "roguish Zionism" of weak, submissive and scattered bands of *dhimmī* Jews, was psychologically unacceptable. By extension this also meant that the very existence of Israel, secured by these victories, was for the Arabs intolerable.

Concurrently with the planning of open armed confrontation, the Arabs resorted to other means as well to bring Israel to its knees. They carried out hit-and-run terrorist attacks against Israel and against Jews in other parts of the world. They organized an economic boycott against Israel extending it also to American and other Western firms which did business with "the Zionist entity." They sought and gained the support of Soviet Russia which, although in 1947 it had voted in the UN for the partition of Palestine and the establishment of a Jewish and an Arab state, had soon thereafter taken a definitely anti-Israel stand, and which discriminated against the Jews within its own borders. They engaged in political work in the UN and its agencies for the purpose of passing as frequently as possible anti-Israel resolutions whose adoption was automatically ensured by the triple alliance of the Arab states, the Communist bloc, and Third World countries, which together wielded an overwhelming majority in the General Assembly.

In each subsequent armed encounter between the Arabs and Israel, the Arabs were better prepared and threw greater forces into battle. Yet the strength of Israel also increased, with the result that each time (in 1956, 1967, and 1973) the Arabs were defeated. Still, they had difficulty in recognizing that they did not have the military capability of beating Israel by force of arms. The psychological breakthrough to the position that, instead of continuing the pattern of arming, fighting, and suffering defeat, it was possible, and even desirable, to conclude a peace treaty with Israel came in Egypt after the 1973 Yom Kippur War. Prior to that event the Arab position was that Israel was unlike other enemies with whom the conclusion of a peace agreement was an honorable way of putting an end to a state of belligerency. Israel, that is, the Jews, were a people humiliated by God, and therefore could not be given the honor of making peace with them. The Syrian scholar Muḥammad Azzah Darwaza expatiated on this subject in his address to the Fourth Conference of the Academy of Islamic Research:

> God branded [the Jews] with the stigma of humility [read: humiliation] and meanness. Allah has sent among them those who torture them severely and will keep on persecuting them up to the Last Day.[25] The Jews announced from time to time that they long for reconciliation with the Arab Muslims. "If the enemy incline towards peace, do thou also incline towards peace, and trust in God." [This] Quranic (8:61) sentence is applied to make peace with an enemy who has his own country and state, but the Jews in Palestine are our enemies who have made their aggression upon a country of the Arab Muslims. The Jews usurped the Arab country with the help of the Imperialist tyrants . . . Therefore we cannot resort to peaceful means in dealing with them as long as they form their state upon the ruins of an Islamic state . . . The Muslims should spare no effort to exterminate their state . . .[26]

In a like vein, Shaykh ᶜAbd al-Ḥamīd ᶜAṭiyya al-Dibrānī, Rector of the Libyan Islamic University, concluded: "Hence, present-day Muslims should never treat with them for peace, since it has been proved beyond doubt that they are a mere gang of robbers and criminals, to whom trust, faith, and conscience mean nothing."[27]

The catalyst for a radical change in this attitude of no negotiations and no peace with Israel was the Yom Kippur war of 1973. Although that war, too, ended with the defeat of Egypt and Syria, Egypt did score an initial success when she launched a surprise attack, crossed over the Suez Canal, and pushed the Israeli units back from the east bank of the canal. Despite what happened subsequently, this registered in Egyptian and Arab consciousness as a great victory, and more than that, a redeeming event. Syrian President Assad, in an address to the Syrian nation broadcast on October 15, 1973, said: "During these glorious ten days . . . We restored for the Arab his self-confidence after healing his wounded dignity . . . You have revived the tradition of our glorious nation . . ." Next day, Egyptian President Sadat, addressing the Egyptian parliament, referred to the same event as "the most glorious days of [our] history . . ."[28] Arab writers and poets spoke in glowing terms about the transformation of the Arabs, as a result of that victory, "from an honorless existence, an existence of beasts and animals, into human beings possessed of honor . . ."[29]

An important effect of the 1973 war, in addition to restoring Arab self-esteem, confidence, and honor, was a temporary impetus towards Arab unity. Syria and Iraq, enmeshed for years in antagonism and mutual denunciations, improved their relations. As Lebanese Arab analysts put it, "There were even reports of possible steps toward Syrian-Iraqi unity, should the fighting be renewed. Yet only weeks before the war there had been heated exchanges between Damascus and Baghdad." When Jordan, which did not take part in the war except for sending small contingents to the Syrian front, declared her commitment to the war, both Tunisia and Algeria restored (on October 14) diplomatic relations with Amman. As against these manifestations, "probably the only fundamental dispute that survived the emphasis on brotherhood was that between King Hussein [of Jordan] and the Palestine resistance movement." On October 12 the Executive Committee of the Palestine Liberation Organization voiced sharp criticism of King Hussein.[30]

At the same time, the October war produced a far-reaching, and seemingly paradoxical change in the Egyptian attitude to Israel. Egypt had borne the brunt of the earlier Arab-Israeli wars, and suffered the most crushing defeat in 1967. But she became in 1973 the only Arab country which, in the course of the repeated Arab-Israeli clashes, succeeded in regaining by force of arms any territory occupied by Israel: an area of several square miles east of the Suez Canal whose entire east bank had been held by Israel since the 1967 war. It was this victory, partial though it was, which changed the Egyptian view of the Israeli adversary. Egypt now felt that it was possible for her to sit down and talk peace with Israel without unduly humiliating herself. Actually, there was nothing paradoxical in this. What happened was that, in the course of a couple of years or so after the October war, Egypt came to the conclusion that, having driven back Israel from part of the Egyptian territory she had occupied in 1967, it was no longer dishonorable or humiliating for Egypt to open negotiations with Israel about the conditions under which Israel would evacuate all of Sinai and return it to Egypt. What is certainly remarkable is that Egypt had nine years earlier hosted the Fourth Conference of the Academy of Islamic Research and probably inspired its "no negotiations and no peace" position vis-à-vis Israel, and that, having initiated in the same spirit the October war with Israel only four years earlier, Egypt should be the one Arab country to take the initiative in seeking a rapprochement and an understanding with Israel. This bold step, whose historical consequences it is still too early to evaluate, resulted in a boycotting of Egypt by almost the entire Arab world, and led ultimately to the assassination of President Sadat by those elements which believed that what he did was nothing short of treason to the cause of the Arab nation.

In any case, in 1977 President Sadat, who had planned and executed the Egyptian attack on Israel's Suez positions on Yom Kippur 1973, undertook what world opinion considered a phenomenal about-face by visiting Jerusalem, addressing the Israeli Knesset (parliament), and establishing direct contact with Israel. This, in turn, opened the door to protracted negotiations between Cairo and Jerusalem, in which American President Jimmy Carter had a crucial role, and which culminated in the Camp David agreement and the Israeli-Egyptian peace treaty. The immediate results of these new Israeli-Egyptian relations included a considerable reduction in the number and strength of Israel's Arab enemies, and, on the psychological plane, the beginning of the end of the "menacing Jew" phase in Arab-Jewish relations, at least as far as the leadership of the most powerful Arab country was concerned.

It can be foreseen that it will take many years before other Arab countries follow Egypt's lead. In the meantime, the image of the Jew as a menace, as a sinister figure, a danger to the world as a whole and to the Arabs in particular, continues to be projected in Arab writings and verbal utterances. As recently as on December 8, 1980, the Jordanian representative at the UN gave succinct expression to this Western-derived Arab image of the Jew as the evil power exploiting equally the Arab world and the rest of humankind. He stated that the natural resources of the Arab world had long been "held in bondage and plundered by [the Jewish] people's cabal, which controls and manipulates the rest of humanity by controlling the money and wealth of the world," and mentioned, by way of example, "people like Lord Rothschild [who] every day, in ironclad secrecy, decide to flash around the world how high the price of gold should be . . ."[31] These, by the way, are the words of the representative of a so-called "moderate" Arab state, which appear moderate indeed when compared to what the more radical Arab states have to say about Israel and the Jews.

THE "PROTOCOLS"

As contact between the Arab world and the West intensified, more and more European anti-Semitic tracts were translated into Arabic, often under governmental aegis, and with the approval of Arab leaders who supplied signed prefaces. The use of the pen as a weapon had been a long-established tradition in Arab culture (remember the *hijā'*!), and before long Arab authors began to launch written attacks against the Jews by utilizing the entire arsenal of Western anti-Semitic arguments. After the establishment of Israel, as Morroe Berger remarked, there was no need any longer for importing anti-Semitic agitation from Europe. Instead, Westernization made the Near East self-sufficient in this field as in many others.[32]

Still, the one anti-Semitic tract which was the heaviest piece in the literary artillery of Arab anti-Semitism was of Western manufacture. It was the infamous *Protocols of the Elders of Zion*. The *Protocols*, concocted in 1897 by an unknown author in Paris working for the Russian secret police, the Okhrana, purports to contain the records of a secret conference held by leaders of world Jewry in Basel, Switzerland, in that year, when the First Zionist Congress actually took place in that city. Their thrust is that the Jews hold the whole world in their grip, controlling and exploiting it with their money, their secret international organization, and their ruthless cunning. First printed in Russian in 1903, then in a fuller version in 1905, the *Protocols* were translated after World War I into many languages.

After the end of the war it was widely recognized in the Western world that the *Protocols* were but a crude anti-Semitic forgery. However, while the career of the *Protocols* thus came to an end in the West, they found a new lease on life in the Arab world, where they have been published between 1927 and 1967 in several Arabic translations and in numerous editions in Egypt, Syria, Lebanon, and Iraq. In addition, abridgements of the *Protocols* were published in several anti-Zionist tracts, and they were quoted in a very large number of political studies dealing with the Palestine problem.[33] In Egypt the *Protocols* were officially considered a genuine historical document, and their full text was printed in Cairo in 1957 in the series "Political Books" published by the governmental Information Office, under the title *Protocol (sic) of the Wise Men of Zion*. The preface, signed by the "Committee for Political Books," states that this secret Zionist document is most important for the Arab reader so as to recognize the full intentions of "world Zionism whose accursed seed, Israel, was sown by imperialism in our land Filastin."[34] A year later, an interview with President Nasser was published in the semi-official Cairo daily *al-Ahrām* (of Sept. 29, 1958), and in the official Egyptian English-language publication of Nasser's speeches and press conferences (1958, 2:30), in which he said to the Indian journalist R. K. Karanjia who interviewed him:

> I wonder if you have read a book, "Protocols of the Learned Elders of Zion." It is very important that you should read it. I will give you a copy. It proves beyond the shadow of a doubt that three hundred Zionists, each one of whom knows all the others, govern the fate of the European continent . . . and that they elect their successors from their entourage."[35]

On December 10, 1963, and January 23, 1964, the Jordanian newspaper *al-Jihād* informed its readers that the Palestine Committee of the Arab League would discuss the publication of the *Protocols* in all languages, so as to call the attention of world opinion to the truth in the plots and aims of Zionism. And on August 23, 1967, the Egyptian newspaper *al-Akhbār* wrote that the Supreme Council for Islamic Affairs had decided to publish a book, which would include the *Protocols*, and to distribute it in English and French translations.[36]

The credence given even by Muslim scholars to the authenticity of the *Protocols* was illustrated at the Fourth Islamic academic conference to which reference has repeatedly been made above. One of those who presented papers was Kamāl Aḥmad ᶜAwn, vice-principal of the Egyptian Tanta Institute, who mentioned the *Protocols* and the Talmud in one breath as two authentic expressions of the Jewish mentality: "I shall quote neither the Talmud . . . nor the Protocols of Zionist sages, seeing that the Jews may deny both of them." ᶜAwn then proceeded to assert that "Abraham was a true Arabian who emigrated with his tribe from the heart of the Arabian Peninsula to Iraq whence he emigrated after his divine mission to the land of the Canaanites in Syria . . . Thus Abraham was a true Arabian . . ."[37]

A remarkable testimony to the extent to which, in addition to the *Protocols*, also other anti-Semitic stereotypes and libels, long discredited and discarded in the Western world, have found a new home in Arab lands was supplied by utterances of King Fayṣal (reigned 1964–1975) of Saudi Arabia. He accepted the *Protocols* "at face value, as proving all that his father [King Ibn Saud] had ever said about the perfidy of the Jewish race. Copies of the *Protocols* were given out in Fayṣal's reign as bedside reading to guests in Saudi hotels." In his conversation with American Secretary of State Henry

Kissinger in November, 1973, Fayṣal first reiterated the old bromide that "Before the Jewish State was established there existed nothing to harm the good relations between Arabs and Jews . . ." and then launched into a vehement anti-Jewish diatribe.[38]

In an interview Fu'ād al-Sayyid, a reporter of the Egyptian illustrated weekly *al-Muṣawwar*, was granted by King Fayṣal in the summer of 1972, the king said, among other things:

> Israel has had wicked intentions since ancient times. Her purpose is to destroy all the other religions. It was proved from history that they were the people who started the crusades in the period of Ṣalāḥ al-Dīn al-Ayyūbī, so that that war should result in the weakening of both the Muslims and the Christians. They hold the other religions lower than their own religion, and the people who follow those religions are considered by them to be on a lower level than they. As an example of the gratification of their thirst for revenge, they have a day on which they mix the blood of the non-Jews with bread and eat it. It happened about two years ago when I was on a visit to Paris that the police came across five murdered children, and their blood had been drained. It was clear that some Jews had killed them so as to take their blood and mix it with the bread which they eat on that day. This will show you the extent of their hatred and malice against the non-Jews.[39]

Here we have a blatant example of the uncritical adoption of the worst old European anti-Semitic canards, including the blood-libel, with the added note of personal reminiscence.[40] As for his reference to the Crusades, the king's knowledge of history is somewhat hazy: he confuses the beginnings of the Crusades in the late eleventh century with the time of Saladin who defeated the Crusaders in Palestine about a century later. But he is consistent in his anti-Semitism when he alleges that the Jews (who, in fact, suffered as much from the Crusades as the Arabs) "started" the Crusades for the purpose of weakening both the Muslims and the Christians. However, what is most saddening in this incident is not so much the rabid anti-Semitism of the Arab king which is known from other sources as well, but that an Egyptian newspaper should have published it at all, and if so, should have done it without any comment as to the absurdities of the king's statements. One can perhaps see in the publication of this interview a manifestation of the strongly anti-Israel atmosphere in Egypt in the years in which she made her preparations for the Yom Kippur war of 1973.

A dozen years after the Saudi king's blood-libel, the delegate of Saudi

Arabia to a UN seminar on religious tolerance reechoed and amplified King Fayṣal's statement about Jewish thirst for gentile blood. Addressing the seminar on December 5, 1984, in Geneva, Dr. Maʿrūf al-Dawalībī, Counsellor to the Royal Court in Riyadh, recounted as an established fact, and in gory detail, the 1840 Damascus blood-libel, and told how the Jews had slaughtered Father Albert Thomas and his servant, "gathered" their blood for ritual purposes, and then cut their bodies into pieces. Dr. Dawalībī also "quoted" the Talmud to the effect that "if a Jew does not drink every year the blood of a non-Jewish man, he will be damned for eternity." Then, mixing the terms "Jew" and "Israeli," he quoted the Jewish barber allegedly involved in the murder of Father Thomas, as having said that "a Jewish physician is not allowed to give true medicine to someone who is not Israeli, except for medical experiments as it is done with dogs." The Talmud, according to the authority of the barber, to which Dr. Dawalībī gives full credence, also "says that the whole world is the property of Israel, and that the wealth, the blood, and the souls of the non-Israelis are allowed and are theirs." This, according to Dr. Dawalībī, was "the reason which has caused the discrimination and oppression against the Jews" throughout history.[41]

As for Egypt, the shades of the *Protocols* continued to haunt it even after the peace agreement with Israel. In the June 26, 1982, issue of the Egyptian daily *Akhbār al-Yawm*, Muḥammad Ṭanṭāwī conflates the notorious and imaginary "Elders of Zion" with the delegates to the first Zionist Congress. He writes:

> Logic and reason are weapons with which we have to face Israeli conspiracies in the area. Those are old conspiracies that were formulated in the first congress of the Elders of Zion which met in 1897 in Switzerland. At that congress there were three hundred Zionists. . . . If we look at these resolutions of the Elders of Zion, we see that the secret plan of the Zionists is to conquer the world.[42]

In a similar vein, although without reference to the "Elders of Zion," Anis Mansour wrote, after the Israeli invasion of Lebanon, in another Egyptian weekly, the *Uktūbār* ("October") magazine: "Israel today . . . managed to exterminate two nations—the Lebanese and the Palestinian . . . Israel has not forgotten what Hitler did to the Jews, although what Hitler did is very modest if we compare it to what they did in Beirut."[43]

The foregoing examples should suffice to show the depth of the anti-Jewish and anti-Israel feelings—it is difficult to distinguish between the two—which have in recent times agitated some of the Arab leaders and writers. In order to complete the picture, it would be necessary to supplement this presentation with at least a few indications as to the manner in which Arab populations in various countries view the Jews and Israel. Regrettably, the absence of both public opinion polls and sociological studies on the issue in Arab countries makes this impossible. Failing that, one can make only a few general observations.

One is that in Arab countries there are practically no channels through which the people could inform the leadership of their opinions and wishes. Not only are there no public opinion polls, but elections are, as a rule, little more than ritual exercises. The only way for the people to express what they want is to hold street demonstrations, as we have seen as recently as in October, 1984, when riots took place in several Egyptian towns because of the increase in the prices of basic commodities such as bread—whereupon the price increases were promptly rescinded. This being the situation, Arab governments, even if they wanted to do so, have no way to ascertain the wishes of the people. Which means that governmental decisions, which inevitably affect the lives of the people, are being made with little knowledge of what the people want.

The second observation is that Arab leaders, whether traditional such as kings, emirs, and sheiks, or modern such as the semi-dictatorial presidents of the Arab republics, exert a stronger influence on public opinion than is the case in the Western democracies. In the West, with their two-party or multiparty systems, pronouncements of the incumbent leaders are frequently disputed and contradicted by the leaders of the opposition, so that both sides must constantly compete for the ears and minds of the population which is their electorate. In Arab countries, the press, the radio, and the television serve only the incumbent leadership, whose persuasive powers are therefore not counterbalanced by a presentation of disparate points of view. Hence one can assume that the virulent anti-Israel and anti-Jewish stance of most Arab leaders has been, and is being, echoed to a considerable extent by the people. Taking both the above points together, one must conclude that any future change in the Arab attitude to Israel and the Jews will have to come from the Arab leaders, to which popular sentiment can be expected to respond positively.

Keeping in mind the above considerations, it is clear that it is the conflict over Palestine that is in the center of all or most of the Arabs' recent anti-Jewish sentiments. As long as the Jews did not control Palestine, did not plan to get Palestine, and did not even claim any rights to Palestine, they could safely be treated as *dhimmīs*, and the Arab attitude to them could find its full expression in contempt. Once however the Jews claimed, fought for, and obtained Palestine, contempt for them became a clearly inappropriate sentiment, and was replaced by hatred, an entirely new feature in the millennial Arab-Jewish relations. Whether the Egyptian-Israeli peace agreement will have the effect of mitigating, and ultimately eliminating, this new Arab anti-Jewish attitude, only time will tell.

It is time now to turn to the focal point of the contemporary Arab-Jewish conflict: the claim both peoples are convinced they have to the possession of Palestine.

THE JEWISH CLAIM

The small strip of land which lies between the Jordan River and the Mediterranean became the locus of some of the greatest religious events in the history of man after a minor wandering Aramean chieftain named Abram (later Abraham) felt impelled by a divine voice to leave his home in Haran in Mesopotamia, and go, with his wife Sarai (Sarah), his nephew Lot, and other followers, to the land of Canaan. It is a remarkable fact that the first words which, according to the biblical narrative, the Lord addressed to Abraham were not, as we would have expected it, something to the effect that "I am the Lord God whom alone thou shalt serve from now on . . ." but, without any introduction or self-identification of the divine speaker, the abrupt command, "Get thee out of thy country . . . unto the land that I will show thee. And I will make of thee a great nation . . ." (Gen. 12:1–2).

Next, after Abraham arrives in Canaan, "unto the place of Shechem" (today Nablus) the Lord again appears to Abraham and tells him, "Unto thy seed will I give this land" (Gen. 12:7). Ever since this divine promise the fate of the children of Abraham, Isaac, and Jacob was inseparably tied to the land which in their consciousness assumed the character of the Land of Promise.

Scholars today are of the opinion that the biblical stories of Abraham reflect conditions which obtained in the seventeenth or sixteenth century B.C.E., and even if their historicity remains doubtful, they must contain legendary or anecdotal reformulations of events that actually took place in that period. What is more important for the millennial Jewish attachment to the Holy Land is that in Jewish consciousness and memory that land was promised, and repeatedly promised, to the seed of Abraham (Gen. 17:8), then of his son Isaac (Gen. 26:2), and then of Isaac's son Jacob (Gen. 28:13–14), and that the Jews always have felt that the land was theirs by strength of this divine triple promise, even before they actually took possession of it.

The children of Jacob, renamed Israel, had to undergo first the bitter experience of the Egyptian slavery, which tradition considers to have lasted four hundred years,[44] before they were liberated by the great lawgiver Moses, and led into Canaan by his disciple and successor Joshua. Scholars today have come to the conclusion that not all the Hebrew tribes were in Egypt, and that not all of those who were in Egypt left that land of slavery at one particular time under one leader, but that there was a protracted period of migration of Hebrew tribes from Egypt to Canaan, that the conquest of Canaan was not accomplished under one leader within a short period of time, but was a gradual process, and that the Hebrew tribes which came from Egypt were joined in Canaan by brother tribes who had never left the country. But these scholarly modifications or rectifications of biblical tradition are of minor importance in relation to the basic mythical charter which the traditional account provides, and which tells of the great seminal and formative events of the Egyptian slavery, the miraculous redemptive Exodus, the parting of the sea, the awesome revelation on Mount Sinai, and the conquest of Canaan which God enabled the twelve tribes to achieve in fulfillment of His promise.

After the days of the Israelite judges, those charismatic leaders who continued the struggle against the remaining inhabitants of Canaan in the twelfth and eleventh centuries B.C.E., followed the hundred-year period of the united Israelite kingdom under Saul, David, and Solomon (ca. 1024–928 B.C.E.), and then the era of the two Hebrew monarchies of Israel (928–721 B.C.E.) and Judah (928–586 B.C.E.), during which twenty kings ruled in each. The defeat of Judah by the Babylonians in 586 B.C.E. marked the beginning of the so-called Babylonian Exile, which was followed forty-eight years later by the return under Cyrus the Great, and the establishment of the Second Jewish Commonwealth which, in turn, was destroyed by the Romans 608 years later, in 70 C.E.

What is significant in these thirteen centuries of Hebrew and Jewish history in the Land of Israel is that in Jewish consciousness the two periods, separated by the brief Babylonian captivity, became identified as those of the First Temple and the Second Temple respectively. That is to say, what remained important for the Jewish psyche for two millennia after the victory of the Romans over the Jews was not the existence of Hebrew and Jewish kingdoms, which, in any case, were ruled more often than not by kings judged by a pious posterity idolatrous and therefore evil, but that the Temple of Jerusalem stood and functioned as the central sanctuary and place of worship for the Jews of both Palestine and the ever widening Diaspora. I am tempted to quote at least some of the fascinating legends contained in the Talmud, the Midrash, and later Jewish literature about the global, in fact, cosmic, function of the Jerusalem Temple, but I have to refrain since such quotations would lead us far afield from our present subject.[45] But let me mention only in most general terms that those legends are expressive of the firm conviction of the people and their teachers that the regular performance of the Temple ritual was a guarantee of the very existence of the world, and of the proper functioning of the forces of nature, including the fertility of fields, animals, and men. The sacrificial ritual in the Jerusalem Temple could, of course, be carried out only by Jewish priests which, in turn, required that Jerusalem, and the land of which it was the capital, be under Jewish control.

Soon after the destruction of the Jerusalem Temple by the Romans, the rabbis substituted prayers for sacrifices, and those prayers, recited three times every day by all observant Jews (and until the Jewish Enlightenment all Jews were observant), contain these supplications as parts of the main prayer, the Eighteen Benedictions (in my literal translation):

> Sound the great *shofar* (ram's horn) for our freedom, and raise up a banner to gather our exiles, and gather us from the four corners of the earth. Blessed art Thou, O Lord, who gathereth the exiled of His people Israel. . . . And to Jerusalem Thy city return in compassion, and dwell in her as Thou hast spoken, and rebuild her soon in our days, rebuilding her for all eternity, and speedily establish in her midst the throne of David. Blessed art Thou, O Lord, who rebuildeth Jerusalem. . . . And may our eyes see Thy return to Zion in compassion. Blessed art Thou, O Lord, who returneth His Shekhina to Zion.

Those who know the importance of prayer in Jewish life and its central role as a life-sustaining force in the midst of the trials and tribulations of the long centuries of exile in Christian and Muslim lands, can appreciate the depth and strength of the Jewish longing for Zion, for Jerusalem, for the Land of Israel, which their prayers both expressed and kept alive. In that longing, as the above quotations from the daily prayers show, religious sentiments and national aspirations were inseparably intertwined.

Reality, however, fell far short of dreams and desires. In the long centuries after the Roman exile of 70 C.E., the Jewish population of Eretz Israel at first gradually diminished, then shrank to a few communities mainly in the four holy cities of Jerusalem, Hebron, Safed and Tiberias, although in every age individual Jews or small groups managed to translate their yearning into action and settled in the Holy Land. However, reduced numbers never meant a reduced importance of the Land of Israel in Jewish life. Spiritually, Eretz Israel remained the home of the Jewish people in every country of the Diaspora and in every age. Intellectual and religious developments that took place in the Jewish community of Eretz Israel influenced and even modified Jewish life in the Diaspora. Many of the major works of Jewish religious literature were produced in the Land of Israel. They include the Mishna (compiled ca. 200 C.E.), the Jerusalem Talmud (ca. 425 C.E.), numerous Midrashim (fifth to sixth centuries C.E.), the religious poetry of Eleazar Kallir (seventh or eighth century), and the system of vocalization of Hebrew texts, which was developed in Tiberias, in the ninth century, and which enabled the Jews to read the Bible and the prayers with a great degree of accuracy. The writings of the sixteenth-century Safed masters (Isaac Luria, Ḥayyim Vital, Moses Cordovero, and others) made the Kabbala a popular mass movement among all three major divisions of the Jewish people, the Oriental (Middle Eastern) Jews in Arab lands, the Sephardim in the Ottoman Empire and northwestern Europe, and the Ashkenazim in Central and Eastern Europe. Sixteenth-century Safed was also the place where Joseph Caro (who, incidentally, was also a leading Kabbalist) wrote his *Shulḥan ʿArukh*, the last great code of Jewish law, which is considered authoritative to this day by all Jews except those of Reform persuasion. And Solomon Alqabetz, the author of the famous Sabbath-song *Lekha Dodi*, sung to this day in all synagogues every Friday evening, also lived in Safed at the same time. In the seventeenth century it was in Gaza, at the time the home of a sizable Jewish community, that Shabbatai Zevi (1626–1676) first felt in himself the stirrings of a messianic mission, which, before its final debacle in 1666, developed into the greatest messianic movement experienced by the Jewish people.

In the early eighteenth century there was increased Jewish immigration to Eretz Israel. This movement began with a convoy of fifteen hundred Jews led by Judah Ḥasid and Ḥayyim Malakh, of whom one thousand arrived in Jerusalem in 1700 (five hundred had died on the way). Because of financial problems encountered in Jerusalem, subsequent immigrants preferred to settle in the other three holy cities. In general, the great insecurity in the country, the incessant skirmishes among various ethnic groups, the cruelty and rapacity of the Turkish pashas and their underlings, made life for the Jews in eighteenth- and nineteenth-century Palestine extremely difficult, even hazardous. The total population in 1800 is estimated at three hundred thousand, of whom twenty-five thousand were Christians belonging to various sects, and five thousand were Jews, mostly Sephardim.

Sizable Jewish immigration from East Europe began in 1882, when the Jewish population numbered twenty-four thousand. By November 2, 1917, when the British Government issued the Balfour Declaration, this number had been augmented by some sixty-five thousand Jewish immigrants, almost all of them from East Europe. In the three decades that were to pass until the declaration of Israel's independence on May 14, 1948, another 450,000 Jewish immigrants had arrived, so that on the day of Israel's birth the *Yishuv* (the Jewish population of Palestine) numbered about 650,000. Thereafter the immigration, and with it the population increase, was much more rapid. On her thirty-fifth birthday (1983), Israel had a Jewish population of about 3.5 million.

One British, and three international documents conferred upon the Jews the right to establish a national home, and ultimately a state of their own, in Palestine. In the Balfour Declaration the British Government undertook to facilitate the establishment of a Jewish national home in Palestine. On April 24, 1920, the Supreme Council of the Peace Conference at San Remo resolved that the mandate over Palestine be conferred on Britain, charging her with the establishment of a Jewish national home in Palestine as laid down in the Balfour Declaration. On July 22, 1922, the League of Nations Council confirmed the Palestine Mandate, citing the Balfour Declaration, and recognizing the "historical connection of the Jewish people with Palestine . . . and the grounds for reconstituting their National Home in that country." Twenty-five years later the United Nations took up the Palestine problem, and on November 29, 1947, its General Assembly resolved by a vote of thirty-three to thirteen, with ten abstentions, the establishment in Palestine of two states, one Jewish and one Arab, with Jerusalem and its environs as an international zone. The British Government announced that it would withdraw its forces on May 15, 1948, and the day before that the Jewish People's Council approved the Proclamation of Independence which declared the establishment of the State of Israel.

To summarize: The Jewish claim to Palestine rests on religious, historical, political, emotional, and international-legal foundations, which are often interconnected. The religious-historical foundations are the belief in the divine promise repeatedly recorded in the Bible. The historical-political foundations are the actual dominion exercised over the land by the biblical Hebrews and their heirs the Jews for thirteen centuries, from the conquest of Canaan in the thirteenth to twelfth century B.C.E. to the destruction of the Second Jewish Commonwealth by the Romans in 70 C.E., and the continued Jewish presence in the country ever since. The religious-emotional foundations consist of the intense sentimental attachment of the Jews to the Land of Israel, as expressed in their daily prayers and in their messianic hopes for Redemption and Return. The international-legal foundations consist of the Balfour Declaration, the mandate over Palestine conferred by the League of Nations on Britain, and the United Nations resolution to set up a Jewish state in part of Palestine.

THE ARAB CLAIM

The earliest basis of the Arab claim to Palestine is its conquest by the Arab general ᶜAmr ibn al-ᶜĀṣ in 634, that is, some 565 years after the Jews had lost sovereignty over their land. Jerusalem, which fell to the Arabs in 638, was known to them at the time as Īliyā, from the Latin name of the city Aelia, or from the name of the prophet Elijah (in Hebrew Eliyahu), that is, the sanctuary of Elijah. They also called it Bayt al-Maqdis, from the Hebrew *bet hamiqdash*, or the Aramaic *bet maqdsha*, meaning "House of the Sanctuary." By the tenth century, however, the short name al-Quds, "The Holy," had become established. Arab legend has it that some Jews showed the Caliph ᶜUmar the site of the ancient Temple of Jerusalem, which was purposely concealed by the Christians under heaps of rubbish. ᶜUmar cleared the site, laid bare the Holy Rock, and prayed at it. (However, see the story told by Ṭabarī which is quoted below.) During the rule of the Caliph Muᶜāwiya (ca. 602–680) the Arabs began to use the site as a place of worship, and the building of the mosque, known to this day as "The Dome of the Rock," was begun. It was completed under ᶜAbd al-Malik ibn Marwān (reigned 685–705), the first Umayyad caliph, and had since been renovated and restored several times. It stands today in the middle of the Ḥaram al-Sharīf, "The Noble Sanctuary," and is one of the finest monuments of Arab architecture.

The Arab tradition that Palestine was definitely conquered by the Arabs under the rule of ᶜUmar has been shown by historians to be in need of revision, just as was the biblical tradition of the conquest of Canaan under Joshua. It has been established that for six centuries after ᶜUmar, that is, from the seventh to the thirteenth century, Jerusalem itself was contested between the Arabs, or rather Muslims, and the Christians, as well as by many Muslim princes and factions among themselves.[46] To detail the changes in the political and military control exercised over Palestine by one external power after the other, and the administrative changes which cut the country into different slices in different periods, would require special and lengthy study which would lead us far beyond the subject of the present book. What we can do briefly is to make one general statement: in the nine centuries from the conquest of Palestine by ᶜAmr ibn al-ᶜĀṣ to its conquest by the Turks there was never a period of any duration in which Palestine would have been an independent and united country under Arab rule. However, what we are primarily interested in in the present context are the feelings of the Arabs about Palestine, which, as the feelings of the Jews about it, are something quite different from the actual history of the country as can be established by scholarly research.

For many centuries religious sentiments took the first place among the Arab feelings about Palestine. Palestine, as they knew from the Koran and tradition, was the land in which lived Abraham, an extremely important ancestral figure for the Arabs (see chapter 2). To possess the land which Abraham roamed, assumed for them great religious significance. Especially important in Arab eyes was to have control over Hebron, known to the Arabs as Khalīl, that is, "Friend," because it was the town in which Abraham, the *khalīl Allāh*, "friend of God," was buried, together with most members of his family. It is interesting to note that this epithet, *khalīl Allāh*, is the Muslim Arab reflection of the Jewish Midrashic explanation of the biblical name of the city, Ḥevron. The name, the Midrash says, was derived from the epithet of Abraham who was called *ḥaver*, friend.[47] However, while Jerusalem was known to the Arabs from the time of Muhammad, they learned about Hebron only considerably later, while the Jews, who were quite numerous in the Hebron area in the first centuries of Islam, had conducted active worship at the tomb of Abraham for generations prior to the Arab conquest of Palestine.[48] Later Muslim tradition, in order to put the Arab connection with Hebron on firmer ground, claimed that Muhammad was ordered by God to pray on Mount Sinai, in Hebron, and in Bethlehem—all Jewish holy places—before reaching Jerusalem.

Jerusalem, of course, came to figure most prominently in Muslim-Arab religious tradition. Early Islamic scholars took certain verses in the Koran as referring to Jerusalem. Foremost among these passages is *sūra* 17 : 1 which tells of the night journey of Muhammad and which opens with the words, "Praise be to Him who caused His servant to go by night from the Sacred Mosque to the Farthest Mosque whose environs We have blessed that We show him Our signs . . ." (my translation). This verse was taken to mean that Muhammad was transported in a miraculous night journey from Mecca to Jerusalem. Later Arab legend embellished this brief reference, and told about Muhammad having completed the long journey from Mecca to Jerusalem and back in a single night, on the back of a miraculous steed, al-Burāq, occasionally described as white and winged. When he arrived in Jerusalem, the legend goes on, Muhammad dismounted, and tied al-Burāq to the Rock, the ancient sacred rock about which there is an abundance of Jewish legends, making it the Even Sh'tiyya, "Foundation Stone," of the world, and upon which stood the Holy of Holies of Solomon's Temple. Muhammad prayed, then remounted, and al-Burāq took him up to heaven, kicking itself off the rock, and leaving on its surface its hoofprint, which was pointed out to me in 1933 when I first visited the site.

The Koranic passages and the later legendary traditions combined to make Jerusalem with its al-Ḥaram al-Sharīf, the third holiest place for Islam, after Mecca and Medina. Not to be in possession of Jerusalem is a situation intolerable to Muslim religious sensibilities. As one of the recently deceased kings of Saudi Arabia said, it was his great hope and desire to be able to prostrate himself in the Noble Sanctuary in Jerusalem, meaning, of course, in a Jerusalem restored to Muslim rule.

In view of this solid entrenchment in Muslim tradition of Jerusalem as a holy place it is interesting to note that the earliest Arab attitude on the question of the sanctity of the Jerusalem temple area was negative. Bernard Lewis has pointed out that in early Islam stories circulated whose purpose was to demonstrate that to venerate Jerusalem as a holy city was a sign of Jewish influence and therefore wrong. One of the stories of this type is told by Ṭabarī, the great ninth-century historian, who describes the visit ᶜUmar paid to the newly conquered city of Īliyā. While there he asked Kaᶜb al-Aḥbār, his expert on things Jewish, where to establish the place of prayer. Kaᶜb answered, "By the Rock." But ᶜUmar objected, reproached Kaᶜb of "following after Judaism," and declared that "We were not commanded concerning the Rock, but we were commanded concerning the Kaʿba (in Mecca)."[49] Despite such initial objections—even if the story is apocryphal, it shows that there was a trend opposing the adoption by the Muslims of the Jewish veneration of Jerusalem—subsequently the Rock took its place as the third holiest sanctuary in Islam. Thus religious sentiment, whatever its origin, became an Islamic motivating force to strive for the establishment of Muslim, that is, Arab, dominion over Jerusalem, and by extension over all of Palestine.

While there is thus undoubtedly a certain parallel between the Jewish and the Muslim religious sentiments concerning Palestine, there are important differences between them of which one must not lose sight. For the Muslims, the two most important holy cities are Mecca and Medina. One is where Muhammad was born, the other is where he died; and in both places he spent all his life. Jerusalem for them is only the third holy place, and it is holy only because, according to Koranic tradition, Muhammad paid one single visit to the site of the ancient Jewish temple. For the Jews there is only one Holy City, Jerusalem, which is the locus and focus of their entire religious and national history. Muslim tradition does not claim that God promised the Land of Canaan to the children of Ishmael or to the children of the other great Arab ancestral figure, Qaḥṭān. In Muslim tradition Palestine does not figure as the ancestral homeland of the Arabs—that place of honor is reserved for Arabia. Muslim tradition, although a Messiah-like figure, that of the *mahdī*, plays an important role in it, does not attribute to him a return, at the head of his people, to Palestine and Jerusalem, while in Jewish religious tradition the Messianic redemption and return to Zion, and the reestablishment in the Holy City of the throne of David are crucial features. That is to say, the Holy Land and the Holy City are incomparably more pivotal for Judaism than for Islam.

Now for the population picture. Statistics of the population of Palestine prior to the British takeover are nonexistent, but the impression one gains from early travelers' reports is that the population must have been very sparse. One estimate puts the total population of the country in 1800 at three hundred thousand, and even that may be too high a figure. In the course of the nineteenth century, with its unsettled conditions, the size of the Arab population apparently did not increase. However, when the Jewish *ʿaliyot* ("waves of immigration") began, in 1882, the Arab population, too, started to increase, and outstripped the Jewish population growth. This was due to two factors. One was the traditionally high birthrate among the

Arabs, averaging about eight live births per woman in the course of her entire reproductive period (ca. fifteen to forty-nine years of age). In traditional circumstances, the high birthrate was counterbalanced by an equally high death rate, with the result that there was no population increase, or only a very slight one. Thus from 1800 to 1914 it is estimated that the Arab population of the area which later was to become western Palestine increased from three hundred thousand to six hundred thousand.[50]

Jewish reconstruction work in the country, including the introduction of sanitation and medical services, although it began only on a small scale, nevertheless resulted in a gradual improvement of health conditions. These developments led to a drop in the Arab infant, child, and adult death rates, while the traditional pattern of high birthrate continued. Consequently, the Arab population of Palestine began to exhibit a growing natural increase. By 1941 increase surpassed 3 percent annually, and thereafter continued to rise.[51] In 1947, the United Nations Special Committee on Palestine stated in its report that

> the rate of increase of the Moslem Arabs in Palestine was the highest registered statistically anywhere in the world, a phenomenon attributed to a high rate of pregnancy together with a considerable decline in the infant mortality rate, the latter brought about by the improvement in living conditions and public health services.[52]

The other factor was Arab immigration to Palestine from the neighboring countries. The improving economic conditions and employment opportunities created in Palestine by what the Jewish community of Palestine liked to refer to as *binyan ha'aretz*, "building of the land," attracted Arabs from Syria, Lebanon, Transjordan, and Egypt. The exact number of Arab immigrants is unknown, but according to the official British figures it was about 36,000 in the twenty years between 1922 and 1942.[53] This figure, however, has to be augmented by that of the illegal immigrants. While the British mandatory authorities were generally able to control Jewish immigration which came in through Mediterranean ports of entry, they were unable to exercise any control over the Arab immigrants who could cross at will the long and unguarded land frontiers between western Palestine and Lebanon, Syria, Transjordan, and Egypt. It is estimated that the actual total Arab immigration to Palestine from 1922 to 1947 amounted to about one hundred thousand. A study carried out by Fred M. Gottheil showed that from 1922 to 1931 a total of 54,790 Arabs immigrated into those parts of

Palestine that in 1948 became Israel, while 4,677 Arab immigrants settled in what subsequently became the West Bank and Gaza.[54] Within the areas in which there was the major Jewish population concentration, the most attractive places for Arab immigrants were the mixed Arab-Jewish cities. The Peel commission in its 1937 report noted that the Arab population increase was largest in Haifa (86 percent), Jaffa (62 percent), and Jerusalem (37 percent), while the purely Arab towns, such as Nablus and Hebron, increased only by 7 percent, and in Gaza there was actually a drop of 2 percent.[55]

A complementary factor was the almost total absence of Arab emigration from Palestine. From 1920 to 1931 only 9,272 non-Jews left Palestine, while in the same period over 103,000 persons emigrated from Syria and Lebanon. The obvious main reason for this marked difference, and for the attraction of Palestine for Arab immigrants, lay in the much better economic conditions enjoyed by the Arabs in Palestine than in the neighboring countries. The per capita income of the Palestinian Arabs rose from LP (Palestine Pounds) 10–12 in 1920, to LP 27 in 1937, in which year the comparable figure for Egypt was LP 12, for Syria and Lebanon LP 16, and for Iraq LP 10.[56] Economic development brought along with it cultural and educational progress, so that the Palestinian Arabs became the most advanced Arab community as far as living standards, educational level, health conditions, and demographic rates were concerned. And parallel with the improvement in quality of life went the intensification of national aspirations, and the emergence of Arab leaders who began to engage in anti-Jewish agitation.

Whatever their antecedents, by the time Israel was established, the Arabs constituted two-thirds of the total population of western Palestine. They were an Arab population like that of any other Arab country. They were attached to their towns, villages, homes and fields in the same manner in which Arabs in other countries were to theirs. While Palestinian nationalistic feelings, as opposed to the consciousness of being Arabs, were still largely absent among them, anti-Jewish sentiments were not. Even though Arab quality of life was considerably better in Palestine than in other Arab countries, this was a factor that remained unknown to most Arabs who had no opportunity to compare their standard of living with that of Arabs beyond the borders of Palestine. Only when and where Arab immigrants from other countries came and settled among them, did people in their immediate environment become aware that their circumstances were attractive to outsiders. What most of them did know, because they could not help noticing it all around them, was that the Jews enjoyed a standard of living higher than their own, and this produced resentment.

Added to this was the fact that new, formerly unknown, problems arose. The improving sanitary conditions, with the greater availability of medical services, resulted in an increase in the number of children who remained alive in the average Arab family. This, in turn, created a new type of economic problem, especially in the villages, where the limited land holdings now proved insufficient to provide a basis of livelihood for the more numerous upcoming generation. Traditional Muslim laws of inheritance provided for a distribution of the father's estate among all his children, with the sons receiving a full share each and the daughters half a share each. This worked fine for many generations, as long as the surviving children were not more than two, on the average. What the surviving son lost from the estate of his father by having to give up one-third of it to his sister, he received back from the estate of another man whose daughter he married. In this manner the same amount of land was worked by roughly the same number of people generation after generation. Once, however, the number of surviving children rose to more than two per married couple, this system proved unworkable, because the parcel of land each of them received was too small to support a man and his family. In this situation some of the sons felt that it was better to strike out on their own; they sold, or entrusted the cultivation of, their piece of land to a brother, and left the village. A similar population movement took place also among the nomads, with the consequence that the Arab population of the cities came to be composed of a growing element of ex-fellaheen and ex-bedouin laborers. A certain fraction of these footloose young men was attracted to terrorist or other radical formations which appealed to them because of the livelihood they provided, and even more so because of their ideology which gave a collective expression to these young men's feelings of uprootedness. The Arabic term *shabāb*, "young men," or "youth," when used in Palestine, usually referred to a group of such uprooted, often idle, dissatisfied, and violence-prone young men. In view of the fact that, until quite recently, practically the only way the Palestinian Arabs could express their aspirations and resentments was through street demonstrations, the *shabāb* came to play a disproportionate and highly visible role in Palestinian Arab political life, and the success of Arab political leaders often depended primarily on their ability to influence, usually to inflame, the *shabāb*. In the 1936–39 Palestinian Arab revolt, although it involved broader population groups, these deracinated young men played a considerable role.

The best presentation of the Arab claim to Palestine is the one given by George Antonius, a Palestinian Christian Arab intellectual leader and eloquent exponent of the Arab cause. In his well-known book *The Arab Awakening*, considered by many students of Arab nationalism the "classic study" of the subject, Antonius argues that the Arab rights to Palestine

> are derived from actual and long-standing possession, and rest upon the strongest human foundations. Their connexion with Palestine goes back uninterruptedly to the earliest historical times, for the term 'Arab' denotes nowadays not merely the incomers from the Arabian Peninsula who occupied the country in the seventh century, but also the older populations who intermarried with their conquerors, acquired their speech, customs and ways of thought and became permanently arabised. The traditions of the present inhabitants are as deeply rooted in their geographical surroundings as in their adoptive culture, and it is a fallacy to imagine that they could be induced to transplant themselves, even to other Arabs surroundings . . . Any solution based on the forcible expulsion of the peasantry from the countryside in which they have their homesteads and their trees, their shrines and graveyards, and all the memories and affections that go with life on the soil, is bound to be forcibly resisted.

Then Antonius goes on to present the political basis of the Arab claim to Palestine. Here he refers to the various promises made by Britain to the Arabs during World War I and to statements of British intentions, and interprets them as "a binding recognition of Arab political rights" to Palestine. Finally, summing up his arguments, he states,

> In other words, the Arab claims rest on two distinct foundations: the natural right of a settled population, in the great majority agricultural, to remain in possession of the land of its birthright; and the acquired political rights which followed from the disappearance of Turkish sovereignty and from the Arab share in its overthrow, and which Great Britain is under a contractual obligation to recognise and uphold.[57]

These arguments, while they do not reflect the Arab position during and immediately following World War I, can be considered a cogent summation of the Arab feelings about Palestine in 1938, when Antonius wrote his book.

PALESTINIAN ARAB NATIONALISM

Much has been written about the spread of the idea of nationalism from Europe into the Arab world, and about the subsequent polarization of Arab nationalism between particularistic local nationalisms (in countries which the Western powers carved out of the Arab dominions of the Ottoman Empire), on the one hand, and the pan-Arab nationalism which embraced all the Arabic-speaking peoples, on the other.[58] Some of the independent Arab states are today fifty or more years old, but the tension between these two poles of Arab nationalism has never been resolved. In fact, it has become a major additional factor in the age-old Arab conflict proneness.[59]

It is remarkable how rapidly the population of each of the newly created Arab states developed a national consciousness and patriotic feelings of its own. This process was facilitated in the major Arab states by historical memories that the leadership soon learned how to utilize. Sentiments in French mandatory, and later independent, Syria were thus related back to the great days when Syria, with Damascus as its splendid capital, was the center of the great Umayyad caliphate, while the newly reestablished Iraq saw herself as heir to the ʿAbbāsid empire whose center was the Iraqi capital of Baghdad. However, no other Arab country had as solid a basis for priding itself of its glorious past as Egypt, which, although its greatest age lay far back in the millennia of the *jāhiliyya*, nevertheless came to view that early Pharaonic period as part of its national history.

In Palestine, such attempts at establishing a great Arab national past ran into a vexing problem. Since Palestine had never been an independent Arab country, its period of pride had to be sought in the biblical Israelite age. As we have seen in an earlier chapter, the Arabs considered themselves heirs of Abraham the *ḥanīf*, and claimed that Abraham, with his son Ishmael, was the founder of the sanctuary at Mecca. One writer even claimed that Abraham himself was an "Arabian." Thus the more general claim could be made, even though it remained tenuous at best, that Palestine was the scene of part of Arab prehistory. The difficulty arose in connection with the long period between Abraham (whose Arab progeny settled in Arabia) and the end of the Hebrew monarchy, during which there was no Arab presence in Palestine, while the Banu Isra'il ("Children of Israel") were undeniably masters of the land. Hence, in contrast to Egypt, the Arabs could not claim that they had also in Palestine a national history going back to the long millennia of the *jāhiliyya*.

The Arabic name for Palestine, *Filasṭīn* (colloquially *Falasṭīn*), is derived from the Greek *Palaistine*, which, in turn, was based on the biblical name *P'leshet*, Philistaea, with the more frequent adjectival form *P'lishti*, plural *P'lishtim*, Philistine(s). The Arabic name Filasṭīn appeared first in 634, when the Arab conquerors overran the territories known under Byzantine rule as Palaestina Prima and Palaestina Secunda. The first, which comprised the southern part of Palestine, was renamed by the Arabs Jund Filasṭīn, "district of Palestine," with Lydda as its capital, while Palaestina Secunda, consisting of the northern part of the country, was renamed by them Jund Urdunn, "district of Jordan," with Tiberias as its capital. Both *jund*s were parts of the larger Umayyad empire. Similarly under the ᶜAbbāsids (from 950 on), the two *jund*s, together with Syria, were but a province of their empire. In 969 Palestine was conquered by the Egyptian Fāṭimids. In 1099 the Crusaders captured Jerusalem and other parts of Palestine. After their defeat and the recapture of Jerusalem by Ṣalāḥ al-Dīn (Saladin) in 1187, the territories west of the Jordan continued under Mameluk rule until 1516, when they fell to the Ottomans who held it for four hundred years. The Ottomans divided Palestine for administrative purposes into the *sanjak*s (districts) of Gaza, Jerusalem, Nablus, Lajjun, and Safed, and made all these *sanjak*s a part of the *eyālet* (*vilayet*) of Damascus, which in practice meant that under them Palestine was part of Syria.

The first expression of the Arab endeavor to throw off the Turkish yoke was the formation in 1875 of a secret Arab society in Beirut, Lebanon, with branches established subsequently in Damascus, Tripoli, and Sidon. In 1882 followed the abortive revolt of Aḥmad ᶜArabī (ᶜUrābī) Pasha in Egypt, whose suppression marked the beginning of British rule in Egypt. Although these early manifestations of Arab nationalism were ruthlessly crushed by the Turkish Sultan ᶜAbd al-Ḥamīd (reigned 1876–1908), Arab calls for an Arab revival continued. Foremost among those who worked for the Arab cause was the Aleppan Muslim Arab writer ᶜAbd al-Raḥmān al-Kawākibī (1849–1903), who argued in his book *The Excellences of the Arabs* (1901) that the Arabs, rather than the Turks, were the legitimate rulers of Islam, and that only the Arabs could represent Islam in its purity. He also called for a separation of religion and state, and thus was a precursor of modern secular Pan-Arabism which embraces both Muslim and Christian Arabs. In 1904 Syrian Arab émigrés living in Paris founded the Ligue de la Patrie Arabe ("League for the Arab Homeland"), whose aim was the liberation of Arab lands from Turkish domination.

Several Palestinian Arab activists and writers participated in the Arab liberation movement. Najīb ᶜAzūrī, a Syrian Christian, who served as Turkish deputy pasha in Jerusalem and was a leader of the Ligue, published in 1905 a book in Paris titled *Le reveil de la nation Arabe dans l'Asie Turque* ("The Revival of the Arab Nation in Turkish Asia"). This book had an important role in the early stages of the Arab national movement, and foresaw the struggle which was to develop between "the awakening Arab nation and the latent efforts of the Jews to reconstitute on a large scale the ancient kingdom of Israel. These two movements are destined to fight each other continually."[60] In the same year ʿAzūrī, together with French authors and journalists, launched the monthly *L'Independence Arabe*, of which eighteen issues were published before it ceased publication in 1906. In 1909 five Syrian and two Palestinian students founded in Paris the secret society Jamʿiyyat al-Umma al-ʿArabiyya al-Fatāt ("Club of the Young Arab Nation"), whose aim was Arab independence. Among the other Arab groupings organized mainly by Syrians, the best known was the Ḥizb al-Lāmarkaziyya al-Idāriyya al-ʿUthmānī ("Party of the Ottoman Administrative Decentralization"), which was founded in Cairo in 1912. All these political stirrings, which aimed at the liberation of the entire "Arab homeland," and in which local Arab nationalism played no role, came to a halt during the four years of World War I.[61]

A specifically Palestinian Arab nationalism was slow to come. At first there arose differences over economic interests between Arab and Jewish workers. The Jewish "colonists" of the First ʿAliya (1882–1904) employed cheap Arab labor on their farms, and when the Jewish workers who arrived with the Second ʿAliya (1904–1914) demanded that the Jewish farmers should employ Jewish laborers, it came to localized clashes between Jewish and Arab workers, as in Jaffa, in 1908. The Arabs recognized, however, that the establishment of Jewish settlements was to the economic advantage of the Arabs who lived in the vicinity, and they "often expressed the wish that the Jews should buy land in their area and settle near them."[62]

A decisive change in Arab attitudes took place after the Turkish revolt of July 1908 which resulted in the ousting of Sultan ʿAbd al-Ḥamīd and the formation of a Turkish parliament in which, of the 245 deputies, 60 were Arabs, including three who represented the *sanjak* of Jerusalem. Although the Arab presence in this new Turkish parliament was very scanty in proportion to the Arab population in the Ottoman Empire (there were 10.5 million Arabs as against 7.5 million Turks "in racial terms"), this new political situation enabled the Palestinian Arabs to engage openly in nationalistic activities. The leadership of this movement was in the hands of Palestinian Greek Orthodox Christian Arabs, who founded two periodicals (in 1908 the weekly *Al-Karmel* in Haifa, and in 1911 the daily *Al-Falasṭīn* in Jaffa), both of which became active disseminators of anti-Jewish propaganda. The Palestinian Arab members of the Turkish parliament began to speak up against the Jewish settlement work in Palestine. New Palestinian Arab officials with strong nationalistic leanings were appointed to key positions in the Turkish administration of Palestine, and began to place obstacles in the way of the Jewish endeavors.

Although the attitude of the Young Turk leaders toward Jews and Zionism was quite positive (several of them had been educated in the Alliance Israélite school in Salonika), they were apprehensive lest the Zionist settlement work in Palestine ultimately lead to a secession of that part of the Turkish-controlled lands. They therefore preferred to see Jewish settlement in other parts of the country, such as Macedonia and Izmir (Smyrna). They also feared that Jewish immigration to Palestine might arouse resentment among the Arabs. These fears were nourished by such manifestations as the cable of protest (published by the leading Constantinople papers in 1910) sent by the heads of the Arab communities (six Christians and one Muslim) in Nazareth, in reaction to the purchase by the Jews of land at al-Fūla (the site of the present Afulah-Merhavya area in Israel). The cable claimed that "the Zionists plan to drive us off the land, and these purposes of theirs are matters of life and death to us." Arab spokesmen also demanded of Talᶜat Bey, the Turkish Minister of the Interior, that he refrain from facilitating the entry of Jews into Palestine, and prohibit the purchase of Arab lands by Jews. In 1911 the minuscule Jewish community of Palestine was the object of virulent attack in the Turkish parliament by three Arab deputies from Jerusalem who accused the Jews of training their young people in arms, organizing as independent entities, and endangering the Arab population of Palestine and the Ottoman Empire. This was followed by another cable signed by one hundred fifty Arab notables and sent to the Turkish parliament, protesting land purchases by Jews.[63]

At the same time Arab nationalist leaders recognized that their cause could benefit from Jewish help. In June 1913 was held in Paris the first conference of Arab nationalists which was an overt anti-Turkish demonstration, and in preparation for which Arab approaches were made to the Jews with a view to setting up an Arab-Jewish alliance. In the course of these contacts it appeared that most Arab leaders in Cairo and Beirut took a positive view of Zionism, were basically in favor of Jewish immigration to Syria and Palestine, and expressed their understanding of "the valuable assistance that the capital, the diligence, and the intelligence of the Jews can provide to the accelerated development of the [Arab] areas . . ."[64] of Turkey. Similar statements were published by other members of the Cairo and Beirut Arab committees. As for immigration, Aḥmad Mukhtār Bayham, of the Beirut committee, declared, "The entry of Jews—yes! But the entry of Turks—no!" And ʿAbd al-Ḥamīd Zahrāwī, president of the Paris Arab conference, stated:

> Because they [the Jews] are our brothers in race, and we regard them as Syrians who were forced to leave the country at one time but whose hearts always beat together with ours, we are certain that our Jewish brothers the world over will know how to help us so that our common interest may succeed and our common country will develop both materially and morally. . . .[65]

However, despite these declarations of sympathy for the Jews, no formal agreement was reached between the Jewish and the Arab leaders concerning such crucial issues for the Zionists as Jewish immigration to, and land purchases in, Palestine. In early 1914 the Palestinian Arab press stepped up its propaganda against Jewish immigration. At the same time, Arab leaders began, for the first time, to make use of what can be called "double exposure" to which later some of them, for instance, Yasir Arafat, were to resort with considerable mastery. Thus Saʿīd al-Ḥusaynī, a former mayor of Jerusalem and deputy for Jerusalem in the Turkish parliament, made frequent anti-Zionist statements in parliament, but asserted in private that all his declarations and speeches "were nothing but propaganda aimed at Arab public opinion, and they would only make it easier for [him] to help the Jews, as no one would suspect [him] of taking bribes from them."[66] The factual situation was that the Arab representatives were increasingly inclined to view Jewish immigration to and settlement in Palestine as a danger to the Arabs. Nevertheless, feelers were being sent out from both sides, and meetings planned, without, however, a readiness on the part of either of them to commit itself to a binding agreement. This is where matters stood on the eve of World War I.

The war broke out in August, 1914, and three months later Turkey entered it on the side of Germany. In Palestine, both Arabs and Jews suffered from the emergency regulations, forced conscription into the Turkish army, famine, and harsh Turkish measures of repression. On October 1, 1914, Turkey abolished the "capitulations," which had provided protection to the Jews who were not Turkish citizens, and within a year over eleven thousand Jews felt compelled or actually were compelled to leave Palestine. The Turkish stance towards the Arabs who were suspected of separatist aspirations was equally harsh. In 1916, twenty-two leaders of the Arab national movement were hanged in Damascus and Beirut. Hangings took place also in Jerusalem. In April, 1917, when the British launched their offensive in the south of Palestine, all the nine thousand Jewish inhabitants of Tel Aviv-Jaffa were expelled, most of them to the Galilee. As a result of these measures and the hardships the *yishuv* had to face, its numbers were reduced from eighty-five thousand in 1914 to fifty-six thousand in 1918. Both Zionist settlement work and Palestinian Arab national aspirations were forced to lie dormant in the trying war years during which no less than 350,000 persons, or 10 percent of the total population of Syria (which included Lebanon and Palestine), died of starvation.[67]

The issuance on November 2, 1917, of the Balfour Declaration in which Britain undertook to facilitate the establishment of a Jewish national home in Palestine created apprehension among the Palestinian Arabs. Within a year the first Palestinian Arab political organs came into being: The Muslim-Christian Society, the Arab Club, and the Literary Club. In 1919 these societies met in Jerusalem in a countrywide conference, and resolved that Palestine was "Southern Syria," and that the only way to combat Zionism was through unity with Damascus.[68] In March, 1920, when the All-Syrian Congress proclaimed Fayṣal king of United Syria (including Lebanon and Palestine), enthusiastic demonstrations took place in Palestine, and the Nabī Mūsā festival in April of that year became an occasion for anti-Jewish riots. At this juncture, if there were any rising local Palestinian Arab national aspirations, they were given little if any expression.

Simultaneously with these anti-Jewish manifestations, there were also Arab expressions of sympathy with the Jewish endeavors. On March 23, 1918, *al-Qibla*, the official organ of King (formerly Sharīf) Ḥusayn ibn ʿAlī of the Ḥijāz, who had proclaimed in 1916 the Arabian revolt against Turkey, published an article, written by Ḥusayn himself, appealing to the Arabs of Palestine to be hospitable to the Jews, accept them as brothers, and to cooperate with them for the common good.[69] In January, 1919, Ḥusayn's son Fayṣal signed an agreement with Chaim Weizmann, president of the World Zionist Organization, which in effect endorsed the Balfour Declaration. A few weeks later Fayṣal reiterated this endorsement in a letter he wrote on March 1, 1919, to Felix Frankfurter.

In July, 1920, when the Hāshimite regime collapsed in Syria, the Palestinian Arabs turned their attention to their immediate area. In their December 1920 conference they formulated two new resolutions: one contained an absolute rejection of Zionism, and the other the demand of the establishment of a local government in Palestine to be elected by the prewar inhabitants of the country. With these an independent Palestinian Arab nationalism, as distinct from that of Syria or any other Arab country, was born.

The political work of the executive committee elected by the conference consisted of formulating demands, presenting protests, and organizing strikes. It was not as radical as to support the Arab riots of May 1921 which were organized by the remnant of more extremist Arab formations and in which forty-seven Jews were killed in Jaffa and elsewhere. Also in 1921 the Palestinian Muslim Supreme Council was created, and in 1922 Ḥājj Amīn al-Ḥusaynī (who was to become the foremost Palestinian Arab champion of anti-Zionism and later collaborated with Hitler), the newly elected mufti of Jerusalem, became its head. From this time on Palestinian Arab nationalism expressed itself almost exclusively in activities against Zionism and the *yishuv*.

From the 1920s on the leadership of Arab Palestine was disputed between the two most prominent families of Jerusalem, the Ḥusaynīs and the Nashāshībīs. The former was headed by the mufti, the latter by Rāghib Bey Nashāshībī, the mayor of Jerusalem. The sharp rivalry between the two families and their followers weakened the effectiveness of their anti-Zionist activities, and enabled the formation of additional groupings, such as that of the Pan-Arabist Ḥizb al-Istiqlāl ("Independence Party") in 1931, led by members of various families; the Ḥizb al-Iṣlāḥ ("Reform Party"), in 1934, led by Dr. Ḥusayn al-Khālidī, who succeeded in capturing the mayoralty of Jerusalem from the Nashāshībīs; and the Ḥizb al-Kutla al-Waṭaniyya ("National Bloc Party") of Nablus in 1935. The Ḥusaynī and Nashāshībī groups themselves underwent an evolutionary process from traditional-familial to political, and in 1934 the Nashāshībī faction was formally constituted as the Ḥizb al-Difāᶜ al-Waṭanī ("National Defense Party"), while in the following year the Ḥusaynīs followed suit by organizing themselves into the Ḥizb al-ᶜArabī al-Filasṭīnī ("Palestinian Arab Party"). In April 1936 all these parties agreed to unite into the Al-Lajna al-ᶜArabiyya al-ᶜUlyā ("Arab Higher Committee") in order to coordinate their struggle against the British mandatory government and the Jews of Palestine. The dominant personality in the committee was the mufti, Ḥājj Amīn al-Ḥusaynī. The Committee engaged in two types of activities: it organized a country-wide Arab strike, and sponsored Arab mercenary formations to engage in hit-and-run attacks against Jews. An Iraqi contingent, led by German-trained Fawzī Kawukjī, was imported to spearhead these terrorist attacks and to impose a central command upon them. Nevertheless Arab factionalism continued, with the result that many more Arabs than Jews were killed by Arabs. In October, 1936, under British pressure, the Arab Higher Committee agreed to stop the bloodshed, and made Kawukjī and other band leaders leave the country. Nevertheless sporadic attacks continued, and when in the summer of 1937 a British district commissioner was murdered, the mandatory government outlawed the Arab Higher Committee. The mufti thereupon fled abroad, other Arab leaders were exiled, and the Palestinian Arabs were left, in effect, without effective leadership.

The years of World War II were a period of quiescence as far as Palestinian Arab nationalism was concerned. After the war two Arab paramilitary organizations were founded, the Futuwwa ("Manliness"), under Ḥusaynī leadership, and al-Najada ("Valor") sponsored by the Muslim Brotherhood. The two merged in 1946.

Soon after its foundation in 1945 the Arab League began to intervene in Palestinian affairs and to conduct a concentrated anti-Zionist campaign. As the work of the League developed, it overshadowed in significance that of the Palestinian Arab leadership, which lost much of the independent field of activities it had commanded until 1945. Henceforth the Palestinian Arabs were no longer the main representatives of their own cause. It was the Arab League which represented their interests, became their spokesman, fought their political battles for them, and, in effect, told them what to do. At first this appeared to be an advantage: the opponents of the Jews of Palestine and of the World Zionist Organization were no longer the relatively weak Palestinian Arabs, but the much more powerful Arab League with its expanding membership and growing influence. The disadvantages of the situation became clear only after the emergence of the Palestine Liberation Organization (PLO), which claimed to be the sole and independent representative of the Arabs of Palestine, but which, in effect, was buffeted between the major Arab states and became a pawn in their own struggle for position and competition for leadership in the Arab world.

It is easier to agree on something to fight against than on something to work for. Much in modern Arab history has testified to the truth of this observation, but nothing more than the Palestine problem. When the Palestine partition resolution came up for the vote at the United Nations General Assembly, all six Arab member states (Egypt, Iraq, Lebanon, Saudi

Arabia, Syria and Yemen) voted against it because they rejected the allocation of part of Palestine to a Jewish state. But no agreement among them was forthcoming as to what should be the political status of that part of western Palestine that the UN partition plan allocated to a future Arab state. The Arabs were unable to reach an agreement even on such procedural issues as whether or not to testify before the United Nations Special Committee on Palestine (UNSCOP), which was appointed by the UN for the purpose of submitting recommendations as to the solution of the Palestine problem and which held hearings in the summer of 1947. The Arab states did testify, but the Palestinian Arab Higher Committee (which had been reconstituted after the war) boycotted it. When the UN General Assembly passed the partition resolution, the Arab Higher Committee announced its resistance to it and its determination to prevent its implementation by force of arms.

The four Arab neighbors of mandatory Palestine (Syria, Lebanon, Transjordan, and Egypt) concurred, and decided to send armed contingents against whatever force the *yishuv* would be able to muster. From November 29, 1947 (the date of the UN partition resolution) to May 14, 1948 (the date of Israel's declaration of independence) local Palestinian Arab leaders organized armed groups and began to attack the Jews especially on open roads and in isolated settlements, with the help of the Palestine Liberation Army that had been trained outside Palestine and was commanded by the same Fawzī Kawukjī who had had a leading role in the Arab revolt of 1936. In April 1948, by which time the Jews had shown that they could hold their own against such irregulars, the neighboring Arab states began to plan for an attack on Jewish Palestine from all sides, and on May 15 they launched their assault without, however, organizing a unified command. By undertaking the responsibility for eliminating the newborn Jewish state, the Arab states, in effect, further reduced the importance and role of the Palestinian Arab Higher Committee, which was led, in the absence of the mufti, by another member of the Ḥusaynī clan, Jamāl al-Ḥusaynī.

From this time on it could be foreseen that the Arab state in Palestine, provided for in the UN partition resolution, would never come into being. Of the Arab combatant states two, Egypt and Transjordan, succeeded in occupying parts of the territory of mandatory western Palestine, and remained in occupation after cease-fire agreements were reached with Israel. It soon became evident that Transjordan had no intention to deliver into the hands of a future Palestinian Arab government the West Bank in whose possession it found itself, and that the attitude of Egypt was the same with reference to the Gaza Strip. It was likewise clear that no consensus would be forthcoming among the other Arab states concerning these two Arab-held territories. The Arab states never made a concerted effort to establish, or at least declare, a Palestinian Arab state in these areas, which they could have done without at the same time giving up the Arab claim to the rest of western Palestine. True, Egypt did make a halfhearted move by sponsoring a so-called "All-Palestinian Arab Government," which was proclaimed on September 20, 1948, in Gaza under the mufti's leadership, but this step had no practical significance in view of Transjordan's refusal to recognize it. Thus what happened was that the political clock was in effect turned back to premandatory times, and the Arabs of Palestine were again ruled by outsiders. Whatever national ambitions for independence they may have had at the time were simply ignored by the two Arab occupying states, exactly as they were by Israel.

As for Transjordan, its parliament unanimously resolved in December 1948 to "incorporate" the West Bank, which at the time had a resident Arab population of 500,000 plus 465,000 refugees from those parts of Palestine which became the State of Israel. At the same time they also changed the name of their country from Transjordan to the Hashimite Kingdom of Jordan, echoing thereby the old Arab name of the "Jund of Jordan," a territory that also straddled both banks of the Jordan River. The addition of 965,000 persons tripled the kingdom's population, so that from that time on two out of every three persons in the state of Jordan were Palestinians. Although the political committee of the Arab League unanimously condemned Jordan for having taken this step, and Egypt even insisted on expelling her sister kingdom from the League, the British recognition of the annexation laid the issue at rest. However, King Abdallah had to pay with his life for this aggrandizement of his domain: on July 20, 1951, he was assassinated in Jerusalem by henchmen of the mufti.

For two decades (1948–1967) Palestinian Arab nationalism lay dormant. The West Bank was treated by Jordan as a dependency, and so was the Gaza Strip by Egypt. The question of granting independence to these Palestinian Arab areas, which Jordan and Egypt could have done at will anytime, simply did not arise. The Arabs themselves on the West Bank and in Gaza, although chafing under Jordanian and Egyptian rule, did not manifest any initiative that would have attested to an awakening Palestinian

Arab nationalism. As stated in a volume prepared by the Beirut An-Nahar Arab Report Research Staff, with an understandable shift of emphasis,

> Between 1948 and 1967 the world at large forgot about the Palestine cause . . . The areas still under Arab control were not then considered an adequate base for the creation of a Palestinian state. Instead, the West Bank was incorporated into Jordan, while the Gaza Strip remained under Egyptian military rule . . . The Palestinians as such were lost to sight.[70]

What this carefully phrased statement actually means is that under Jordanian and Egyptian rule the Palestinian Arabs did not feel that any effort at independence would be tolerated by Amman and Cairo. This being the situation, any initiative for the revival of Palestinian Arab nationalism had to come from the outside, from those Arab governments that controlled the fate of the West Bank and the Gaza Strip. Looking back at that period, Palestinian Arab leaders themselves have recognized that the idea of "reviving the Palestinian entity" emerged as a result of the wish of Arab leaders outside Palestine, and especially President Nasser, to keep the Palestine problem alive.[71] In September 1963 the Council of the Arab League initiated the setting up of an organization for the "Palestinian people" by declaring that "the time has come for the Palestinian people to take the responsibility for the solution of its problem."[72] It was not until 1964—fully sixteen years after Jordan and Egypt had gained control over those two areas—that the Palestine Liberation Organization and the Palestine Liberation Army were formed, in order "to serve as a Palestinian political entity and to juxtapose the Israeli existence with a Palestinian one,"[73] as stated by Ẓāhir Mukhsan, one of the PLO-Saiqa leaders. Nevertheless, after the formation of the PLO it took another ten years for the Arab states to recognize it as the official spokesman for the Palestinians.

The major catalyst in the emergence of Palestinian Arab nationalism was unquestionably the Six-Day War of 1967, which gave Israel control over both the West Bank and the Gaza Strip. This has been clearly recognized by the leaders of various Palestinian militant organizations. To quote Ẓāhir Mukhsan again, he stated that in consequence of the June 1967 war the PLO "acquired content . . . [and] became a symbol of the resilience of the Palestinian people . . ."[74] After that war, the entire area of what had been western Palestine under the British mandate was in Israeli hands. This new situation meant that the Arabs of the West Bank and Gaza, including refugees from Israel, were, for the first time in twenty years, free to give vent to their nationalistic feelings which they had had to keep carefully under control while they were under Arab rule. The fact is that from 1948 to 1967 all overt and vociferous expressions of Palestinian Arab national ambitions were avoided for fear that the Jordanian and Egyptian authorities would resent such manifestations as separatistic aspirations. Hence even the PLO was satisfied from its foundation until 1967 with terrorist acts against Israel—which were unexceptionable from a Jordanian and Egyptian point of view—and did not claim Palestinian Arab self-determination, but served primarily as a tool in the hands of the Arab rulers.

As two Arab students of the history of the Palestinian resistance put it,

> The defeat of the Arab governments in the 1967 war . . . had two major results: (1) the Palestinians decided they could no longer depend on others [read: the Arab states] to champion their cause, and began to act on their own through the newly formed resistance organizations; and (2) the Arab governments began to talk of the formation of a smaller Palestinian state in the pre-1948 Palestine territory of the West Bank and the Gaza Strip.[75]

It was not until May 1968, almost a year after the Six-Day War, that the Palestinian National Council, meeting in Cairo, drafted a Palestinian National Covenant, which defined the national goals of the Palestinian Arabs. This document, which remains to this day (1984) the charter of the PLO, declared that the Palestinians would struggle for the liberation of all of Palestine, that the whole country belonged to the Palestinians alone, and that only those Jews who had lived in Palestine prior to the beginning of the "Zionist invasion" would be considered Palestinians and allowed to live in liberated Palestine.[76] With that Palestinian Arab nationalism reached its full maturity, and revealed itself, at least in this Covenant, in a most extreme form by proclaiming in effect that its aim was to put an end to the existence of Israel and expel practically its entire Jewish population. At the same time, the Covenant imitates other Arab constitutions by paying lip service to the generally upheld Arab idealistic notion that there is a "Great Arab Homeland" of which Palestine is an integral part, and an "Arab Nation" which includes the Palestinians. In October 1974, at an Arab summit meeting in Rabat, Morocco, the PLO reached the zenith of its political career: the heads of twenty Arab states unanimously recognized the PLO as the sole representative of the Palestinian people.

This is not the place to describe the divisions and stresses within the Palestinian Arab national movement, the constant infighting between its various factions, the rapidly changing political affiliations which pull them or parts of them, once into this, and once into that, Arab camp, and the shifting of their center of gravity from one Arab state to another. With all these tensions and vacillations, Palestinian Arab nationalism, as distinct from the nationalisms of the Arab states surrounding Israel, is today a factor that both Israel and the Arab states must reckon with.

In the early 1980s the Arabs of Palestine continued to suffer from the shortcomings that had plagued them ever since the end of Turkish rule: lack of unity, lack of leaders of stature with a capacity to rally the whole population, and lack of agreement on what to work for rather than on what to fight against. Despite the Rabat resolution, the PLO was splintered and weakened. King Hussein, the PLO leadership, the Arabs in the Israeli-occupied territories, and all the Arab states agreed that they were against Israel, that they wanted Israel to give up Gaza and the West Bank, and even more (if not all) of her present area. But what was to happen with the Palestinian territories if and when they were liberated? On this crucial issue the interested Arab parties were sharply divided. King Hussein wanted them to be returned under Jordanian rule. The PLO wanted to make them into an independent Palestinian state from which to continue its fight against Israel. What the Palestinians themselves wanted was unknown. In all probability there was no uniform opinion among them, and certainly no Arab authority (or Israel, for that matter) had ever asked them, or had even tried to set up an apparatus for ascertaining their views.

It was pointed out by historians and students of Arab affairs that the Arabs of Palestine in the 1980s were a people in a diaspora, similar in certain respects to the Jewish diaspora prior to the establishment of the State of Israel. This situation had two tragic aspects. One was that in re-acquiring their old homeland, the Jews, willy-nilly, caused the exile and dispersion of a major part of the Palestinian Arab population, which until 1948 had been the majority in western Palestine. The other was that unless she was willing to commit political suicide, Israel could not agree to admitting large numbers of Arabs whom events had turned into refugees (or, rather, as the years wore on, their children and grandchildren), nor to reducing her boundaries to the indefensible territorial configuration that had been hers until the 1967 war.

THE ARABS IN ISRAEL

The Arabs in general had long been used to living under foreign rule. Until the end of World War I most Arab countries were dominated by the

Ottoman Turks, and a few by France and England; thereafter, until the end of World War II, all Arab countries, with the exception of Saudi Arabia and Yemen, were ruled by the three European colonial powers of England, France, and Italy. But, despite the foreign rule, the Arabs in each of their countries constituted the majority population (this held good even for the North African countries with their very large Berber contingents), lived in an essentially Arab society, had their own Arabic schools, and were (at least most of them) the carriers of traditional Arab culture, and the proud followers of what they regarded the only true religion, Islam. In Israel, in 1948, the Arabs almost overnight became a minority in a country in which for many centuries they had been the overwhelming majority even though they did not enjoy self-rule. As far as population, society, and culture were concerned, Palestine until the establishment of Israel, and certainly until the large-scale Zionist immigration in the interwar period, was as much an Arab country as were Syria, Iraq, or Egypt.

With the independence of Israel this had suddenly changed. And not only did the Arabs become a minority in the land which they believed and felt to be their country, but right away there began a process of penetration of non-Arab influences the like of which neither they, nor Arabs in any other country, had ever before experienced. Elementary education was made compulsory under Israeli law, and although the language of tuition remained Arabic in the Arab schools, one of the subjects all Arab children had to take was Hebrew language. Then, before long, more and more Israeli Arabs found employment in the Jewish sector of the economy, more and more commuted daily to nearby Jewish cities, towns, and villages, where they earned much more than they could in their own economic sector, and in these circumstances a working knowledge of Hebrew, easily acquired inasmuch as it is linguistically similar to Arabic, proved an advantage.

Every improvement in their living standard tied the Arabs more and more to the economy of Jewish Israel, and brought them closer to its society and culture. Arab towns and villages were supplied by Jewish companies with water and electricity. The Israeli radio and television broadcasted Arabic programs which presented an Israeli perspective, and showed what was done in Israel in general, and what Israel did for its Arabs in particular, in a favorable light. Most trying for the self-esteem of the Muslim majority among the Israeli Arabs was the fact that even their religious institutions, such as the mosques and the *sharīʿa* (religious) courts, could continue to function only by sufferance of the Israeli, that is, Jewish, government authority. In brief, although in no segment of Israeli Arab society had things reached a stage even in the 1980s where one could speak of the onset of Arab deculturation, that is, a decline of their traditional Arab culture, it soon became clear that what was happening was that the Israeli Arabs were rapidly becoming bicultural: while retaining their traditional Arab culture, they acquired more and more of the modern Israeli-Hebrew culture. At the time of this writing (1985), this process is still in full swing.

Much has been written in recent years about the Arabs in Israel. Books, monographs, and articles abound about the problems the Arabs of Israel represent for the country at present, and will represent in the future, when, due to their very high natural increase, they will constitute an increasing percentage of the total population; about the ongoing improvements in their condition as a result of the steady extension of Israeli health, educational, and social services to the Arab sector; about the rapid process of their political emancipation which by 1985 had made them the politically freest, most conscious, and most active Arab population in any country of the Middle East; about their either planned or spontaneous, but in any case rapidly intensifying, participation in the Israeli economy as a result of which their standard of living rose above that of the Arabs in the neighboring countries. The numerous studies on these and similar subjects have also made the Israeli Arabs by far the most-researched and best-known Arab population of any country.

Yet with all these studies analyzing and interpreting the Israeli Arabs, the picture one gets of them is an incomplete one. What it means for Israel to have a sizable and rapidly growing Arab population is well enough known. What it means for the Arabs to constitute a sizable and rapidly growing population in a Jewish state is known much less well. When it comes to analyzing and interpreting their own reaction to living as a religious, national, linguistic, and ethnic minority in a state which is neither Muslim nor Arab, the Arabs of Israel in the first half of the 1980s still formed a rather inarticulate community. Despite the example of several Arab universities and colleges in the West Bank, whose population in general was less educated than the Israeli Arabs, the latter have not yet founded a single institution of higher learning of their own, but instead attended in growing numbers Jewish universities in Israel, and other schools in Arab and non-Arab countries.[77] Moreover, although Israeli Arab intellectuals have begun to turn to such fields as the social sciences, and are certainly acquainted with the writings of Israeli Jewish sociologists and anthropologists on the Israeli Arabs (much of which is published in English), they have not yet begun to produce significant studies of their own which would throw light on, by telling the inside story of, the Israeli Arabs' perception of Israeli society and culture, and their own place in them. The absence of such studies makes an understanding of the Israeli Arab position more difficult for both themselves and outsiders.

The few studies of their condition in Israel undertaken by Israeli Arabs tend to be political tracts. In the past, too, political writing used to be one of the most frequently employed genre by Palestinian Arab writers.[78] Their new political studies are, as a rule, strongly critical of the Israeli government and its treatment of the Arabs. An example is the book *The Arabs in Israel*, written by Sabri Jiryis, a Palestinian Christian Arab, a graduate of the Law School of the Hebrew University of Jerusalem, who was the legal representative of the Palestinian Arab al-Arḍ ("The Land") movement,[79] and was an Israeli citizen until he emigrated to Lebanon. His book was first published in Hebrew in Haifa, in 1966, then in Arabic translation, and in 1968 in English as one of the monograph series of the Institute for Palestine Studies in Beirut, Lebanon. While Jiryis does not deny that "desirable developments" have taken place in the life of the Arabs in Israel, he argues that Israel's claims concerning these developments are exaggerated, and that in certain fields they took place "in spite of the negative attitude of the [Israeli] authorities." He finds that a "comparison between the services provided by the government to Arabs and Jews shows how great the discrimination has been" against the former. His conclusion is that the domestic policy of Israel towards the Arabs living in the country is one of "racial discrimination and repression," and that it is "a failure" as a direct result of Israel's faulty management, of its negative attitude, and "of the destructive activities of its rulers."[80] In toto, the book is a sharp attack on the Israeli government, and the Israeli Jewish Arabist Ori Stendel found that it "is made up of bitter calumnies against the government of Israel, facts related out of context, and blatant falsehood."[81] One may add that the very fact that such a book could be published and circulated in Israel seems to indicate that the "repression" of the Arabs of which it complains did not include a denial of freedom of expression.

However, it is not only Arab spokesmen and political authors who consider the condition of the Israeli Arabs unsatisfactory and accuse the Israeli government of discrimination against the Arab minority in the country. Some Israeli Jewish social scientists agree, at least partly, with these claims. Among them is Henry Rosenfeld, an anthropologist at Haifa University, who considers justified the Israeli Arabs' complaint that they are discriminated against, and refers in this connection to such governmental actions as the large-scale confiscation of land owned by legal Arab residents.[82] He also finds that "the conceptualization of the level of social development of the Arabs in ethnic terms . . . did not express acknowledgment of different and equal (Jewish and Arab) cultures, but of superior and inferior national groups with qualitatively different cultures. This could be accommodated to a policy of controls, justified Jewish patronage, political manipulations, supervision of living, hierarchical relations in government offices, and so forth." Translated into simpler English, what Rosenfeld says is that the Arabs and their culture are regarded by the Jews of Israel as inferior, and that this view serves as justification of governmental control and manipulation of the Arabs. Rosenfeld also argues that national discrimination and class limitations were factors in the politicization of the Arab minority in Israel, and that "discrimination against the Arabs is expressed in national categories and concepts . . ." As for the Arab reaction to this situation, Rosenfeld observes that it "is not in the direction of intensifying contradictions or of direct confrontation (along the 'tragic' lines of 'an irreconcilable conflict between two national entities') but rather aims at political, economic, and national equality, that is, of closing of gaps in the social framework of the existing state."[83]

Despite such controversies, there are some hard facts about which there can be no disagreement. To begin with, statistical data about the standard of living of the Israeli Arabs show that by the 1980s, although it has not yet reached the level of the Israeli Jews, it had risen above that of the Arabs in the neighboring countries. The average Israeli Arab had a higher income, consumed a better and more balanced diet, enjoyed better housing, was better clothed, used more appliances, and benefitted from better health and medical services than his fellow Arabs across the border. Most importantly, the Israeli Arabs had a lower infant, child, and general mortality, a higher life expectancy, and a higher natural increase than the Arabs in other countries. Their average natural increase between 1950 and 1975 was 4 percent annually—higher than that of any Arab country. As a result, the number of the Israeli Arabs (including the Druze) increased from 173,400 (11 percent of the total population) in 1951, to 575,900 (15.8 percent of the total) in

1975, and 712,500 (17.4 percent of the total) in 1983.[84] If the 4 percent annual Arab natural increase continues, the Arab population of Israel will double in seventeen years.

The statistics show similar improvements in the field of education. The reduction of the traditional Arab illiteracy has proceeded at a much faster rate in Israel than in the neighboring Arab countries, due to the strict enforcement of the law of general and compulsory elementary education. In 1954 34 percent of the Arab men and 79 percent of the Arab women in Israel were illiterate; by 1975 the rate for men was reduced to 10 percent, and that for women to 36 percent.[85] The still relatively high illiteracy of Arab women is an indication, not so much of the residual reluctance among the Muslims to send their daughters to school as of the survival of members of the old generation of women in which illiteracy was widespread. These literacy rates are much higher than those of the Arab countries. Even in Lebanon which, with its large Christian Arab population is by far the best-educated Arab country, the male illiteracy rate in 1970 was 21.5 percent and the female 42.1 percent.[86]

As indicated above, the spread of literacy among the Israeli Arabs is accompanied by an increase in the knowledge of Hebrew, and by one more, powerfully acculturative, process: the growing employment of Arabs in the Jewish sector of the economy. These, again, are statistically established facts. Outside the realm of statistics, but well within the scope of observable phenomena, lies the reaction of the Israeli Arabs to their "Israelization." One of the few studies on this subject was done by Mark A. Tessler, who conducted field work among the Arabs in Israel in 1974. Tessler terms the Israeli Arabs a "non-assimilating" minority, and finds that there is an "unnarrowed cultural distance" between Arabs and Jews in Israel. This conclusion, based on interviews with 348 Israeli Arabs, is puzzling, inasmuch as the data Tessler adduces show an inconsistency, in fact, an ambivalence, in the Israeli Arabs' attitude to the State of Israel and its dominant Hebrew-Jewish culture. Some of the responses manifest antagonism, while others indicate a definite trend toward rapprochement with Jewish Israel. On the one hand, only 23 percent of the interviewees said that they feel more comfortable in Israel than they would in an Arab or Palestinian state (30 percent said it made no difference), and 55 percent considered Israel's creation in 1948 to have been illegal. On the other, 53 percent stated that the term "Israeli" described them "very well" or "fairly well," and 40 percent said that they felt closer to Jews in Israel than to Arabs in distant lands such as Algeria or Morocco. The Arab cultural rapprochement to Jewish Israel was expressed in such responses as the rejection by 50 percent of the proposal that it was unacceptable for a married woman to go out socially in public if her husband was not with her, and by the fact that most of the respondents selected Hebrew radio and television programs as often as they did programs in Arabic. It seems especially significant that 55 percent felt that it was important for their children to study the history of Judaism, that 65 percent felt the same about studying the history of Zionism, and that 78 percent said they would not object if their children attended a Jewish high school. In view of these findings Tessler observes that "the rejection by many Israeli Arabs of some aspects of traditional Arab culture is unmistakable, suggesting that the distance between Jews and Arabs in Israel is reduced in some areas." Nevertheless he concludes that "no plausible outcome of the struggle among [the] cultural and religious factions would bring about a situation in which non-Jews can share fully the mission of the state." The data presented do not seem to justify this conclusion.[87]

The trend towards the reduction of the cultural and socioeconomic distance between the Israeli Arabs and the Jewish majority suffices to produce in the mind of concerned Arab political and cultural leaders serious fears that it might lead in the course of time to a loss of the Palestinian Arab culture which differed only slightly from that of the Arabs of neighboring Lebanon, Syria, and Jordan. Such fears might lead to a serious dissatisfaction with the situation in which the Israeli Arabs find themselves, and this despite all the unquestionable material advantages life in Israel has for the Arabs as against life in those neighboring countries.

These cultural apprehensions are aggravated by psychological circumstances. The foregoing discussions in this book have amply shown that a) the Arabs have been conditioned by their religion, tradition, and history to have an especially disdainful attitude to the Jews whom for many centuries they had only known as *dhimmīs*; b) never in the course of their history in the far-flung countries inhabited by them had Arabs ever had the experience of living under Jewish rule; and c) although many Arabs are still unfamiliar with their own history, whatever knowledge they do have of the Koran and of Islam is enough to inculcate them with the feeling that a situation in which Jews rule over Arabs is anomalous, is against the will of Allah as revealed to the Prophet Muhammad, and simply must not be tolerated. If this conviction has so far not led to stronger manifestations of Arab resistance to Israeli rule than it had in the course of the last several decades, the reason for this lies in the fact that the Arabs are also pragmatists, and, if not in thought and word, certainly in action, have always recognized and accepted the limitations of the possible.

The absence of action, however, does not mean lack of desire to act. Given an opportunity, such as they did not have in 1956, 1967, and 1973, one can expect that most Israeli Arabs will, in the event of a renewed Arab-Israeli conflict, side with their Arab brethren rather than with Israel. One can also add that the basic unreadiness to reconcile themselves to life under Israeli rule was in the 1980s still a part of the Israeli Arab mentality. One could foresee that whatever further improvements would be made by Israel in the material aspects of the life of the Israeli Arabs would in themselves scarcely affect it. Such improvement should be made by all means, parallel with improvements in the standard of living of the population in general, and even over and above them, so as to reduce as rapidly as possible the still existing gap between the Jews and the Arabs. This is a necessary, but by no means sufficient, condition of the diminution of Arab resentment at having to live under Jewish rule. But, as far as the ultimate elimination of that resentment is concerned, it would seem that only internal psychocultural developments in the Israeli Arab population itself will be able to bring it about. Concretely, what I mean is that first the Israeli Arabs will have to absorb enough of the Israeli-Hebrew culture and values to erase from their psyche the age-old Arab contempt for the Jewish *dhimmī*s. This is not something that can be imposed upon the Arabs from the outside by legislative or administrative measures. It can come about only gradually as a result of the de facto symbiosis of Arabs and Jews, of the daily contact between the two communities, and of the growing recognition among the Arabs that Israel is a democratic society in whose life they can have a fair share despite all the historical differences between them and the Jews.

One important factor which militates against the "Israelization" of the Israeli Arabs remains to be mentioned. It is their growing radicalization which is the outcome of the contact with the West Bank Arabs made possible by the 1967 occupation of the West Bank and Gaza by Israel, and of the increase in Arab self-assurance following the 1973 Yom Kippur War. Among the West Bank Arabs themselves the 1973 events brought about a profound political-ideological radicalization, a weakening of the old, traditional leadership, the emergence of new, young counter-elites, and a strengthening of their support of the PLO.[88] Among the Israeli Arabs there was only an echo of these developments, which was weak compared to their force in the West Bank, but strong enough to demonstrate anew to the Israeli government that the process of integration of the Arabs into the Israeli nation was still fraught with problems and difficulties.

Nevertheless, the "Israelization" of the Arabs of Israel, which has already begun to take place, can be expected to continue. It can also be foreseen that it will duplicate, but in a reverse direction, the "biblicalization" of the pagan Arab world that was brought about by the genius of Muhammad. Muhammad, by appropriating the great ancestor figure of Abraham, other key biblical characters, and numerous biblical tenets, transformed, once and for all, the Arab world, and created a new Arab version of the by-then old Hebrew monotheism. The Israeli Arabs, by acquiring modern Hebrew Israeli culture, are thereby transforming themselves before our very eyes into a radically new coinage in the Arab world: into an Arab people whose cultural physiognomy will have two sides, an Arab and a Hebrew. The reversal of the direction in modern Israel as against what took place in classical Arabia can be expected to be due to the radical differences in the Arab experience in the two periods. Muhammad's attitude to the Children of Israel proceeded from an initial respect and admiration for them as the heirs of biblical revelation and shifted to increasing resentment over their rejection of him as a prophet of God and of his teachings as the completion of the revelation God had made to Abraham. The present-day Israeli Arabs' attitude to contemporary Israel has no choice but proceeds in the opposite direction: from the traditional Arab contempt for the Jewish *dhimmīs* to a respect for the people of Israel which will inevitably develop as a by-product of the growing Arab familiarity with, and understanding of, the nonmaterial aspects of Israeli-Hebrew culture. One can hardly maintain a contemptuous attitude to a people whose culture one has absorbed and values internalized. Herein, I believe, lies the key to the "Israelization" of the Israeli Arabs: in the realm of culture and values, and beyond them, in the common Abrahamic substratum of the proto-historic traditions of both peoples. The more the Israeli Arabs become part of Israeli life, and the more Israel becomes part of the life of the Arabs who live within her boundaries, the more they will be able to liberate themselves from that particular feature in their religious tradition that at present still renders it an indignity for them to live under Jewish-Israeli rule.

Once this comes about—and it *can* come about without unduly impinging on the many valuable aspects of Muslim-Arab culture—the Arabs of Israel will be able to reach a positive reassessment of their position as fully equal partners in the democratic and liberal State of Israel, and to consider themselves Israeli Arabs in the same full sense as the Arabs in America consider themselves American Arabs.

I am confident that such a development is bound to take place in the not too distant future. In the meantime, all we can do is to work for, hope for, and pray for peace among the Seed of Abraham.

10

Summation and Conclusion

Having reached the end of our rapid journey through thirteen centuries of Arab-Jewish relations, I want to wind up with a summation and some additional conclusions.

The Arab attitude to the Jews crystallized in the Medinan period of Muhammad's life. It was in Medina that he completed the appropriation of the Jewish myth of origin, and made Abraham the forerunner of Islam, the founder of the sanctuary in Mecca, and the father of the Arabs. He also adopted and adapted major features of the Jewish religious ritual, and several biblical and Midrashic stories. Convinced that by reshaping it he brought to completion the old Jewish biblical religion when the Jews of Medina refused to acknowlege him as the "seal of the prophets," in fact, as any kind of a prophet at all, he turned resolutely against them. As a source of spiritual tradition, he felt, he had exhausted them. As a reservoir of likely converts they proved a disappointment. They opposed him, and he became their bitter enemy. He developed the thesis that the Jews maliciously falsified their own Scripture, and were, even in antiquity, an evil, rebellious people upon whom God visited severe punishment because of their sins. These having been their antecedents, the Jews deserved nothing but abasement and humiliation, and were expected to be grateful that the Muslims allowed them at all to live in the House of Islam.

In the first several centuries after Muhammad, as Muslim scholarship and legalism developed, the rules of conduct the Jews had to obey were laid down in meticulous detail and increasing severity. Yet at the same time also internal Muslim processes of differentiation began: the one *dīn*, religion, of Muhammad branched out into the major sects of the Shīʿites and Sunnites, and, among the latter four different *madhhab*s, schools of jurisprudence, arose. With these developments, and even more so with the break-up of the united caliphate into several separate Arab kingdoms, the Muslim attitude toward the Jews also underwent a fragmentation. In some countries and in certain sects there developed a softer, in others a harsher, attitude toward, and treatment of, the Jews. In some places and periods the restrictions imposed upon the Jews and codified in the so-called "Covenant of ʿUmar," were strictly enforced by the authorities, in others often largely disregarded. Where the liberal point of view prevailed, not only was the position of the Jews generally better, but some Jews could and did rise to highest office in the royal courts.

While the *ʿulamāʾ* in general either remained ignorant of or were reluctant to acknowledge the debt their religion owed the Jews for what Western scholars called "the Jewish foundations of Islam," that debt was amply repaid by the Arabs during the great efflorescence of their culture in the early Middle Ages. There can be no doubt but that the parallel flowering of Arab and Jewish cultures in Syria, Iraq, Egypt, Morocco, and Spain owed more to Arab than to Jewish initiative. This is shown, among other things, by the fact that in all lines of cultural endeavor there always was a time lag between the onset of the upward curve among the Arabs and the start of the same trend among the Jews. But once they followed in the footsteps of the Arab grammarians, exegetes, philosophers, poets, doctors, and scientists, the Jews excelled in all these fields to no lesser a degree than the Arabs, and in some, such as translation and cartography, even eclipsed them.

By the time the decline in medieval Arab culture set in, the Jews had established a foothold in Europe, and thus were able to shift their center of gravity from the Arab East to the Christian West. The most obvious manifestation of this shifting was the increase in numbers of the Ashkenazi division of the Jewish people as against that Jewish contingent that lived in Arab (and other Muslim) lands, and which, until about 1000 C.E., constituted the majority of the Jewish people. Simultaneously, the cultural élan passed from the Sephardi and Oriental Jews to the Ashkenazim, with the result that when the Arab countries eventually entered their period of cultural stagnation, the Sephardi and Oriental Jews—who, incidentally, lagged behind the Arabs in the onset of their cultural decline just as they were tardy in the beginning of their cultural rise—were able to pass the torch to their Ashkenazi brethren, while the Arabs had no like recourse.

Before all that happened, however, the Jews in Arab lands had produced a huge literature in Arabic (in most cases using the Hebrew alphabet, which, with some slight additions, was totally suitable to reproduce the

Arabic script), compared to which what they wrote in Hebrew and Aramaic, their own two old languages, was relatively meager. Reading, or even merely surveying, the literary production of the Jews in Arabic, one wonders how a people living under conditions of *dhilla*, humiliation, could have developed such an intensive and rich cultural activity. The explanation seems to lie in the fact that the humiliation often remained merely a Muslim religious requirement that in the reality of joint Arab-Jewish life was disregarded. A complementary explanation is that even in those places and times where and when the humiliation of the Jews was actually insisted upon by their Arab overlords, the specific psychological responses developed by the Jews as defense mechanisms, or rather means of survival, enabled them to seek and find refuge in religious, scholarly, and other intellectual endeavors even in the midst of the most trying circumstances. Since the Arab cultural environment was one in which intellectual activity was highly valued, the Jewish scholarly output did not remain unknown to their Arab contemporaries. To be aware, though, did not necessarily mean to be appreciative, and, in fact, we find that the Arab savants' views of their Jewish colleagues (and of the Jews and Jewish religion in general) ranged from the virulently antagonistic exemplified by Ibn Ḥazm to the emphatically sympathetic as illustrated by Ṣaᶜid al-Andalusī.

While no similarly sharp contrasts can be found between the treatment meted out to Jews in one Arab country and another, there were considerable differences in the overall attitudes of the Arab potentates and populations to their Jewish *dhimmīs*. Yemen can be considered as a country in which humiliation was a permanent, unchanging, and dominant element in both the popular and official Arab attitude to the Jews. Although even there, as we know from documents published by Professor Ratzhabi, the Jews could apply to the country's legal authorities to obtain redress if they felt they had suffered wrongs beyond the customary "abasement and humiliation." In comparison with Yemen, in Morocco there were great temporal and local variations of the Jewish condition, ranging, or even rapidly swinging, from murderous attacks to friendship and mutual help.

The commonality between the Arabs and the Jews was most conspicuously expressed in folk religion. Most of the component elements of this great and all-pervasive cultural complex were shared by members of both communities. Both believed in, and resorted to prophylactic measures against, the jinn, the evil eye, and defilement, and both venerated saints, frequently the very same saints, and knew many tales about the cures they had performed and the miracles they had wrought. Whether there was any positive correlation between the commonality of Arab-Jewish folk culture and the attitude of the Arab majority to the Jewish minority, is one of those highly worthwhile issues which still await investigation.

A sharp contrast to the general Arab-Jewish commonality of folk religion is represented by the attitudes of the two communities to the feminine in the divine. Although the Hebrew term *Shekhina* was taken over by Muhammad and Islam from Judaism in the Arabicized form of *Sakīna*, the Jewish mystical-mythical concept of the Shekhina as the feminine aspect of God, and—as it developed in Kabbalism—the feminine counterpart of the masculine deity, has remained excluded from both official Islam and Muslim-Arab folk religion. In official Islam, as represented in the *ḥadīth*, in Koran exegesis, in the *sharīʿa*, and in religious philosophy, Allah is a purely spiritual being, genderless, and without any human-like attributes. In popular Islam He is a sublime father figure, conceived, rather vaguely, in a male image. In both official and popular Islam the divine entourage of the angels is likewise imagined as a male company. Only such subordinated figures as the houris of paradise are conceived of as females, and so are some of the jinn whose extrahuman world duplicates that of man in being composed of males and females, as well as of Muslims, Jews, Christians, and pagans. Even Ṣūfism, the great and influential mystical development in Islam, although the love relationship between man and god plays a central role in it, does not allow of any sexual aspect in its mystical gestalt of the deity.

The total absence of the feminine from the divine realm has its counterpart in the Muslim exclusion of women from most of the important officially prescribed religious observances. This, in turn, created among Muslim women a religious vacuum that was filled by popular beliefs and rituals, such as those centering upon the *zār* exorcisms, the sum total of which amounts to a veritable women's religion, frowned upon but nevertheless tolerated by the *ʿulamā'*.

In Jewish mysticism, whose main development took place in a Muslim Arab environment or on its peripheries, the feminine aspect of the divinity came to play a central role. In Moses de Leon's *Zohar* and in the teachings of the sixteenth-century Safed Kabbalists, despite their mystical-speculative nature, the Shekhina (or Matronit) came dangerously close to an image of a feminine deity, distinct from, and occasionally even contraposed to, God, the masculine divine king. The religious life of the Jews in Arab lands (as well as of the Kabbalistically influenced Ashkenazim in Europe) was punctuated by endlessly repeated short prayers, the so-called *kawwanot*, or sacred "intentions," aimed at bringing about the unification of God the King and the Shekhina who had suffered a tragic separation when the Jerusalem Temple was destroyed. Sexual intercourse between man and wife was given special sanctity in the requirement that it be performed with the *kawwana* of achieving, or at least aiding, that great cosmic-spiritual purpose. These aspects of rabbinically sanctioned popular Judaism assured woman an important place in religious life, over and above the formal requirement that she perform numerous *mitzvot*, religious commandments, and rites. This having been the case, the Jewish woman experienced nothing comparable to the Muslim woman's craving for religious satisfaction, and, consequently, no special women's religion ever developed in Judaism as it did in Islam.

An overarching social outcome of these dissimilarities between Islam and Judaism with respect of the feminine in the divine and the participation of women in the official religious practice was the difference between the position of women in Arab and in Jewish society. Among the Arabs, just as the feminine was excluded from the divine realm, so women were excluded and segregated from the society of men. Among the Jews, who accorded a role to the feminine in the divinity, women were given a place in social life. Although the Jews could not avoid being influenced by the Arabs with regard to their treatment of the women—just as they could not prevent many other Arab cultural influences from penetrating the *mellāḥ*—nevertheless the segregation of women and their relegation to an inferior position never reached the same degree among the Jews as among the Arabs. This variance gave the *mellāḥ* a different social tone from that of the *medīna*. It also enabled both the Jewish women and their menfolk to respond more readily to modernization than their Arab counterparts, once they came into contact with the Western world.

Westernization brought about also a change in the Arabs' attitude to the Jews. The age-old view of the *dhimmīs* as weak, defenseless, and hence contemptible people had to be modified in the light of the Westerners' more positive attitude to the Jews, and the increasing evidence of Jewish influence, and what the Arabs perceived as Jewish power, in Europe. Such evidence began to reach the Arab world in the nineteenth century. After being kept in subjection by Islam for thirteen centuries, the Jew became within a few decades metamorphosed into a figure seen as a threat to the Arabs. This sinister, powerful, and malicious Jew was presented to the Arab world in the shape of the conspiratorial "Elders of Zion" whose "Protocols," made available in Arabic, had a frightening impact, and contributed materially to transforming the traditional Arab disdain for the humble *dhimmī* into a hatred of the menacing Jew.

This new Arab attitude to the Jews came to a point in the Palestine issue. As the Jews began to immigrate to Palestine, as they obtained international recognition of their claim to their ancient homeland, and, finally, as they received the UN's approval for setting up a state of their own in Palestine, hatred of the Jews gained added justification in the eyes of the Arabs, and hardened into the resolve to eject the Jewish state from their midst, just as their ancestors got rid of the Crusaders several centuries earlier. At the same time, the establishment of Israel and especially her victories over the Arabs became the catalyst for the emergence of a Palestinian Arab nationalism, one of whose aims was to put an end to Israel's existence.

As long as Israel won military victories, the Arabs' indignation, consternation, and dismay over the anomaly of a *dhimmī*-turned-menace defeating them were so intense that they felt it was simply impossible for them to sit down with Israel to talk peace. When Egypt gained an initial victory in the Yom Kippur War with her surprise attack, which, as President Herzog of Israel put it, was an "outstanding Arab military success,"[1] Egyptian President Sadat felt that now it was possible to face Israel across the negotiating table as one would any other adversary after the clamor of battle had subsided. Those successes of the first few days of the war not only redeemed Egypt and restored Arab honor, but transformed Israel in her eyes from the embodiment of sinister evil, to an enemy with whom one can seek an understanding without dishonoring oneself. Hence, psychologically, the road was opened to the Camp David agreement, although, understandably, much external persuasion was also needed before negotiations could begin.

The events triggered directly or indirectly by the foundation of Israel have transformed the Arab world dramatically. On the one hand, the Arabs have learned to use the oil weapon, and several oil-producing Arab countries have since 1973 accumulated unimagined wealth that they have used to inaugurate a great process of technological development. On the other, for the first time in their history of thirteen centuries the Arabs have no Jews, or almost none, living among them. By the 1970s, only in four Arab countries did the number of the remaining Jews exceed one thousand. At present the position of the Jews in those four countries varies greatly. In Morocco (seventeen thousand Jews in 1982) their position is satisfactory. Whenever it appears necessary, they are provided police protection to prevent mob action against them. They are free to leave the country if they wish to, and their continued voluntary sojourn has been used by King Ḥasan as an argument in his attempts—motivated no doubt by his recognition of the usefulness of the Jews for the country—to persuade those Jews who had left to return, offering them also various inducements. So far this royal generosity evoked only a feeble response among the Moroccan Jews either in France or in Israel. In Syria (four thousand Jews in 1982) the Jews would like to leave but are not permitted to. They are, in effect, hostages of the government, and are constrained (or feel constrained, which amounts to almost the same thing) to make occasionally public declarations of their loyalty to Syria and of their opposition to Israel. Syria's prohibition of Jewish emigration is comparable to that of the Soviet Union, but at least it has the appearance of a more rational motivation: inasmuch as it is officially at war with Israel, Syria can claim that it does not allow the emigration of its Jews since they might go to Israel and strengthen the hand of her enemy. In Tunisia (thirty-seven hundred Jews in 1982) the position of the Jews is much worse than in Morocco, but better than in Syria. The young Tunisians generally manifest a harsher attitude toward the Jews than their elders. As a curiosity it may be mentioned that the Tunisian government encourages the colorful LaG baᶜOmer celebrations on the Island of Jerba because they are a tourist attraction. As to the situation of the Jews in Yemen (twelve hundred in 1982), no information is available.[2]

Apart from these few exceptions, the Arab world in the second half of the twentieth century has become practically *Judenrein*, as a result of the emigration of close to eight hundred thousand Jews after 1948. The subjoined table gives a country-by-country numerical breakdown of this great new Jewish exodus from the Arab Middle East.

Estimated Number of Jews in the Arab Countries in 1948 and 1982

Country	1948	1982	Decrease
Morocco	286,000	17,000	269,000
Algeria	140,000	300	139,700
Tunisia	71,000	3,700	67,300
Libya	35,000	—	35,000
Egypt	75,000	200	74,800
Iraq	125,000	200	124,800
Syria-Lebanon	20,000	4,250	15,750
Yemen-Aden	53,000	1,200	51,000
Total	805,000	26,850	778,150

Sources: *American Jewish Year Book for 1948–49 and 1984*; *Encyclopaedia Judaica*, s.v. Iraq, 8:1149.

Thus for the first time since the days of Muhammad and the great Arab conquests of the Near East and North Africa, the Arabs have no ubiquitous *dhimmīs*. The presence of the Jews which, as I put it earlier in this book, served as a leaven in Arab society and culture, has come to an end. What will be the consequences of this new situation for Arab culture cannot be gauged, nor even guessed at this stage.

In the meantime, however, a much more potent leaven, or, rather, irritant, has been implanted into the very midst of the Arab world in the form of the new Jewish state. We have seen in chapter 9 the vehement Arab reactions to this development, and the stimulant it provided for the emergence of a Palestinian Arab nationalism. For the Arab world as a whole, the existence of Israel and the desire to destroy, or at least weaken, the "Zionist entity" came to serve as the impetus for a number of developments whose impact has been felt in the last two decades in a major part of the world, and especially in the Western world, but whose ultimate significance still lies in the future. Without the outrage they felt at their repeated defeat by Israel and the aid certain Western countries rendered the Jewish state in her life-and-death struggle with them, the Arabs may never have had the temerity to resort to the oil weapon, and would not have accumulated untold wealth. Without their newly won riches they would not have been able to acquire huge arsenals of modern weapons. Without the inflow of oil money Saudi Arabia and the Gulf states would not have undergone their astounding technological modernization, could not have built their new cities and new industries, and would not have become important factors in the world's financial markets. Likewise, without these developments the Arab states would have had neither the thrust nor the means to embark upon the large-scale educational efforts which are at present laying the foundations for a future Arab cultural renaissance. One is therefore justified in observing that the Jews, removed from the Arab lands and concentrated in Israel, together with their Ashkenazi brethren who had come from Europe, proved even more of a leaven for the Arab world than they had been while living as protected and despised *dhimmīs* in each and every corner of the House of Islam.

The struggle between Israel and the Arabs, which has by now been going on for close to four decades, gave rise to a hatred of Israel and Zionism which has become an institutionalized feature in the ideology, the attitude, and the phraseology of the leadership of most Arab states, and the media utilized by them. This has gone so far that any enemy, even an opposing

Arab or Muslim country, is almost automatically designated as "Zionist." After the Muslim Brotherhood's attack on the Aleppo Artillery Academy on June 16, 1979, in which thirty-two cadets were killed and fifty-four wounded, the Damascus monthly *Flash of Syria* quoted Brig. Adnan Dabbagh, the Syrian Interior Minister, as having stated in a television address that "the criminals were acting as agents of American imperialism and Zionism," and that "this criminal act serves only 'Israel' and the enemies of the Arab nation."[3] Among the more recent examples of this absurd identification are the mutual accusations of Iraq and Iran to the effect that the opponent is aided and abetted by, and serves the interests of, "Zionism." It almost appears as if those who claim to speak for the Arab countries were caught in some kind of Orwellian syndrome, in which a daily two-minute "hate Israel" period has become a psychological must. When viewed against this disheartening background, the Egyptian-Israel peace agreement signified as great a psychological breakaway for Egypt as it was a political milestone for Israel.

The establishment of Israel was the greatest historical watershed of all times in Jewish-Arab relations. It made the almost complete evacuation of the Arab lands by the Jews both possible, and, in the event, inevitable. It brought within a few years some 670,000 Jews into Israel from Arab and other Muslim lands. The completion of this great new exodus marked the end of thirteen centuries of Arab-Jewish symbiosis. At this moment it is still too early to evaluate that long chapter in Jewish history which thus came to a close. But if I may be permitted to give my personal impression as I try to visualize what the Jews gained and lost, what they enjoyed and suffered, in their life under Islam, I would say the following:

They gained, first of all, a new cultural élan, and a broadening of their intellectual horizon. They acquired the linguistic tools with which to create an astoundingly rich and many-sided literature. They were given the stimulus to develop a new aspect of their religion, that of Kabbalistic mysticism, while creating also a series of halakhic codes which standardized, and fixed for all generations to come, the rules of their religious law. Ultimately, they acquired the ability to move on into the newly upcoming world of Christian Europe, where they were to undergo great sufferings, but where they were able to leave behind the Middle Ages in which the Arab world was to remain caught mentally until the nineteenth century.

The last-mentioned point leads me to a consideration of what the Jews lost by being concentrated for many centuries in the House of Islam. As long as Arab culture flourished, they lost nothing by living there rather than in Europe. But the Arab decline inevitably pulled down with it the Jews as well. That part of the Jewish people which remained living in Arab (and other Muslim) lands followed, after a time lag of one or two centuries, the Muslim majority into its period of stagnation. While I would certainly not go as far as Spengler, who coined the term "fellah peoples" to designate the latter-day heirs of his ancient "Magian culture," a glance at the history of the Arabs from the fifteenth century on, and of the Jews in Arab lands from the seventeenth, shows that the cultural flowering of both peoples had come to an end by those dates. Fortunately for the Jews, their Ashkenazi division was by that time ready to lead Jewish history into new fields of cultural achievement.

As for the joys and sufferings of the Jews under Islam, there were many. Modern research into Jewish history in Arab lands has shown that both of the two older contrasting views about the position of the Jews under Islam were, if not totally wrong, certainly one-sided. Life in the House of Islam had for the Jews pleasures and pains, existing simultaneously side by side, or alternating in rapid succession. Jewish history, even if one does not embrace what Salo Baron termed its "lachrymose view," does not allow us to ignore the fact that it has abounded in suffering and tragedy. However, from this point of view, compared to what Christian Europe did to the Jews, culminating in the Nazi holocaust, Jewish life under Islam must appear as infinitely better than under the Cross. On the other hand, while in parts of Europe enlightenment and emancipation eased the burden of being Jewish, and led in the nineteenth century to the social liberation and the cultural rejuvenation of the Jews, in most Arab countries they continued to be considered *dhimmī*s until their very exodus, which tells their whole story in a word.

For thirteen centuries the Arabs had tolerated the Jews in each and every corner of their realm, except in the central part of Arabia. From now on they will learn to live with few Jews in their lands, but with the irritating presence of a small Jewish state in the midst of the vast world area they call the Arab homeland.

Notes

NOTES TO THE PREFACE

1. First published in October, 1947, as No. 67 of the Titles in the *Memoir Series* of the American Anthropological Association.

2. First edition published in 1962, by the University of Pennsylvania Press, Philadelphia.

3. First edition published in 1973, by Charles Scribner's Sons, New York.

4. First edition published in 1977, by Charles Scribner's Sons, New York.

NOTES TO CHAPTER ONE: JEWS AND ARABS VIEW THEIR PREHISTORY

1. Cf. Robert Graves and Raphael Patai, *Hebrew Myths*, New York: Greenwich House, distributed by Crown Publishers, 1983 (first published in 1964), pp. 100 ff.

2. Ibid., pp. 120 ff.

3. Cf. Raphael Patai, *The Arab Mind*, revised edition, New York: Scribner's, 1983, p. 77.

4. Cf. Ignaz Goldziher, "Djāhiliyya," in *Encyclopaedia of Islam*, first ed.

5. Cf. the story of Abraham and Ishmael in the next chapter.

6. Patai, *The Arab Mind*, p. 89, and sources there.

7. Patai, *The Arab Mind*, pp. 85–86, and sources there.

8. Cf. *Encyclopaedia of Islam*, 2d ed. (hereafter EI^2), s.v. Ayyām al-ʿArab.

9. Cf. Patai, *The Arab Mind*, pp. 122–23, and sources there.

10. Cf. Patai, *The Arab Mind*, p. 123.

11. Cf. Tosefta ʿAvoda Zara 8:4; B. Sanhedrin 56–60; Maimonides, *Yad haḤazaqa*, Hilkhot M'lakhim 8:10; 9:1; 10:12.

NOTES TO CHAPTER TWO: ABRAHAM IN JEWISH AND ARAB TRADITION

1. W. F. Albright, *American Journal of Semitic Languages* 77 (1923), 125–33; F. M. Th. Boehl, *Mededeelingen der Kon. Nederl. Akademie d. Wetenschappen, Nieuwe Reeks* 9, no. 10 (1947) 17ff.; *Encyclopedia Miqrait*, Jerusalem, 1955, 1:449, s.v. Amraphel.

2. M. D. Cassuto, *Enc. Miqrait* 1:61ff., s.v. Abraham.

3. In Louis Ginzberg, *Legends of the Jews*, vol. 1, Philadelphia: The Jewish Publication Society of America, 1909, the legends about Abraham take up 126 pages, not counting the 63 pages of notes in vol. 5.

4. It is not clear to me on what does H. A. R. Gibb base his assumption, unsupported by documentation, that "it would seem that Abraham and Ishmael were already traditionally regarded as the founders of . . . the Kaaba" in the days of Muhammad. Cf. his *Mohammedanism*, New York: Mentor Books, 1955, p. 44.

5. Only a very few of the more important studies can be mentioned here: Abraham Geiger, *Was hat Mohammed aus dem Judenthume aufgenommen*, 1833, also in English, *Judaism and Islam*; Gustav Weil, *Biblische Legenden der Muselmänner*, Frankfurt, 1845; Charles C. Torrey, *The Jewish Foundation of Islam*, 1933; J. A. Montgomery, *Arabia and the Bible*, 2nd ed., 1969.

6. Cf. S. D. Goitein, *Jews and Arabs*, New York: Schocken Books, 1964, p. 49: "It must not be inferred . . . that the Jews of al-Medina were very observant or learned."

7. Later, Arab religious scholars, e.g., Ibn Ḥazm, took apparent pleasure in pointing out inaccuracies and contradictions in the Bible. Cf. chapter 4.

8. Ginzberg, *Legends of the Jews* 1:195ff.

9. Cf. EI[2], s.v. Āzar.

10. Koran 2:125–29, transl. by M. Pickthall, New York: Mentor Books, 1953, p. 44.

11. Cf. *Enc. Miqrait*, s.v. Yishmael.

12. Josephus Flavius, *Antiquities of the Jews* 1:12:2.

13. Ibid., 1:12:4.

14. Ibid., 1:15:1.

15. Bukhārī, Ṭabarī, etc. Cf. Gustav Weil, *The Bible, the Koran, and the Talmud*, New York: Harper, 1846, pp. 88–91; M. Grünbaum, *Neue Beiträge zur semitischen Sagenkunde*, Leiden: Brill, 1893, pp. 107–8.

16. David Rieder, *Pseudo-Jonathan: Targum Jonathan ben Uziel on the Pentateuch*, no place, no publisher, printed in Jerusalem, 1974, p. 29.

17. Pirqe R. Eliᶜezer, ch. 30. Cf. a more elaborate version in *Sefer haYashar* (twelfth century), ed. Lazarus Goldschmidt, Berlin: Benjamin Harz, 1923, pp. 70–72.

18. Cf. Raphael Patai, *Society, Culture and Change in the Middle East*, 3rd ed., Philadelphia: University of Pennsylvania Press, 1971, pp. 181–83.

19. Cf. *Enc. Miqrait*, s.v. Yoqṭan.

20. Cf. EI[2], s.v. Ḳaḥṭān; Patai, *Society, Culture*, pp. 189–90, and the schematic genealogical table on p. 190.

21. Cf. EI[2], s.v. Hūd.

22. Cf. EI[2], s.v. Ḳaḥṭān.

23. Cf. EI[2], s.v. ᶜAdnān.

24. Patai, *Society, Culture*, pp. 183–86, 206–8, 217–21; EI[2], s.v., Ḳays-ᶜAylān.

25. EI[2], s.v. Djāhiliyya.

26. D. S. Margoliouth, *The Relations between Arabs and Israelites prior to the Rise of Islam*, London: Humphrey Milford, Oxford University Press, 1924, pp. 72ff.

27. Ignaz Goldziher, *Die Richtungen der Islamischen Koranauslegung*, Leiden: Brill, 1920, pp. 79–81.

28. EI^2, s.v. Isḥāḳ.

29. Cf. al-Bayḍāwī (thirteenth century), commentary on Koran 37 : 101–2, and cf. M. Grünbaum, *Neue Beiträge*, pp. 107–8.

NOTES TO CHAPTER THREE: JEWS IN ARAB LANDS

1. H. A. R. Gibb, *Mohammedanism*, New York: Mentor Books, 1955, p. 46.

2. Cf. *Encyclopaedia of Islam*, 2nd ed. (hereafter EI^2), s.v. Maysir.

3. In EI^2 s.v. al-Farazdaḳ.

4. Cf. H. A. R. Gibb, *Arabic Literature*, Oxford: Clarendon Press, 1963, p. 44.

5. Marmaduke Pickthall's translation.

6. For further details, cf. EI^2, s.v. Djabrā'īl.

7. Cf. G. Vajda's article in EI^2, s.v. Ahl al-Kitāb.

8. EI^2, s.v. Kāfir.

9. Shīrāzī, *Tanbīh*, ed. A. W. T. Juynboll, Leiden, 1879, pp. 287ff.; as cited by Reuben Levy, *The Social Structure of Islam*, Cambridge University Press, 1957, p. 254.

10. Levy, op. cit., pp. 254–55.

11. For literature about them, cf. EI^2, s.vv. Hutaym and Ṣulayb.

12. Levy, op. cit., pp. 57–66.

13. Cf. *Encyclopaedia Judaica*, Jerusalem, 1972, s.v. Iraq.

14. Cf. A. S. Tritton, *The Caliphs and Their Non-Muslim Subjects* (reprint), London, 1970, pp. 115–26.

15. Cf. Yedida K. Stillman, "The Wardrobe of a Jewish Bride in Medieval Egypt," in Issachar Ben-Ami and Dov Noy (eds.), *Studies in Marriage Customs* (Folklore Research Center Studies IV), Jerusalem: The Magnes Press–The Hebrew University, 1974, pp. 297–304.

16. Moshe Ma'oz, *Reform in Syria and Palestine: The Impact of the Tanzimat on Politics and Society*, Oxford: Clarendon Press, 1968, pp. 205, 231; *idem*, *Anti-Jewishness in Official Arab Literature and Communications Media* (in Hebrew), Shazar Library–The Institute of Contemporary Jewry–The Hebrew University of Jerusalem, 1975, p. 26.

17. Abraham Yaʿari, *Massaʿot Sh'liaḥ Tz'fat*, Jerusalem, 1942, p. 19.

18. Ma'oz, *Reform*, pp. 207–8.

19. Cf. Raphael Patai, *Society, Culture and Change in the Middle East*, 3rd ed., Philadelphia: University of Pennsylvania Press, 1971, pp. 251ff.

20. EI^2, s.v. al-Ḥākim.

21. Jāḥiẓ, *Kitāb al-Bayān wa al-Tabyīn*, 2 vols., Cairo, 1313 H., 1 : 168, as quoted by Levy, op. cit., p. 66.

22. Raphael Patai, *The Arab Mind*, 2nd ed., New York: Scribner's, 1983, pp. 358, 362, 365, tables 2, 6, and 8; UNESCO *Statistical Yearbook 1984*, pp. I-20, III-58.

23. EI², s.v. Baghdad, p. 901a.

24. Petaḥia of Regensburg, *Sibbuv*, ed. Grünhut, pp. 8–10. My translation from the Hebrew.

25. This aspect of the personality of Maimonides is discussed in R. Patai, *The Jewish Mind*, New York: Scribner's, 1976, pp. 130–33.

26. Abraham Eliyahu Harkavy (ed.), *Zikkaron laRishonim* I, St. Petersburg, 1891, pp. 154–55.

27. Ibid., p. 143.

28. Ibid., pp. 144–45, 166–67.

29. EI², s.v. Hidjā'.

30. Harkavy, op. cit., p. 228.

31. Cf. Patai, *The Jewish Mind*, pp. 115–20, 133–34.

32. Thus by ᶜAḍud al-Dīn al-Ījī, in his *Kitāb al-Mawāqif fī ᶜIlm al-Kalām* ("The Book of Positions in the Science of the Kalām"), cf. EI², s.vv. al-Īdjī, ᶜIlm al-Kalām.

33. Maimonides, *Iggeret Teman* ("Letter to Yemen"), as quoted in *Encyclopaedia Judaica*, 1972, s.v. Saadyah Gaon.

NOTES TO CHAPTER FOUR: CORDOVA—THE ARAB CAMELOT

1. Pascual de Gayangos (translator), *The History of the Muhammedan Dynasties in Spain*, 2 vols., London: Oriental Translation Fund, 1840–43 ("extracted from the Nafhut-Tib min Ghosni-l-Andalusi-r-Rattib by Ahmad ibn Mohammed al-Makkari"), pp. 205, 209, 214–15.

2. Ibid., pp. 217ff., 229. According to Ibn Bashkuwāl, ibid., p. 229, there were 300 attendants.

3. Quoted by Philip K. Hitti, *History of the Arabs*, 10th ed., New York: St. Martin's Press, 1970, p. 527.

4. Gayangos I: 121ff., 157.

5. As quoted by Hitti, *History of the Arabs*, pp. 526–27. The above description of Cordova is largely based on Hitti, pp. 520–36, 557–601; EI², s.v. Ḳurṭuba; Gayangos 1:200–49; E. Lévi-Provençal, *Histoire de l'Espagne Musulmane*, vol. 2, *Le Califat Umaiyade de Cordoue* (912–1031), Paris: Maisonneuve, 1950.

6. This, incidentally, illustrates the fundamental difference between the Jewish position in the medieval Arab world and in the modern West. In the former, the works of an Arabic-writing Jewish scholar and author were part and parcel of Jewish scholarship and Jewish literature; in the latter, the works of a Jewish author written in German or English belong to German and English literature, respectively, even though both Jewish and anti-Jewish critics often are at pains to point out the "Jewishness" or the Jewish features in them.

7. The above summary of Ibn Ḥazm's philosophy is based largely on R. Arnaldez's excellent and detailed article in EI², s.v. Ibn Ḥazm.

8. Ibid.

9. Cf. Ernest Renan, *Averroes et l'averroisme*, Paris, 1852; rev. ed. by H. Psichari, Paris, 1949.

10. Cf. George F. Hourani, *Averroes on the Harmony of Religion and Philosophy*, London, 1961.

11. Ibn Rushd frequently makes the distinction between scholars and ordinary men or the masses. Philosophy, he held, should be the reserve of scholars. On a similar intellectual elitism of Maimonides, cf. R. Patai, *The Jewish Mind*, New York: Scribner's, 1977, pp. 130–33.

12. Cf. Stuart MacClintock, in *The Encyclopedia of Philosophy*, New York: Macmillan and Free Press, 1967, s.v. Averroes.

13. EI^2, s.v. Ibn ʿAbd Rabbih.

14. EI^2, s.v. Ibn Ḥayyān.

15. As quoted by Hitti, *History of the Arabs*, p. 535.

16. Ibid., pp. 514–15; cf. Lévi-Provençal, *Histoire* 1:271; *Civilisation*, 69ff.

17. Hitti, *History of the Arabs*, p. 241; Eliyahu Ashtor, *The Jews in Moslem Spain*, Philadelphia: The Jewish Publication Society of America, 1973, 1:388. Cf. Gustav Flügel, *Die grammatischen Schulen der Araber*, Leipzig, 1862 (Deutsche Morgenländische Gesellschaft, Abhandlungen, vol. 2, no. 4), p. 18; EI^2, s.v. Fiʿl.

18. Ashtor, 1:249–50.

19. Ibid., 1:229, 236.

20. Ibid., 1:252–54.

21. Cf. Samuel haNagid, *Shire Milḥama* ("War Songs"), ed. A. M. Haberman, Tel Aviv; Maḥb'rot Sifrut, 1948.

22. Cf. Israel Zinberg, *A History of Jewish Literature*, vol. 1, Cleveland and London: Case Western Reserve University, 1972, pp. 27, 33.

23. Cf. Benjamin L. Gordon, *Medieval and Renaissance Medicine*, New York: Philosophical Library, 1959, p. 235.

24. Cf. Leo Strauss, "The Literary Character of the *Guide* . . ." in Salo W. Baron (ed.), *Essays on Maimonides*, New York: Columbia University Press, 1941; *idem*, "Introduction to Maimonides' *Guide* . . ." in Shlomo Pines (translator), *Maimonides, Guide of the Perplexed*, Chicago: University of Chicago Press, 1963.

25. Cf. also Patai, *The Jewish Mind*, pp. 96ff. for a general picture of Jewish culture in Muslim Spain.

26. Ibid.

27. Cf. the studies mentioned in chapter 2, n. 5

28. Samuel Poznanski, "Karaite Miscellanies," *Jewish Quarterly Review* 8 (1896), 681–84, and M. Steinschneider, "Introduction to the Arabic Literature of the Jews," ibid. 11 (1899), 606. Cf. also *Encyclopaedia Judaica* (1975), s.v. Daniel ben Moses al-Qumisi.

29. The above summary of Ibn Ḥazm's views on Jews and Judaism is based on Moshe Perlmann, "Eleventh Century Andalusian Authors on the Jews of Granada," American Academy of Jewish Research, *Proceedings* 18 (1948–49), pp. 270–83.

30. According to Koran 2:61–65 and 7:166, God turned the sinners among

the Children of Israel into apes; and according to Koran 5 : 65 He turned them into apes and pigs. Other Arab writers, too, use the term *qird* to designate the Jews.

31. Perlmann, "Eleventh Century . . ." pp. 284–86.

32. Ibid., pp. 288–89.

33. Eliyahu Ashtor, *Qorot haY'hudim biS'farad haMuslimit*, Jerusalem: Qiryat Sefer, 1966², 1 : 204ff; 2 (1966): 84–120.

34. The title page of this edition reads (in my translation): Categories of the Nations of Abu al-Qāsim Ṣāᶜid ibn Aḥmad al-Andalusī, who died in 463 H., scientific, philosophical, social, physical, which is a study about the state of the nations, and the quality of their kings, and their customs, and their characters, and their culture, and their religions, and their traits, and their habitations, and their ways of life, and the house of their emigration, and about the nations which are concerned with the sciences and those which do not concern themselves with them, and about their famous scholars and their philosophical and scientific ideas. Egypt. Printed at the expense of ᶜAlī Muḥammad Abū Ṭālib in Egypt, Printing Press of Muḥammad Muḥammad Maẓhar.

35. Reading *wayusammūn* instead of *wayasmaᶜūn*.

36. I.e., every nineteen lunar years are seven lunar months shorter than nineteen solar years.

37. I.e., 1 hour $X\frac{876}{1080}$, or 876 of 1080 parts of an hour.

38. I.e., $\frac{204}{1080}$ parts of an hour.

39. Māsarjuwayh or Māsarjis (early eighth century) was the first translator of medical works into Arabic, and authored two books of his own, one on food and one on *al-ᶜAqāqīr* ("Simples"). Cf. Patai, *The Jewish Mind*, p. 100, and p. 549, n. 2.

40. Ahrun al-Qāṣṣ ("Aaron the Preacher"), whose *Kunnāsh* ("Scrapbook" or "Principles," a medical pandect) is often quoted by pharmacological writers, had great reputation as a scholar. His book, which he wrote in Greek, was translated into Syriac, and Māsarjuwayh translated it into Arabic. Cf. Bar Hebraeus (1226–1286), *The Chronography*, transl. E. A. W. Budge, Oxford, 1932, p. 57; Jāhiẓ, *Kitāb al-Ḥayawān*, Cairo, 1356 H., 1 : 250; EI², 1 : 213a.

41. Isḥāq ibn Sulaymān, surnamed al-Isrā'īlī (ca. 855–932), physician and philosopher, was born in Egypt, emigrated when about fifty to Qayrawān, capital of the Maghrib, where ᶜUbayd Allāh al-Mahdī, the founder of the Fāṭimid dynasty, appointed him court physician. He wrote numerous philosophical books in Arabic, several of which were translated into Latin and printed in *Omnia Opera Isaac*, 1515. Cf. *Enc. Judaica*, s.v. Israeli, Isaac ben Solomon.

42. Isḥāq ibn ᶜImrān (late ninth century–early tenth century), wrote the *Kitāb al-Mālīkhūliyya* ("Book of Melancholy"), translated into Latin by Constantinus Africanus (1010/15–1087) as *De melancholia*. Al-Andalusī discusses him elsewhere in his *Ṭabaqāt al-Umam*.

43. Sahl ibn Bishr Ḥabīb (died ca. 820) wrote, in addition to the books mentioned above, the *Kitāb al-Aḥkām* ("Book of Rules"), which dealt with the

principles of astrology, and was rendered into Hebrew by an unknown translator under the title *K'lalim* ("Principles" or "Rules"). In the late Middle Ages it was translated into Latin.

44. That is, Ḥasdai ibn Shaprut, cf. above.

45. Arab chroniclers refer by the term *fitna* to the times of troubles which followed the death of ᶜAbd al-Raḥmān Sanshol in 1009. Cf. EI², s.v. Fitna.

46. M'naḥem ibn al-Fawāl (eleventh century) was a physician and philosopher. Lucien Leclerc, who misspells his name as Mounadjam ben al Kaoual, says of him: "He was a Jew of Saragossa, a skilful physician and adept of philosophy." See Leclerc, *Histoire de la médecine arabe*, Paris: Leroux, 1876, 1:548.

47. Abu al-Walīd Marwān (Yona) ibn Jannāḥ (born Cordova, 985/90–died Saragossa, before 1050) is well known for his outstanding work in Hebrew grammar, cf. Patai, *The Jewish Mind*, pp. 112–13. His treatise mentioned by al-Andalusī is not extant.

48. Isḥāq ibn Qusṭār or Qasṭār or Saqatar (982–1057), also known as Ibn Yasos, was a physician and philologist. Cf. Steinschneider, ZDMG 9:838; *Hebr. Bibliogr.* 20, 9; JQR 11 (1899): 607; Wilhelm Bacher, in Winter und Wünsche, *Die jüdische Literatur* 2:183, 262, 326; Leclerc 1:548; Heinrich Graetz, *History of the Jews* 3:273.

49. Al-Muwaffaq Mujāhid al-ᶜĀmirī and his son Iqbāl al-Dawla ᶜAlī were "slave emirs," cf. Dozy, *Histoire des Musulmans d'Espagne* 3, *passim*.

50. I.e., Solomon ibn Gabirol (1021–1053), whose major metaphysical work, written in Arabic, was preserved in a medieval (twelfth century) Latin translation under the title *Fons Vitae*, with the author's name disfigured to Avicebron. The book became very popular and it was long believed to have been the work of a Christian author. Ibn Gabirol's ethical work, *Kitāb Iṣlāḥ al-Akhlāq* ("The Book of Betterment of Characters") is extant.

51. This Ḥasdai (born ca. 1040) was a grandson of Ḥasdai ibn Shaprut. He was a poet who wrote only in Arabic and of whom an Arab critic wrote, "He did not compose verses but miracles." He also mastered music in both theory and practice, and specialized in speculative philosophy. In 1066 he became the vizier of the king of Saragossa. Cf. Graetz, *Hist.*, 3:280.

52. Saᶜīd ibn Yaᶜqūb al-Fayyūmī is Saᶜadia Gaon, who is discussed above in chapter 3.

53. Abū Kathīr Yaḥyā ibn Zakariyya al-Ṭābarānī (i.e., "of Tiberias"), cf. Steinschneider, "Introduction to the Arabic Literature of the Jews," JQR 11 (1899), p. 116.

54. Dā'ūd al-Qūmisī. A David Abū Sulaymān al-Qūmisī (died ca. 945), a Karaite scholar, lived in Jerusalem. Al-Andalusī may have known of him from al-Masᶜūdī, who mentions that Dā'ūd al-Qūmisī translated the Bible into Arabic with a commentary. Cf. M. Steinschneider, *Jewish Quarterly Review* 11(1899): 606; *Enc. Judaica*, s.v. Daniel ben Moses al-Qumisi.

55. Ibrāhīm Abū Saᶜd ibn Sahl al-Tustarī (died 1048) appears in Jewish sources as Abraham ben Yashar. He was from Tustar (or Shustar) in southwestern Persia, lived in Egypt, and was a financier and courtier. He sold the Caliph al-Ẓāhir

(reigned 1021–36) a Negro slave-girl who subsequently became the mother of the later Caliph al-Mustanṣir. At the age of seven, when al-Mustanṣir succeeded his father, his mother became very influential in state affairs, and al-Tustarī was one of her trusted advisers. On his recommendation, Ṣadaqa ibn Yūsuf al-Falāḥī, a Jewish convert to Islam, was appointed vizier. In 1048 Ṣadaqa had al-Tustarī assassinated. Cf. *Enc. Jud.*, s.v. Abu Saʿd al-Tustari.

56. On the *mutakallimūn*, the Muslim rational philosophers, see EI^2, s.v. ʿIlm al-kalām.

57. Abū Ibrāhīm (ibn) Ismā'īl ibn Yūsuf known as al-Ghazāl. Al-Ghazāl is a copyist's error for Naghrela, known by his Hebrew name as Sh'muel haNagid (993–1055/56), see above.

58. Cf. *Fihrist*, p. 22, and Ibn Khaldūn, *al-Muqaddima*, ed. Quatremère, 2:179.

59. Cf. Salo W. Baron, *A Social and Religious History of the Jews*, vol. 8, Philadelphia: The Jewish Publication Society of America, 1958, pp. 192ff.

NOTES TO CHAPTER FIVE: YEMEN AND MOROCCO—A STUDY IN CONTRAST

1. My calculations on the basis of figures published in the *Statistical Abstract of Israel* 23 (1972), for the year 1970.

2. Israel Central Bureau of Statistics, *Juvenile Delinquency*, 1970. Special Series, no. 408, p. 26.

3. *Encyclopaedia Judaica*, Jerusalem, 1972, s.v. Israel.

4. EI^2, s.v. Kaʿb al-Aḥbār.

5. EI^1, s.v. Wahb ibn Munabbih.

6. A. Shivtiel, Wilfred Lockwood, and R. B. Serjeant, "The Jews of Ṣanʿā'," in R. B. Serjeant and Ronald Lewcock (eds.), *Ṣanʿā': An Islamic City*, London: World of Islam Festival Trust, 1983, p. 421, quoting Aḥmad b. Yaḥyā al-Murṭada, *Kitāb al-Azhar*, Beirut, 1973, p. 322, reproduced here with slight stylistic changes. Cf. also Erich Brauer, *Ethnologie der jemenitischen Juden*, Heidelberg, 1934, quoting Yavn'eli, who gives a longer list of restrictions.

7. Shivtiel, loc. cit.

8. Ibid., p. 394.

9. Ibid.

10. Ibid.

11. Ibid., p. 422.

12. Ibid.

13. Ibid., p. 423.

14. Y'huda Ratzhabi, *Bo'i Teman*, Tel Aviv, 1967, p. 202.

15. Shivtiel, op. cit., p. 424.

16. Ibid., note 205.

17. Ibid., pp. 425–26.

18. In 1961, that is, twelve years after their arrival in Israel, 78.8 percent of the male, and 37.7 percent of the female Yemenite Jewish immigrants aged four-

teen and over were literate. The breakdown of the data according to age groups shows an impressive growth of literacy in the last half century prior to their emigration: of the Yemenite males who at the time of their immigration to Israel were sixty years old or older, only 57.1 percent were literate, while among those who were fourteen years old or younger 95.7 percent were literate. The corresponding percentages for the female immigrants are even more impressive: they were 1.8 percent and 80.9 percent respectively. Among the Moroccan Jewish immigrants the picture was very similar. These figures, even those for the 60 plus age group, compare favorably with those of the Arabs: in Yemen in 1962 only 5 percent of the male, and none of the female, population over fifteen years of age was literate, while in Morocco in 1971 the corresponding percentages were 33.6 percent and 9.8 percent respectively. Cf. State of Israel, Central Bureau of Statistics, *Languages, Literacy and Educational Attainment*, part III, Jerusalem, 1966, pp. 2–12; R. Patai, *The Arab Mind*, 1983, table six (foll. p. 356).

19. Cf. Y'huda Ratzhabi, "Darda'im" (in Hebrew), *Edoth: A Quarterly for Folklore and Ethnology*, Jerusalem, 1946, 1:3, pp. 165–80; English summary, pp. 195–96.

20. Raphael Patai, *The Jewish Mind*, New York: Scribner's, 1977, p. 385. The Yemenite Jews are the most thoroughly studied Middle Eastern Jewish community. Among the recent books (all in Hebrew) are: Yosef Tobi, *The Jews of Yemen in the 19th Century*, Tel Aviv: Afikim, 1976; Israel Yeshaᶜyahu and Yosef Tobi (eds.), *The Jews of Yemen: Studies and Researches*, Jerusalem: Yad Izhak Ben-Zvi, 1975; S. D. Goitein, *The Yemenites: History, Communal Organization, Spiritual Life*, Jerusalem: Yad Izhak Ben-Zvi and the Hebrew University, 1983.

21. S. D. Goitein, *Jews and Arabs*, New York: Schocken Books, 1955, pp. 73, 75.

22. Cf. Harold D. Nelson (ed.), *Morocco: A Country Study*, Washington, D.C.: American University, 1978, p. 101.

23. Ibid., pp. x, 5, 134.

24. Norman A. Stillman, *The Jews of Arab Lands*, Philadelphia: The Jewish Publication Society of America, 1979, p. 101.

25. André Chouraqui, *Marche vers l'Occident: Les juifs d'afrique du nord*, Paris: Presses Universitaires de France, 1952, pp. 183–84.

26. As far back as about 1900 George Edmund Holt gave an elaborate account of how the Muslims and Jews of Morocco were addicted to lying. The Muslims "lie unmitigatedly in open court [of law] unless facing the east," and as for the Jews, they considered it proper behavior to lie to a non-Jew; they "go them one better if their hands are not washed and their heads covered . . ." Cf. George Edmund Holt, *Morocco the Bizarre*, New York: McBride, Nast & Co., 1914, pp. 59–60, 73–74.

27. Ibid., pp. 192–97.

28. Nelson, p. 60.

29. Ibid., pp. 73–74.

30. Stillman, pp. 281–83, 286.

31. Cf. text in Stillman, pp. 371–73.

32. Cf. Raphael Patai, "HaFolqlor w'haEtnologiya shel ʿAm Yisrael," *Edoth*, Jerusalem, 1 : 1 : 1–12 (October, 1945); "Problems and Tasks of Jewish Folklore and Ethnology," *Journal of American Folklore* 59, no. 231, pp. 25–39 (Jan.–March, 1946); reprinted in R. Patai, *On Jewish Folklore*, Detroit: Wayne State University Press, 1983, pp. 17–34.

33. S. D. Goitein, *From the Land of Sheba*, New York: Schocken Books, 1973, pp. 38, 44–45, 56–57.

34. Dov Noy, *Jefet Schwili erzählt*, Berlin: Walter de Gruyter, 1963, pp. 340–43 and 87–90 (in this order).

35. R. Y'huda ben R. Aharon Yarimi, *MeAggadot Teman*, Jerusalem, no date, p. 101.

36. Norman A. Stillman, "Muslims and Jews in Morocco," *The Jerusalem Quarterly* 5 (Fall, 1977), pp. 79–80.

37. Francoise Legey, *Contes et legendes populaires du Maroc, recueillés a Marrakech*, Paris: Leroux, 1926, p. 293, tale no. 86.

38. Cf. EI^2, s.v. Djuḥā.

39. J. Scelles-Millie, *Contes sahariens du Souf*, Paris: Maisonneuve et Larose, 1963, p. 265.

40. Ibid., pp. 159ff., 165, 167 n., 260.

41. Dov Noy, *Moroccan Jewish Folktales*, New York: Herzl Press, 1965, pp. 18, 41, 98, 150, 177.

42. Stillman, "Muslims and Jews," pp. 81–82.

43. Pierre Flamand, *Quelques manifestations de l'ésprit populaire dans les juiveries du Sud-Marocain*, Casablanca, Morocco: Imprimeries Reunies, n.d. (ca. 1958), pp. 113–14.

44. Moshe Shokeid, "Jewish Existence in a Berber Environment," in Shlomo Deshen and Walter P. Zenner (eds.), *Jewish Societies in the Middle East*, Washington, D.C.: University Press of America, 1982, p. 105.

45. Ibid., p. 117.

46. Yaʿqov Moshe Toledano, *Ner haMaʿarav*, Jerusalem, 1911, pp. 64ff.

47. Allan R. Meyers, "Patronage and Protection," in Deshen-Zenner, p. 90.

48. George Edmund Holt, *Morocco the Bizarre*, New York: McBride, Nast & Co., 1914, p. 133. Emphasis in the original.

49. Shokeid, op. cit., pp. 113–17.

50. David Hart, *The Aith Waryagar of the Moroccan Rif*, Tucson, Arizona: University of Arizona Press, 1976, pp. 279–80.

51. Lawrence Rosen, "Muslim–Jewish Relations in a Moroccan City," *International Journal of Middle Eastern Studies* 3 (1972): 435–49.

52. Mrs. W. B. Harris, *Tafilet*, Edinburgh and London, 1895, pp. 97ff., as cited by Edward Westermarck, *Ritual and Belief in Morocco*, London: Macmillan, 1926, 1:535–36.

53. Westermarck, op. cit., 1:536.

54. Meyers, op. cit. pp. 85ff.

55. Westermarck, op. cit., 1:518–64.

56. Meyers, p. 98.

57. Hart, pp. 279–80.

58. Rosen, pp. 444–45.

59. Dorothy Willner, *Nation Building and Community in Israel*, Princeton, N.J.: Princeton University Press, 1969, pp. 263, 297–98.

60. Cf. Raphael Patai, The Druze: *enfants terribles* of the Middle East? London: Institute of Jewish Affairs, Research Report, no. 3, March 1984.

61. Moshe Shokeid, *The Dual Heritage*, Manchester University Press, 1971, pp. 19–20, 22, 23, 24, 27.

62. Ferdinand Ossendowski, *The Fire of the Desert Folk: An Account of a Journey Through Morocco*, New York: Dutton, 1926, pp. 104–5.

63. H. Z. Hirschberg, *MeEretz M'vo haShemesh*, p. 112. My translation from the Hebrew.

64. Shokeid, *The Dual Heritage*, 113–17.

65. EI^{2}, s.v. Ḥarṭānī; Hirschberg, *MeEretz*, pp. 109–10; Richard V. Weekes (ed.), *Muslim Peoples: A World Ethnographic Survey*, Westport, Conn.: Greenwood Press, 1978, p. 102; Raphael Patai, "The Culture Areas of the Middle East," in Wolfgang Weissleder (ed.), *The Nomadic Alternative* (a volume in the *World Anthropology* series), The Hague—Paris: Mouton, 1978, p. 14.

66. On the contempt in which the smiths and the Negroes are held by the Moors of the Sahara, cf. Lloyd Cabot Briggs, *Tribes of the Sahara*, Cambridge: Harvard University Press, 1960, pp. 233–35.

67. Shokeid, in Deshen–Zenner, pp. 109, 110, 111, 114, 116, 117, 118, 119.

68. H. Z. Hirschberg, *Toldot haY'hudim b'Afriqa haTz'fonit*, Jerusalem: Mossad Bialik, 1965, 1:129.

69. Patai, "Culture Areas . . . ," pp. 13–14, and map on p. 6.

70. Scelles-Millie, pp. 143–46, 151. Also Hirschberg, *MeEretz*, p. 112, remarks on the lighter coloration of the Jews in the Atlas Mountains.

71. Brauer, *Ethnologie*, pp. 52, 328, 336.

72. Vicomte Ch. de Foucauld, *Reconnaissance au Maroc 1883–1884*, Paris: Challamel et Cie., 1888, p. 397.

73. On Foucauld's anti-Jewish sentiments cf. Hirschberg, *MeEretz*, p. 174.

74. Issachar Ben Ami, *Y'hude Maroqo*, Jerusalem: Rubin Mass, 1975, pp. 59, 102, 109, 110. Cf. also pp. 165–66, the folk story which presents the inadvertent breaking of a pitcher of *maḥya* as a major catastrophe.

75. Hirschberg, *MeEretz*, pp. 108, 154, 158–59, 174, 236.

76. R. Feuerstein and M. Rischel, *Yalde haMellāḥ: HaPiggur haTarbuti etzel Yalde Maroqo uMashma^{c}uto haHinnukhit* ("The Children of the Mellāḥ: The Cultural Retardation among the Children of Morocco and Its Educational Significance"), Jerusalem: Department of Child and Youth Immigration, The Jewish Agency, the Szold Institute for the Children and Youth, 1963, p. 62. My translation.

77. EI^{2}, s.v. *khamr*, and EI^{1}, s.v. *sharab*.

78. Reuben Levy, *The Social Structure of Islam*, 2nd ed., Cambridge University Press, 1957, pp. 240, 247, 250–51, 336.

79. Foucauld, *Reconnaissance*, p. 400.

80. Raphael Patai, *Society, Culture and Change in the Middle East*, 3rd ed., Philadelphia: University of Pennsylvania Press, 1971, pp. 412ff.; *The Arab Mind*, New York: Scribner's, 1983, pp. 25ff., 59–60.

81. Westermarck, *Ritual and Belief in Morocco*, 1:600; 2:135, 136, 138–40, 142, 143, 147.

82. Westermarck, *Marriage Ceremonies in Morocco*, p. 356; *Ritual and Belief*, 1:588.

83. Feuerstein and Rischel, pp. 70–71.

84. Patai, *The Arab Mind*, pp. 225, 311, 312.

85. Feuerstein and Rischel, p. 72.

86. R. Patai, *The Vanished Worlds of Jewry*, London: Weidenfeld and Nicolson, and New York: Macmillan, 1981, p. 105.

87. R. Patai, *Israel Between East and West*, p. 295.

88. R. Patai, *Society, Culture and Change*, p. 403.

89. Rivka Bar-Yosef, Lecture at a conference of school supervisors in Israel. Mimeographed stenogram published by the Pedagogical Secretariat of the Ministry of Education and Culture, Jerusalem, November, 1957, p. 62.

90. Ibid.

91. *Encyclopaedia Judaica*, 5:1099.

92. Cf. Herbert S. Lewis, "Yemenite Ethnicity in Israel," *The Jewish Journal of Sociology* (London) 26:1 (June, 1984), p. 11.

93. Rivka Bar-Yosef, op. cit., pp. 60–62.

94. Patai, *Israel Between East and West*, pp. 295–96.

95. R. Patai, *Cultures in Conflict*, New York: Herzl Press, 1958, 1961.

96. Feuerstein and Rischel, pp. 232–33.

NOTES TO CHAPTER SIX: JEWISH AND ARAB FOLK CULTURE

1. Edward William Lane, *The Manners and Customs of the Modern Egyptians*, New York: Everyman's Library, no date, p. 241.

2. In 1966 there were, according to the census, two million Copts in Egypt, constituting some seven percent of the total population. Cf. EI^2, s.v. Ḳibṭ. It will be of interest to note that while the number of the Copts decreased in Egypt since the early nineteenth century, the total population of the country in 1820 was 2,000,000; in 1847–48, ca. 4,500,000; in 1950, 20,000,000; and in 1980, 43,000,000. That is, in 150 years the population increased 21 fold.

3. Lane, *Modern Egyptians*, p. 478.

4. On the jinn among the Muslims cf. Edward Westermarck, *Ritual and Belief in Morocco*, London: Macmillan, 1926, 1:262–413; EI^2, s.v. Djinn, and literature there, 2:548. On demons in Jewish belief and folklore, cf. Micha Joseph Bin Gorion, *Mimekor Yisrael: Classical Jewish Folktales* (trans. I. M. Lask), Bloomington and London: Indiana University Press, 1976, index, s.v. Demons.

5. André Chouraqui, *Marche vers l'Occident: Les Juifs d'Afrique du Nord*, Paris: Presses Universitaires de France, 1952, p. 199. Marabouts are Muslim holy men;

dervishes are Muslim religious mendicants; *f'qih* (literal Arabic *faqīh*) is a Muslim wise man; *deguez* (pl. *degaguez*) and *rᶜfafa* are saintly medicine men.

6. Cf. Taufik Canaan, *Dämonenglaube im Lande der Bibel* (Morgenland, Heft 21), Leipzig: J. C. Hinrich, 1964.

7. See below, "magic."

8. Westermarck, *Ritual and Belief*, 1:402, and literature in fn. 1; Issachar Ben Ami, *Y'hude Maroqo*, Jerusalem: Rubin Mass, 1975, p. 165.

9. Cf. S. Seligman, *Der böse Blick und Verwandtes*, Berlin: Hermann Barsdorf, 1910, 2 vols. (still a classic). On the evil eye in Morocco, cf. Westermarck, *Ritual and Belief*, 1:414–78.

10. Westermarck, *Ritual and Belief*, 1:430.

11. Ibid., 1:433.

12. Ludwig Blau, *Das altjüdische Zauberwesen*, pp. 153ff; Westermarck, *Ritual and Belief*, 1:426–78; S. Seligmann, *Der böse Blick und Verwandtes*.

13. Westermarck, *Ritual and Belief*, 1:448–49.

14. Cf. plates, Westermarck, *Ritual and Belief*, 1:452.

15. Ibid., 1:445–47.

16. Ibid., 1:462, 465. In my own amulet collection I have numerous examples of Arab and Jewish amulets of various types.

17. Cf. Gerschom Scholem's instructive article in *Encyclopaedia Judaica*, Jerusalem, 1972, s.v. Magen David, and literature listed there.

18. Cf. Raphael Patai, *Gates to the Old City*, New York: Avon Books, 1980, and Detroit, Michigan: Wayne State University Press, 1981, pp. 185–89.

19. Muḥammad ibn Isḥāq (ca. 1000), *Fihrist*; cf. EI¹, s.v. Siḥr.

20. Cf. EI¹, s.v. Budūḥ.

21. Dozy, *Suppl.* 2:775b; EI¹, s.v. Siḥr, p. 414.

22. Cf. Yosef Dan, "Magic," in *Enc. Judaica* 11:715.

23. Eijub Abela, "Beiträge zur Kenntniss abergläubischer Gebräuche in Syrien," *Zeitschrift des deutschen Palästina-Vereins* 7 (1884), p. 106.

24. Ludwig Blau, *Das altjüdische Zauberwesen*, Strassburg 1898, p. 159.

25. Cf. sources in R. Patai, *On Jewish Folklore*, Detroit, Mich.: Wayne State Univ. Press, 1983, p. 359.

26. Cf. sources in Patai, op. cit., pp. 394, 437.

27. Patai, op. cit., p. 403.

28. Ibid., pp. 368–69, 426.

29. Sources, ibid., pp. 376, 428.

30. Published by Wayne State University Press, Detroit, Michigan, 1983.

31. Cf. Westermarck, *Ritual and Belief*, 2:370–433.

32. Ibid., 2:427.

33. Françoise Legey, *The Folklore of Morocco*, London: Allen & Unwin, 1935, pp. 175, 107.

34. Westermarck, *Ritual and Belief*, 2:426–27.

35. Cf. sources in Patai, *On Jewish Folklore*, p. 358.

36. A late-nineteenth-century handbook by R. Raphael Ohana, entitled

Mar'eh haY'ladim ("The Children's Mirror"), 3rd ed., Jerusalem, 1909, pp. 35b, 78b, as quoted in Patai, *On Jewish Folklore*, p. 358.

37. R. Yaʿaqov Moshe Toledano, *Yam haGadol* ("The Great Sea"), Cairo, 1931, pp. 81–85.

38. At present about half of the Jerbans are Ibāḍīs (following the local form of Ibāḍism called Wahbism), while the other half is Mālikī orthodox Muslim. Cf. EI², s.vv. Djarba and Ibāḍiyya.

39. Cf. R. Dozy and M. J. de Goeje, *Description de l'Afrique et de l'Espagne par Edrisi*, Leiden, 1866, p. 127.

40. Maimonides, *Igrot uSh'elot uT'shuvot*, Amsterdam: Proops, 1712, p. 3a. My translation from Hebrew. Cf. Patai, *The Jewish Mind*, p. 464; H. Z. Hirschberg, *Toldot haY'hudim b'Afriqa haTz'fonit* (A History of the Jews in North Africa), Jerusalem: Mosad Bialik, 1965, 1:123.

41. Edward Westermarck, *Marriage Ceremonies in Morocco*, London: Macmillan, 1914.

42. Issachar Ben-Ami, "Le Mariage Traditionnel chez les Juifs Marocains," in Issachar Ben-Ami and Dov Noy (eds.), *Studies in Marriage Customs*, Jerusalem: The Magnes Press–The Hebrew University, 1974, pp. 9–103.

43. Westermarck, *Marriage Ceremonies in Morocco*, p. 241.

44. Ben-Ami, "Le Mariage . . . ," p. 71.

45. Westermarck, *Ritual and Belief*, 1:199; 2:5.

46. Ben-Ami, p. 10.

47. L. Voinot, *Pelerinages judéo-musulmans du Maroc*, Paris, 1948, p. 125.

48. Jean Mathieu et R. Manneville, *Accoucheuses musulmanes traditionnelles de Casablanca*, Publications de l'Institute des Hautes Etudes Marocaines 53, Paris, 1952, p. 10.

49. S. D. Goitein, *A Mediterranean Society: The Jewish Communities of the Arab World as Portrayed in the Documents of the Cairo Geniza*, Berkeley and Los Angeles: The University of California Press, and New York: Columbia University Press, 4 vols., 1967–1983, 3:154, 156, 157, 169, 175, 182, 183, 187, 196, 316–19, 358; 4:199–200.

50. Raphael Patai, *Sex and Family in the Bible and the Middle East*, New York: Doubleday, 1959, pp. 188–92.

51. Amnon Cohen, *Jewish Life Under Islam: Jerusalem in the Sixteenth Century*, Cambridge, Mass.: Harvard University Press, 1984, pp. 128–35, 169–88.

52. R. Patai, *On Jewish Folklore*, pp. 348–56.

53. Cf. sources in Westermarck, *Ritual and Belief*, 2:313, n. 2.

54. Ibid.

55. Cf. T. Schrire, *Hebrew Amulets: Their Decipherment and Interpretation*, London: Routledge & Kegan Paul, 1966. Contains numerous illustrations and a bibliography, to which add Michael L. Rodkinson, *History of Amulets, Charms, and Talismans*, New York, 1893, although this book discusses primarily the *tephillin*.

56. Cf. Westermarck, *Ritual and Belief*, 1:216.

57. On the veneration of saints among the Jews in Morocco and in Israel, and legends they told about the saints, cf. Issachar Ben-Ami, "Folk-Veneration of

Saints Among the Moroccan Jews," in Shelomo Morag, Issachar Ben-Ami, Norman A. Stillman (eds.), *Studies in Judaism and Islam*, Jerusalem: Magnes Press–The Hebrew University, 1981, pp. 283–344.

58. Cf., e.g., C. B. Klunzinger, *Upper Egypt: Its People and Its Products*, London: Blackie & Son, 1878, pp. 393–94.

59. Lane, *Arabian Society in the Middle Ages*, p. 70; I. Goldziher, *Muhammedanische Studien*, Halle a. S., 1890, 2:312; Westermarck, *Ritual and Belief*, 1:174 (Morocco); J. W. McPherson, *The Moulids of Egypt*, Cairo, 1941, pp. 46–47 (Egypt), etc.

60. Cf. Moses Alshekh (d. ca. 1607), *Ḥelqat M'ḥoqeq* (Commentary on Job), Venice, 1603, on Job 30:23; cf. *Enc. Jud.*, s.v. Hillula. On the *mawālid* in various countries cf. Lane, *Arabian Society*, pp. 71ff.; Goldziher, *Muh. Studien* 2:312; Westermarck, *Ritual and Belief*, 1:175–78 (Morocco); McPherson, *Moulids of Egypt*, pp. 129–319 (126 Egyptian mawālid); Harold B. Barclay, *Buurri Al Lamaab*, Ithaca, N. Y.: Cornell Univ. Press, 1964, pp. 182–88 (*ziyāra*s and *mawālid* in Sudan); Taufik Canaan, *Mohammedan Saints and Sanctuaries in Palestine*, London: Luzac, 1927; Michael Ish-Shalom, *Qivre Avot*, Jerusalem: Palestine Institute of Folklore and Ethnology, 1947.

61. Lane, *Modern Egyptians*, p. 241.

62. Cf. Goldziher, *Muh. Studien*, pp. 329–30; cf. also pp. 275–378; Westermarck, *Ritual and Belief*, 1:35.

63. M. Cl. Huart, *Journal Asiatique* 2 (1878): 479ff.

64. Yāqūt, *Muᶜjam al-Buldān*, 2:308.

65. Goldziher took the description of this cult from John Mills, *Three Months' Residence at Nablus and an Account of the Modern Samaritans*, London: John Murray, 1864, p. 32.

66. Al-Qazwīnī, *Āthār al-Bilād*, p. 194; Yāqūt, *Muᶜjam*, 3:759.

67. Cf. Raphael Patai, *Man and Temple in Ancient Jewish Myth and Ritual*, 2nd ed., New York: Ktav, 1967, pp. 184–86. Cf. also Patai, "The 'Control of Rain' in Ancient Palestine," *Hebrew Union College Annual* 14 (1939), p. 282, notes 159, 160.

68. Edmond Doutté, *Magie et religion dans l'Afrique du Nord*, Algiers, 1909, p. 593; Westermarck, *Ritual and Belief*, 2:252, 255.

69. André Chouraqui, *Marche vers l'Occident: Les Juifs d'Afrique du Nord*, Paris: Presses Universitaires de France, 1952, p. 294.

70. McPherson, *Moulids of Egypt*, pp. 36, 142, 322.

71. Cf. *L'Univers israélite*, Oct. 7, 1932, as quoted by Chouraqui, p. 294.

72. Westermarck, *Ritual and Belief*, 1:195–96; Edmond Doutté, *Missions au Maroc—En Tribu*, Paris, 1914, pp. 208ff., 72.

73. Louis de Chenier, *The Present State of the Empire of Morocco*, London, 1788, 1:190f., as cited by Westermarck, *Ritual and Belief*, n. 2.

74. Louis Voinot, *Pélerinages judéo-musulmans du Maroc* (Institut des Hautes Etudes Marocains, Notes et Documents IV), Paris: Editions Larose, 1948, pp. 17–82, 98.

75. Cf. H. Z. Hirschberg, *MeEretz M'vo haShemesh* (English title: Inside

Maghreb: The Jews of North Africa), Jerusalem: Youth Department of the Zionist Organization, 1957, pp. 151–60.

76. Voinot, *Pélerinages*, pp. 125–27.

77. Canaan, *Mohammedan Saints.*

78. Ibid., pp. 294–95.

79. Ish-Shalom, *Qivre Avot*, Jerusalem: Palestine Institute of Folklore and Ethnology.

80. Cf. 1948. *Enc. Jud.*, s.v. Holy places, pp. 925–26.

81. Ish-Shalom, *Qivre Avot*, p. 177.

82. The Israel Museum, Jerusalem, published this painting in the form of a 25 × 36 inch colored poster.

83. R. Ḥayyim Vital, *Sefer Shaᶜar haKawwanot*, vol. 2, Tel Aviv, 1963, p. 191. My translation.

84. Lane, *Modern Egyptians*, p. 55.

85. Westermarck, *Ritual and Belief*, 1:69; 2:410, 412–13.

86. Those of Wezzan and Tlemcen have been described by Chouraqui, pp. 299–300. The *hillula* or R. Shimᶜon ben Yoḥai on the eve of LaG baᶜOmer in Tetuan are described by Hermann Cohn, *Moeurs des Juifs et des Arabes de Tétuan*, Paris: Librarie Lipschutz, 1927, p. 17.

87. George L. Harris (ed.), *Iraq: Its People, Its Society, Its Culture*, New Haven: HRAF Press, 1958, p. 61; EI^2, s.v. Karbalā.

88. Cf. the vivid description of Elizabeth Warnock Fernea, *Guests of the Sheik*, New York: Doubleday, 1969, pp. 199–245.

89. Cf. Louis Massignon, *Essai sur les origines du lexique technique de la mystique Musulman*, Paris: J. Vrin, 1954, p. 402 (*shabaḥ*).

90. Fernea, *Guests of the Sheik*, pp. 203–7.

91. Cf. A. Ben-Yaᶜaqov, "The ᶜĪd el-Ziyāra in Baghdad," *Edoth* (Jerusalem) 1:1 (Oct. 1945), pp. 37–40.

92. Cf. David Suleiman Sassoon, *Massaᶜ Bavel* (Travel to Iraq), Jerusalem, 1955, p. 292, with a picture of the hand in question. Cf. also index, s.v. *qever*, about many other Jewish saints' tombs in Iraq.

93. Westermarck, *Ritual and Belief*, 1:110; 2:80–86, 133–58, 161, 172f. Cf. Doutté, *Magie et religion*, pp. 499ff., 506f.; Emile Laoust, in *Hesperis*, Paris, 1921, 1:257f.

94. Westermarck, *Ritual and Belief*, 2:134.

95. Ibid., 2:135.

96. Ibid., 2:137.

97. Ibid., 2:138–39.

98. Ibid., 2:139.

99. Ibid., 2:139–40.

100. Ibid., 2:141–42.

101. Ibid., 2:143–45.

102. Ibid., 2:255.

103. Sir James George Frazer, *The Magic Art*, London: Macmillan, 1932, 1:285.

104. Cf. Alfred Bel, "Quelques rites pour obtenir le pluie en temps de sécheresse chez les musulmans maghribiens," in *Receuil de mémoires et de textes publié en l'honneur de xive Congrés des orientalistes*, Algiers, 1905, pp. 60f.; Doutté, *Magie et religion*, p. 593.

105. The reason for this belief was not that the Jews had more children than the Muslims, but that more of their children, once born, remained alive, due to somewhat better hygienic conditions which, in turn, resulted from certain features in Jewish folk tradition.

106. Westermarck, *Ritual and Belief* 2:252.

107. Bel, "Quelques rites," p. 80; cf. also p. 67; Doutté, *Magie et religion*, p. 586.

108. Bel, "Quelques rites," pp. 65, 67, 91; Doutté, *Magie et religion*, pp. 586, 588; Laoust, *Mots et choses berberes*, Paris, 1920, pp. 204ff.; Westermarck, *Ritual and Belief*, 2:258, 262, 268, 281.

109. Cf. R. Patai, *Man and Temple*, pp. 184–86.

110. Bel, "Quelques rites," pp. 55, 56, 59, 79; Westermarck, *Ritual and Belief*, 2:259, 266, 267.

111. *Massekhet Sofrim* 14:18; Y. *Yebamot* 12c top; Y. *Baba Metzia* 11b mid.

112. Voinot, *Pélerinages*, pp. 123–27.

113. Maimonides, *Yad haḤazaqa*, Hilkhot ʿAkum, ch. 11.

NOTES TO CHAPTER SEVEN: THE FEMININE IN THE DIVINE

1. Cf. the detailed discussion of this phenomenon in R. Patai, *The Hebrew Goddess*, New York: Avon Books, 1978, pp. 16–58.

2. Cf. *Seder ʿAvodat Yisrael*, Roedelheim, 1868, pp. 87ff. My translation.

3. Cf. L. Gardet, "Allāh," in EI^2, 1:411–12.

4. Cf. sources in R. Patai, *The Arab Mind*, 2d ed., New York: Scribner's, 1983, p. 333.

5. The subject is dealt with in detail in Patai, *The Hebrew Goddess*.

6. *P'siqta diRav Kahana* (fifth century C.E.), ed. Mandelbaum, 1:235.

7. B. Rosh haShana 31a; cf. Patai, *The Hebrew Goddess*, pp. 106–7.

8. Patai, op. cit., pp. 107–8.

9. Ibid., pp. 108–9.

10. Num. Rab. 12:6.

11. Lev. Rab. 6:1; Patai, op. cit., p. 112.

12. Midrash Mishle, ed. Buber, p. 47a; Patai, op. cit., p. 112. Cf. also B'reshit Rabbati (11th century), ed. Albeck, p. 27 in the name of R. Akiba (second century C.E.), which says that God "removed Himself and His Shekhina" from the evil generation of Enoch, cf. Patai, op. cit., p. 113.

13. Ignaz Goldziher, "Über den Ausdruck 'Sakīna'," in his *Abhandlungen zur arabischen Philologie* I, Leiden: Brill, 1896, p. 178.

14. Patai, op. cit., p. 114.

15. Nāṣir Khusraw, *Sefer nāmeh*, ed. Charles Schefer, Paris: Ernest Leroux 1881, p. 28, translation p. 87.

16. Num. Rab. 12:6.
17. B. Qid. 70b; B. Ned. 38a.
18. Sources in Patai, *The Hebrew Goddess*, p. 109.
19. Goldziher, op. cit., p. 182. My translation from the Arabic.
20. Cf. *Encyclopaedia Judaica*, Jerusalem, 1972, s.v. Bat Kol.
21. Goldziher, op. cit., pp. 183ff.
22. Ibid., pp. 190–93.
23. Patai, op. cit., pp. 99–100, 103, 111.
24. Goldziher, op. cit., pp. 193–94, quoting Muslim 5:297.
25. Pirqe Avot 3:2.
26. EI^1, s.v. Sakīna.
27. EI^2, s.v. Djanna.
28. EI^2, s.v. Bektāshiyya.
29. Cf. R. A. Nicholson, *Studies in Islamic Mysticism*, Cambridge, 1921 (reprint Delhi, 1976), pp. 170, 173, 180, 189–266.
30. Ibid., p. 184.
31. EI^2, s.v. Ibn al-ᶜArabī.
32. A. J. Arberry, *Sufism: An Account of the Mystics of Islam*, London: Unwin Paperbacks, 1979, pp. 21, 27–28, 98–99, 102.
33. Thus according to the 1954 declaration of Pope Pius XII, cf. *New Catholic Encyclopaedia*, s. vv. Mariology and Mary, Blessed Virgin.
34. Cf. Koran 5:116; cf. 4:169/171.
35. Zohar 1:49a; 3:74b. Cf. Patai, *The Hebrew Goddess*, p. 161. On father and mother in the divinity according to the Kabbala, cf. ibid., pp. 126–29, 135–42.
36. The maidens accompanying the Matronit are referred to elsewhere as well in the Zohar. Cf., e.g., Zohar 2:394: "The Matronit merits to come to her husband [God] only with those virginal maidens who accompany her, and lead her, until she reaches her husband . . . in order to bring her to join her husband."
37. Midrash haNeᶜelam on Lam. Zohar Ḥadash, with the Sullam commentary, vol. 21, Tel Aviv, 1965, pp. 15–17.
38. Zohar 3:69a; cf. Patai, *The Hebrew Goddess*, p. 166.
39. Zohar, loc. cit.
40. Zohar 2:89a-b. Cf. Patai, op. cit., p. 163.
41. Patai, op. cit., pp. 162–65.
42. *Sefer haKawwanot* ("The Book of Concentrations"), Venice, 1620; Constantinople, 1720; etc.
43. Cf. sources in Patai, *The Hebrew Goddess*, pp. 167–68.
44. *Seder T'filla mikol haShana ᶜim Kawwanot ha'Ari* ("The Order of Prayer for the Whole Year with the Concentrations of the Holy Lion [i.e. Isaac Luria]"), Koretz, 1794, p. 263b (last page of the book).
45. *Sefer haKawwanot*, p. 26a.
46. Ibid., p. 23a.
47. Y'ḥi'el Mikhael Epstein, *Seder T'filla Derekh Y'shara* ("Order of Prayer The Straight Road"), Frankfurt a.M., 1697, pp. 10a, 10b; cf. also pp. 23b, 24a, b, etc.

48. Cf. references in Seligman Isaac Beer (1825–1897), *Seder ᶜAvodat Yisrael* ("The Order of the Service of Israel"), Roedelheim, 1868, p. 55.

49. Cf. *Siddur Ishe Yisrael* ("Prayer Book Fires of Israel"), reprint, Jerusalem, n.d., p. 17a.

50. *Siddur Otzar haT'fillot* ("Prayer Book Treasury of Prayers"), Vilna, 1914.

51. *Siddur Bet Yaᶜaqov heḤadash* ("The New House of Jacob Prayer Book"), Vienna: H. Ziegelheim, no date, p. 4.

52. *Siddur T'filla k'Minhag S'farad* ("Prayer Book According to the Sephardi Custom"), with explanations by R. Moshe Cordovero, Przemysl, 1892; reprinted Jerusalem, 1964, p. 22b. The "brains" (or marrow) mentioned are an important concept in the Lurianic Kabbala. It refers to a mystical substance with which both the "Small of Face" (God) and the Shekhina must be provided in order to advance from a lower to a higher stage in the unfolding of the divine configuration. I am indebted to Dr. Martin Samuel Cohen of the University of Heidelberg, Germany, for his elucidation of this point.

53. *Siddur Bet Yaᶜaqov heḤadash*, pp. 32, 34, 324–25, 374, 387.

54. Ibid., pp. 157–58.

55. Ibid., p. 374.

56. Ibid., p. 387.

57. Ibid., pp. 389, 404, 408, 413, 422, 435, 449, 450, 457–58, 462, 465.

58. E.g., *Siddur Tora Or v'Shaᶜar haKolel . . . Nusaḥ haAri* ("Prayer Book The Tora is Light and the Universal Gate . . . Version of Isaac Luria") contains numerous additional references to the Shekhina. The following is a sampling of other prayer books containing the "unifications" and other references to the Shekhina:

Seder l'Shalosh R'galim k'Minhag haS'faradim ("Order for the Three Pilgrims' Festivals According to the Sephardi Custom"), no place, 1857.

Seder Or Zaruᶜa T'filla l'Khol haShana k'Minhag S'farad ("Order Sown Light Prayer for the Whole Year According to the Custom of Spain"), Jerusalem, 1897, repr. 1966.

Seder Shaᶜar haShamayim ("Order Gate of Heaven . . . Version of Spain"), New York, 1954 (on p. 277 the unification of God and the Shekhina is stated to be the purpose of circumcision).

Siddur T'filla ("Prayer Book") of the Yemenite Rabbi Shalom Sharᶜabi, Jerusalem, 1964 (reprint).

Siddur Or miTziyon, Nusaḥ S'farad ("Prayer Book Light from Zion, Version of Spain"), Jerusalem, 1968.

Siddur T'fillat Y'sharim ᶜim Sharḥ fī al-ᶜArabī ("Prayer Book The Prayer of the Righteous Ones, with a Commentary in Arabic as Spoken in Baghdad and Its Environs and the Cities of India and China . . ."), edited and translated by Ṣāliḥ Yaᶜqūb Manṣūr, Jerusalem, 1938.

Seder Minḥa vᶜArvit l'Shalosh R'galim ("Order of the Afternoon and Evening Prayers for the Three Pilgrims' Festivals . . . According to the Custom of Baghdad"), edited by Yitzḥaq Yosef Ḥayyim Aᶜbūdī, Livorno: Sh'lomo Belforte, 1935. On p. 90a the blessing recited when seeing leafy trees is stated to have as its purpose "the unification of God and the Shekhina . . ."

59. Gershom G. Scholem, *Major Trends in Jewish Mysticism*, New York: Schocken Books, 1961, pp. 285–86.

60. Zohar 1:110. My translation.

61. Mohammed Marmaduke Pickthall's translation. See his *The Meaning of the Glorious Koran*, New York: A Mentor Book, 1953, p. 304.

62. Reuben Levy, *The Social Structure of Islam*, Cambridge: At the University Press, 1957, p. 130.

63. Ibid., p. 131.

64. Bayḍāwī on Koran 4:38, as quoted by Levy, *Social Structure of Islam*, pp. 98–99.

65. Dorothy Van Ess, *Fatima and Her Sisters*, New York: John Day, 1961, pp. 134–35; Elizabeth Warnock Fernea, *Guests of the Sheik*, Garden City, N.Y.: Doubleday Anchor Books, 1969, pp. 105–15.

66. Cf. R. Patai, *Society, Culture and Change in the Middle East*, Philadelphia: University of Pennsylvania Press, 1971, p. 464.

67. Cf. sources, ibid., pp. 465, 529–30; cf. also Edward Westermarck, *Ritual and Belief in Morocco*, London: Macmillan, 1926, 1:345ff., 379.

68. Patai, *Society, Culture and Change*, pp. 465–68.

69. Ibid., p. 468. Subsequently Vincent Crapanzano applied the categories Apollonian and Dionysian to Muslim religious manifestations, cf. his *The Ḥamadsha: A Study in Moroccan Ethnopsychiatry*, Berkeley-Los Angeles-London: University of California Press, 1973, p. 226.

70. Harold B. Barclay, *Buurri Al Lamaab: A Suburban Village in the Sudan*, Ithaca, N.Y.: Cornell University Press, 1964, p. 203; cf. pp. 196–97, 201–2, 204–5.

71. Patai, *Society, Culture and Change*, p. 468.

72. Westermarck, *Ritual and Belief*, 1:393–94, 396–98, 400, 402; Crapanzano, *The Ḥamadsha*, pp. 146–48; *idem*, "Mohammad and Dawia: Possession in Morocco," in Crapanzano and Vivian Garrison (eds.), *Case Studies in Spirit Possession*, New York-London: John Wiley, 1977, p. 144.

73. Crapanzano, *Ḥamadsha*, pp. 44–45, 143–46; "Mohammed and Dawia," pp. 144–45.

74. Westermarck, *Ritual and Belief*, 1:395.

75. J. Leibovitch, *Annales du Service des Antiquités de l'Egypte* 41 (1942): 77–86; James B. Pritchard (ed.), *Ancient Near Eastern Texts Relating to the Old Testament*, 2d ed., Princeton, N.J.: Princeton University Press, 1955, pp. 133, 250; R. Patai, *The Hebrew Goddess*, pp. 44, 48.

76. Westermarck, *Ritual and Belief*, 1:396.

77. Crapanzano, *Ḥamadsha*, pp. 142, 146.

78. Ibid., pp. 8–9, 56, 224.

79. Ibid., pp. 37–38. Cf. the profusion of data collected by Westermarck, *Ritual and Belief*, index, s. vv. *jinn* and *jnun*.

80. Crapanzano, *Ḥamadsha*, pp. 224–25.

81. Ibid., pp. 75, 89–90, 145.

82. Cf. the texts of these *aryāḥ* in Crapanzano, *Ḥamadsha*, pp. 145, 147–49.

83. Crapanzano, ibid., pp. 86–87, 98, 162–66.

84. Lucie Wood Saunders, "Variants in Zar Experience in an Egyptian Village," in Crapanzano and Garrison, op. cit., pp. 177–92.

85. Josephus Flavius, *Ant.* 8:2:5.

86. Testament of Solomon, ed. Chester Charlton McCown, Leipzig: Hinrichs, 1922, index, s.v. Ornias.

87. *Enc. Judaica* (1972), 5:1531–32, s.v. Demons.

88. Cf. Ḥayyim Vital, *Sefer haḤezyonot* ("Book of Visions"); Samuel Vital, *Shaᶜar haGilgulim* ("Gate of Transmigrations"), 1875, 1912, etc. Cf. R. Patai, "Exorcism and Xenoglossia Among the Safed Kabbalists," *Journal of American Folklore*, 1978, pp. 82233; *idem*, "The Love Factor in a Hebrew-Arabic Conjuration," *The Jewish Quarterly Review*, n.s. 70, no. 4 (1980), pp. 239–53.

89. S. R. Mizraḥi, *Maᶜase Nora shel haRuaḥ* ("Terrible Story of the Spirit"), 1904; M. Sassoon, *Sippur Nora shel haDibbuq* ("Terrible Tale of the Dibbuq"), 1966; cf. G. Scholem, "Dibbuk," in *Enc. Judaica* 6:19–21.

NOTES TO CHAPTER EIGHT: WOMEN—JEWISH AND ARAB

1. This, incidentally, is a key verse which has been taken by certain religious sects as scriptural proof that God is both male and female; for otherwise how could the first man and woman be said to have been created "in the image of God"?

2. Cf. Savina J. Teubal, *Sarah the Priestess: The First Matriarch of Genesis*, Athens, Ohio: Swallow Press, 1984.

3. Gen. Rab. 18:2; 45:5. Cf. the *ḥadīth* about the character of woman being determined by her being formed out of a crooked rib, cf. below.

4. William Robertson Smith, *Kinship and Marriage in Early Arabia*, Cambridge, 1885, pp. 122–40.

5. R. Patai, *Society, Culture and Change in the Middle East*, Philadelphia: University of Pennsylvania Press, 1971, p. 122.

6. Reuben Levy, *The Social Structure of Islam*, 2nd ed., Cambridge University Press, 1957, p. 92.

7. First two quotes in this paragraph are from Thomas Patrick Hughes, *A Dictionary of Islam*, Lahore, 1965, pp. 678–79. The third and fourth are from the same source, p. 671.

8. Cf. Levy, op. cit., pp. 124–29.

9. Elizabeth Warnock Fernea, *Guests of the Sheik*, New York: Doubleday Anchor Books, 1969, p. 164.

10. Goldziher, *Muhammedanische Studien* 2:302.

11. Edward William Lane, *The Manners and Customs of the Modern Egyptians*, London: Everyman's Library, no date, pp. 435–37.

12. Nabih Amin Faris and Mohammed Tawfik Husayn, *The Crescent in Crisis: An Interpretive Study of the Modern Arab World*, Lawrence, Kansas: University of Kansas Press, 1955, p. 46.

13. Nejla Izzeddin, *The Arab World: Past, Present, and Future*, Chicago, Ill.: Regnery, 1953, pp. 57–58.

14. *Averroes' Commentary on Plato's Republic*, ed. with a translation by E. I. J. Rosenthal, Cambridge University Press, 1956, p. 166. The first three additions in square brackets are by Rosenthal, the fourth one is added by me.

15. Goitein, *A Mediterranean Society*, 3:323.

16. I say "perhaps," because Tertullian (ca. 160–ca. 230), the North African ecclesiastical writer, also mentions in his *De virg. vel.*, 17 (as cited by Yedida K. Stillman, "Libās," in EI^2 5:733) that Arabian women appeared in public totally enveloped in their mantle so that only one eye was left free.

17. Eliezer Grünhut (ed.), *Sibbuv haRav Rabbi P'taḥya miRegensburg*, Part I, Frankfurt a.M., 1905 (reprinted in Israel, 1967), pp. 8–10. The Hebrew text has *q'ri'a*, "reading," both times, but the author evidently means *miqra*, Scripture, i.e., Bible study.

18. Moshe Perlmann (editor and translator), Samaw'al al-Maghribī, *Ifḥām al-Yahūd* ("Silencing of the Jews"), New York: American Academy for Jewish Research, Proceedings 32, 1964, p. 75.

19. Goitein, *Mediterranean Society* 3:345, 355.

20. Grünhut, *Sibbuv*, loc. cit.

21. Pedro Cantera Vaca, *Relacion de Oran*, 1631–36, in P. Jimenez de Gregorio, *Hispania* 22 (1962), pp. 93–114; as cited by H. Z. Hirschberg, *Toldot haY'hudim biTz'fom Afriqa* ("History of the Jews in North Africa"), Jerusalem: Mossad Bialik, 1965, 2:104.

22. Alexander Russell, *The Natural History of Aleppo*, 2d. ed., London, 1756, 2:58–64; as quoted by Norman A. Stillman, *The Jews of Arab Lands: A History and Source Book*, Philadelphia: The Jewish Publication Society of America, 1979, p. 320.

23. William Lemprière, *A Tour from Gibraltar to Tangier* . . . , London, 1791, p. 198; as quoted by Stillman, op. cit., pp. 313–14.

24. Lane, *Modern Egyptians*, pp. 559, 561.

25. Lemprière, op. cit., p. 198; Lane, op. cit., p. 561.

26. William C. Prime, *Tent Life in the Holy Land*, New York, 1857, pp. 434–35; as quoted by Stillman, op. cit., p. 353.

27. Cf. photograph of a Jewish woman in her home in Rabat, early twentieth century, wearing the traditional *ḥayk* (in literary Arabic *ḥā'ik*), a long white outer garment covering the body, head, and face, and leaving only the eyes open, in L. Goulven, *Les Mellahs de Rabat-Sale*, Paris: Geuthner, 1927, reproduced in Stillman, op. cit., illustration no. 32 following p. 392.

28. Maimonides, *Mishne Tora* (*Yad haḤazaqa*), Hilkhot M'lakhim, 1:5.

29. Reuben Levy, *The Social Structure of Islam*, p. 99.

30. H. Z. Hirschberg, *Toldot haY'hudim*, 1:136.

31. Ibid., 1:139–40, and sources there, p. 359, n. 121.

32. Ibid., 1:137.

33. Cf. above, chapter 6, "Naming." Goitein, *Mediterranean Society* 3:154, 156, 157, 169, 175, 182, 183, 187, 358; 4:199–200.

34. Patai, *Sex and Family in the Bible and the Middle East*, Garden City, N.Y.: Doubleday, 1959, pp. 188–92.

35. Goitein, op. cit., 3:359.
36. Ibid., 3:323.
37. Lane, *Modern Egyptians*, p. 96.
38. Goitein, op. cit., 3: 185. Cf. also the *ḥadīth* quoted above.
39. Cf., e.g., Charles M. Doughty, *Travels in Arabia Deserta*, New York, 1937, 1:231, 236.
40. Cf. sources in Patai, *Society, Culture and Change in the Middle East*, Philadelphia: University of Pennsylvania Press, 1971, pp. 413–17.
41. G. Lecomte, "Falaḳa," in EI², 2:763–64.
42. Cf. Elkan Nathan Adler, *Jewish Travellers*, London: Routledge, 1930, p. 81.
43. Alois Musil, *Arabia Petraea*, Vienna, 1908, 3:211.
44. Hilma Granqvist, *Marriage Conditions in a Palestinian Village*, Helsingfors: Societas Scientiarum Fennica, 1935, 2: 167–68.
45. As quoted by Goitein, *Mediterranean Society*, 3: 185.
46. Goitein, op. cit., 3: 184–89.
47. Ibid., p. 157.
48. Maimonides, *Mishne Tora (Yad haḤazaqa)*, Hilkhot Ishut 21:3, 10. My translation.
49. Khalīl ibn Isḥāq, *Mukhtaṣar* ("Abstract"), transl. Perron, *Exposition scientifique de l'Algerie*, Paris, 1877, 13: 130; as cited by R. Levy, *The Social Structure of Islam*, pp. 99–100.
50. Abraham ben David of Posquieres, "Hasagot," in Maimonides, *Mishne Tora*, Jessnitz, 1736, 2:59a (Hilkhot Ishut 21: 10).
51. Cited in Goitein, *Mediterranean Society* 3: 184.
52. *Shulḥan ᶜArukh, Even ha ᶜEzer* 154:3.
53. Patai, *The Arab Mind*, 2d ed., New York: Scribners, 1983, p. 362, tables 2 and 6.
54. Cf. Patai, *Israel Between East and West*, 2d. ed., Westport, Conn.: Greenwood, 1970, p. 141, and sources there.
55. Ibid., p. 358.
56. Bet Barukh Levin, Center for the Study of the Labor Movement in Israel, *Mizzug Galuyot*, mimeographed, May, 1967, p. 17.
57. A. Chouraqui, *Marche vers l'Occident: Les Juifs d'Afrique du Nord*, Paris: Presses Universitaires de France, 1952, pp. 328, 336.
58. Milton Jacobs, *A Study of Culture Stability and Change: The Moroccan Jewess* (a dissertation abstract), Washington, D.C.: Catholic University of America, 1956, p. 46.
59. Cf. UNESCO *Statistical Yearbook 1984*, pp. III–20ff. The figures as given are somewhat misleading inasmuch as they represent gross enrollment ratios reached by dividing the number of girls of *all ages* enrolled in primary schools with the total number of girls in the primary school age-group. If, in addition to girls in this age-group also older girls are enrolled in primary schools (as is inevitably the case in countries where female education is newly introduced), this can considerably increase the gross enrollment ratio and boost it to well over 100 percent. Thus

the ratio for Iraq (1982) was 103, for Lebanon (1981) 114, for Qatar (1982) 112, and for the United Arab Emirates (1982) 131. For Jordan (1981) it was 100. For Israel (1982), despite its traditionally great emphasis on education, it was 96. The exceedingly high ratios in the Arab countries listed here as well as above in the text make their reliability appear questionable.

60. Ibid., pp. 118ff., 327ff.

61. Ibid., p. 330.

62. Peter Mansfield, *The New Arabians*, Chicago: J. C. Ferguson, and New York: Doubleday, 1981, pp. 27–32.

63. Patai, *The Arab Mind*, p. 333.

64. Ibid., pp. 332–33.

65. In accordance with the dictum attributed to ʿUmar, "let there be no two religions in Arabia," cf. A. J. Wensinck, *A Handbook of Early Muhammadan Tradition*, Leiden: Brill, 1927, p. 204; Hughes, *Dictionary of Islam*, 1965, p. 653. The banning of Jews was not observed one hundred percent even in Saudi Arabia. In the southwestern parts of the country, near the Yemenite border, for example, in Najrān, dozens of Jewish families lived until they emigrated to Israel in 1948/49. Philby, who visited Najrān in the 1930s, describes his encounter with Jews there who according to him numbered eighty persons. He observes that the Jews of Najrān "had lived for generations on terms of perfect amity with some of the most ferocious tribes in Arabia, and had had little to complain of. Indeed the Arabs could not dispense with their valuable services to the community, for, in addition to making jewelry and trinkets for the women, they were the only gunsmiths and armourers in the district." See H. St. J. B. Philby, *Arabian Highlands*, Ithaca, N.Y.: Cornell University Press, 1952, p. 232. Cf. also pp. 277–81 where he gives details of the life of the Jews in Najrān.

66. Yedida K. Stillman, "Libās," EI[2] 5:740.

NOTES TO CHAPTER NINE: ARABS UNDER JEWISH RULE—A HISTORICAL ANOMALY

1. Cf. Adnan A. Aïta, *Le Conflit d'Alexandretta et le Société des Nations* (University of Geneva doctoral thesis, no. 464), Damascus: Editions Librairie Universelle, 1947, p. 5. Cf. also Avedis K. Sanjian, "The Sanjak of Alexandretta (Hatay): Its Impact on Syrian-Turkish Relations (1939–1956), *Middle East Journal* 1956, p. 389. Literature on Alexandretta is listed in the article "Iskandarun" in EI[2].

2. Cf. Sanjian, op. cit., pp. 379, 382.

3. Ibid., pp. 381–82, quoting a UN document.

4. Aïta, op. cit., p. 109.

5. Sanjian, op. cit., pp. 382–86.

6. George Lenczowski, *The Middle East in World Affairs*, 4th ed., Ithaca-London: Cornell University Press, 1980, pp. 336–37; cf. also Sanjian, op. cit., p. 389.

7. Sanjian, op. cit., p. 393.

8. Ibid., p. 394.

9. Cf. *The New York Times*, Nov. 11, 1975. It is of interest to note that Dr. Sayed Nofal, an Egyptian religious scholar, stated in Sept. 1968 in his address to the Fourth Conference of the Academy of Islamic Research held in Cairo that "Zionism is colonialism and racism which ought to be liquidated . . ." Cf. p. 55 of the source quoted in note 19 below.

10. Lenczowski, op. cit., pp. 739–40.

11. Philip K. Hitti, *History of the Arabs*, New York: St. Martin's Press, 1981, p. 726.

12. Ibid., pp. 732–35 : EI[2] s.v. Durūz.

13. Cf. Joshua Blau (ed.), *Teshuvot haRambam*, Jerusalem: Meqitze Nirdamim, 1947, pp. 284–85, no. 149.

14. Cf. documents published by Norman A. Stillman, *The Jews of Arab Lands*, Philadelphia: The Jewish Publication Society of America, 1979, pp. 357–61.

15. See text, ibid., pp. 371–73.

16. Cf. sources quoted in R. Patai, *The Arab Mind*, p. 51.

17. Ibid., pp. 51–52.

18. A. J. Barker, *Arab-Israeli Wars*, New York: Hippocrane Books, 1980, p. 19; Chaim Herzog, *The Arab-Israeli Wars*, New York: Vintage Books, 1984, pp. 20–23.

19. Cf. D. F. Green's introductory comments in D. F. Green (ed.), *Arab Theologians on Jews and Israel*: Extracts from the Proceedings of the Fourth Conference of the Academy of Islamic Research. Geneva: Editions de l'Avenir, 1971, pp. 2–3. The conference proceedings were published in Arabic in three volumes, and in English in one volume by the Academy of Islamic Research, under the title *The Fourth Conference of the Academy of Islamic Research*, Rajab 1388–September 1968, Cairo: General Organization for Government Printing Offices, 1970. The extracts reprinted by Green are photographic reproductions from this volume. Printer's errors and English stylistic peculiarities were left as they appeared in the original both in Green's book and in the excerpts I quote from it.

20. *The Fourth Conference*, p. 2; Green, op. cit., p. 9.

21. *The Fourth Conference*, pp. 125–26; Green, pp. 46–47.

22. Ibid.

23. Hussein of Jordan, *My "War" with Israel*, as told to, and with additional material by Vick Vance and Pierre Lauer, New York: William Morrow, 1969, pp. 82–83.

24. As quoted by Abdallah Kannoun, a member of the Academy of Islamic Research, cf. *The Fourth Conference*, p. 260; Green, p. 50.

25. Reference to Koran 7 : 167, which reads: ". . . thy Lord proclaimed that He would raise against them till the Day of Resurrection those who would lay on them a cruel torment." Pickthall's translation.

26. *The Fourth Conference*, pp. 470, 492, 495: Green, pp. 27, 30, 31.

27. *The Fourth Conference*, p. 526; Green, p. 35.

28. Cf. the texts of these addresses in Riad N. El-Rayyes and Dunia Nahas (eds.), *The October War: Documents, Personalities, Analyses and Maps*, Beirut, Lebanon: An-Nahar Press Services, 1973, pp. 268, 280–281.

29. From a poem by Yūsuf Idrīs (born 1927), the well-known Egyptian playwright and novelist, entitled *al-Khalāṣ* ("The Deliverance"), published in the Egyptian daily *al-Ahrām* on October 12, 1973. My translation. Cf. also the analysis of the Arab reaction to the October War in R. Patai, *The Arab Mind*, 2d ed., pp. 314–21.

30. El-Rayyes and Nahas, op. cit., pp. 114–15, 120–22.

31. As quoted by Jehuda Bauer, "Anti-Semitism Today—A Fiction or a Fact," *Midstream* 30:8 (October, 1984): 28.

32. Morroe Berger, *The Arab World Today*, Garden City, N.Y.: Doubleday, 1962, p. 262.

33. Cf. the list of these publications in Y'hoshafat Harkabi, *ᶜEmdat ha ᶜAravim b'Sikhsukh Yisrael-ᶜArav* ("The Position of the Arabs in the Israel-Arab Conflict"), Tel Aviv: Dvir, 1968, pp. 487–90.

34. As quoted in Hebrew by Harkabi, op. cit., p. 214.

35. R. K. Karanjia, *The Arab Dawn*, Bombay, 1958, appendix, p. 330; as quoted in Harkabi, *Arab Attitudes to Israel* (the English version of the Hebrew book quoted in footnote 33 above), New York: Hart Publ. Co., 1972, p. 235.

36. Ibid., p. 218. Cf. also pp. 212–19, where there is a detailed discussion of the manifold uses of the *Protocols* in Arab propaganda, and even in school books.

37. *The Fourth Conference*, pp. 362–63; Green, p. 14.

38. Robert Lacey, *The Kingdom*, New York and London: Harcourt Brace Jovanovich, 1981, pp. 385–86, 418. Kissinger himself describes briefly in his memoirs the address to which King Fayṣal treated him, and characterizes it as King Fayṣal's "standard speech." In it the king spoke about the Jewish-Communist conspiracy whose purpose was "to undermine the civilized world as we know it," and which "was now trying to take over the American government." Kissinger adds that "the speech on Communism and Zionism, however bizarre it sounded to Western visitors, was clearly deeply felt." Cf. Henry Kissinger, *Years of Upheaval*, Boston-Toronto: Little Brown, 1982, pp. 661–62.

39. Cf. *Al-Muṣawwar*, Alexandria, Egypt, August 4, 1972, issue.

40. I tried to find out whether this statement was perhaps a distortion of some criminal event that actually took place in Paris during a visit of King Fayṣal. At my request, Mlle Nelly Gutman, director of the Centre d'Etudes et de Recherche sur l'Anti-sémitism Contemporain of Paris inquired at the French Ministry of Foreign Affairs, and was informed that the only visit of King Fayṣal of which the ministry had a record took place on May 14–18, 1973, and not in 1970, as the king states in the interview. As for the finding of the bodies of five murdered children at any time during those years, inquiry at the French Home Office, Ministry of Justice, and the police could not elicit any information.

41. Address by Dr. Maᶜrūf al-Dawalībī, Counsellor to the Royal Court in Riyadh, Saudi Arabia, delivered on Dec. 5, 1984, to the UN Seminar on the Encouragement of Understanding, Tolerance, and Respect in Matters Relating to Freedom of Religion or Belief. Transcript of the simultaneous English translation, prepared by the Permanent Mission of Israel to the office of the United Nations in Geneva. The seminar was organized by the UN Center of Human Rights.

42. As quoted by Bauer, "Anti-Semitism Today," p. 26.

43. Anis Mansour, in *October* magazine of August 8, 1982, as quoted by Bauer, loc. cit.

44. The Bible, as well as later Jewish authors, had a special fondness for a period of four hundred years. Thus both the First Temple of Jerusalem and the Second were stated to have stood for four hundred years, although actually the First Temple stood for 370 years, and the Second for 587 years. If the Egyptian slavery actually lasted four hundred years, each of the four generations which spanned it (Levi-Kehat-Amram-Moses) must have lasted a hundred years.

45. Cf. the discussion of these subjects in R. Patai, *Man and Temple in Ancient Jewish Myth and Ritual*, 2d ed., New York: Ktav, 1967.

46. S. D. Goitein, "al-Ḳuds," in EI^2 5:322.

47. Genesis Rabba 84; B. Menaḥot 53b.

48. M. Sharon, "al-Khalīl," in EI^2 4:956.

49. Cf. Bernard Lewis, *The Jews of Islam*, Princeton University Press, 1984, p. 71. To my regret this book came to my hands too late to take full account of it.

50. "Israel, State of," in *Enc. Judaica* 9:487.

51. Roberto Bachi, "Demografiya," in *HaEntziqlopediya haʿIvrit* (1957), 6:705.

52. Aharon Cohen, *Israel and the Arab World*, New York: Funk and Wagnalls, 1970, pp. 224–25.

53. "Israel, State of," in *Enc. Judaica* 9:1023.

54. Fred M. Gottheil, "Arab Immigration into Pre-State Israel: 1922–1931," in Michael Curtis et al. (eds.), *The Palestinians: People, History, Politics*, New Brunswick, N.J.: Transaction Books, 1975, p. 34.

55. As quoted by Aharon Cohen, op. cit., p. 225. After completing the above chapter, two recently published books came to my attention which deal with the problem of Arab population figures in pre-Israel Palestine. They are Arieh L. Avineri, *The Claim of Dispossession: Jewish Land-Settlement and the Arabs 1878–1948*, New Brunswick and London: Transaction Books, 1984; and Joan Peters, *From Time Immemorial: The Origins of the Arab-Jewish Conflict over Palestine*, New York: Harper and Row, 1984. Both books, each within its own specific context, present basically the same argument about the relatively recent arrival in Palestine of a considerable part of its Arab population, and the historical untenability of the Arab claim of having been in possession of the country for thirteen centuries.

56. Alfred Bonne, as cited by Aharon Cohen, op. cit., p. 226.

57. George Antonius, *The Arab Awakening*, New York: G. P. Putnam, 1946, pp. 390–91. The book was written in 1938.

58. Cf. the useful bibliography in Curtis, *The Palestinians*, pp. 269–72.

59. For more on this subject, cf. R. Patai, *The Arab Mind*, pp. 219–27, 335–37.

60. As quoted by Shlomo Avineri, "Political and Social Aspects of Israeli and Arab Nationalism," *Midstream*, Jan. 1973, pp. 41–45. For the emergence and history of political parties in Arab lands, cf. Elie Kadouri, "Ḥizb," in EI^2 3:514–26, with extensive bibliography on pp. 525–26.

61. Cf. Cohen, op. cit., pp. 51ff.; Kadouri, op. cit.

62. Cf. sources in Cohen, op. cit., pp. 63–64.

63. Ibid., pp. 70–80. For another, more recent, detailed account of the Palestinian Arab attitude to Zionism prior to World War I, see Neville J. Mandel, *The Arabs and Zionism Before World War I*, Berkeley-Los Angeles-London: The University of California Press, 1976. Mandel concludes that the roots of Arab antagonism to Zionism went back to the pre-1914 period, and that it was an existing trend which the Balfour Declaration greatly aggravated.

64. Statement by Rafīq Bey al-ʿAẓm, approved by the Cairo Committee of Muslim and Christian Arabs, and published in *Le Jeune Turc* of Paris and in the Arab press. Cf. Cohen, op. cit., p. 94.

65. Published in *Le Jeune Turc*, as quoted by Cohen, op. cit., p. 97.

66. Cohen, op. cit., p. 103.

67. Ibid., pp. 79, 113.

68. Cf. sources in Yehoshua Porat, "The Palestinian-Arab Nationalist Movement," in Curtis, op. cit., p. 124. Cf. also Moshe Maʿoz, "Palestinian Arab Nationalism: The West Bank Dimension," (xeroxed), no. 18 of The Woodrow Wilson Center International Studies Program, Washington, D.C., Oct. 8, 1980, p. 7.

69. Antonius, *The Arab Awakening*, p. 269.

70. Riad N. El-Rayyes and Dunia Nahas (eds.), *Guerrillas for Palestine: A Study of the Palestinian Commando Organization*, compiled by An-Nahar Arab Report Research Staff, Beirut, Lebanon: An-Nahar Press Service, 1974, p. 225.

71. *Palestinian Leaders Discuss the New Challenges for the Resistance*, Beirut: Palestine Research Center, April, 1974. Reprinted in Curtis, op. cit., p. 167.

72. As quoted by Chaim I. Waxman, "Varieties of Palestinian Nationalism," Middle East Information Series 25 (Winter 1973–74), New York: American Association for Peace in the Middle East. Reprinted in Curtis, op. cit., p. 114.

73. Curtis, op. cit., p. 167.

74. Loc. cit.

75. El-Rayyes and Nahas, *Guerrillas*, pp. 225, 227–28.

76. Cf. the analysis of the Palestinian National Covenant by Y. Harkabi, "The Palestinian National Covenant," in *Maʿariv*, Tel Aviv, Dec. 12, 1969; English translation in Curtis, op. cit., pp. 143ff.

77. On the rapid growth of the number of Arab university and college students in Israel, and on the intellectual and political position of the Arab intelligentsia in Israel, cf. Eli Rekhess, "The Intelligentsia" (in Hebrew), in Aharon Layish (ed.), *The Arabs in Israel: Continuity and Change*, Jerusalem: The Magnes Press, The Hebrew University, 1981, pp. 180–96.

78. Cf. the brief review of Adnan Mohammed Abu-Ghazaleh, *Arab Cultural Nationalism in Palestine during the British Mandate*, Beirut: The Institute for Palestine Studies and the University of Libya, 1973, and especially chapter 3, "Popular Writing" (pp. 39–57), ch. 4, "Literary Writing" (pp. 58–69), ch. 5, "Historical Writing" (pp. 70–87), and the bibliography (pp. 103–114).

79. Cf. Jacob M. Landau, "Al-Ard Group" in Jacob M. Landau (ed.), *Man, State, and Society in the Contemporary Middle East*, New York: Praeger Publishers,

1972, pp. 196–207. Landau finds that al-Arḍ's criticism of the Israeli government was characterized by aggressiveness, admiration for Nasser, incitement of the Israeli Arabs, and one-sidedness in stressing the negative side and completely ignoring all government assistance to the Arab minority.

80. Sabri Jiryis, *The Arabs in Israel*, Beirut, 1968, Monograph series of the Institute for Palestine Studies, pp. 119, 173, 175. The book was published in a 2nd, augmented edition, in New York and London: Monthly Review Press, 1976, with a foreword by Noam Chomsky.

81. Ori Stendel, "The Rise of New Political Currents in the Arab Section in Israel 1948–1974," in Moshe Maᶜoz (ed.), *Palestinian Arab Politics*, Jerusalem Academic Press, 1975, p. 138.

82. Henry Rosenfeld, "The Class Situation of the Arab National Minority in Israel," in *Comparative Studies in Society and History: An International Quarterly* 20 : 3 (July 1978), p. 390. According to one estimate quoted by Rosenfeld 40 percent of the land owned by legal Arab residents was confiscated by the authorities; according to another, the Arabs were left with no more than 30 to 40 percent of the land that was theirs before the state's establishment.

83. Ibid., pp. 392, 399, 404.

84. Uziel O. Schmelz, "Vital Statistics and Population Growth" (in Hebrew), in Layish, op. cit., pp. 14, 17–18, 41; *Statistical Abstract of Israel 1984*, no. 35, p. 52.

85. Uziel O. Schmelz, "Labour Force" (in Hebrew), in Layish, op. cit., p. 48.

86. Cf. sources in R. Patai, *The Arab Mind*, 2d ed., table 6 foll. p. 356.

87. Mark A. Tessler, "The Identity of Religious Minorities in Non-Secular States . . ." in *Comparative Studies in Society and History: An International Quarterly* 20 : 3 (July 1978), pp. 359, 366, 368–70.

88. Moshe Maᶜoz, *Anti-Jewishness in Official Arab Literature and Communications Media* (in Hebrew), Jerusalem: Shazar Library, The Hebrew University, 1975, pp. 28–29. For a political history of the Jordanian period of the West Bank, cf. Amnon Cohen, *Political Parties in the West Bank Under the Hashemite Regime* (in Hebrew), Jerusalem, 1980.

NOTES TO CHAPTER TEN: SUMMATION AND CONCLUSION

1. Cf. Chaim Herzog, *The Arab-Israeli Wars*, New York: Vintage Books, a Division of Random House, 1984, p. 315, and again on p. 375.

2. Cf. Abraham Karlikow, "Jews in Arab Countries," in *American Jewish Year Book 1978*, pp. 485–99.

3. *Flash of Syria*, no. 85, Damascus, July 1979, p. 7. The "Zionist enemy" or "Zionist entity" is mentioned on practically every page of that issue.

Index

Arabic names and words beginning with the article *al-* are listed under the letter following the article. The source of foreign words and phrases listed in this index is indicated in parentheses, using these abbreviations:

A – Arabic	Ge – German	P – Persian
Aram – Aramaic	Gr – Greek	S – Spanish
B – Berber	H – Hebrew	T – Turkish
F – French	L – Latin	